WHY ADJUDICATE?

WHY ADJUDICATE?

ENFORCING TRADE RULES IN THE WTO

Christina L. Davis

PRINCETON UNIVERSITY PRESS   PRINCETON AND OXFORD

Library of Congress Cataloging-in-Publication Data

Davis, Christina L., 1971–
    Why adjudicate? : enforcing trade rules in the WTO / Christina L. Davis.
p. cm.
Includes bibliographical references and index.
ISBN 978-0-691-15275-2 (hardcover) – ISBN 978-0-691-15276-9 (pbk.)
1. World Trade Organization.   2. Foreign trade regulation.
3. Administrative procedure.   I. Title.
    HF1385.D38 2012
    382′.92–dc23
                        2011040102

British Library Cataloging-in-Publication Data is available

This book has been composed in Sabon

Printed on acid-free paper. ∞

Typeset by S R Nova Pvt Ltd, Bangalore, India
Printed in the United States of America

10 9 8 7 6 5 4 3 2 1

To Kosuke, Keiji, and Misaki

Contents

Figures

Tables

Acknowledgments

READING ROBERT HUDEC'S BOOK *Enforcing International Trade Law: The Evolution of the Modern GATT Legal System* sparked my interest in trade adjudication. Although a legal scholar, Hudec had a deep appreciation for the political obstacles that shape use of the law. Competing interests within and between states give rise to inconsistent laws and trade disputes, and Hudec observed that in this context, law takes on a dimension of political theater. My book explains the process through which leaders performing for a domestic audience are more likely to turn to legal dispute settlement, and it shows how legal action provides information that allows the two sides to work out their differences. I never had the opportunity to meet Robert Hudec, but I hope he would have found some parts of this book interesting.

More directly, this project has developed through the critical questions and feedback over many years from scholars who have long been at the forefront of studying trade disputes. I thank Chad Bown, Marc Busch, and Greg Shaffer for extensive comments on the manuscript and earlier papers. Eric Reinhardt raised several important questions early on in the project that influenced my thinking about trade disputes, and he provides a service to the field by making his data on GATT disputes available. I owe much that I know about Japanese trade policy to long conversations with Ichirō Araki and Tsuyoshi Kawase, who also introduced me to the wider network of trade experts in Japan. Many scholars and practitioners shared insights from their own research and experience with WTO dispute settlement. I am grateful to Peter Allgeier, Joshua Bolten, Stephen Chaudoin, Jeffrey Dunoff, James Durling, Roberto Enchandi, Gary Horlick, Keisuke Iida, Merit Janow, Moonhawk Kim, Akira Kotera, Giovanni Maggi, Clarita Costa Maia, Ken Matsumoto, Mitsuō Matsushita, Leo Palma, Saadia Pekkanen, Amelia Porges, Timothy Reif, Stephanie Rickard, Sōichirō Sakuma, Jeffrey Schott, Susan Schwab, Richard Steinberg, Carmen Suro-Bredie, Yoichi Suzuki, Alan Sykes, Akihiko Tamura, Daniel Tarullo, Shintarō Watanabe, Bruce Wilson, and Masaru Yamada. Others who asked to remain anonymous are not mentioned here by name, but contributed greatly to my research through their generosity in taking time away from their hectic schedules to grant me an interview.

The broader scholarly community has given valuable feedback. I would like to acknowledge my gratitude to Karen Alter, Sarah Brooks, Jeff Colgan, Cédric Dupont, Manfred Elsig, Songying Fang, Jeffry

Frieden, Kishore Gawande, Judith Goldstein, Lucy Goodhart, Saori Katada, Daniel Kono, Jack Levy, Mark Manger, Ed Mansfield, Lisa Martin, Megumi Naoi, Sharyn O'Halloran, Elizabeth Perry, Jon Pevehouse, Peter Rosendorff, Anne Sartori, Kenneth Scheve, Leonard Schoppa, Beth Simmons, Randall Stone, Jordan Tama, Alexander Thompson, Michael Tomz, and James Vreeland. Susan Pharr has been a dedicated advisor; she has overseen my undergraduate senior thesis and doctoral studies, and offered wisdom to help me during my uncertain times as assistant professor. I appreciate her willingness to continue to read my papers and guide my career development.

I am grateful for the opportunity to present parts of the book at Columbia University, The Graduate Institute in Geneva, Harvard University, Humboldt University in Berlin, Northwestern University, Ohio State University, Oxford University, Rutgers University, Sophia University in Tokyo, Stanford University, UCLA, University of Pennsylvania, University of Virginia, Yale University, and several academic conferences. At Princeton, the International Relations Colloquium offered an important venue to present early versions of my research. Excellent questions from the students and faculty at all of these institutions led me to clarify my argument and strengthen the evidence.

Colleagues and visiting scholars at Princeton University contributed to a rich intellectual environment. Joanne Gowa gave the right mix of criticism and support to keep me going through this long project. Always ready to exchange comments on our research or share stories about our children, she has been the ideal mentor and a great friend during my years at Princeton. Amy Borovoy, Amaney Jamal, and Sophie Meunier offered encouragement and advice on how to more effectively communicate my ideas and shared in those lighter moments necessary to keep everything in perspective. Robert Keohane, Helen Milner, and Andrew Moravcsik provided useful comments that challenged me to think more broadly when I became too focused on the intricacies of trade disputes. I was fortunate to have Stephen Kaplan and Krzysztof Pelc across the hall during my final year of completing the project, as they gave detailed comments on the manuscript and kept asking when I would be finished. Daniela Campello, Leany Lemos, and Valeria Silva helped me to understand the politics of Brazilian trade policies both through sharing their knowledge and introducing me to officials in Brazil.

The book involved substantial data collection, for which I relied on many research assistants. First and foremost, Raymond Hicks has been an invaluable source of advice and made it almost too easy to add more variables to the analysis with his efficient help collecting data. I cannot thank him enough for the countless times he quickly responded to my questions and requests—often going beyond what I had thought to ask for. In addition, I appreciate the work by many undergraduate and graduate students who diligently coded trade reports and provided background research for the case studies: Ryan Brutger, Wamiq Chowdhury, Courtenay Dunn, Jonathan Elist, Crystal Frierson, Mariko Hayashi, Mark Jia, Ann Lee, Lubna Malik, Jennifer Oh, Anbinh Phan, Eri Saikawa, John Stevenson, Jason Weinreb, Meredith Wilf, and Derek Wong. I thank Wendy Hansen for sharing her data on industry associations, and I thank Doug Weber at the Center for Responsive Politics for assistance with data on political contributions.

John Odell taught me to see the politics behind negotiation strategies from a broader perspective. His leadership brought out the best in each of the submissions for an edited volume on trade negotiations during a series of conferences, and I am happy to be able to publish an abridged version of my contribution to that volume as chapter seven in this book. I thank Cambridge University Press for permission to reprint parts of "Do WTO Rules Create a Level Playing Field for Developing Countries? Lessons from Peru and Vietnam." from John Odell, ed. *Negotiating Trade: Developing Countries in the WTO and NAFTA.* (Cambridge: Cambridge University Press, 2006), pp. 219–56.

I am greatly indebted to Sarah Blodgett Bermeo, who coauthored with me the paper "Who Files? Developing Country Participation in the GATT/WTO," *Journal of Politics* 71, no. 3 (July 2009): 1033-49. Data from that article is included in the dataset analyzed in chapter three. Sarah also worked as a research assistant for the book project and provided useful input as a scholarly critic and friend.

Yuki Shirato was involved with this project from its inception in 2003, when we first began to work on a paper about why Japan's steel industry advocated using WTO dispute settlement against foreign trade barriers even as the electronics industry remained passive. This led to our coauthored article "Firms, Governments, and WTO Adjudication: Japan's Selection of WTO Disputes," *World Politics* 59, no. 2 (January 2007): 274-313. Insights from our collaborative work and the data we created together are carried into the analysis of chapter five in this book. As he moved from working at Keidanren to being a student at business and law school, Yuki has given me a window on a wider range of questions beyond political science and offered valuable feedback on my ideas.

Funding support for the research was generously awarded by an Abe Fellowship, the Cyril E. Black Preceptor award, and Princeton University. Two years of sabbatical leave granted by Princeton University allowed me time to focus on my research. I greatly appreciate the courtesy of Aiji Tanaka and the Center for Global Political Economy at Waseda

University to make office space available to me during extended visits to Japan for research during the summers of 2009 and 2010.

At Princeton University Press, Chuck Myers encouraged the project and helped me to focus on the core questions of why states litigate and how it matters. Ben Holmes ably oversaw the production process. I am grateful to Joseph Dahm for excellent copyediting of the manuscript, and thank Richard Comfort for compiling the index. I appreciate the suggestions from two anonymous reviewers.

My deepest gratitude is for my family, who made it possible for me to balance the demands of completing the book while also being a wife and mother. My parents Alton and Carole Davis and my parents-in-law Takashi and Fumiko Imai patiently listened to all of my worries and helped in any way they could despite living far away. Words are inadequate to express my thanks to Kosuke Imai. Whether teaching me the logic of causal inference and matching analysis or taking on more tasks at home to allow me time for work, he has always been there for me as intellectual partner and supportive husband. I dedicate the book to Kosuke and our children. Keiji and Misaki were born and grew from infant to school age during the years it has taken to complete this book. I hope that some of the lessons it contains on dispute settlement will help them to manage their own relations!

Abbreviations

ACCJ	American Chamber of Commerce in Japan
ACWL	Advisory Centre on WTO Law
AD	Antidumping
APEC	Asia-Pacific Economic Cooperation
ASEAN	Association of Southeast Asian Nations
BTA	Bilateral Trade Agreement
CFA	Catfish Farmers of America
CRP	Center for Responsive Politics
DOC	Department of Commerce
DPI	Database of Political Institutions
DPJ	Democratic Party of Japan
DS	dispute settlement
DSU	Dispute Settlement Understanding
EC	European Community
ECJ	European Court of Justice
EU	European Union
FDI	foreign direct investment
FTA	free trade agreement
GATS	General Agreement on Trade in Services
GATT	General Agreement on Tariffs and Trade
GDP	gross domestic product
ICJ	International Court of Justice
IIPA	International Intellectual Property Alliance
IMF	International Monetary Fund
IPR	intellectual property rights
ISIC	International Standard Industry Classification
ITC	International Trade Commission
ITO	International Trade Organization
JCCT	Joint Commission on Commerce and Trade (U.S.–China)
JFTC	Japan Fair Trade Commission
LDC	least developed country
LDP	Liberal Democratic Party (Japan)
METI	Ministry of Economy, Trade, and Industry (Japan)
MFN	most favored nation
MITI	Ministry of International Trade and Industry (Japan)
MOFA	Ministry of Foreign Affairs (Japan)
NAFTA	North American Free Trade Agreement
NAICS	North American Industry Classification System

NSC   Nippon Steel Corporation
NTB   nontariff barrier
NTE   National Trade Estimate Report
ODA   official development assistance
OECD   Organisation for Economic Co-operation and Development
PAC   political action committee
PARC   Policy Affairs Research Council (Japan)
PR   proportional representation
PTA   preferential trade agreement
RTAA   Reciprocal Trade Agreement Act
SED   Strategic Economic Dialogue (U.S.–China)
TBT   Agreement on Technical Barriers to Trade
TRIMs   Agreement on Trade-Related Investment Measures
TRIPS   Agreement on Trade-Related Aspects of Intellectual
                Property Rights
UNCTAD   United Nations Conference on Trade and Development
UNICE   Union of Industrial and Employers' Confederations
                of Europe
USTR   United States Trade Representative
VASEP   Vietnam Association of Seafood Producers
VAT   value-added tax
VER   voluntary export restraint
WTO   World Trade Organization

WHY ADJUDICATE?

1

Introduction

WHY DO STATES turn to international courts to resolve their disputes? Liberal protesters on the streets condemn international organizations as servants of corporate interests, while conservative skeptics of international law reject intervention into state decision making by international bureaucrats. Governments of both large and small states have reason to avoid courts. Powerful states like the United States and EU have tools for leverage in bilateral negotiations. Whether offering side payments or threatening unilateral sanctions, they can influence the behavior of smaller states without need for a third party. At the same time, small developing countries fear legalization will merely introduce another tool where they lack capacity and cannot defend their interests. It is not as if filing a lawsuit mobilizes a police force. For all of their "court-like" appearance, international courts are fundamentally different from domestic courts because they lack the authority to impose their rulings in an anarchic international system. Moreover, using courts is costly. Hiring lawyers, preparing formal briefs, and taking a dispute into the public arena cost time and money and also risk injuring diplomatic relations. Nonetheless, we observe a clear trend toward legalization as more areas of international affairs are regulated by international law, and the number and authority of international courts have grown. States are increasingly turning to courts to solve disputes.

They do so in order to achieve better outcomes. The choice of adjudication represents a shift in process—not abdication of sovereignty.[1] Governments negotiate international rules and decide when and how to enforce them. Often states retain gatekeeper status over which legal complaints are filed. They have discretion over whether to comply with rulings issued against them by international judges. Governments give up some control when they enter formal dispute settlement and open themselves to third-party involvement, but this sacrifice of autonomy comes as a deliberate choice.

Understanding the decision to use legal enforcement is critical for evaluating how international institutions shape state behavior. The

---

[1] The literature interchangeably uses the terms *litigation* and *adjudication*. Following Abbott et al. (2000) and Trachtman (1999) I will generally use the term *adjudication*.

effectiveness of any legal system depends upon the actions of the police, prosecutor, and judge. One must consider the interaction of law with the probability of enforcement. Given the same set of legal commitments and punishment standard, challenges to every small infraction push the system toward strict compliance while imperfect enforcement induces weak compliance. In the absence of a central prosecutor or police force, most international regimes depend upon member states to monitor the policies of other states and to challenge specific violations. What are the incentives for states to take on this enforcement role?

This book argues that states use international adjudication in order to manage domestic political pressure and pursue international cooperation. The decision to invoke international law in a dispute does not proceed automatically on merits of the case alone. While the stakes in the outcome and legal standard for each case are important factors in the decision to enforce rules, these are not the only criteria. One must recognize the intensely political nature of filing a lawsuit against another country. Addressing a dispute in a legal venue raises new costs for the state in terms of legal preparation, diplomatic relations, and risk of precedent that could affect a wider range of issues. Some actors may prefer negotiations that allow flexibility in terms of when and how to resolve the dispute between two states without formal procedures, third parties, and publicity. As a result, many cases that could be taken to court are instead negotiated. Those states with domestic constraints on executive autonomy, however, will find it hard to accept negotiated compromises. In democracies, and especially those democracies with sharp partisan divisions and institutional checks and balances in the structure of government, the executive faces demands from the legislature to demonstrate its effort to enforce the agreements ratified by the legislature. The executive here includes the president or prime minister and the bureaucracy. Domestic constraints that encourage visible accountability limit the flexibility for an executive to reach informal compromises. Engaging in political theater by initiating legal action against a foreign government proves to be an effective strategy not only for dealing with foreign governments but also for managing domestic pressure. Willingness to bear the costs of going to court signals that the government gives priority to enforcement. As a result, incentives to use courts arise from their usefulness as a political tool and not only from their role to interpret the law and allocate punishment.

This book will test the implications of political demand for adjudication in analysis of when and how states have used adjudication to resolve trade disputes. I develop a theory about domestic constraints to explain why democratic states are more likely to file legal complaints against trade barriers and select their cases based on the political influence of the affected industry. Checks on executive autonomy in the domestic institutional framework encourage the government to be responsive to industry interests. Choosing adjudication as a trade strategy allows the government to visibly demonstrate enforcement actions to its domestic audience and signal strong resolve to a trade partner. Adjudication functions as a response to domestic pressure that promotes settlement of trade disputes by providing information about preferences.

The question of how states maintain cooperation in anarchy without centralized enforcement has been a major theme in international relations scholarship. Leading theories account for why states agree to a rule framework. Powerful states have incentives to provide public goods that benefit systemic stability and have the capacity to supply centralized enforcement (e.g., Gilpin, 1981; Kindleberger, 1986). In the face of market failures that could prevent cooperation, states establish institutions that lower transaction costs (Keohane, 1984). Distributional conditions along with the externalities of the issue influence how these institutions are designed to balance the interests of states (Martin, 1992b; Koremenos, Lipson, and Snidal, 2001). Legalization, defined in terms of the obligation for compliance, precision of rules, and delegation to third-party dispute settlement, represents one dimension of variation in the form of international institutions (Abbott et al., 2000, p. 401).[2]

High levels of legalization that include delegation to third-party dispute settlement are evident across security, human rights, and economic issue areas. War crimes have been challenged by international tribunals since the Nuremberg Trials and more recently by the International Criminal Court. The International Court of Justice has a varied set of cases including territorial disputes and claims regarding mistreatment of foreign nationals. The UN Convention on the Law of the Sea refers disputes that cannot be resolved amicably to the International Tribunal for the Law of the Seas. The European Human Rights Convention established a court that has a large docket of cases brought by individuals against their own governments. Regional integration has deepened as economic regulations for a common market are enforced by courts: the European Court of Justice is the most prominent regional court, but many other regional communities including the Andean Pact and Mercosur in Latin America and the Common Market of Eastern and Southern Africa have courts that hear cases related to economic disputes among member states. Bilateral investment treaties provide for dispute settlement by third parties such as the International Court of Arbitration or International Centre for Settlement of Investment Disputes. Finally, trade, as the area that is the subject of this book, offers an example of

---

[2] See a special issue of the journal *International Organization* (Goldstein et al., 2000) for comprehensive analysis of the concept of legalization and its application across issue areas.

legalization with hundreds of trade disputes addressed in a formal dispute settlement process by members of the General Agreement on Tariffs and Trade (GATT) and now the World Trade Organization (WTO).

The legalization of international affairs has attracted growing attention, but there is a need to explain why states use courts. Research has primarily focused on when states comply with their commitments (Chayes and Chayes, 1995; Downs, Rocke, and Barsoom, 1996; Simmons, 2000). Less attention has been given to how other states respond to violations. When the harm from cheating and benefits of cooperation are shared broadly across states, enforcement represents a public good where each state may seek to free ride on actions of others rather than "play the role of policeman" (Axelrod and Keohane, 1986, p. 235). One of the main functions of international institutions is to provide information about compliance in order to increase the reputational costs of noncompliance (Keohane, 1984; Dai, 2007). Yet many regimes rely upon decentralized enforcement. The states that challenge violations play an important role in establishing regime effectiveness because their actions trigger the material and reputational mechanisms for compliance in the institution.

Litigation also serves domestic purposes. Democratization and legalization have grown as two parallel trends in international politics. The increase in the number of democratic states since 1970 has been accompanied by an increase in the use of international courts across a range of policy areas from human rights to trade and investment. The close connection between democracy and judicial institutions within a state is widely recognized (e.g., Larkins, 1996; Widner, 2001; La Porta et al., 2004; Stephenson, 2003). More recently it has become evident that democratic states also show an affinity for the use of courts to resolve international disputes. The advanced industrial democracies have taken the leading role in the establishment of international courts. Democratic regime type increases the likelihood that a pair of states will seek legal dispute settlement of a territorial dispute (Allee and Huth, 2006). In the area of trade adjudication, research has highlighted the positive relationship between democracy and trade complaints in both the GATT and WTO periods (Busch, 2000; Reinhardt, 2000; Davis and Bermeo, 2009; Sattler and Bernauer, forthcoming). Indeed, during the first decade of WTO adjudication, authoritarian governments brought only ten disputes.[3] The democratic preference for legalized dispute settlement is one dimension of a broader complementarity between

---

[3] This counts distinct dispute matters with a WTO complaint filed between 1995 and 2004. Authoritarian governments are classified as those with a score below 6 on the polity 2 measure of democratic institutions.

democracy and multilateralism highlighted in several recent studies (e.g., Moravcsik, 2000; Mansfield and Pevehouse, 2006; Keohane, Moravcsik, and Macedo, 2009; Simmons, 2009).

The emergence of China as a major player in the trading system raises new questions. China has begun to take part in adjudication as both complainant and defendant in several cases. Although it filed only one complaint during its first five years as a new WTO member, China initiated five cases over the period 2008–10. Such action demonstrates that authoritarian states may also use international courts. Domestic constraints arise within the authoritarian context, and future research must explore more carefully such variation. Nonetheless, WTO adjudication by China continues to lag behind its democratic counterparts and is small relative to the growing share of protection measures imposed on Chinese exports. According to one measure of trade barriers, Chinese exports at the global level face nearly four times the level of barriers imposed against the exports from other countries (Bown, 2010, p. 5). Such high levels of protection give rise to potential demand for adjudication. Against this backdrop, the five cases by China over three years are moderate relative to the six cases filed by the EU and the nine cases filed by the United States during the same period. Notably, other developing countries such as Brazil and Argentina have in past years initiated as many as five cases in one year! Finally, it is illustrative to compare China and Taiwan WTO challenges of antidumping investigations against their firms since they joined the WTO at nearly the same time (December 2001 and January 2002, respectively), and this is the most frequently challenged type of trade barrier in WTO adjudication. At first glance, the authoritarian government of China appears more active with five complaints against antidumping investigations relative to two complaints by the democratic government of Taiwan. Yet China confronted 410 investigations and Taiwan only 92, making Taiwan nearly twice as likely as China to use adjudication against any given barrier.[4] While China's evolving approach to trade enforcement strategies is important to watch carefully, the overall pattern across countries remains one in which democracies are the leading litigators.

This book will focus on the use of adjudication in the enforcement of trade rules. Both the theory and empirical analysis compare the choice of adjudication to the alternative to resolve disputes outside of the legal forum. I ask two questions: Under what conditions do states choose legal

---

[4] The data here for the period through the end of 2008 are from Bown (2009a, pp. 81–82), who describes variation in which European Community challenges 19 percent of initiations against its firms relative to India challenging 7 percent, both of which are much higher than either Taiwan or China.

venues for dispute settlement, and how does the legal context change the outcome? My answers will highlight the role of domestic politics to generate demand for adjudication as an enforcement strategy.

The Enforcement of International Trade Law

Trade represents a promising area to examine the role of courts in international affairs. The multilateral trade regime now regulates over $24 trillion in trade on the basis of formal treaty agreements.[5] Although much research focuses on the role of the WTO in liberalizing bilateral trade flows (Rose, 2004; Gowa and Kim, 2005; Goldstein, Rivers, and Tomz, 2007), the WTO conflict resolution mechanism plays a critical role in the ability of states to reach agreements and maintain cooperation (Kovenock and Thursby, 1992; Maggi, 1999; Busch and Reinhardt, 2002; Rosendorff, 2005). Increasing levels of trade that accompany liberalization generate both wealth and conflict as states confront each other with demands for market access and protection for sensitive industries. States established the GATT and then the WTO in order to manage this conflict through a common set of negotiated multilateral rules and a formal process for dispute settlement.

The question of enforcement arises after states conclude a liberalization agreement through negotiating rules and then disagree over whether a trade partner is in compliance with those rules. Such disputes may arise through either a failure of implementation in which exporters never gained the promised market access or through a new barrier that has been imposed in response to changed economic or political conditions. The disputed measure may represent a clear violation of rules or a policy where there could be different interpretations of the agreement. These barriers that present potential inconsistency with the rules may be overlooked by trade partners, negotiated in bilateral talks or multilateral committees, or raised for adjudication. The three steps of liberalization, cheating, and enforcement are interrelated. Low levels of liberalization would be less likely to lead to widespread cheating since compliance is easy, and as a result enforcement would rarely be a problem (Downs, Rocke, and Barsoom, 1996). Deep liberalization commitments are more likely to give rise to incentives for cheating and

---

[5] According to *International Trade Statistics 2010* (data for charts 8 and 10 at http:// www.wto.org, accessed February 17, 2011), WTO members' total merchandise trade was $17.86 trillion and total trade in commercial services was $6.24 trillion for 2009 (trade measured as exports plus imports among WTO members, excluding intra-EU trade). This represents 93.7 percent of world trade in merchandise and 94.8 percent of trade in services.

encounter serious enforcement challenges, but states would not have accepted such commitments in the first place without some assurance regarding enforcement (Fearon, 1998). While recognizing the feedback between enforcement and liberalization promises in the first stage and between enforcement and the likelihood of cheating in the second stage, explaining the question of why states make liberalization commitments and why they subsequently impose protection is not my main purpose. Rather, I am interested to explain when and how states choose to enforce rules. By examining the variation in demand for enforcement within a single issue area and existing rules framework, I am able to take into account many factors that influence the first two stages even as my central argument focuses on the final stage of enforcement decisions.

Background on Adjudication of Trade Disputes

The General Agreement on Tariffs and Trade (GATT) began as a provisional agreement in 1947 with informal consultations to resolve disputes, but within less than a decade practice had evolved to rely upon an appointed panel of experts who issued independent rulings on formal legal complaints about noncompliance. Although commonly referred to as *dispute settlement*, this is simply "a nice sort of nonadversarial, nonthreatening, look-at-the-positive-side phrase for what most people would call a lawsuit" according to Hudec (1987, p. 214). The ability of the defendant to block the establishment of the panel or adoption of a ruling limited the enforcement capacity of states under GATT, but its dispute procedures were nonetheless invoked in over two hundred cases, and states generally complied with rulings (Hudec, 1993). Dispute settlement became more legalistic when the World Trade Organization (WTO) replaced the GATT procedures with a reformed dispute settlement understanding that ended the de facto veto right of defendants and added a standing Appellate Body of judges to review panel decisions.[6] Now a highly legalized dispute settlement process enforces regulations over a wide range of economic policies for a membership of more than 150 states. Since its establishment in 1995, states have addressed over four hundred trade disputes within the WTO dispute settlement process.[7] The issues before the court have ranged from the labeling of sardines to the amount of subsidies received by Boeing and Airbus.

---

[6] For analysis of changes from GATT to WTO see Jackson (1997); Barton et al. (2006); Krueger (1998).

[7] The WTO has assigned a distinct dispute number for 419 disputes as of the end of 2010. Sometimes a new number is assigned for a repeat filing on the same issue, so the actual number of distinct disputes is slightly lower.

The WTO dispute settlement system is a technical legal process. The initial complaint consists of a request for consultations stating the legal basis for the complaint by one or more member government against a specific trade policy measure taken by another member government. All complaints are public information and become part of the official record of WTO disputes. Consultations take place as confidential negotiations in Geneva between the two parties. If settlement is not reached the Dispute Settlement Body will approve the request from the complainant for a panel, which is composed of three or five independent experts chosen in consultation with complainant and defendant. The panel process then requires written submissions from both parties to the panel. These submissions are complex legal arguments about the interpretation of WTO law and the facts related to the trade impact of the policy.[8] The three meetings of the panel include opening and closing statements from the two parties and any third parties with interest in the case, and response to questions from the panel. The process can be ended through mutual agreement at any stage. In the case of an appeal of the panel ruling, both sides again present new submissions to the Appellate Body before a final ruling is issued on the case. A small number of cases continue with further proceedings to evaluate compliance and arbitrate an amount for authorized sanctions. Panel and Appellate Body rulings are detailed legal documents that are typically hundreds of pages in length.

Costly Enforcement

The trade regime relies on decentralized enforcement in which states bring forward claims. In contrast with domestic legal systems, there is no central public prosecutor. Some treaty organizations, such as the International Atomic Energy Agency in the Non-proliferation Treaty regime, provide centralized monitoring to coordinate enforcement actions.[9] Although the Trade Policy Review Mechanism of the WTO provides information on member policies, it has not been used as a means to reveal noncompliance (Hoekman and Mavroidis, 2000; Patel, 2008).

---

[8] Although the written submissions are generally not public documents, some governments such as the United States make them publicly available (see http://www.ustr.gov/Trade_Agreements/Monitoring_Enforcement/Dispute_Settlement/WTO/Section_Index.html). The first U.S. submission as complainant for one relatively minor case, "Mexico—Definitive Antidumping Measures on Beef and Rice," was 91 pages in length. Its first submission as defendant for the case, "United States—Definitive Safeguards Measures on Imports of Certain Steel Products," was 373 pages in length.

[9] See Dai (2002) for discussion of the conditions that lead to different institutional design in monitoring functions.

The WTO Secretariat explicitly remains neutral on member inquiries about compliance questions, and the reviews are too infrequent to represent an alarm system alerting members about noncompliance. Only panels and the Appellate Body render judgments on compliance, and these are in response to member complaints. While strategic action by the court as an agent is possible in the ruling phase, the court cannot solicit or refuse to hear a case. This institutional design means states remain the central actor for enforcement because only states have the authority to enforce the agreement through filing a complaint under the dispute settlement provisions of the agreement. As a result, enforcement will be only as great as the willingness and capacity of states to monitor and challenge the trade barriers of their trade partners.

If enforcement were costless, we would see all violations brought forward as complaints. Instead, the number of potential trade disputes is large, and only a small proportion are raised for adjudication. Although there have been over four hundred WTO complaints, many more WTO inconsistent policies are not challenged. The barriers are either ignored or addressed in other venues. For example, the United States National Trade Estimate Report, which monitors the trade barriers of U.S. trade partners that harm U.S. exports, listed 126 trade barriers by Japan during the years 1995 to 2004, of which only 6 were addressed in WTO dispute settlement. Most were addressed in other negotiation venues, but these often continued to be reported as serious problems without resolution of the complaint. Partial progress is reported for some cases, but 41 barriers continued to be reported after more than two years of negotiations and no report of any progress to resolve the complaint. Yet the United States is the *most* active complainant in WTO dispute settlement! The number of potential WTO disputes that are never filed may be even larger for developing countries, which face greater obstacles to filing cases. Costs at the level of industry and government inhibit filing many potential cases.

Failure of export industries to mobilize for government intervention against foreign trade barriers may contribute to imperfect enforcement of trade agreements. Governments rely upon industry to inform them of foreign trade barriers, and WTO adjudication typically goes forward as a public-private partnership in which industry demand begins the process (Shaffer, 2003). The affected industries represent a critical "enforcement constituency" (Iida, 2006, p. 29). To initiate the process, they must identify barriers, determine the economic value of replacing the barrier with WTO-consistent policy, and use resources to lobby government (Bown, 2009a). So the question is, when will an export industry have incentives to lobby its government to challenge foreign trade barriers? Export industries may find that a trade barrier represents too small of a hindrance to justify mobilization. Competitive markets generate a collective action problem—when the foreign trade barrier is nondiscriminatory, its removal would equally benefit all exporters so that no individual firm has incentive to mobilize for its removal. Those in high-velocity business environments will face opportunity costs for lobbying and enforcement strategies that take years to achieve results (Davis and Shirato, 2007). For example, the Japanese firm NEC chose not to ask its government to challenge U.S. antidumping duties on its supercomputers in the WTO because it had already moved on with other strategies to improve market share and did not want to wait for the WTO verdict (ibid., p. 303). Finally, firms that have invested in building good relations with foreign governments and developing their market image with buyers in foreign markets worry that lobbying in favor of legal action could produce backlash in other areas against their interests. These factors reduce enforcement levels where industry interests are insufficient to produce mobilization. Cheating by the trade partner may go unobserved by a government because their industry fails to inform them of the negative impact, or the government will give low priority to the matter if their own industry responds passively to inquiry about the problem.

Nonetheless, many export interests do lobby to demand government intervention against foreign trade barriers. In some cases, export firms do not face collective action problems for mobilization because they compete in oligopolistic markets (e.g., aircraft manufacturers) or face narrow discriminatory trade barriers (e.g., antidumping duties that are assessed on specific firms).[10] Less diversified industries with a narrow range of products and long time horizons such as steel and agriculture will find it worthwhile to invest in lobbying for trade barrier removal. Industry associations help to overcome collective action problems. In a poor country like Pakistan, coordination by the All Pakistan Textile Mills Association led to the necessary support of industry to split the burden of legal fees with the government for a WTO case against U.S. restrictions on cotton yarn exports filed in April 2000 (Hussain, 2005, p. 465). Mobilization is most likely against barriers for industries that are a principal supplier, meaning that they have a sufficiently large share of the market to recoup benefits from improved access even when exporters from other countries could free ride on their effort. Powerful associations that represent a broad set of export interests (e.g., the American Chamber of Commerce, UNICE, and Keidanren) lobby for removal of barriers that may not cause severe damage to any single

---

[10] See Bown (2009a, pp. 100–104) for list of firms associated with backing specific WTO disputes.

industry but nonetheless worsen the export environment. Dai (2007, p. 56) argues that the ready availability of industry as low-cost monitors willing to inform governments about noncompliance accounts for why states chose a decentralized compliance mechanism in the WTO.

A second factor behind imperfect enforcement is the government role as a filter. In these cases, the harmed export industry may lobby for action against a foreign trade barrier but its government chooses not to act. Officials from countries as diverse as the United States and Canada to Costa Rica and Pakistan said during interviews that they face more potential cases raised by industry than the government will decide to file. Governments do not have the same incentives as their export industry to challenge foreign trade barriers. In a comprehensive study of economic negotiations, Odell (2000, p. 25) demonstrates that officials pursue multiple objectives including economic gains for the industry as well as relational influence with foreign countries and domestic political interests.

Adjudication raises costs related to administrative burden, legal precedent, and diplomatic stakes that concern the government more than industry. Legal fees for hiring an international law firm to handle case preparation are typically about $1 million but vary greatly depending on the case (the United States and EU sometimes hire outside legal assistance, and it is routine for Japan and even some developing countries to do so as well). Some of these costs are shared with the affected industry, but government personnel and financial resources are still dedicated to support the litigation effort.[11] Precedent represents a double-edged sword—winning the ruling may come back to haunt the government as a precedent against its own policies on related issues in the future (Busch, 2007, p. 743). Governments also worry about the risk of losing the ruling, which represents a worse outcome than the status quo because a behavior that had been questionable before the ruling now stands publicly legitimated to be adopted by others.

Diplomatic stakes represent a key reason for imperfect enforcement. Srinivasan and Levy (1996) show in a simple model that governments may favor lower use of a dispute system to challenge foreign trade barriers than demanded by their export industry because the government has a utility function that includes political relations with a trade partner in addition to their shared utility with their export industry for removal of the foreign barrier. Leaders may want to overlook the sins of their trade partners in "tacit collusion" where both agree to tolerate some

---

[11] This burden accounts for the evidence that many developing countries struggle to use legal enforcement to their advantage (e.g., Kim, 2008; Davis and Bermeo, 2009).

cheating (Hoekman and Mavroidis, 2000, p. 529).[12] They may fear that challenging a trade partner's barrier would be linked to other economic policies, whether by countersuits in WTO adjudication or in other policy areas.[13] The public nature of suing a trade partner can contribute to acrimonious rhetoric harmful to diplomatic relations. The country imposing a trade barrier provokes resentment from producers in the trade partner whose interests are harmed, but may nonetheless be hostile to the decision of the trade partner to challenge the measure in public as a violation. The tendency to view complaints as a diplomatic insult is not new with the WTO—the view of legal complaints as aggressive actions had suppressed the number of GATT complaints in the 1960s, and it led some members during Tokyo Round negotiations to call for specific wording in the new understanding on dispute settlement noting that complaints should not be intended or considered as contentious acts (Hudec, 1980, p. 178). The WTO Dispute Settlement Understanding (article 3.10) states, "It is understood that requests for conciliation and the use of the dispute settlement procedures should not be intended or considered as contentious acts." The sense that this provision is necessary acknowledges the fear of negative consequences. Beyond this formal exhortation there is little the regime can do to prevent the kinds of subtle linkages feared by industry and governments that contemplate suing a trade partner. The foreign government could easily adopt small measures that may worsen the business environment for exporters or investors related to the dispute or those in completely different economic sectors without engaging in actual violation of rules. A tense summit between leaders or rebuff of a foreign policy initiative would be even more difficult to directly connect with a trade dispute, but officials acknowledge concerns that such ripple effects could occur.

Restraint motivated by diplomatic relations can affect both large and small states. Concern about maintaining good relations with its allies during the Cold War led the United States to tolerate some trade violations under the GATT regime as a small cost in a larger grand strategy (Low, 1993). For example, the development of the European Common Market and especially its Common Agricultural Policy harmed some U.S. economic interests and raised several points of violation with GATT rules, but also represented a pillar of U.S. foreign policy to

---

[12] This follows the logic of efficient breach in contract theory where not all provisions are completely enforced. The literature has mostly focused on the formal exceptions written into agreements such as safeguard policies and restraints on punitive measures (e.g., (Rosendorff and Milner, 2001; Schwartz and Sykes, 2002; Downs and Rocke, 1995). Lax enforcement represents a more informal means of achieving flexibility in agreements.

[13] Busch and Reinhardt (2002, p. 464) list examples of *countersuits* in GATT/WTO adjudication.

support the integration and strength of Europe as an ally against the Soviet Union. The decision not to challenge the onset of these policies was as much about foreign policy as economic interests or international law. Smaller countries feel even more need to think twice about the possible diplomatic ramifications of suing trade partners. For developing countries, dependence on foreign aid has been shown to reduce initiation of WTO complaints (Bown, 2005a).

The potential for trade disputes to exacerbate diplomatic relations is clear from a few examples. Alter (2003, p. 789) notes that the long-standing U.S. conflict with Europe's ban against hormone-treated beef "continues to anger US beef producers, while raising the ire of the European public." When the United States filed two WTO complaints alleging that China offered inadequate protection of intellectual property rights, the Chinese spokesman for the Ministry of Commerce protested that "the decision runs contrary to the consensus between the leaders of the two nations about strengthening bilateral trade ties and properly solving trade disputes. It will seriously undermine the cooperative relations the two nations have established in the field and will adversely affect bilateral trade."[14] Although such protests may be more rhetorical than serious, governments still feel a need to take into account potential harm to diplomatic relations from their trade policy actions. Interviews with trade lawyers and officials involved in disputes suggest that diplomatic concerns are a factor that can either delay the timing for when a case is initiated or prevent one altogether.[15]

Diplomatic stakes are more likely to deter enforcement actions than to deter defection from the trade agreement by a protectionist trade partner because of the differences in policy-making venue. Trade barriers are typically enacted as a domestic economic policy. The policy process privileges the affected producer groups. The regulatory agencies in charge of trade remedies or the legislature that authorizes new standards or subsidies are favorable to serving producer interests. Enforcement of trade agreements, however, is conducted as foreign economic policy. Here the executive holds agenda control. While typically an executive is more pro–free trade than a legislature for the negotiation of trade agreements, their greater sensitivity to diplomatic relations makes the executive less tough on enforcement. This point will be further developed in this book as a key variable for why domestic constraints may shift preferences for enforcement.

---

[14] Xinhua news report, "China Expresses Regret, Dissatisfaction over U.S. Complaints at WTO," April 10, 2007, available at People's Daily Online, http://english.people.com.cn/.

[15] Interviews with USTR official and a lawyer at leading international law firm, Geneva, October 2007.

As an action within agreed upon rules, however, WTO adjudication is *less costly than unilateral retaliation*. From the perspective of both diplomatic relations and the consumer loss incurred by raising tariffs, market closure is an extreme tactic to gain market access. Threatening complete withdrawal from the trade regime (as in the "grim trigger" strategy that upholds cooperation over repeated games) is so costly that it does not represent a credible response to a single act of defection by a trade partner raising a trade barrier. In a more proportional "tit-for-tat" response, states may simply raise their own tariff on similar goods to those harmed by the partner's trade barrier. Yet even a proportional punishment strategy encounters problems. Small states lack the power to make effective threats, and raising tariffs would harm their own interests. Large states with sufficient market share to influence world prices and benefit from setting an optimal tariff nonetheless have reasons to be cautious about unilateral retaliation. At the international level, trade partners resent the perception that another state is acting as judge and jury to punish what they may consider a justifiable policy. Threats can provoke negative backlash as the target state domestic audience unifies in opposition to foreign criticism (Odell, 1993). Unilateral retaliation may spiral into a trade war if the partner responds with its own "tit-for-tat" sanctions. The risk of excessive response in retaliation looms large, especially for states sensitive to interest group pressures. Retaliatory policies have the potential to become a vehicle for a log roll between export industries seeking competitive advantage through lowering foreign barriers and import-competing domestic industries seeking to use the retaliatory tariffs for protection.

The costs of unilateral retaliation for both the large state choosing to use it and the smaller states fearful of its abuse were a primary motivation for strengthening adjudication as an alternative strategy. As the United States experienced domestic pressure to address its growing trade deficit in the 1980s, aggressive trade enforcement actions were demanded by Congress and industry. Macroeconomic conditions were the driving force of trade imbalances, but politically the demand for retaliation against foreign protection had a more powerful appeal than recommendations for policies to encourage domestic savings (Bergsten and Noland, 1993). The use of unilateral retaliation by the United States had moderate success in opening foreign markets but was met by hostility of trade partners (Bayard and Elliott, 1994). The costs of unilateral retaliation produced a convergence of interests for reforms of dispute settlement system in the Uruguay Round negotiations as the United States advocated a strengthened legal system for adjudication of disputes in the hopes it would legitimize enforcement efforts, while its trade partners sought a strengthened legal system to restrain U.S. unilateral measures (Barton et al., 2006, p. 71).[16]

The WTO rules make unilateral retaliation even more costly by framing the act as a violation of international trade law punishable by sanctions. Bayard and Elliott (1994, p. 351) conclude their study of U.S. trade retaliation policies to say that the strengthened WTO dispute system presented the United States with a choice of whether it would act as a "sheriff, aggressively enforcing multilateral rules from within the system" or a "vigilante, turning its back on the system and using force to pursue its unilateral demands." This was tested most explicitly in the 1995 U.S.-Japan negotiations in which the United States issued demands for guarantees of increased market share in the Japanese auto and auto parts market. When the breakdown of bilateral negotiations led the U.S. government to threaten retaliation against Japanese auto exports to the United States, Japan filed a WTO complaint against the U.S. retaliation measures. Recognizing it would lose the case, the United States instead backed down on its major demands to make a deal. Separately the EU won a WTO ruling that mandated retaliation measures could only follow WTO rulings.[17] The WTO has raised the costs of unilateral retaliation to the point where this no longer represents a routine trade policy strategy even for the United States. At the same time, filing a complaint in the dispute settlement process represents a moderate-cost trade strategy that allows a government to take enforcement action without resorting to unilateral trade sanctions.

Forum Choice for Trade Disputes

While a growing literature examines WTO adjudication, little research compares adjudication with alternative strategies. Research has focused largely on explaining why states implement WTO-inconsistent policies and the outcomes of observed legal disputes (e.g., Busch, 2000; Reinhardt, 2001; Rosendorff, 2005; Bown, 2004b, c; Guzman and Simmons, 2002). Several studies examine why some trade issues are taken before

---

[16] The United States had often justified unilateral actions with reference to the weakness of the GATT dispute system that allowed defendants to block negative panel rulings. Trade partners wanted to remove this excuse with the establishment of a robust adjudication process (Hudec, 1993, p. 193).

[17] "United States—Sections 301–310 of the Trade Act of 1974" (WTO DS152). The complaint was filed November 1998 and the panel ruling adopted January 2000. The ruling found that the U.S. law itself was not a violation, but noted that this conformity was contingent on the United States implementing Section 301 in conjunction with a WTO ruling and authorization of retaliation. See http://www.wto.org/ english/tratop_e/dispu_e/cases_e/ds152_e.htm.

formal WTO adjudication (e.g., Horn, Mavroidis, and Nordstrom, 1999; Reinhardt, 2000; Bown, 2005a; Busch and Reinhardt, 2002; Allee, 2003; Sattler and Bernauer, forthcoming), but more research is needed that compares alternative strategies (Davis and Shirato, 2007). Positive assessments of WTO adjudication as an effective means of dispute settlement in its early years have since given way to more cautious evaluations as several prominent cases have dragged on without resolution (Butler and Hauser, 2000; Iida, 2004). The American Law Institute Project on WTO Case Law offers detailed analysis of effectiveness from legal and economic perspectives for the major WTO cases.[18] The reports highlight a more nuanced view of successes and failures in the record of cases with legal rulings. The complaints filed for adjudication, however, represent a small fraction of the total number of policies in violation of WTO agreements. We can evaluate the effectiveness of adjudication only in comparison with outcomes that would have been achieved had an alternative strategy been chosen for the same issue.

In trade policy, the parallel process of creating regional trade associations, participating in the multilateral trade system, and concluding bilateral arrangements has resulted in overlapping jurisdictions (Davis, 2009). Many trade issues could be addressed in any one of these negotiation forums, or in informal bilateral negotiations. For example, U.S. agricultural exports to Japan have long faced quarantine measures that restrict import of several products. The United States filed multiple legal complaints at the WTO against measures affecting apples while relying on diplomatic meetings at the bilateral level and technical discussions among agriculture department officials to address the import ban prohibiting U.S. potatoes.[19] U.S. complaints about European subsidies to its aircraft industry were addressed through both multilateral negotiations and bilateral talks for nearly four decades with intervening periods of litigation in the late 1980s, more bilateral talks in 1990s, and a return to litigation that has continued from 2004 to 2011. What determines why disputes are sometimes brought into the formal legal process while others are negotiated in different venues and some are ignored? While no two cases are identical, it is important to consider which differences are most important to affect the choice of enforcement strategy. Would

---

[18] These case reports are published in the January issue of *World Trade Review*.

[19] Two disputes related to quarantine policies for apples led to rulings against Japan by the Appellate Body (WT/DS76/AB/R, February 22, 1999, "Japan-Measures Affecting Agricultural Products"; WT/DS245/AB/R, November 26, 2003, "Japan-Measures Affecting the Importation of Apples"). The 2000 USTR National Trade Estimate Report (p. 203) documents the U.S. complaint about Japan's policy to ban import of fresh potatoes from the United States as way to prevent introduction of golden nematode virus.

the nature of the trade barrier, economic stakes, or political pressures be most relevant to account for the divergent approaches in each case?

The standard response would be that states go to court when they need a third party to determine whether a policy is a violation. Courts perform two functions. First, rulings help states to interpret the trade agreement. Given the complexity of issues and large number of members, trade agreements are negotiated as incomplete contracts that leave open gaps for flexible interpretation. From this perspective, trade disputes are taken to court when there is uncertainty about the law. Second, rulings permit the injured party to take retaliatory action against those who commit a violation. Some states deliberately cheat even while they remain committed to the agreement because they face changing domestic political or economic conditions. For example, rising import competition leads some states to impose trade barriers. Third-party authorization of proportional countermeasures allows flexibility to punish the single defection and facilitate return to normal business (Schwartz and Sykes, 2002; Lawrence, 2003; Rosendorff, 2005). According to this logic, litigation is driven by the demand for protection and compensation.

These explanations suggest that we should account for the variation observed in enforcement strategies toward the trade dispute examples previously mentioned in terms of law and economics. From the law-based perspective, one could emphasize that legal status of Japan's apple quarantine was more complex than its potato import ban, and disagreement over the law prevented either side from making a settlement until there had been an Appellate Body ruling. Rules for subsidies have been problematic because vague definitions leave room for interpretation over which set of domestic policies constitute subsidies. The aircraft case raised concerns that both sides could be found to violate rules. From the economic-based perspective, the level of import competition and export stakes matter such that rising import competition for Japanese apple growers mandated Japanese support for trade barriers and U.S. export stakes justified its high enforcement action for apple industry. For the aircraft dispute, the erosion of U.S. market share and release of new European models shifted strategies. Such conditions were indeed important for the cases and drive some of the overall pattern in trade enforcement. But the next section will highlight why law and economics alone are insufficient to understand when and why states use courts to address their trade disputes. Differences in the political influence of the specific industries and shifts in legislative attention to trade enforcement issues were also important for the choices in these specific disputes and more generally.

Puzzles in the Pattern of Trade Adjudication

Several puzzles appear in the empirical pattern of trade disputes that suggest the need to look beyond the role of courts to provide legal clarity and allocate punishment. More than half of all WTO disputes are settled during the period after filing a legal complaint but before a panel issues a ruling on the legal claim.[20] For these cases, the adjudication process has not taken on any role to interpret the law or authorize retaliation. Furthermore, there is little uncertainty about the legal outcome for those cases that proceed to a formal ruling by a panel: nearly 90 percent of panel rulings have found that the challenged policy is in violation of the agreements.[21] The high pro-plaintiff pattern of WTO rulings goes against litigation theories that parties would settle out of court all of the obvious legal cases such that courts would be asked to issue rulings only for those cases close to the legal standard, which would produce on average a 50-percent win rate (Priest and Klein, 1984). One might suspect that the high violation rate reflects intransigence by the defendant. Yet retaliation against noncompliance is rare. In all but a handful of cases the defendant changes the policy within the required period before authorization of retaliation takes place. Through the end of 2010 there had been eighteen instances in which the WTO authorized retaliation, and countries had gone forward to implement retaliation in only nine of these cases. In sum, the role of the panels and Appellate Body to provide legal interpretation that leads to authorization of retaliation appears to be quite modest for most disputes.

The pattern of which states use adjudication raises further questions for standard explanations based on power and interest. In economic negotiations, market size is the most relevant measure of power. When bargaining over market access, those with a larger market have more to

---

[20] Busch and Reinhardt (2003, p. 724) find that 58 percent of WTO cases between 1995 and 2000 were dropped or resolved before a panel ruling. From 1995 to the end of 2010, 126 panel rulings (excluding multiple rulings on a complaint to avoid double counting) had been circulated to members relative to 419 complaints registered at WTO. Since cases filed in 2009 and 2010 would still be working through the legal process and multiple complaints by countries are often grouped into a single panel ruling, the appropriate denominator for comparison with 126 rulings is 286 distinct "matters" subject to complaint by one or more countries over the period 1995–2008. From this set of cases with potential to have had ruling, 56 percent have been dropped or settled through mutual agreement without a panel ruling. The data for rulings and complaints grouped by matter are from worldtradelaw.net, accessed February 24, 2011.

[21] A summary of the 126 adopted reports for standard WTO disputes shows that 111 (88 percent) involved at least one finding of violation with agreements. See http://www.worldtradelaw.net/dsc/database/violationlist.asp, accessed August 3, 2011.

offer as both carrot and stick. In addition, foreign policy tools connected to alliances, foreign aid, and other sources of influence may also confer power resources through linkage tactics. Across any of these measures, the United States and EU stand out as the dominant powers within the trade system. Despite having leverage to generate strong "outside options" in bilateral negotiations, the United States and EU have filed more complaints than any other government. While one could explain their role as trade police in terms of free trade interests and provision of a public good through enforcement of multilateral rules, such an explanation is inconsistent with the fact that the United States and EU are also the most frequent targets of complaints. Moreover, smaller states are also active. In recent years, over half of the states filing complaints have been developing countries. Adjudication appears to be used as a tool by both powerful and weak states.

Enforcement policies respond to industry demand for the removal of foreign trade barriers. A trade interest explanation suggests that states challenge barriers that affect sufficient economic value to justify the cost of enforcement action. States with many large export industries are more likely to file cases because they encounter more trade barriers that meet this threshold.[22] Important cross-national variation in dispute patterns, however, does not fit the predictions of a trade interest model. For example, the Japanese export sector is large relative to its modest use of adjudication, and despite a small economy, the Philippines has used adjudication more often than its larger neighbors Indonesia and Malaysia. In addition, the variation over time in use of adjudication by a large trading state like the United States, which has filed as many as seventeen cases in some years and as few as one case in other years, cannot be explained by the relatively small shifts of trade volumes.

Interest may fail to produce action if governments do not believe they can bring a change in the offending policy. Those who emphasize the role of retaliation as the force behind compliance with trade agreements suggest that market power matters because it provides more force behind the threat of retaliation.[23] Yet the emergence of several small developing

---

[22] Horn, Mavroidis, and Nordstrom (1999) use a measure of trade diversity to show that states with a larger trade portfolio initiate more WTO disputes. Sattler and Bernauer (forthcoming) show that "gravity" in terms of trade flows between states and their economic size are significant variables to explain which states initiate more cases, with similar results when measuring export diversity.

[23] Bown (2004b, 2005a) finds that states with greater retaliatory power to restrict imports from the defendant in a dispute are more likely to initiate a dispute and gain larger trade liberalization outcomes.

countries that are repeat players in WTO adjudication counters the idea
that retaliatory capacity is a necessary condition for active enforcement
policies (Davis and Bermeo, 2009). Contrary to the expectations of
power arguments, developing countries are not reluctant to challenge the
violation of larger trading partners; Guzman and Simmons (2005) show
that poor states are more likely to file against rich countries because there
is more at stake when a trade barrier restricts access to a large market.
Fundamentally, power offers an incomplete explanation of why states
use adjudication because powerful states have credible retaliatory threats
outside of the legal venue.

Overview

This book presents a theory to explain why democratic institutions for
accountability encourage use of adjudication to resolve trade disputes.
I argue that adjudication serves as a release valve that allows governments to respond to multiple competing interests while avoiding a
trade war. On the complainant side, governments file a formal legal
complaint for WTO adjudication as a costly signal to domestic and
foreign audiences of the government's support for exporter interests that
have been harmed by foreign protectionism. On the defendant side too,
allowing oneself to be dragged into court signals support for importer
interests that benefit from the trade barrier.

Use of adjudication as a signaling mechanism is most likely in
democracies where different interests between the executive and legislature generate uncertainty about whether the government will deliver
on market-opening commitments. The key independent variable is constraints on executive autonomy by the legislature. An autonomous executive will have more flexibility to reach negotiated agreements without
the need to resort to public litigation as a costly signal. Constraints on
the executive reduce the flexibility to accept negotiated compromises and
generate demand for visible accountability. These constraints can arise
in a presidential system where the executive faces strong checks and
balances from the legislature and may face an opposition party majority.
Yet even parliamentary systems can experience high constraints when
there is fragmentation among parties in the legislature and coalition rule
that forces the executive to respond to demands from multiple parties.
The division of interests at home increases constraints on the executive
for many policy issues including foreign economic policy. Legal action
offers a visible measure of effort that helps the executive demonstrate to a
skeptical legislature its resolve to defend domestic industry. I hypothesize
that democratic states will have the greatest demand for adjudication

and initiation of cases will vary as a function of electoral balance and government structure. Executives who must govern within a context of constraints arising from partisan and/or institutional divisions will be more litigious than their counterparts who enjoy a majority in the legislature and wide discretion over policy.

My argument about the role of domestic constraints also explains why governments select cases for WTO adjudication according to political influence rather than just economic and legal criteria. Domestic export industries and their representatives in the legislature suspect the executive will be too dovish in negotiations with foreign trade partners and/or the foreign government will not comply. Uncertainty about whether the government can deliver market access reduces the incentives for export industries to offer political contributions and other forms of support. This credibility problem may lead a government to file a WTO dispute as a costly signal of their commitment to the domestic interest group. At the same time, the import industry of the respondent state influences forum choice by encouraging resistance to settlement. Here too, adjudication signals commitment to the industry. As a result, interest group pressure on both sides of a trade dispute pushes politicized trade topics into dispute adjudication.

Chapter 2 develops the argument described above and places it within the context of the related literature. The empirical chapters test my argument at the cross-national level and through comparison of U.S. and Japanese trade policies. In chapter 3, statistical analysis of the use of adjudication by eighty-one states over thirty years from 1975 to 2004 shows that democracies are more likely to file legal complaints while controlling for their market size and trade structure. I use the data to examine different dimensions of democratic politics and evaluate whether demand for adjudication reflects electoral preference for free trade, legal norms, or accountability mechanisms arising from legislative constraints on executive autonomy. The domestic constraints hypothesis receives support from evidence that states with high checks and balances at home are the most frequent users of adjudication. I also show that the same dynamic generates a positive correlation between democracy and the likelihood of a state to be targeted as a defendant in WTO disputes. These findings at the country level are then extended to dyadic data of bilateral relationships to show that domestic politics in terms of institutions of the complainant and defendant and geopolitics in terms of alliance relations between trade partners shape the pattern of disputes.

The empirical analysis of U.S. and Japanese trade policy provides closer examination of policy processes and outcomes. These two countries are similar as two of the largest advanced industrial economies that both enjoy stable democratic governance and commitment to rule of law. But they present a useful contrast because they lie at opposite extremes among the advanced industrial democracies in terms of legislative constraints on trade policy. Both chapter 4 and chapter 5 begin with qualitative assessment of the policy context for trade policy based on examining trade legislation, testimony in the legislature, and interviews of business and government officials. The evidence demonstrates how Congress grants conditional authority to the executive on trade policy. In this context of low delegation from the legislature to the executive the theory predicts more frequent use and politicization in selection of cases for WTO adjudication. By contrast, the Japanese legislature grants considerable autonomy to the bureaucracy for management of foreign trade policy. As a result, there should be lower demand for adjudication and less politicization of case selection. In a parallel structure the chapters then incorporate statistical analysis of enforcement strategies. Using original data based on U.S. and Japanese government reports about foreign trade barriers, I analyze why some potential trade disputes are ignored or negotiated in alternative venues while others are raised for formal adjudication in the WTO. Whereas the United States has been very active in WTO adjudication and consistently uses this strategy for industries that are major sources of political contributions and during periods of divided government, Japan follows a more selective adjudication strategy and initiates only a few cases for large industries with less obvious political influence on selection. The insights are further tested in case studies about specific disputes.

The U.S. case studies show how Congress intervenes to shape U.S. adjudication choices. First, Kodak's battle with Fuji Film for access to the Japanese market illustrates how politicization by an influential firm and its allies in Congress pushed the administration to file a case even when there was a high risk of losing the legal battle (as it did). More complex dynamics arose for the second case study, the Boeing-Airbus dispute. The long saga of U.S. trade policy toward European subsidies for the commercial aircraft industry has culminated in both sides claiming a legal victory in the Boeing-Airbus WTO disputes, but there were decades of false starts with disagreement among industry and Congress and within the administration about the best approach to a threat to the leading export industry. The case study examines each decision juncture since 1970 that raised the question of whether to use adjudication against European aircraft subsidies. By 2004, with Airbus as the new market leader, Boeing came around to favor adjudication, and the political pressure rose as the issue became a topic in the presidential campaign and subject of a Senate resolution demanding action. The United States filed a WTO complaint in 2004 that opened up seven years of adjudication. The case study helps to illustrate across one issue over time how variation in political pressure influences the choice of trade strategy. The final case study of U.S. policy looks across a set of issues with one trade partner. China now takes the place as the lead punching bag for the congressional criticism of foreign trade policy, and here too the administration has used adjudication to manage domestic pressure. The administration refuses congressional demands to take legal action against China for its undervalued currency policy, but carefully selects cases to raise for adjudication on other issues as part of a strategy to defuse political pressure to "do something" against China. The disputes over Chinese industrial policy for semiconductors and automobiles and enforcement of intellectual property rights have a broader purpose than to advance a specific legal claim or economic interest. They are signals that the administration is not afraid to challenge China when it does not comply with the rules, and this tough message is equally important to reassure Congress as it is to warn the Chinese. Each of the case studies also examines the outcomes in terms of how adjudication helped to diffuse political pressure at home and improve bargaining at the international level with trade partners.

The Japanese case studies in chapter 5 demonstrate the absence of political pressure on foreign economic policy. The government has initiated several WTO complaints on U.S. antidumping policies that harm the Japanese steel industry. When filing complaints, bureaucrats and industry take the lead with little interest from the legislature. Whereas U.S. officials face pressure to get tough with China, Japan has been able to pursue patient negotiations without the need to resort to adjudication to satisfy domestic demands. A cultural aversion to litigation could contribute to less frequent use of WTO adjudication by Japan, but this explanation seems implausible given that the Japanese government was a central advocate for legalization of the WTO dispute system and that variation over time in Japan's complaints follows the shift in political constraints.

Where the early chapters focus on how political constraints shape selection of cases for legal complaints, chapters 6 and 7 turn to assess the impact of using the legal process. Chapter 6, with quantitative data from the United States, and chapter 7, with qualitative evidence for developing countries, show that when comparing similar kinds of disputes and trade partners, states gained better outcomes through the dispute mechanism. Building on the model of forum choice and data on potential trade disputes, chapter 6 evaluates the effectiveness of the different strategies for bringing policy change and ending disputes. Conditioning on the fact that the most politicized cases are selected for WTO adjudication, the legal forum is quite effective to resolve disputes. I apply statistical techniques of matching to the sample of negotiated trade barriers to adjust for their propensity to be raised in adjudication, and then conduct regression analysis of dispute outcomes in terms of policy change. The results show that adjudication increases the probability of progress to resolve the complaint by one-third. Furthermore, a duration model that controls for the variables that influence strategy selection shows that adjudication is correlated with a reduction in the time to removal of the barrier.

Chapter 7 demonstrates how even poor states benefit from adjudication. I follow the logic of the book that one must assess the choice of law relative to what would have transpired if the case did not go to the legal venue. Evidence is from a controlled case comparison of a dispute by Peru against EU labeling policies for sardines and a dispute by Vietnam against U.S. labeling policies for catfish. The two small states had identical legal text in trade agreements as the basis for their claim to change the discriminatory labeling rules against fish exports, and both were involved in an asymmetric dispute with a major trading partner. But since Vietnam was not yet a WTO member at the time, it could not follow the same strategy as Peru to file a WTO complaint. Thus in this case study, I take the different choice of enforcement strategy as exogenous and highlight how the use of adjudication by Peru allowed it to win the requested change from Europe while Vietnam's demands were entirely ignored by the United States.[24]

The conclusion chapter reviews the theory about the political role of adjudication. It explores the tension in how adjudication represents both conflict and cooperation between states as they escalate a trade dispute but do so within agreed upon rules. The tendency to sue friends reflects this dynamic—within a broadly cooperative relationship trade adjudication can be part of business as usual. Yet the case studies for both the United States and Japan revealed that adjudication against China as a potential rival brought fears of unwanted tensions arising from the public action of filing legal complaints. A final section extends the implications of the argument for a broader theory of legalization in international relations.

By looking at domestic and international institutions, I show how the two levels fit together. Market failures that domestic problems generate can be resolved through the use of international institutions. This occurs not just in terms of how states design the charter of an international institution, but in their ongoing effort to enforce agreements and maintain cooperation. The political conditions that

---

[24] This case study is a revised version of a chapter that first appeared as Davis (2006).

generate demand for strong enforcement could undermine cooperation, but when they are channeled through dispute settlement they provide leverage for higher levels of enforcement. My conclusions challenge the view of courts as primarily an instrument for legal interpretation and allocation of punishment and highlight their role to mediate domestic political pressure and provide information helpful to settlement.

2

Domestic Constraints and Active Enforcement

THE CENTRAL GOAL of this book is to develop a theory of political demand for legalization with a focus on the role of adjudication in international trade disputes. Legal disputes occupy a middle ground between international conflict and cooperation. The resort to legal action represents a bargaining failure necessitated when two parties cannot resolve their disagreement through negotiation. It is a second best strategy because hiring legal experts, presenting arguments in a public disagreement, and waiting for a third-party ruling raise transaction costs. Nevertheless, the decision also represents cooperation because the parties follow rules to resolve their disagreement rather than take unilateral measures. This chapter will explain how courts play an important role in the ability of democratic politicians to support international commitments. I develop hypotheses about how variation in domestic politics affects the demand for use of adjudication to resolve disputes.

Existing theoretical frameworks are unable to explain the pattern of enforcement within the trade regime. An extension of realist theories would point to an expectation for powerful states to act as the enforcing actor. Power arguments fail to account for why the United States must use international courts to solve its trade disputes when its market power should guarantee credible threats to enforce bilateral bargaining outcomes.[1] Rational institutionalist theories suggest enforcement activities would focus on pursuit of mutual gains in areas where there are complex issues with positive externalities such as intellectual property rights protection. Instead agricultural issues, which do not involve complex economic problems or generate valuable spin-offs, form nearly a third of all disputes, and only a small share have addressed intellectual property rights protection. The economic theory of trade agreements as a repeated prisoners' dilemma that is *self-enforcing* provides little role for dispute settlement. Theories that present trade agreements as incomplete contracts attribute dispute settlement mechanisms as clarifying interpretation

---

[1] As noted in chapter 1, market size (GDP) offers the most relevant measure of power in economic negotiations. Those with larger markets have more carrots and sticks in negotiations. More specific measures for any given dispute could refer to the bilateral export balance or aid flows that offer direct retaliatory capacity.

of agreements. The occurrence of hundreds of trade disputes that almost always lead to a violation ruling indicates that the dispute mechanism is doing more than to resolve legal uncertainty. In sum, the pattern of who files, the selection of issues, and the outcomes of cases challenges the expectations of existing theories.

Taking a closer look at the domestic political origins of trade disputes is necessary to explain the demand for adjudication. The logic of tied hands and two-level games in bargaining has shaped a large research agenda that brings together analysis of domestic politics and international relations (e.g., Schelling, 1960; Putnam, 1988; Milner, 1997; Odell, 2000; Martin, 2000). In particular, existing scholarship highlights the role for domestic politics in the area of trade. Democratic governance has been shown to increase trade cooperation in terms of openness and the number of trade agreements (Milner and Kubota, 2005; Mansfield, Milner, and Rosendorff, 2002). Democratic states rely on external monitoring and enforcement threat as part of a commitment device to support liberalization commitments (Reinhardt, 2003). Variation within democratic polities also shapes outcomes. Research on U.S. trade policy shows that partisanship and the willingness of Congress to delegate authority to the president influence protection levels (Lohmann and O'Halloran, 1994; Bailey, Goldstein, and Weingast, 1997).

This chapter will develop an explanation for how political pressures that shape conditions for liberalizing trade policy also affect enforcement. The executive must demonstrate resolve to act as a tough negotiator on behalf of export interests in order to maintain support for liberalization in the legislature and among industry. This dynamic generates demand for trade adjudication as a costly signal of commitment to defend the market access gains that were promised in the agreement. By increasing the credibility of enforcement, the international organization helps governments to make domestic commitments.

The executive and legislature have different interests for enforcement. While both seek to promote exports and prevent cheating, responsiveness to industry complaints about foreign trade barriers and sensitivity to diplomatic repercussions from aggressive trade policies influence their choice of strategy. A smaller constituency base, shorter time horizons, and low involvement in foreign policy decisions make legislators more responsive to industry interests. In contrast, a national constituency and responsibility for foreign policy make the executive weigh tradeoffs between economic interests and potential negative impact for other policy issues that may arise from enforcement actions (e.g., harm to diplomatic relations, opportunity costs for pursuit of other trade policy goals, risk of bad precedent). Thus the legislature favors tough enforcement actions and the executive will be more cautious about challenging violations of trade partners. Adjudication offers a middle route between negotiation and trade war that helps states to manage these domestic pressures.

Some states will face greater pressures to use this tool in their foreign economic policy. When a gap exists between legislative and executive preferences, conditional delegation forces the executive to demonstrate commitment to enforce agreements. Taking the visible and costly action of adjudication allows an executive to reveal its type as a willing agent for tough trade enforcement. This dynamic increases the use of adjudication and politicizes the selection of cases. States with unified government structure and preferences will have less need to engage in litigation, and will do so only when trade partner resistance and economic interests justify the action. My theory suggests trade enforcement will vary as a function of domestic political conditions. Where constraints limiting executive discretion promote protection policies at home (Lohmann and O'Halloran, 1994), they simultaneously push for more aggressive policies to open foreign markets.

To illustrate, consider the different prism through which the U.S. president and U.S. Congress viewed Chinese policies on intellectual property and currency in September 2010. The U.S. president and executive agencies coordinating across issues had to consider the possibility that a trade war could derail efforts to coordinate with China on economic policies during upcoming meetings at the IMF and G20 Summit and interfere with sensitive foreign policy efforts regarding the hard-won cooperation of China with UN sanctions against Iran's nuclear program. The primary concern for members of Congress was the fear that workers were losing jobs due to unfair trade policies. While the president hoped to address industry and worker complaints and Congress supported foreign policy goals, the two branches approached the same issue of how to address the trade impact of Chinese policies with different priorities. That month the House of Representatives passed legislation to restrict imports from China and the USTR initiated a WTO dispute to challenge a protectionist barrier by China against U.S. exports.[2]

This chapter develops the argument that will be evaluated in subsequent chapters. First, the initial section reviews the multilateral trade

---

[2] The resolution, HR2378, "Currency Reform for Fair Trade Act," was passed on September 29, 2010 by a vote of 348 to 79. It calls for treating undervalued currency as a subsidy that could trigger use of countervailing duties. The WTO complaint, DS414, "China Countervailing and Anti-Dumping Duties on Grain Oriented Flat-rolled Electrical Steel from the United States," was filed September 15, 2010. It challenged the duties China had imposed on U.S. steel imports as a response to subsidies provided industries under the American Recovery and Reinvestment Act of 2009.

regime and its enforcement role. The second section presents the core argument of the book to explain why governments use forum choice to signal resolve. The third section derives testable hypotheses about why democratic states and those with higher constraints on executive autonomy will be more likely to use adjudication.

Trade Institutions and Liberalization

The literature offers three perspectives on the role of multilateral institutions to promote cooperation for trade liberalization. The first portrays multilateral trade agreements as a solution to a prisoners' dilemma that works by reducing incentives to cheat. A second perspective on asymmetric information offers insights into why bargaining failures give rise to legal disputes. The third examines how trade agreements help states to make a domestic commitment to liberalization.

These theories build on assumptions about the societal basis of trade policy preferences. Those who expect to benefit from the gains of trade will mobilize to support policies for openness. Theories predict variation in support for free trade in terms of the comparative advantage of industries and factor abundance (e.g., Rogowski, 1989; Hiscox, 2002; Scheve and Slaughter, 2001). Looking beyond the aggregate interest of society, the endogenous protection literature examines how lobbying by special interests can bias policies toward protection (e.g., Magee, Brock, and Young, 1989; Grossman and Helpman, 2002). From this starting point that preferences and organization of interests matter, I focus on the role of institutions. While preferences alone may account for large historical patterns in the shifts of protection and free trade, they do not offer guidance for the specific strategies adopted to achieve these goals. At the level of midrange theorizing about the form of cooperation, attention to institutions is necessary to explain why two actors with similar economic interests may nonetheless opt for quite different approaches to the question of enforcing rules with partners.

Multilateral Enforcement and Retaliation

Trade liberalization has been driven forward by the reciprocal exchange of market access. Similar to other cooperation dilemmas, reciprocal trade liberalization depends upon both an initial bargain over the terms for market access and expectations for subsequent enforcement of compliance with the rules. The distributional terms of a trade agreement reflect the balance of gains and losses across export and import industries for each participant. Yet states commit to reciprocal trade liberalization under conditions of uncertainty. Vulnerability arises because a state that implements the agreement exposes its import sectors to new competition while the gains for its export sector depend upon foreign market liberalization. If trade partners fail to deliver the promised market access, the liberalizing state is left with an unsatisfactory outcome. This is the classic portrayal in the cooperation literature of trade as a prisoners' dilemma. Large states have incentives to use a tariff to improve their terms of trade while forcing costs onto their trade partners, and all states may face domestic political pressures to protect home industries. By raising trade barriers, they defect from the agreement. This produces suboptimal outcomes for all when other states engage in the same strategy. In repeated interactions such as trade politics, cooperation may be possible because a state can respond to such cheating with retaliation in the next period (Oye, 1985). Problems observing such cheating or costs associated with the implementation of punishment, however, may prevent effective enforcement. Theories have accounted for the emergence of cooperation by the use of international institutions that establish robust enforcement mechanisms in order to reduce the uncertainty about compliance (Keohane, 1984; Martin, 1992a).

Fearon (1998) highlights that states will bring their concerns about compliance into the initial bargaining over outcomes. The challenge is to create the right balance between each state wanting others to comply all the time while they can choose to comply conditionally. On the one hand, if compliance is entirely discretionary with weak enforcement provisions, states have no incentive to offer concessions because they can expect few gains. On the other hand, rigid enforcement would lead states to refuse agreements or make shallow commitments given domestic uncertainty about their own future preferences.[3]

The multilateral trade regime was established to help states commit to maintain open markets. By accepting membership states revealed information about their preference for free trade. Following on the logic that trade represents a prisoners' dilemma, the role of the trade agreement is to allow states to achieve more efficient outcomes by coordinating on tariff levels that will be self-enforcing because the losses incurred by cheating and facing retaliation would be greater than the short-term benefits of protection (e.g., Mayer, 1981; Staiger, 1995; Bagwell and Staiger, 2002). States conclude trade agreements in order to achieve mutual gains from liberalization while avoiding a trade war.

[3] Both scenarios would represent shallow cooperation that could arise if states have weak preferences for cooperation and/or high fear of cheating (Downs, Rocke, and Barsoom, 1996).

Institutional design has helped states to balance the need for compliance and flexibility by authorizing deviation from rules under specified conditions. In the trade regime, escape clause measures such as safeguard policies that allow states to increase tariffs in response to an import surge are one such institutional mechanism for flexibility (Rosendorff and Milner, 2001). From a contract theory perspective, these exceptions reflect the notion of *efficient breach*.[4] The logic motivating authorized deviation from the terms of the agreement is aptly described by Dam (1970, p. 80) in his classic study of the GATT regime: "It is better, for example, that 100 commitments should be made and that 10 should be withdrawn than that only 50 commitments should be made and that all of them should be kept." Nonetheless, the temptation to abuse such exceptions and commit outright violations or genuine confusion about interpretation of rules will give rise to charges of noncompliance.

The dispute settlement mechanism plays a central role in managing such conflict. Most scholarship emphasizes the retaliatory power behind the legal procedures. States comply with trade agreements because the agreement creates a context of repeated interaction. Cheating in one period will be less tempting given the likelihood of punishment that reduces gains over subsequent periods. In a logic described by former GATT Director General Arthur Dunkel as a "balance of terror" (Bagwell and Staiger, 2002, p. 100), states sustain cooperation for open markets by threatening to close their markets. The threat to unilaterally withdraw from cooperation by returning tariffs to their preagreement levels underlies enforcement according to the repeated game logic that upholds cooperation in models of trade as a prisoners' dilemma.[5] Such a threat of massive retaliation, however, is not credible for enforcement of minor infractions against an agreement. How do states address individual trade barriers that are significant for an industry but would not justify withdrawal from the regime? Single acts of unilateral punishment for a particular trade measure are not expected within the trade regime. The implementation of such retaliation risks setting off a spiral of responses that could lead to a trade war. The dispute settlement system addresses this problem. *Rule-based retaliation* in the dispute settlement process occurs when states use authorized forms of retaliation to induce

---

[4] See Schwartz and Sykes (2002) for application of contract theory to describe the structure of GATT. Kucik and Reinhardt (2008) demonstrate that antidumping provisions, one of the leading flexibility mechanisms, increase liberalization.

[5] Bagwell and Staiger (2002, p. 96) describe this balance in which the multilateral dispute process operates by "limiting the use of retaliation along the equilibrium path and repositioning retaliation as an off-equilibrium-path threat that enforces equilibrium-path rules."

compliance or rebalance concessions to compensate for noncompliance after they have received authorization from a panel.[6] The moderate level of punitive measures against violations enhances stability in the system by accommodating temporary noncompliance driven by political necessity (Rosendorff, 2005; Lawrence, 2003).

The third-party investigation of violation claims in a multilateral dispute system provides information to guide retaliation. It would be too costly for states to specify every possible condition, and so the GATT and WTO agreements represent incomplete contracts that offer broad parameters for acceptable policies with many areas of vague language that can give rise to differences of interpretation.[7] The rulings issued in the dispute settlement process fill gaps in the interpretation of agreements. When a government adopts a policy in response to new circumstances unforeseen at the time of making commitments there may be grounds for two parties to disagree about the compliance of the measure. For example, as new products are developed they can raise complex questions for tariff classification. In one dispute, European regulators classified set-top boxes with communication functions under the higher tariff for electronics while the United States, Japan, and Taiwan contended they should fall under the zero-tariff commitments for information technology.[8] Not only were there no tariff commitments for the exact product at hand, but WTO rules do not explain how to address products that could be classified under different categories. The use of expert panels and a standing body of judges in the WTO Appellate Body provides an authoritative determination of policy status. In this case, the ruling found the European regulation to be in violation and called for a change of the tariff classification. Other members of the agreement who are not directly involved in the dispute are informed so that there can be a greater aggregation of enforcement power through a reputation mechanism (Maggi, 1999). For the example given above,

[6] For example, the United States was authorized by the dispute settlement body in 1999 to raise tariffs on $116.8 million worth of European imports per year as retaliation to enforce the violation ruling against the EU ban on import of hormone-treated beef (Canada was authorized to raise tariffs on $11.3 million per year in its dispute against the same measure since it had lower value of exports affected by the measure). In view of continued noncompliance the United States imposed the tariffs until 2011 as a form of compensation for the nullification of benefits it expected to receive when it negotiated liberalization commitments.

[7] See Battigalli and Maggi (2002) on the determinants of rigidity and discretion in contracts.

[8] "European Communities and Its Member States Tariff Treatment of Certain Information Technology Products" (DS375, 376, 377), request for consultations filed May 28, 2008, panel ruling adopted September 21, 2010.

twelve countries had filed as third parties in the dispute.[9] All of the membership also observes the case in the sense that they consent to adoption of the ruling in the Dispute Settlement Body. Determination of violations in a legal process can induce compliance pressure through invoking international obligation as an incentive above and beyond retaliation concerns (Jackson, 1997; Kovenock and Thursby, 1992).

The empirical record of enforcement raises questions about the emphasis on retaliation. The prisoners' dilemma logic suggests that violations should be met with punishment in all cases. Instead, we observe that many violations are overlooked and retaliation has been rare. Low (1993), who now serves as director of economic research at the WTO, describes a "conspiracy of noncompliance" during the GATT period of the trade regime in which members collectively ignored each other's violation of the trade agreement. Whether it was European preferences for former colonies or Japan's ban against rice imports, many inconsistent policies were not raised in legal complaints. Moreover, those violations that were challenged through GATT dispute settlement were largely resolved successfully without retaliation—there was only one case with authorization of retaliatory measures (Hudec, 1993). Anticipation of retaliation could shape the pattern of disputes if states choose not to impose protection against trade partners who can retaliate in response. Evidence during the GATT period shows that states were more likely to implement legal forms of protection against trade partners that had retaliatory power and reserve their illegal protection for trade partners with less retaliatory power (Bown, 2004c). Nonetheless, both the United States and Europe as the largest markets with the greatest retaliatory capacity on many dimensions (market size, aid and foreign policy leverage) faced countless violations that led them to actively use dispute settlement. The efforts by the United States to use its retaliatory capacity in the form of unilateral action to coerce trade partners had modest results, achieving U.S. goals only half of the time (Bayard and Elliott, 1994, p. 64).

The establishment of strengthened dispute settlement provisions in the WTO channeled more disputes into the rule-based system as one observes the decline of unilateral retaliation and increase of formal complaints filed against violations. Nonetheless, retaliation remains infrequent (as of January 2011, only eight WTO disputes had led to suspension of concessions). The design of the WTO dispute settlement mechanism restrains retaliation by regulating its use within fixed procedures and

[9] See (Busch and Reinhardt, 2006) for analysis of effects of third-party paticipation on the conduct of disputes.

keeping retaliation proportional to the lost trade. This calls for thinking about adjudication from a perspective that looks beyond the threat of punishment.

Asymmetric Information and Bargaining Failure

The logic of the terms-of-trade-driven externality as motivation for trade agreements emphasizes that trade agreements are welfare enhancing. If compliance were observable, no disputes would occur. The threat of retaliation would deter violations or motivate efficient bargaining to reach a mutually satisfactory renegotiation of commitments. Yet there has been a steady stream of trade disputes—over four hundred WTO complaints have been filed between 1995 and 2010. While this is a tiny number of contested policy measures relative to the thousands of tariffs and regulations in each of the more than 150 member states, clearly disputes do arise.

As governments face new economic or political circumstances, they may choose to defect from their commitments. Several theories for why new disputes arise focus on this dynamic in which rational governments raise trade barriers in response to some exogenous shock (Bown, 2004c; Rosendorff, 2005; Maggi and Staiger, 2008). Often these responses in turn generate questions about interpretation of the agreement. This can lead states to invoke the legal dispute mechanism as an interpretive tool to clarify legal obligations and/or punishment mechanism to rebalance reciprocity. Other disputes involve failures to implement the agreement that may persist until trade partners decide to force the issue with legal action.

The legal disputes are puzzling because states incur additional costs in terms of resources and diplomatic relations when they choose to resolve their disagreement by adjudication. These costs give states an interest to reach a bilateral settlement without adjudication. As in studies of war, states with perfect information should avoid the costs of actually fighting war by reaching the settlement dictated by the relevant variables of power and interest (Fearon, 1995). Visible enforcement actions through filing complaints in WTO adjudication represent bargaining failures. The empirical pattern of trade disputes is that states first negotiate issues informally and take legal steps only when they are unable to reach an agreement.

In part, bargaining failures could arise because of resistance from import-competing industries in the defendant states that have a vested interest in the disputed trade barrier (Iida, 2003). In particular, a cost-benefit analysis that takes into consideration how delay is positive for the defendant and negative for the complainant offers one explanation for the unusual pro-complainant ruling pattern observed in WTO adjudication (Guzman, 2002). This may account for the cases that are dragged out to the end of the adjudication process even when the defendant can clearly anticipate that it is likely to lose the panel ruling. States that seek political cover for a policy change against the interests of entrenched groups will prefer to make concessions after a legal ruling rather than in a voluntary setting.[10]

The U.S. imposition of safeguards to protect its steel industry is often given as such an example. After having made election promises to help the steel industry as part of a surprising victory in West Virginia, President George Bush felt obligated to approve the request for a safeguard measure raising tariffs against imports. Speaking about the decision later, Joshua Bolten who served as White House chief of staff at the time, said that the president "wanted us to find the best way to help the industry gain a breathing space and become competitive while reducing the harm to trade relations."[11] They knew when imposing the safeguard measure in March 2002 that it would be challenged with a WTO complaint (indeed eight members would file complaints against the measure), and also fully planned to end the measure. Bolten said, "The WTO ruling helped politically to set the timing for bringing it to an end." One month after the measure was ruled a violation by the Appellate Body, the United States withdrew the safeguard.

Half of WTO disputes, however, reach a settlement before a violation ruling, which means the pursuit of political cover for concessions by the defendant is only a partial explanation. Moreover, for the disputes with entrenched trade partner resistance where defiance is all too predictable, complainant persistence in going to trial seems puzzling. Why would a state pay the costs of going to court when knowing the other would not comply? Making a deal to accept a side-payment concession from the other party without paying litigation costs would seem preferable to both sides.

The answer may lie in information asymmetries. Under uncertainty, actors can make mistakes that prevent reaching agreement. Three possible sources of uncertainty exist: power, law, and resolve. Viewing adjudication as a bargaining failure presents a puzzle for power-oriented explanations of trade policy. On the one hand, power in terms of retaliation capacity correlates with better outcomes in WTO adjudication (Bown, 2004b; Busch and Reinhardt, 2003). The largest states, the United States and EU, file the largest number of complaints as they

---

[10] See Davis (2003) for evidence of this in trade disputes, and see Allee and Huth (2006) for evidence from territorial disputes.

[11] Interview by author, Princeton, New Jersey, May 12, 2010.

enforce their own interests in the trade agreement. On the other hand, states with more power should be able to achieve settlement without adjudication. The United States and EU file cases against Argentina and the Philippines as well as against each other. The fact that even the states with the highest capacity to retaliate nonetheless resort to adjudication to solve their trade problems suggests that it is not uncertainty about power that explains use of adjudication.

In the context of adjudication, anticipation of legal victory is also a consideration. One explanation for the occurrence of legal disputes is parallel to the rationalist accounts of war arising from divergent expectations.[12] The logic is that costly battles (wars or trials) occur because both sides think they will win. In their classic study of selection models for litigation, Priest and Klein (1984) emphasize that trials occur when actors' expectations about the likelihood of victory diverge—otherwise they should negotiate a settlement. They draw the implication that only very close cases will go to trial, producing a tendency toward a 50 percent trial win rate. Other models assume that defendants are better informed, creating a screening effect in which the guilty settle early and only defendants who have strong cases (knowing they are innocent) will pursue trial (Grossman and Katz, 1983; Hylton, 1993). This would increase the defendant win rate.[13] In contrast to the 50 percent win rate expected by the Priest and Klein (1984) model or the high defendant win rate expected by the asymmetric information model, WTO adjudication shows a high plaintiff win rate. In an examination of cases from 1995 to 2002, Guzman (2002) shows that 90 percent of rulings find that the defendant violated WTO rules.[14] This suggests that it is not uncertainty about the legal ruling alone that drives WTO enforcement.

Finally, states face uncertainty about resolve. Even when a state possesses the capacity to coerce compliance through unilateral retaliation, the political costs to exercising power could create uncertainty about

---

[12] See Morrow (1989) as one example of the literature on uncertainty and war initiation. Fey and Ramsay (2007) critique the logic that mutual optimism alone could account for war.

[13] Empirical support has been found in tests that examine variation of informational demands to assess legal cases across issue areas (i.e., tort disputes versus civil rights) (e.g., Eisenberg, 1990; Hylton, 1993; Waldfogel, 1998).

[14] Each ruling consists of multiple legal conclusions, allowing for the common occurrence of a mixed ruling that supports some of the arguments of the defendant even while finding overall that the measure is in violation of the agreement. Nonetheless, among disputes between industrial states 95 percent of legal claims are won (Horn and Mavroidis, 2008, p. 24). The lower win rate for developing countries (58 percent) could reflect less skills for their legal teams.

whether a state will enforce its claim through unilateral measures.[15] The asymmetric information problem arises because states do not know whether their adversary is bluffing. Negotiators seeking the best deal possible have incentives to misrepresent their position until at the extreme every widget is portrayed as serving national interest and political survival. Miscalculation about opponent resolve can lead to bargaining failures as states offer inadequate concessions for a mutually acceptable agreement.

There are enough cases of tolerating noncompliance for defendants to hope that they will get away with a protectionist measure and low-ball offers in early negotiations. Whether one considers the United States decision not to challenge Airbus subsidies during early years of development and the slow and patient negotiations regarding Japanese and Korean quarantine restrictions against U.S. beef exports related to fears about mad cow disease (bovine spongiform encephalopathy), even the trade barriers that affect important industries of powerful countries are not always challenged by either legal complaint or retaliation threats. Uncertainty over resolve will be even greater in disputes that involve small countries with fewer resources. A Costa Rican trade official remarked that in cases filed against the U.S. barriers on its textile exports and against Trinidad and Tobago barriers on its pasta exports, taking legal action was necessary to show that they were serious about the problem.[16]

Trade Agreements as Domestic Commitments

In addition to their impact on incentives for cooperation at the international level, trade agreements help governments to make domestic commitments in the face of lobbying pressure. Political economy research has long shown that trade policy is subject to capture by politically influential groups (Schattschneider, 1935; Magee, Brock, and Young, 1989; Grossman and Helpman, 1994). Governments face a time-inconsistency problem where inefficient industries may fail to change investment patterns when they think lobbying can extend their protection

[15] Reinhardt (2001) argues that challenger resolve increases in the early stage of dispute settlement because of the expectation that a legal ruling will offer leverage to force compliance, presumably at less cost to itself. This argument highlights how the calculation of resolve is critical to explain dispute settlement patterns such as the tendency for early settlement before the actual ruling.

[16] Roberto Enchandi, senior Costa Rican trade ministry official and Ambassador to the EU, telephone interview by author, August 11, 2008.

(Staiger and Tabellini, 1999; Maggi and Rodriquez-Clare, 1998, 2007).[17] This implies that a government susceptible to interest group pressure will join trade agreements as a commitment device to insulate itself from political pressure for protection. Democratic governments are the most likely to join trade agreements because they face a tradeoff between free trade policies favored by aggregate interests of voters and special interest politics (Mansfield, Milner, and Rosendorff, 2002).

From the perspective of domestic commitment arguments, adjudication serves a monitoring role. Voters are not well informed about changes of their government's trade policies, but will learn of protectionist measures when injured foreign governments utilize the trade agreement enforcement provisions. The public announcement of violation rulings acts as an "alarm" to inform the domestic audience (Mansfield, Milner, and Rosendorff, 2002). This information transmission is first triggered when another country files the complaint to challenge a measure; Chaudoin (2011) shows that media coverage for trade barriers increases following the initiation of a WTO dispute. A liberal leader can also use the threat of potential foreign retaliation to advance a policy reform agenda against a resistant legislature (Reinhardt, 2003). Domestic commitment arguments assume that enforcement will occur but do not explore under what conditions foreign governments will enforce the agreement.[18]

Trade agreements may also provide a domestic commitment strategy vis-à-vis export industries. Without guarantees of enforcement, would export industries change investment strategies to take advantage of promised market access opportunities? The decisions to expand production, enter new contracts, or launch foreign joint ventures or direct investment involve sunk costs that could be forfeited if foreign governments later renege on their promises. To the extent that the trade agreement makes enforcement more likely, export industries will be more willing to make these adjustments.

The following section will build on these central insights that states seek multilateral trade institutions to avoid trade wars and use them as a domestic commitment device. Whereas the existing literature on trade enforcement portrays punishment and legal interpretation as the mechanisms by which dispute settlement promotes cooperation, I will

[17] The arguments apply to exporters when used to evaluate strategic trade policy rationale for subsidies. See Grossman and Maggi (1998) for analysis of conditions under which private pressures for strategic trade policy could support a government incentive to make a free trade commitment.

[18] For example, Maggi and Rodriquez-Clare (1998, p. 576) note that their work does not address issues of reciprocal liberalization or imperfect enforcement of agreements.

show that the legal process also functions as a signaling mechanism that facilitates domestic commitments and efficient bargaining between states.

Political Origins of Demand for Trade Enforcement

This section will explain how the use of international adjudication helps to solve the domestic commitment problem that arises in the presence of divided interests within a state over the appropriate level of enforcement. First I explain why the difference in sensitivity to export interest lobbying and diplomatic concerns makes the legislature prefer a high level of enforcement while the executive prefers moderate enforcement that overlooks some noncompliance in trade agreements by trade partners. Second I discuss how this potential for divided interests between the legislature and executive introduces uncertainty at the domestic level over trade enforcement. A legislature that ratifies an agreement may be concerned about the level of enforcement activity that will be undertaken by its government—will the executive play the tough cop role to ensure that trade partners live up to their side of the agreement? Without reassurance about enforcement, the legislature will be willing to accept only low levels of liberalization. In order to achieve higher levels of liberalization, an executive must be able to signal that it will act as a tough enforcement agent for the agreement.[19] Adjudication provides a tool that addresses the executive's dilemma to play tough cop without harming diplomatic relations.

Trade Enforcement as Viewed by Legislature and Executive

The domestic politics of trade policy are commonly examined in a principal agent framework. In this context, the median legislator represents the principal who delegates authority to the executive to act as an agent in the negotiation of trade policy. The executive is treated here as a unitary actor representing a common position based on decisions of the president/prime minister and the relevant departments/ministries supporting the cabinet.[20] On the one hand, the authority to change trade

---

[19] Solving commitment problems is necessary for a broad range of economic reforms and can be addressed through tying hands or signaling type (e.g., Rodrik, 1989; Keefer and Stasavage, 2003).

[20] See, for example, Lohmann and O'Halloran (1994) and Milner and Rosendorff (1996). Studies of both U.S. and EU trade policy emphasize the importance of the conditions placed on the grant of authority to the executive (Destler, 2005; Meunier, 2005). On treating the executive as a unitary actor, see Milner (1997, p. 34). The case studies in chapters 4 and 5 will explore more closely divisions within the executive branch.

policy is vested in the legislature. On the other hand, there are efficiency gains from having a single representative for negotiations and from the specialized knowledge of foreign government policies and international trade law that is accumulated within the trade ministry of the executive branch. As the costs of decision making rise with issue complexity, the legislature finds it optimal to rely on agents who specialize and develop the necessary competence. Thus the legislature faces a trade off between the greater efficiency of allowing the bureaucracy to have flexibility and the desire to lock in behavior against either bureaucratic drift or future political intervention by opponents (Moe, 1990, p. 228).

The legislature favors tough enforcement as a function of responsiveness to export industry demands. Legislators seek reelection, and their interest in trade enforcement reflects their effort to maximize political contributions and job gains for the export industries in their constituencies. Small district size makes legislators susceptible to particularistic demands. Visible actions to address foreign protectionism allow credit claiming at home for the economic gains from exports, even if the trade volumes directly affected by such enforcement actions are small. More fundamentally, legislators require tangible gains from reciprocal liberalization to support the decision to open domestic markets (Gilligan, 1997; Bailey, Goldstein, and Weingast, 1997). Every act of cheating by a trade partner represents withdrawal of reciprocal benefits. The GATT treaty explicitly recognizes the need to balance concessions in the terms for renegotiation of commitments—if a state wants to raise a tariff its trade partners are entitled to withdraw equivalent concessions through raising their own tariffs.[21] The trade barriers challenged by enforcement actions represent an attempt by the foreign partner to renege on the original commitment without such compensation.

Two factors make the executive more cautious about enforcement than the legislature. First, the executive is more likely to hold strong preferences for free trade. The national constituency of the executive creates incentives to focus on improving national welfare, which can be best served through free trade.[22] Support of free trade ironically

[21] There were nearly two hundred cases of renegotiation between 1958 to 1994 under the terms of GATT Article XXVIII. Renegotiation of commitments has been rare since establishment of the WTO with only eight cases between 1995 to 1999 (Hoda, 2002, pp. 88, 107).

[22] There are different variations within this argument: constituency size reduces the influence of narrow interests calling for protection (Schattschneider, 1935; Lohmann and O'Halloran, 1994) and increases the incentives for provision of public goods such as trade (Nielson, 2003; Bueno de Mesquita et al., 2003). A related argument by Ehrlich (2007) suggests that differences in institutional access points makes the legislature more protectionist than the executive. For a critical view, see Hiscox (1999) and Karol (2007).

makes the executive less concerned about enforcement because the original decision to open domestic markets was not conditional on foreign government behavior. While the executive favors reciprocal liberalization, allowing for some cheating on trade agreements by foreign governments is still seen as preferable to retaliation that would entail closing domestic markets. The free trade preferences of the executive dictate against increasing tariffs as part of retaliation.[23] In addition, complete enforcement of trade agreements may not maximize liberalization levels. The notion of "efficient breach" allows for the possibility that imperfect enforcement may be optimal.[24] If a government holds trade partners to the letter of every term in the agreement all the time, whether by repeated legal challenges or unilateral actions, it increases the tension in the system. This may reduce the ability of trade partners to negotiate future liberalization.

Second, the executive has greater sensitivity to diplomatic relations and includes both diplomatic and economic factors in cost-benefit analysis of trade strategy.[25] Foreign policy is primarily the jurisdiction of the executive. Legislatures are influential in foreign policy matters by means of authority over treaty ratification and budget allocation. Nonetheless, the executive is directly responsible to manage diplomatic relations and is more likely to be held accountable by the electorate for problems in foreign affairs. This makes the executive evaluate security or other foreign policy goals that are tangential to the trade policy itself. Indeed foreign policy motivations may lie behind the choice of trade partners (Mansfield and Bronson, 1997). Yet while foreign policy considerations could motivate establishing agreements, they do not motivate tough enforcement. On the contrary, acting as the trade police ticketing neighbors for every speeding violation may harm bilateral political relations. Consequently, the executive faces a tradeoff when weighing the interests of a specific export industry against the interests of system stability and diplomatic relations. Aggregate welfare and diplomatic

---

[23] Although bluffing would alleviate the need to suffer costs from retaliation, concern about reputation creates incentives against bluffing (Sartori, 2002).

[24] Similar to the logic behind arguments that flexibility provisions (safeguards, escape clauses, antidumping provisions) increase liberalization levels and system stability (Downs and Rocke, 1995; Rosendorff and Milner, 2001; Schwartz and Sykes, 2002; Kucik and Reinhardt, 2008), imperfect enforcement may sustain higher levels of overall liberalization.

[25] The greater attention to foreign policy matters by presidents in the context of U.S. trade policy has been widely discussed (e.g., Lake, 1988; Nelson, 1989; Baldwin, 1998; Dam, 2001). In parliamentary systems as well, foreign policy is primarily the responsibility of the cabinet and prime minister. Either a president or a prime minister may be punished if judged to be an ineffectual leader in foreign affairs, whereas few members of the legislature need hold such fears.

relations benefit from negotiation of multilateral trade agreements but may be harmed by tough enforcement.

These divisions are readily apparent in U.S. trade policy. Chapter 4 will highlight several cases in which members of Congress have been at the forefront of calls for strong enforcement. When Kodak claimed that market barriers prevented exports of photographic film to Japan in 1995, it found supporters in Congress who urged the threat of economic sanctions to force concessions from Japan. Concern within the executive branch about further upsetting diplomatic relations at a rocky time in U.S.-Japan alliance talks dictated choice of a less aggressive strategy.

But we also see other governments that confront the tradeoff between representing a specific interest harmed by a trade barrier and broader trade or foreign policy goals. An example from Canada is illustrative. When the EU imposed a ban on import of seal products in 2009, it caused widespread outrage in Canada where the seal hunt has support as a cultural tradition and as a small but influential industry in the eastern coastal region. A representative of the Canadian sealers association called for the government to ban a European product, stating, "If we're going to have a trade war, let's go tit for tat."[26] The Canadian House of Commons held a special emergency debate on the ban, which was widely condemned by members. Several parliamentarians urged the government to challenge the EU measure as a WTO violation, and some went so far as to call for the government to link the matter to negotiations for a free trade agreement with Europe.[27] A representative of the Bloc Quebecois in the House of Commons, Raynald Blais, made the following statement:

> We have to respond in kind. There are many places where we can act: the G7, G8, G20, and so forth. We could also bring this issue up in the incipient negotiations over a free trade agreement between the European Union and Canada. There are places where we can act, but we need to do so with more vigour. This means that the government needs to have teamwork. We parliamentarians can work together collegially as a team, but the government has to do it as a team too.

A leading member of the Liberal Party representing Nova Scotia criticized the government:

> The Conservatives have failed to take effective action to defend this industry against those who would repeat falsehoods and wild accusations to attack it. The Conservative government must defend

---

[26] *Globe and Mail*, May 6, 2009, p. A4.
[27] 40th Parliament, 2nd session, number 051, May 5, 2009.

the interests of the Canadian seal hunt community. It must defend the interests of northern Canada and Newfoundland and Labrador. The government has a responsibility to take the appropriate action right now to ensure that those interests are defended.... I hope the government uses these FTA discussions with the EU to strengthen the defence of the seal hunt.

The response from the executive branch also condemned the European ban, but highlighted the need for restraint in any response. Trade minister Stockwell Day said the government would not take retaliatory measures that could threaten ongoing talks over the Canada-European Union Comprehensive Economic and Trade Agreement.[28] At a press conference, Prime Minister Stephen Harper criticized the European policy while warning, "We cannot let a single disagreement contaminate and undermine all the other issues."[29] Rather than being diametrically opposed on the question of enforcement, the executive approaches the choice of strategy with wider scope of concern for other interests at stake.

THE CHALLENGE OF ENFORCEMENT PROMISES

Aware of these mixed incentives of the executive, the legislator suspects that the executive will devote insufficient effort as enforcer of trade agreements. The executive faces a credibility problem to show that they will deliver on their promise to improve market access. Whereas protection policies can be easily monitored in the domestic context, the promise to increase market access is more complicated. Removal of foreign trade barriers requires government intervention by means of negotiations with foreign governments.[30] Whether government efforts lead to an increase of exports will depend on both the results of the negotiation and follow-up enforcement efforts as well as market factors. Trade negotiations are conducted at the diplomatic level with

---

[28] *Toronto Star*, May 6, 2009, p. A12.

[29] *Gazette* (Montreal), May 7, 2009, p. B2.

[30] Bagwell and Staiger (2002, p. 31) discuss the assumption in the literature that there is a limitation on the choice of instruments to exclude export promoting policies. Direct export promotion through policies such as export subsidies has been foregone as a result of earlier decisions to ban them in the GATT rules. Goodhart (2006) provides a theory for why the geographic mobility of export industries relative to import industries makes politicians favor import subsidies over export subsidies. Use of export subsidies is notably absent as a major policy tool (Rodrik, 1995; Deardorff and Stern, 1998). There have been occasional disputes over indirect export subsidies, such as the foreign sales corporation tax case raised before the WTO adjudication. The GATT and now WTO have also made explicit exceptions to allow export subsidies for agricultural products, although the Uruguay Round Agriculture Agreement set constraints on the amount.

much of the real deal making occurring in private between government representatives. This creates an asymmetry of information between the executive agency that negotiates and the legislature, which cannot engage directly in negotiations. A negotiator may make concessions that sacrifice the interests of one industry for the sake of other industries, aggregate welfare, or diplomatic concerns. The negotiated agreement may reflect a diplomatic compromise and be followed up by weak enforcement. Or, the negotiator may achieve removal of the trade barrier, but alternative disguised protection policies or poor market conditions limit the increase of exports.

The example of U.S. negotiations with Japan on barriers limiting the import of apples illustrates the challenge of evaluating government efforts to improve market access. Japan agreed to liberalize apple imports in 1971, but a wide and changing set of quarantine restrictions operated as a de facto ban. Over twenty years later the U.S. apple industry submitted a formal petition requesting government help to gain access. After a year of bilateral negotiations Japan agreed to approve the import of certain varieties of U.S. apples in 1994. There was a brief increase of sales of U.S. apples that quickly fell off. The mandated fumigation procedures and other measures were attributed as part of the problem, although commentary also noted the low sales could reflect the weakening Japanese economy, shifting exchange rates, and poor consumer evaluation of the U.S. product.[31] The United States filed a WTO case against Japan that was successfully concluded in 1999, and Japan modified the quarantine requirements. U.S. sales still did not take off. The United States filed another WTO complaint that challenged other parts of the quarantine procedures that had not been covered by the first complaint. The governments reached a mutually agreed solution in 2005, and Japan further loosened its quarantine restrictions. U.S. exports remain modest. Even after removal of the barriers, there simply was not strong market demand.[32] The case illustrates the difficulty to evaluate outcomes given intransigent partner resistance, the potential for multiple layers of trade barriers, and unpredictable market conditions. In 1971, 1994, 1999, and 2005 the U.S. government negotiated four agreements,

[31] "An Apple Bonanza Goes Sour," *Seattle Post-Intelligencer*, May 14, 1997.

[32] What anyone learns upon visiting Japan is that while U.S. apples may be half the price, they are also not as tasty as Japanese apples that have been cultivated through labor-intensive practices (e.g., leaf removal, extended period of tree ripening, individual wrapping for protection during distribution). One study revises the standard approach to estimate the cost of a nontariff barrier by allowing for imperfect substitution given differences in product quality (Yue, Beghin, and Jensen, 2005). The analysis suggests that U.S. apple exports would be substantially less than those forecast by the U.S. government in its trade negotiation claims about the damage from the trade barrier.

none of which produced major trade gains. One view would be that the U.S. government did not engage in sufficient efforts to push Japan to open its market and accepted weak agreements. The other view would be that the U.S. government actively supported its industry in negotiations but achieved poor results because Japan was determined to protect the industry by any means and the market was not receptive to U.S. products.

The problem for industry and their representatives in the legislature is how to distinguish between these two scenarios. Schelling (1980, p. 131) notes that promises depend upon two conditions for enforcement: capacity to punish and ability to discern when punishment is called for. In the context of the promise by a leader to serve industry interests in exchange for political contributions, punishment is possible in future iterations of the exchange through withdrawal of contributions. But the problems noted here impinge on the ability to make an enforceable agreement because the industry cannot tell when it should punish a government for a failure to achieve market access gains. When the government brings back a mediocre deal, they cannot know whether it reflects poor effort or partner resistance. Modest export gains from an agreement could be attributed to inadequate monitoring by the government of the market-opening agreement or unfavorable economic conditions. To address these uncertainties, governments must credibly commit to their domestic lobby that they will negotiate for market access and monitor implementation by the foreign government.

Given the legislature's greater responsiveness to industry concerns, the legislature calls on the executive to demonstrate its willingness to act on behalf of specific industries. Without reassurance that the executive will pursue tough enforcement, the legislature may withdraw its support for future liberalization. The export industries that are harmed by foreign trade barriers themselves may hold back on political contributions and investment decisions if they doubt the willingness of the government to enforce the trade agreements offering market access opportunities. In order to avoid signing empty agreements, legislatures act to constrain the executive.

MONITORING THE EXECUTIVE

The extensive literature on delegation examines incentive structures that enable principals to control the behavior of their agent.[33] Political appointments, budget allocation, administrative reorganization, and legislation are among the commonly examined tools (e.g., Epstein and

---

[33] See Bendor, Glazer, and Hammond (2001) for a review.

O'Halloran, 1999; Wood and Waterman, 1991; Huber and Shipan, 2002; Calvert, McCubbins, and Weingast, 1989). Different forms of monitoring allow the principal to supervise the actions of the agent (McCubbins and Schwartz, 1984). In trade policy, constraints on the executive include mandates for negotiation authority and requirements for transparency (e.g., reports on actions taken). The imposition of deadlines and established procedures for action assures the principal that the bureaucratic agent will implement policies as desired. One form of monitoring is to empower private industry to serve as fire alarms that will alert the legislature to any poor performance by the bureaucracy (McCubbins and Schwartz, 1984). Measures can also be passed to require response to industry complaints as a way to encourage the executive to represent constituency interests.

A legislature chooses how tightly to constrain the bureaucratic agent through various means of supervision and control. At lower levels of delegation, specific statutory instructions are often accompanied by extensive monitoring and intervention by the legislature in bureaucratic decision making (Huber and Shipan, 2002). This brings politicization as politicians micromanage agency affairs. McCubbins, Noll, and Weingast (1987) refer to the ongoing oversight as "deck-stacking" agencies. In contrast, at higher levels of delegation the legislature uses less precise statutory language and minimal monitoring as it grants wide discretion to the administrative agent to achieve broad goals. High delegation implies less politicization as politicians adopt a hands-off relationship toward agency implementation of policy. It is important to note, however, that even high delegation that confers considerable bureaucratic autonomy does not imply that elected politicians are abdicating authority. Rather, high delegation reflects a choice to use less direct instruments of control in order to give the bureaucracy flexibility to effectively pursue its mandate (Moe, 1990).

DIVIDED PREFERENCES LEAD TO LOW DELEGATION

The potential for delegation arises when the legislature holds authority within domestic political institutions. At the most general level, there must be separation of power embedded in the constitution for the legislature to check the executive in decision making. Legislatures in an authoritarian regime have no powers to delegate. In parliamentary democracies, the legislature holds authority given that the composition of the cabinet and policy direction depend on support from parliament. Presidential democracies offer more variation in the relative separation of power between the two branches (Shugart and Haggard, 2001). Yet even for a case where one would expect little room for legislative authority within a strong presidential system, there are pathways for influence. A president who can use decrees for many policies will still require legislative approval for other issues. In the context of foreign economic policies, legislative authority is strongest when commercial policy and treaty approval are clearly vested in the legislature. The U.S. Congress can—and does—veto trade agreements and pass legislation on the conduct of foreign economic policy. Even the relatively weak Brazilian Congress has room for influence; the president can use executive decrees to set many policies, but these can be overturned by Congress; the president must submit signed international agreements to Congress for ratification (most—but not all—are approved), the budget submitted by the president faces amendments by the legislature, committees hold hearings on major foreign policy issues including trade agreements, and the Congress approves personnel appointments (Lemos, 2010). Within the range of their institutional powers, legislatures face a choice of how much authority to delegate to the executive. Their willingness to do so will vary as a function of the gap between the preferences of the legislature and executive.

Close monitoring and constraint of delegation make sense only when preferences between principal and agent diverge. Otherwise the principal should let the agent efficiently manage the appointed tasks. According to the "ally principle" actors delegate more willingly to those who share their preferences (Bendor, Glazer, and Hammond, 2001). This generates an expectation for more delegation of trade authority to the executive in a context of unified preferences than in a context with polarized preferences.

The shift of policy constraints may occur through many channels, both formal and informal. First, a government structure that produces more division of preferences among actors such as the presidential system of checks and balances or minority government in a parliamentary system will systematically have higher levels of constraints as evidenced by more specific legislation (Huber and Shipan, 2002). For example, the United States has legislation that explicitly mandates how the USTR will monitor foreign trade policy and respond to industry requests with deadlines for taking action. In contrast, Japan, a government with unified preferences (until recent years there has been long-time majority rule in a parliamentary system), offers autonomy to trade officials. Its trade law includes only a vague statute related to enforcement that authorizes the trade ministry to impose import barriers if necessary to support its international agreements (these laws are discussed in detail in chapters 4 and 5). Second, there is variation in the informal pressure applied to the agency. Whether through phone calls, public statements, and letters or pressure on the appointment of officials, legislators can express demands to shift policies at the implementation level. The expectation of tighter supervision should lead bureaucratic agents to be responsive to such demands in order to avert the need for new legislated constraints.

Fundamentally, it is the structure of preferences that determines constraints in the principal-agent relationship. The problem is that preferences are not observable. Therefore I make the assumption that we can infer division of preferences as a function of institutional structure and partisan balance. When different government branches have institutional independence and opposition parties are strong, there is wider divergence between the preferences of the executive and legislature. More centralized government structures and dominant ruling parties are associated with homogeneous preferences. Variation in preferences also occurs as partisan balance changes. The connection of institutional structure and partisan balance with policy constraints is well established in the literature. Lohmann and O'Halloran (1994) argue that under divided government in the United States, Congress issues more legislation to constrain the executive's authority on trade policy.[34] Divided government is not limited to the United States or even presidential systems, as coalition governments in a parliamentary system face similar constraints (Laver and Shepsle, 1991). The rising number of parties with distinct policy positions in a coalition adds new demands for debate and coordination to reach agreement on any given issue. The increase of veto players with power to block a policy change has been shown to enhance policy stability and hinder cooperation that requires changes of policy.[35] The policy process itself adjusts to reflect divisions of interest among decision makers. Martin (2000) shows that across different political structures, legislatures delegate less to the executive in foreign affairs policy when there is divided government than when the executive and legislature hold similar preferences. I expect to observe more extensive monitoring of trade policy in government systems with higher levels of divided authority in the structure of institutions and partisan control.

[34] They also make the substantive conclusion that divided government results in more protectionist trade policy, but critics have contested this finding (Karol, 2000; Sherman, 2002). The key distinction is that more attention is needed to partisan preferences, since divided government could yield closer executive legislature preferences if the executive does not share the preferences of his or her party, as in the case of a democratic president with liberal trade preferences who would possibly receive more delegation from a Republican Congress. Both sides of the debate agree that divided *preferences* lead to less delegation.

[35] See Tsebelis (2002) for theory of veto players as a unifying concept for how divisions of preferences shape policy outcomes in similar ways across political systems. Keefer and Stasavage (2003) extend the theory in the context of monetary policy, and Mansfield, Milner, and Pevehouse (2007); Mansfield, Milner and Pevehouse (2008) test implications for PTA formation and depth of regional integration.

LOW DELEGATION LEADS TO MORE ADJUDICATION

Domestic constraints on executive autonomy encourage WTO adjudication. The constraints from the legislature force greater responsiveness to industry concerns, and they also influence the choice among alternative strategies to address those concerns. Negotiators who have less discretion may lack the flexibility to accept compromise agreements during negotiations. Close monitoring of the executive by the legislature creates a rigid trade policy with pressure to "show results," which biases selection of strategies toward those with a high public profile. For an executive in a political context with divided interests, outcomes from negotiation will be met with skepticism by the legislature: is this really the best deal possible, or did the executive give in too easily?

WTO adjudication represents a costly signal for the executive to demonstrate commitment to promote market access.[36] Through accepting self-imposed costs that are tied to fulfilling a promise, an actor increases the credibility of its commitment. In this case, the executive chooses a costly trade strategy in an effort to convince the legislature that it will fulfill its promise to enforce trade agreements in exchange for opening domestic markets. If they instead make a deal in bilateral negotiations, the domestic audience may question the agreement and accuse negotiators of being soft. By publicly suing a trade partner, the executive signals that it places priority on specific export interests and is not going to defer to trade partners for diplomatic reasons. The threat of unilateral retaliation would be another way to signal commitment, but it is too costly for an executive that favors free trade and cares about foreign policy. WTO adjudication offers a middle course between negotiation and unilateral retaliation.

The public nature of suing a trade partner raises diplomatic costs as discussed in chapter 1, but is useful in domestic politics. Negotiations encounter difficulties for domestic accountability because of the lack of transparency. Foreign economic policy is conducted by the executive branch. Trade officials consult frequently with the key legislative committee members, but legislators are not in the room for the negotiation. Even if trade officials issue negotiating demands in public, additional concessions take place in backroom deals. Most trade negotiations represent low-profile activities that attract little attention beyond the

---

[36] A large literature has grown about the role of costly signals as a way to give information about underlying type. Spence (1973) started the focus on this issue in economics with his study about the role of investments in education as a signal of quality to employers. The concept has been extended in international relations to address state efforts to demonstrate high resolve in foreign policy crises (e.g., Martin 1992a; Fearon 1997).

directly affected industries. In contrast, filing a WTO complaint is a high-profile action that enters the public realm. The U.S. media give more coverage to the filing of a WTO complaint against its antidumping investigation than to the original announcement of the investigation itself (Chaudoin, 2011). This is true also for other countries. A trade official in Brazil noted that "WTO disputes are followed like a soccer match with front page headlines when case begins or has a major development. Whether the case is about sugar, cotton, or poultry there is news on front pages when they start."[37] While there will be variation among cases in the level of attention, on average one expects more publicity for WTO complaint than bilateral dispute.

The demand for WTO adjudication as a commitment device will be greatest for governments that face a credibility problem to show they are a tough enforcer of trade agreements. As divided interests reduce levels of delegation to the executive, negotiators face pressure to use visible enforcement strategies that demonstrate to the legislature their willingness to fulfill their mandate. Therefore I expect to observe more adjudication by states with institutional checks and partisan divisions. All states will have some demand for cases that represent the obvious national interest—highly distortionary trade barriers that impact the interests of a major export industry and are clear violations of WTO law. But for states with a credible commitment problem at home, the government will have a lower threshold for filing disputes. Even less significant cases that may have been settled for equal results in a negotiation will nonetheless be raised for WTO adjudication because of the need for a signal to domestic audiences. Periods of greater partisan division would fuel an increase of WTO complaints.

The higher level of control exerted by the legislature also influences the selection of which cases to file for WTO adjudication. The executive's interests favor selecting cases to support broad free trade by challenging the most distortionary trade barriers and those likely to win a ruling that would serve as a useful precedent. The legislature, in contrast, has interests tied to serving the industries that provide votes and contributions, and will favor selecting cases to support these industries. A trade ministry that fears losing authority if it does not please the constituents of the legislature will focus its efforts on politically influential industries. This will create a pattern of WTO cases favoring industries that give large political contributions.

In contrast a unitary government with closer preferences between legislator and executive will enjoy more discretion, which allows for

---

[37] Official of Foreign Ministry, telephone interview by author, April 28, 2011.

flexible negotiations and ability to negotiate compromise settlements without incurring enforcement costs. Across a range of issues, bureaucratic agents favor informal agreements in order to maximize their control without intrusion by legislature or other agencies (Lipson, 1991). In the context of trade disputes, the executive would prefer to have a free hand to choose whether a concession offered by the trade partner is good enough to justify bilateral settlement when weighed against considerations important to the executive such as diplomatic relations and precedent. Only for the cases of highest economic need and precedent value would an unconstrained executive choose adjudication. Executives under domestic constraints, however, will find adjudication to be a very useful tool to balance responsiveness to export interests and sensitivity to broader costs.

This argument suggests there will be political manipulation of WTO disputes, which will be empirically observable as a correlation between domestic political conditions and the use of WTO adjudication. The political pressure for enforcement activities produced by domestic political constraints increases the uncertainty that can prevent efficient international bargaining. One might fear this would make adjudication a futile exercise. The next section will turn to examine how adjudication helps to address this problem and resolve a case load full of politicized disputes.

The Effectiveness of Adjudication to Resolve Disputes

The standard view of WTO adjudication is that it encourages compliance because it increases the costs of defection through retaliation. Maggi (1999) focuses on the role of informing third parties. Others emphasize the role of legal obligation (Jackson, 1997; Kovenock and Thursby, 1992). I argue more attention should be given to the role of adjudication to resolve an asymmetric information problem involving uncertainty about the resolve of actors in a dispute. This relates directly to the problem of domestic pressure, which as I have just described adds incentives for strong enforcement actions.

The incentive to bluff, which increases as a function of the domestic constraints discussed in the previous section, introduces uncertainty at the international level that can prevent states from reaching agreements. Exporters call for the removal of trade barriers as a way to improve their competitive position. The partner that imposed the trade barrier must decide whether to offer a concession in negotiation or stand firm. In the effort to gain a better outcome, both sides have incentives to misrepresent their preferences.[38] In a bargaining setting, players may rationally adopt a hard strategy that makes extreme claims and offers few concessions because they seek a larger share of the stakes.

Uncertainty at the international level about the strategy of the opponent may lead to bargaining failures and litigation. In studies of war, uncertainty about opponent *resolve* is a key variable (e.g., Morrow, 1989). For litigation, resolve includes defendant innocence/guilt and plaintiff litigiousness in terms of costs a plaintiff is willing to pay in order to advance the case. Does the opponent have a good case, and is the opponent and willing to pursue it? Cooter, Marks, and Mnookin (1982) model trials as the result of strategic bargaining over distributional gains. Although a hard strategy to demand a large share of distributional gains increases the likelihood of trial, it can be optimal given the uncertainty about the type of the opponent. The settlement offer depends on the beliefs about whether the opponent has high resolve.

The litigation process is itself a screening mechanism. It can be used by the defendant to learn whether the complainant is "peaceful" or "litigious" (Farber and White, 1994). The former will accept a low offer in early negotiations while the latter will persist to adjudication. This use of adjudication leads to defendants refusing to negotiate settlements until a formal complaint is filed, which can freeze out productive bargaining. At the same time, the complainant needs information about whether the defendant is guilty or innocent. Absent strategic behavior, negotiation reveals this information: innocent defendants will have a higher estimate of their probability of victory at trial and will reject a settlement offer while guilty defendants will accept. In that case, no trial would be necessary. Yet strategic behavior over the extent of damages and uncertainty about the complainant's litigiousness may lead some guilty defendants to reject settlement offers.[39] As a result, trials occur.

In trade disputes, initial negotiations probe the trade partner resolve to maintain the contested trade barrier as a potential defendant. Two factors influence its resistance: the political pressure from its own industry that benefits from the barrier and its calculation of exporter state resolve. If political pressure from the domestic industry is high, concessions are unlikely. Even high costs from a trade dispute would be acceptable to maintain the protection for the industry longer. By design, WTO enforcement remains a weak punitive mechanism. There are no retroactive damages, and authorization of retaliatory measures permits

---

[38] This follows the same logic as Fearon (1995) presents for how incentives to misrepresent can lead to war.

[39] Priest (1985) notes that higher litigation rates above their expected 50 percent rule would reflect bargaining over high stakes and the levels of damages.

only raising tariffs on a proportional amount of trade. Compliance following a violation ruling can restore reputation. Thus strong political pressure in the defendant can prevent settlement. But even when the domestic industry is politically weak and a state would be willing to offer concessions rather than face retaliation, the state may refuse concessions in negotiation if it believes the exporting industry's government lacks resolve. We can assume that there is some support for the barrier or else the government would not have chosen to impose it in the first place. As a result, negotiations are not very informative because defendants may stand firm regardless of whether they face high or low political pressure.

WTO adjudication can operate as a screening mechanism of potential complainants because states that care more about diplomatic relations than export interests will be reluctant to file a complaint against a trade partner. The differential cost of the act of filing makes this step an informative signal about the government's resolve in the trade dispute.[40] For the trade partner whose trade barrier is being challenged, this represents critical information for its decision on whether to make a generous early settlement offer such as the partial or complete removal of the barrier. While the trade partner favors the status quo in which it keeps its trade barrier, for some set of less important industries it would be willing to offer concessions rather than face retaliatory sanctions. Uncertainty about the resolve of the exporting state's government leads the foreign government to initially refuse concessions, but offer them after the foreign government files its complaint.

WTO adjudication provides states a way to convey to trade partners their commitment on a particular issue by means of a strategy that has moderate costs, short of risking a trade war through threats of unilateral retaliation. The filing of a complaint to the WTO substitutes for unilateralism. One sees this logic supported by the fact that the increase in use of adjudication by the United States after establishment of the WTO has been accompanied by a decline in resorting to Section 301 unilateral threats by the United States.

Participants in the trade policy process recognize the political role of adjudication as a reward to powerful interests at home and a signal of resolve to trade partners. A U.S. trade official commented that pressure from Congress on the executive to initiate more WTO disputes reflects the fact that it is an easy response for representatives to tell constituents they are seeking a case. "It really shows you are tough when you go to

---

[40] Gibbons (1992, p. 174) notes in his description of signaling games, "The key idea is that communication can occur if one type of the informed player is willing to send a signal that would be too expensive for another type to send."

court."[41] A WTO official told of cases that were initiated as "candy" to reward industries that had provided key electoral support.[42] A lawyer involved in several WTO cases spoke of instances where officials were reluctant due to concerns about the legal strength of a case, and then initiate because they get "rolled by political pressure."[43] Former Representative William Frenzel, chairman of the President's Advisory Committee for Trade Policy and Negotiations, said that input from politicians and industry can be a factor in the selection of WTO cases. He commented that too often the pressure reflects the view that a small market share can be fixed by being a tough negotiator.[44] These political games are not limited to the United States. The complaint by Canada in 1998 against a French ban on imports of asbestos products was one such case—many recognized that the government had a weak legal case but felt the need to pander to an industry in Quebec after the narrow defeat of the 1995 secession referendum.[45] Given that the reasons for one case being more valued than another can range from contribution levels to geographic region, it can be difficult for foreign governments to recognize politically important cases. Hence they rely on legal complaints to gain information about which challenges should be taken seriously and when to offer concessions to resolve the dispute. Where concessions are impossible because the defendant faces equally influential resistance, the litigation process allows both sides to appear supportive of domestic audiences while continuing efforts to work out an acceptable resolution.

IMPLICATIONS FOR THE DEMOCRATIC DIFFERENCE

Under what conditions will WTO adjudication be necessary to resolve disputes? The effect of domestic constraints discussed in the second section of this chapter worsens the international bargaining problem and creates more demand for adjudication. Under conditions of divided government that generate heightened enforcement pressure, the executive may engage in excessive enforcement actions as part of the signal to domestic audiences. This will include tough rhetoric, resistance to partial concession offers in negotiations, and increased willingness to file complaints for WTO adjudication.

[41] U.S. government official, interview by author, October 26, 2007.

[42] WTO official, telephone interview by author, November 2, 2007.

[43] Lawyer for international trade law firm, interview by author, October 25, 2007.

[44] Interview by author, July 11, 2007.

[45] *Globe and Mail*, August 2, 1999, p. B3. See WTO DS135, "European Communities— Measures Affecting Asbestos and Products Containing Asbestos."

Democracies will bring more issues to the negotiating table than authoritarian governments. As discussed above, legislatures are responsive to industry concerns and less sensitive to diplomatic relations. Empowerment of the legislature through democratic institutions increases enforcement action overall. At the extreme one can observe the United States, where the government produces lengthy lists of complaints about its trade partners and engages in constant negotiations. Authoritarian governments also value export industries, but fewer industries have access to mobilize the government to act for their interest. Free of legislative constraints, the authoritarian executive can ignore complaints from some industries and refuse to raise enforcement cases that could harm diplomatic relations. Given the same number of industry complaints, a democratic government would be more likely to raise all of them in talks with a trade partner.

In the face of a barrage of criticism, trade partners have difficulty sorting out which issues are priorities versus those that are part of a show for domestic consumption. This leads to greater reliance by trade partners on WTO adjudication to screen out when it faces a serious challenge to its trade barrier. To the extent that WTO filing itself is a product of the domestic signaling game, however, it will provide less information to promote quick settlement at the international bargaining table. The home government may have to go further through the dispute process to the point of actual retaliation before the trade partner recognizes the need for a concession to avert a trade war.

This challenges two presumptions in the literature. First, the Schelling conjecture contends that domestic constraints increase bargaining leverage through a logic of tied hands (Schelling, 1960). Some studies have shown how states with less room to maneuver from domestic political constraints have been able to extract more concessions during negotiations even in the face of power asymmetries (Evans, Jacobson, and Putnam, 1993). In contrast, my argument suggests that divisions in domestic authority generate uncertainty, which contributes to bargaining failures in negotiation and requires that a government expend more effort. My conclusions add further support to the argument made by Milner and Rosendorff, who demonstrate domestic divisions reduce bargaining leverage when the legislature is hawkish relative to the executive (Milner, 1997; Milner and Rosendorff, 1997). High constraints on executive autonomy make it more difficult for states to reach any agreement.

Second, the literature on international disputes suggests that democracies are better able to signal their resolve in conflicts because domestic constituents would penalize leaders who back down in a crisis. Fearon (1994, p. 587) argues that political competition makes democratic leaders sensitive to audience costs that arise from being seen as having failed in a critical dispute.[46] He predicts that "high-audience-cost states require less military escalation in disputes to signal their preferences, and are better able to commit themselves to a course of action in a dispute." The logic of this model could be extended to trade disputes. Although it is unlikely that leaders will be thrown out of office for failing in a trade negotiation, it is plausible to expect that a political leader will view trade policy outcomes as delivering potential gains or losses in votes and political contributions that affect his or her survival in office. Thus the extension of the audience cost argument implies that democratic states would effectively signal intentions, and thereby improve their chances to reach negotiated settlements in trade talks without escalation.[47] In contrast, my argument shows that domestic signaling activity distorts the statements and actions of democratic leaders so that they are less able to signal resolve and are *more* likely escalate trade disputes with legal action or unilateral measures. When democratic politics reward escalation, there will be no audience cost mechanism. This implies adjudication will be more necessary for democratic states as a means of signaling their level of resolve.[48]

The conventional wisdom about tied hands and audience costs suggests that democratic states would engage in less adjudication because they would be effective negotiators. Instead, the next chapter will demonstrate that we observe a strong democratic propensity in the filing of WTO disputes. To the extent that adjudication represents the failure to resolve the issue in negotiation, democracies are more conflict prone. Yet since adjudication offers a restraint against trade wars, it helps democratic states rein back the domestic pressures that would otherwise unravel cooperative trade relations.

[46] Of course, one must note that autocrats also fear removal from office by means even more harsh than electoral competition.

[47] On the other hand, Fearon (1997) argues democracies rarely bluff. He contends that their use of audience costs to tie hands produces lock-in effects so that once a democratic state has taken moves to escalate a dispute, it is less able to make concessions. Busch (2000) finds support for both dynamics in his analysis of GATT complaints where he shows that democratic pairs of states are more likely to offer concessions during early consultations and are also more likely to escalate disputes to panel stage. I focus on filing complaints as the first move to escalate from informal negotiation to initiate proceedings for legal action.

[48] The expected positive relationship between democracy and WTO adjudication does not depend on the dyadic interaction of regime type, although disputes between two democracies would be the most likely to escalate as both sides engage in signaling activity to domestic audiences.

TABLE 2.1
Divided Government and Policy Constraints.

Government Structure	Constraints on Executive	Trade Policy Process	Enforcement
Divided	High	Monitoring, industry access, low flexibility	Adjudication
United	Low	Bureaucratic discretion, informal deals	Negotiation

Hypotheses for Trade Strategies

This section connects the theory developed above with the observable implications for trade strategies. The concepts will be operationalized and subjected to empirical evaluation in the subsequent chapters.

Table 2.1 summarizes the expected relationship between domestic political conditions and enforcement strategy. The first distinction characterizes whether institutional structure and partisan balance generate divisions between executive and legislature. Second, the dichotomous high and low categories indicate the relative level of domestic political constraints associated with each government structure. When comparing the context of political institutions, the top row for divided government with high constraints on the executive could describe democratic versus authoritarian rule, the United States relative to Japan, or the U.S. period of divided government relative to a period of unified partisan government. The structure of government in the United States places greater checks on executive autonomy than does the structure in Japan, and partisan differences can further widen the gap.

The following hypotheses evaluate the impact of domestic institutions on choice of WTO adjudication:

> **1.** Cross-national selection of strategy: High domestic constraints on executive autonomy will increase use of adjudication.
>
> **2.** Case selection pattern: In the context of high domestic constraints on the executive, governments will use adjudication for politically influential industries.
>
> **3.** Outcomes: Adjudication will be more likely to bring resolution of trade disputes than alternative trade strategies.

These hypotheses apply to both the challenger and defending sides of trade disputes. Democratic states will be not only more prone to filing complaints against their trade partners, but also more likely to have their own trade barriers challenged by legal complaints. The selection of cases and outcomes will reflect the political pressure in the defendant as the defendant is more prone to resist settlement when there is strong demand for protection by the import-competing industry that lobbied for the trade barrier in the first place. While the dispute is strategic, the theory about domestic constraints does not posit dyadic interaction between the domestic institutional makeup of the two parties in the dispute. Therefore in the next chapter I will conduct two separate analyses to test the role of democratic institutions to influence which states are complainants and which states are challenged as a defendant. Then dyadic analysis is conducted in which the challenger and defender institutions are modeled as having additive effects on the probability of a dispute between the two countries while taking into account the dyadic interaction on other dimensions (e.g., bilateral trade, aid, alliance ties). Analysis to test hypotheses about the decision to challenge a barrier in court (chapters 4 and 5) and the effectiveness of adjudication (chapter 6) will control for variables that increase the resistance of the trade partner such as import penetration levels.

Other factors also influence the choice of trade strategies. As discussed in chapter 1, existing literature on WTO dispute settlement suggests adjudication patterns will reflect power, interest, and law. The observable implications from these alternative perspectives on enforcement are briefly raised here, and will be included as control variables for the empirical analysis. The role of retaliation in dispute settlement offers one perspective for how power may influence trade disputes. Those with larger market size have greater leverage for retaliation if a trade dispute should lead to authorized withdrawal of concessions. Within a specific bilateral relationship, the share of exports sent from the respondent to potential complainant increases the retaliatory capacity of the complainant. Studies highlight the importance of bilateral trade dependence to predict dispute initiation and outcomes in specific cases (Reinhardt, 2000; Bown, 2004b). Bown (2005a, 2005b) also finds that states are less likely to complain when the respondent has resources for counterretaliation outside of the WTO such as through withdrawal of trade preferences or foreign aid. The statistical analysis in chapter 3 that examines cross-national propensity to file complaints for trade disputes will control for GDP as a measure of economic power and include measures of bilateral economic interdependence in the dyadic analysis. In addition, theories that emphasize power imply that retaliatory capacity would determine outcomes regardless of venue choice. A powerful state can use informal or formal mechanisms to coerce compliance in bilateral negotiations by means of threatening denial to its market. To the extent that market power matters, one would not expect adjudication to bring different outcomes. Chapter 6 will assess whether the dispute settlement process is effective to promote resolution when controlling for power. This analysis applies an identification strategy to compare outcomes from legal cases with otherwise similar negotiation cases.

Interest, defined as export stakes for a trade dispute, directly influences both industry and government willingness to consider paying enforcement costs. WTO dispute settlement is used to maintain open markets for exports, and states would have little reason to pursue a dispute in the absence of sufficient export stakes to justify enforcement costs. Horn, Mavroidis, and Nordstrom (2005) show that states with more diversified exports use the dispute adjudication system because they have more potential disputes.[49] The trade interest theory leads one to expect exports at the national and industry levels to account for complaint patterns. The cross-national analysis includes a variable to measure the role of exports in the economy as a control for trade interests, and the case selection analysis controls for the export value of the specific industry. In addition, Guzman and Simmons (2005) look at the interest argument in terms of the value of the defendant market and contend that states will be more likely to file against larger countries because the increase in market access is sufficient to justify the costs of taking action. The GDP measure is expected here to produce the opposite effect from the power arguments as states would be more likely to target larger states.

The legal status of an issue is a starting point for any decision about choice of forum. The core function of the dispute system is to clarify legal obligation.[50] Only those issues that are potentially inconsistent with trade law will be challenged through legal proceedings. Selection models from studies of litigation in law journals emphasize the role of legal uncertainty to generate litigation based on the assumption that defendants and plaintiffs would settle out of court any cases where one side clearly had the stronger legal case. This contrasts with an argument that bureaucratic agencies want to maximize their "win rate" and would choose adjudication only when their legal case will bring

---

[49] See also Sattler and Bernauer (forthcoming).

[50] See Jackson (1997, pp. 109–110) on rule-oriented versus power-oriented settlement. The presumption is that in a rule-oriented system based on international law, decisions are based on fair interpretation of rules and parties approach the dispute in terms of their expectation of this legal judgment rather than their expectation of retaliation. Trachtman (1999) discusses that jurisdiction is strictly limited to WTO law.

certain victory.[51] To further test the two arguments, one would ideally want to compare the legal merits of each trade dispute (both filed complaints and disputes where no complaint was filed). Unable to undertake such extensive legal analysis for the scope of this project, I instead follow the literature on domestic law, which has focused on the comparison of variation in trial rates across areas of law. This leads me to consider which areas of WTO law would be more prone to uncertainty about the ruling. The new agreements in the WTO that regulate standards, intellectual property, investment, and services all represent higher uncertainty because they lack prior precedent in GATT adjudication. In contrast, import barriers have the greatest certainty about law given both the long record of cases and the greater clarity of treaty commitments. The two arguments offer opposite predictions. On the one hand, if legal uncertainty drives litigation, there should be more complaints filed in the former areas of WTO law with new agreements. On the other hand, if choosing the best legal case drives litigation, there should be more complaints filed in the latter areas against import barriers. Overall, the legal merits of specific disputes would not affect which countries file more cases on average, but could influence the decision for a given case. The analyses of case selection in chapters 4 and 5 and dispute effectiveness in chapter 6 include the type of barrier as a proxy for whether it would be an easy legal case.

Conclusion

By connecting the role of domestic and international institutions, this chapter has presented an argument that the adjudication forum provided by the international institution offers a solution to a domestic commitment problem faced by governments. The theory about the political origin of demand for adjudication explains which states use adjudication and their choice of cases. Those states with the most uncertainty about enforcement preferences will have the greatest need to use adjudication and will favor their politically influential industries. The importance of uncertainty about preferences also holds implications for *how* adjudication settles disputes. The courts' role to provide information is more important for screening resolve than for clarification of legal interpretation. States use WTO adjudication as a moderate-cost

---

[51] See Posner (1972) on administrative agencies maximizing win rates. In research on WTO dispute resolution that focuses on one area of law, antidumping and countervailing duty cases, Allee (2003) finds that states are more likely to initiate a WTO case when the legal merits show they are likely to win.

signal that informs domestic audiences and trade partners that they are serious about enforcement.

My argument shows the domestic logic that supports paying the cost of filing a complaint. Even knowing that the defendant state could refuse to lower the trade barrier, the executive may choose to file a case in order to signal its type. Far from easy cases with expected compliance being selected for adjudication, many of the cases will be those hardest for cooperation when interest groups are deeply entrenched with support from their governments.

International courts offer the executive a useful tool for managing domestic pressures. While legislative constraints push the executive toward using courts, this is not against the interests of the executive. Given a choice of ignoring the demands for enforcement from important constituencies, responding to domestic pressure with unilateral enforcement actions, or filing complaints for adjudication, the executive favors going to court. In anticipation of these tradeoffs, executives in democratic states are more likely to advocate legalized dispute settlement when negotiating the provisions for enforcement of the agreement. However, the establishment and design of institutions is an infrequent occurrence, and there are many variables correlated with democracy. These factors make it difficult to evaluate the role of democracy and legislative constraints to explain the structure of international institutions. Therefore, the empirical strategy taken in the next chapters will be to test the implications of the argument for which states use courts and their selection of cases.

3

The Democratic Propensity for Adjudication

THE THEORY PRESENTED in the previous chapter explains democratic demand for legalization as a function of legislative constraints on executive autonomy. States choose to bring their trade disputes to court as a complainant because they need a public venue to show tough enforcement action against foreign trade barriers. Defendants decline to settle prior to legal action for similar reasons, but directed in defense of home trade barriers. Adjudication offers the executive under pressure from the legislature a strategy to visibly demonstrate commitment to domestic industries without risk of a trade war.

My emphasis on the role of divided government to generate the demand for using adjudication calls for analysis that parses out which dimensions of democratic governance influence trade strategies. While democracies as a group would face higher constraints on executive autonomy, there is substantial variation among democracies. Those with higher levels of institutional checks and balances would be expected to use adjudication more often than other democracies. Partisan shifts that introduce divided government and coalition rule would also be expected to increase aggressive enforcement of trade agreements. This chapter offers an empirical test of my argument about domestic constraints.

A prima facie case is readily apparent in the United States to illustrate how divided government corresponds with a higher frequency of complaints. Lohmann and O'Halloran (1994) in their classic article show that divided government in the United States leads to increased levels of protectionism, and it appears to also increase export promotion. The average number of complaints filed by the United States is five per year during periods of divided government compared with an average of two per year during unified partisan control. Figure 3.1 shows the trend over time with peaks during periods of divided government. During the first six years of the WTO when the Clinton administration faced a Republican Congress, the United States accounted for over 20 percent of all complaints filed in the WTO each year. Divided government was not the only reason for a spike in cases during the Clinton era. The early years of the WTO were an unusual period for increased levels of adjudication overall; many cases that had been shelved during the

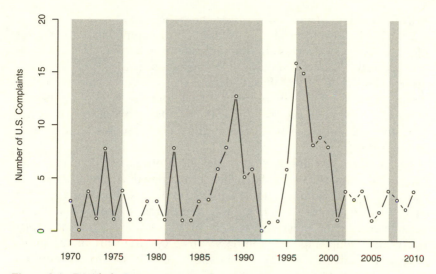

Figure 3.1. Divided Government and U.S. Complaints. The shaded regions indicate periods of divided government in which different parties hold the presidency and majority control in the House of Representatives.

Uruguay Round were now brought up, governments wanted to test the newly strengthened WTO dispute settlement procedures, and compliance problems were prevalent as governments tried to implement new sets of rules. Nonetheless, these factors were equally relevant for all members, and within the larger number of cases the United States took the lead. The U.S. share of WTO adjudication dropped dramatically after the Bush administration came to power, falling below 10 percent of all cases in some years. U.S.-initiated cases grew again to 30 percent of all cases filed in 2007, one year after the Democrats regained control of the House.[1] The effect does not seem limited by the partisanship of the executive—both the Republican administration of Ronald Reagan facing a Democratic Congress and the Democratic administration of Bill Clinton facing a Republican Congress engaged in high activity with several years in which more than five cases were filed. Neither are the U.S. challenges to foreign trade barriers simply a response to the rising trade

[1] The U.S. share of WTO adjudication is calculated as the share of U.S.-initiated complaints relative to all WTO complaints according to the tables available at WorldTradeLaw.net.

deficit. The trade deficit surged over the period 2000 to 2004, even as the Bush administration filed noticeably fewer complaints. Observation of the trade policy process also highlights tension between the legislature and executive. Letters from House Democrats urge the USTR to initiate more cases, while USTR officials defend that they are achieving results without need for more adjudication.[2] This brief overview of the pattern in the United States is suggestive that the balance between legislature and executive may influence adjudication and calls for more comprehensive exploration.

For another close-up, Brazil provides an informative example. During the period from 1975 to 1984, when Brazil remained under authoritarian rule by the military, it filed four complaints. Following election of civilian government in 1985 and democratic consolidation, Brazil became one of the most active users of WTO adjudication as it filed thirty-four complaints between 1985 to 2004. Reforms of the policy process to increase capacity within the executive and to promote coordination with the private sector have supported Brazil's engagement with WTO dispute settlement (Shaffer, Sanchez, and Rosenberg, 2008). The role of the Brazilian Congress to pressure for adjudication is not as direct as seen in the United States. Nonetheless, there is attention to dispute settlement. As in the United States, there are often critical comments in the media and from Congress that the government lets foreign policy goals interfere with economic policies. A trade official said that while he had not heard of specific requests from a member of Congress to file a WTO complaint, there would be media coverage of speeches by members of Congress saying generally that the government "must do something" about trade barriers with Europe or the United States, and after the government files a case members of Congress may say something in mention of the dispute.[3] A search of the records of the Brazilian senate reveals fifteen speakers making reference to WTO disputes.[4] When Brazil's WTO case against U.S. cotton subsidies required a legislative change to authorize cross-retaliation (WTO compliance arbitration authorized Brazil to suspend intellectual property rights protection for U.S. products when the United States failed to comply with the ruling

---

[2] Interviews with House Ways and Means Trade Subcommittee staff member and USTR official, Washington, D.C. August 16, 2007.

[3] Foreign Ministry Official, telephone interview by author, April 28, 2011.

[4] I am grateful to Clarita Costa Maia, analyst at the Brazilian Federal Senate, for conducting this investigation and sharing insights on the Brazilian Congress. The record search counts references by speakers in the senate to WTO complaints involving Brazil as complainant (ten speeches) or as defendent (five speeches) between 1995 and 2011.

within a reasonable period), trade officials consulted with members of Congress to win passage of the measure—this credible threat brought a concession from the United States to directly compensate Brazilian cotton farmers for the injury suffered from U.S. subsidies.[5] The Brazilian case highlights that even while democratization corresponds to a striking upsurge in cases, tracing these to a specific political mechanism is quite difficult. The authority to initiate disputes lies with the executive, and few explicit demands come from Congress. Stepping back to look at more general patterns over a longer time period and number of countries will provide further insight into the political conditions that support active enforcement.

This chapter provides empirical support for the claim that democratic checks and balances generate demand for adjudication. Using statistical analysis of cross-national data from 1975 to 2004 for eighty-one countries, I demonstrate how domestic institutions influence the propensity for using adjudication when controlling for economic size and trade interests. The main analysis will explain the decision to file complaints with attention to different features associated with democratic governance. The first section discusses the argument about domestic constraints in comparison with alternative explanations that democracies choose adjudication to support free trade preferences and to conform with norms for law-guided behavior. The data and variables for statistical analysis are presented in the second section. The third section presents analysis of complainant patterns. Results show that the constraints on the executive imposed by democratic checks and balances correspond to increasing use of adjudication. While it is still possible that electoral incentives for free trade and legal norms contribute to a democratic propensity for adjudication, the statistical analysis shows less support for either of these claims. The fourth section reveals that democratic governments are also more likely to be defendants, and checks on executive autonomy increase the likelihood of being a defendant. The observed pattern in which democracies appear frequently as both challengers and defenders in trade adjudication is consistent with the domestic constraints argument, but the alternative arguments based on democratic free trade preferences or legal norms both imply democracies would be less likely than other governments to appear as defendants. A third set of statistical analysis in the fifth section implements the model with dyadic data to explain variation in which pairs of countries are more likely to litigate. In addition to the role for domestic constraints on

---

[5] Official of Foreign Trade Secretariat, telephone interview by author, April 8, 2011.

both sides of the dispute, alliance relations are an important condition permissive for using adjudication to enforce trade rules.

Why Are Democracies Litigious?

Democratic institutions influence political behavior through multiple channels. I will focus on three: first, divisions of authority create demand for accountability mechanisms in a system of checks and balances; second, electoral competition creates incentives to maximize the general public interest through enforcement of free trade rules; third, democratic values privilege courts as the appropriate venue for dispute settlement. My goal in this section is to discuss how each factor contributes to the democratic propensity toward adjudication of trade disputes.

Checks and Balances

The argument presented in the previous chapter contends that democratic institutions influence trade policy strategies through imposing constraints on the executive that encourage active enforcement. The divisions of authority that arise through institutional separation of power and competition between parties create a credible commitment problem. The commitment problem arises in trade policy because governments open their own market conditional upon a promise of access to foreign markets. It is the job of the executive to guarantee that other states play by the rules, but given that enforcement is costly, the executive will not want to pursue every violation. Domestic constraints push the executive toward higher enforcement levels. In their role to represent their constituencies and respond to industry pressure, the legislature gives more weight to the gains for market access than to the costs of enforcement.

Checks and balances in democratic governance influence trade disputes by means of conditional delegation. Whereas studies of two-level games and international bargaining focus on how legislatures can influence outcomes for negotiations over treaties through the threat to reject ratification or block implementing legislation (e.g., Milner, and Rosendorff, 1996; Milner, 1997; Martin, 2000; Mansfield, Milner and Pevehouse, 2007), these mechanisms are less directly relevant for negotiations over enforcement. Nonetheless, there is a similar logic in the expectation that more constraints reduce bargaining flexibility. Through mandates for public reports, empowerment of private actors, and other means, the legislature imposes constraints to encourage the executive to act on its behalf in pursuit of strong enforcement. As it becomes more difficult to reach negotiated settlements, adjudication becomes more likely.

Democratic accountability mechanisms encourage WTO adjudication directly by increasing the pressure for active enforcement actions, one of which would be filing complaints against potential violations. WTO adjudication is a particularly useful strategy for an executive under enforcement pressure from the legislature because it is costly and public. This represents a visible signal of "tough action" widely reported in the news. Achieving a compromise through bilateral negotiations is less likely to satisfy the domestic audience (the legislature and their industry constituents) that suspects a better outcome may have been possible if only the executive took a tougher stance. In sum, domestic constraints increase enforcement effort and channel this effort into WTO adjudication.

Electoral Incentives

One could alternatively explain high use of WTO adjudication by democracies as a function of the public interest in free trade. Enforcing trade agreements helps to open markets and bring gains for export industries that can strengthen economic performance. The most basic feature of democratic polities is the empowerment of voters to elect their leaders. Those leaders are expected to act in the public interest as they seek election. This provides a powerful incentive for good economic policies to the extent that economic performance is a key dimension on which voters evaluate their leaders. In both authoritarian and democratic regimes, economic conditions influence social stability and regime survival (Haggard and Kaufman, 1995). The key distinction here is that democratic states face broad electoral pressure to conduct reforms to improve economic performance. The large winning coalition necessary to hold office in a democracy encourages the provision of public goods such as free trade (Bueno de Mesquita et al., 2003). Liberal trade policies are one tool for improving economic performance with the gains being greatest from reciprocal liberalization between trade partners. A political leader's need to gain domestic support for policies in a democracy can push for either liberalization or protectionism as a unilateral trade policy, but unambiguously favors reciprocal trade liberalization (Pahre, 2008). Swings of voter opinion have accounted for major shifts in the trade policies of leading democracies (Verdier, 1994). Empirical evidence of democratic preference for free trade includes the role of the United States and Britain as the leading postwar democratic powers to establish the GATT in 1947, the high rate of preferential free trade agreements among democratic states, and greater trade liberalization among developing countries that are democratic (Mansfield, Milner, and Rosendorff, 2000; Mansfield, Milner and Rosendorff, 2002; Milner and Kubota, 2005).

Legal Norms

Democracies are also distinct in their commitment to civil liberties and legal due process. Democracies may be more likely to use international adjudication as a means of dispute settlement because both the government and business groups have greater familiarity with judicial forms of dispute resolution at home. This familiarity builds skills and values that may be transferred to the international level.[6]

The role of adjudication in society is closely tied with the overall political system. In authoritarian regimes that have a functioning judicial system, courts are likely to be constrained in their influence and subject to political intervention. Democratic governance, on the other hand, depends upon an independent judiciary to uphold the rule of law (Larkins, 1996; Widner, 2001). Stephenson (2003) models an independent judiciary as one form of mutual restraint that becomes necessary when there is political competition. He shows empirically that states with greater rates of party turnover and democratic stability have higher levels of judicial independence. Evidence shows that judicial independence has a strong correlation with both political and economic freedom (La Porta et al., 2004). Not only do democracies have better judicial systems, but use of courts becomes common practice. Democratic states have higher rates of litigation (Sarat and Grossman, 1975; Giles and Lancaster, 1989). This is one facet of how democratic political culture supports actions by private actors to make demands of the state to guarantee their rights.

Business interests in democracies gain skills that help to support a litigation strategy. In democratic states, firms become accustomed to providing information to the government and presenting their interests in terms of law and national interest rather than as private deal making (Bernstein and Berger, 1997, pp. 9–10). Firms directly take part in litigation as plaintiffs and defendants. Indeed, business organizations account for the largest share of civil litigation in the United States and other advanced democracies (Galanter, 1975). Such experience prepares the private sector to play its role as a partner with the government in bringing forward a WTO dispute.[7]

---

[6] Doyle (1986); Dixon (1994); Maoz and Russett (1993), and others have made this argument in the context of the democratic peace debate. Gaubatz (1996) contends democracies are more likely to uphold their international commitments because the public and leadership of democracies see law as legitimate and respect its binding nature. Busch (2000) applies a combined argument about norms and audience costs to explain escalation of trade disputes.

[7] Even in the wealthiest and most active WTO participants, the United States and EU, Shaffer (2003) has shown that WTO litigation is often managed through a public-private partnership.

From this perspective, democratic values work through both the public and private sectors to create the belief that adjudication is the most appropriate means to resolve disputes. Even if democratic values do not directly push forward court cases, they may lower resistance to the possibility that adjudication could offer an effective solution.

Testing Alternative Democracy Mechanisms

These three dimensions of democratic institutions—checks and balances, electoral incentives, and democratic norms—could each independently contribute to greater use of adjudication by democratic states. They are not mutually exclusive. Nonetheless, we can probe for which factor is more important through testing observable implications. All three support an overall expectation that democracies would file more cases. But they point to different explanations for why some democracies are more litigious than others and to account for periods of increasing or decreasing use of adjudication. There is considerable variation across democracies. For example, Botswana and Thailand have comparable income with the same level of democracy (polity score of 9 in 2004), but the former has never used adjudication while the latter is a frequent filer (fourteen cases between its accession in 1982 and 2005). When comparing over time, even countries that are consistently active users of adjudication show large fluctuation year to year—since the establishment of the WTO in 1995 the number of cases filed in any particular year by the United States has varied from one to sixteen while Brazil's annual filing has ranged from zero to seven cases.

The argument about democratic accountability implies that the variation among democracies depends upon the extent of divided authority that acts as a check on executive autonomy for trade policy. Rather than democracy per se leading to states, active enforcement policies, checks on executive autonomy generate frequent cases. Authoritarian rulers are the most independent. Yet even within states having democratic political competition there is substantial room for variation in the degree of constraints. These arise from both institutional structure and partisan gap. The continuum would move from the highest level of constraints for a fragmented parliamentary system, followed by a divided presidential system, and more moderate constraints in a unified presidential system or majority rule parliamentary government.

Parliamentary systems have fewer divisions of authority from the perspective that the legislature appoints the executive so that the two branches in principle represent the same interests. When one party holds an outright majority the solid support base in the legislature affords the executive with considerable independence so long as actions maintain the support of their own party. More fragmentation of party strength in the legislature, however, can introduce checks on an executive that must rely upon building permanent or ad hoc coalitions to pass legislation or even to form a government. Indeed, the capacity of the legislature to end the term of the executive through a no-confidence vote affords higher domestic constraint on an executive in a parliamentary system with fragmented party control. Thus parliamentary government can range widely in the degree of divided government (Laver and Shepsle, 1991).

In a presidential system the legislature represents an independent actor with distinct interests arising from different electoral constituencies even in the case that both president and the majority party of the legislature are of the same party. This institutionalizes conflicts of interest between the legislature and executive (Persson, Roland, and Tabellini, 1997). When the president and legislative majority represent different parties, it further divides interests. Democratic accountability pressures are greatest when there are more checks on executive authority. Therefore the differences in political system and partisan balance described here are expected to influence enforcement strategies through their pressure on the executive to demonstrate visible accountability to the legislature for enforcement of trade agreements. Higher levels of domestic constraints on the executive would induce more frequent use of adjudication.

The electoral incentives argument suggests that variation among democracies would depend on partisan orientation and electoral institutions. The political economy literature has focused on how economic interests affect trade policy preferences, which can be used as the basis for expectations about partisan positions on trade. For example, in capital-rich states (the advanced industrial OECD nations), business favors free trade while labor is opposed (Rogowski, 1989; Alt et al., 1996; Scheve and Slaughter, 2001). Evidence supports that in the OECD countries, conservative parties that represent capital owners favor liberalizing trade while liberal parties that represent labor are more protectionist. This offers a starting point for a partisan hypothesis on trade.[8]

It is not clear, however, whether free trade preferences translate directly into support for active enforcement. Enforcement, after all, includes threats of market closure. Conservative parties face a dilemma between support for improved market access abroad and concern about

---

[8] See Milner and Judkins (2004) and Dutt and Mitra (2005). Changes in the interindustry factor mobility may shift trade preferences, as seen by the inconsistent positions of U.S. parties on trade policy over time (Hiscox, 2002). Specific factor models of trade would not connect any partisan orientation to trade. The underlying economic interests of coalitions supporting right and left parties would also differ for developing countries.

the threat to raise tariffs. Liberal parties also have mixed incentives. On the one hand, protectionist sentiments in liberal parties could induce caution about challenging the violations of other states from a "glass house" perspective to avoid attention to their own violations that protect domestic industries. On the other hand, liberal parties may use "fair trade" slogans and complaints about poor compliance by trade partners to slow the rush to free trade. The contrasting positions of the Republican and Democrat presidential candidates in the United States is illustrative: in a speech at an October 2008 event in Washington, D.C., a representative of the Obama campaign said that Senator Obama favored enforcement of existing agreements over the negotiation of new free trade agreements and called for the USTR to reallocate resources and initiate seventeen cases in the coming year (up from four cases in 2007 and three cases in 2008). The trade coordinator of the McCain campaign responded that many disputes could be resolved through quiet diplomacy rather than a "commitment to litigate" and advocated the negotiation of new free trade agreements.[9] The eagerness to litigate came under doubt however as the USTR under the Obama administration initiated only two cases in 2009 and four in 2010. It is a testable proposition whether liberal governments more generally favor enforcement by adjudication.

One must also pay attention to the electoral institutions that filter which interests hold influence. Bueno de Mesquita et al. (2003) suggest that the dimension of democracy that encourages public good provision is the broad size of the winning coalition necessary to support the ruling leadership that chooses policies. They measure the winning coalition size in terms of the competitiveness of recruitment and the inclusiveness of the polity's selectorate. Others have emphasized the role of certain kinds of electoral institutions. Proportional representation (PR) promotes support for free trade by privileging the median voter over special interests (Rogowski, 1987; Mansfield and Busch, 1995).[10] To the extent that WTO adjudication represents a free trade strategy that is a public good, PR systems and those with a large winning coalition would be expected to file more complaints. One could also view WTO adjudication as a private good, however, because it offers benefits to a narrow group

---

[9] Erik, Wasson. "McCain to Seek Trade Compromise; Obama Focus on Enforcement," *Inside Trade*, October 10, 2008.

[10] Rogowski (1987) claims free trade preferences lead to the establishment of PR systems. McGillivray (2004) provides a critique that PR systems lead parties to favor niche groups so that trade policy outcomes depend on the interaction of industry geography and electoral system.

of exporters.[11] This would yield the opposite prediction regarding the effect of PR: to the extent that adjudication represents a response to special interest pressure, PR systems would be less likely to engage in adjudication.

The legal norms argument would suggest that states with a stronger domestic commitment to legal forms of dispute settlement would also be more likely to use adjudication for trade disputes. The strength of legal norms in society can be measured by how well a country protects civil liberties and rule of law. In addition, the role of legal norms to affect the behavior of democracies can be tested as a function of regime duration.[12] New democracies may have less exposure to the norms of rule by law and be more reluctant than their counterparts with longer experience with democratic rule of law. Both rule of law and years of democratic regime duration would be expected to increase use of trade adjudication if international behavior mimics domestic patterns.

Data

The goal of this section is to examine variation over time and across countries in the propensity to initiate adjudication as a function of domestic political constraints while controlling for baseline factors that make some countries more likely to have substantial trade interests. The unit of analysis is the country year for the time period from 1975 to 2004. The period includes two decades of GATT dispute adjudication, which by 1975 had taken on a central role in the trade system, and it includes the first decade of the more legalistic WTO.[13]

Limited data availability for several variables beyond 2004 sets this as the end point of the dataset. The sample of eighty-one countries includes all members of the GATT/WTO as of 2004 with the exception of the thirty-one "least developed countries" (LDCs) and five for which data

---

[11] Some cases are broad in scope without excludable benefits such as the U.S. case against Chinese IPR violations that stands to help all exporters to China. Other cases have a smaller group of beneficiaries, such as the Boeing-Airbus cases. See Rickard (2010) for theory on why private good logic prevails on defendants decision to violate trade rules and evidence that governments with majoritarian electoral system are more likely to violate trade rules than those with PR.

[12] A similar test of democratic norms can be found in the democratic peace literature (Maoz and Russett, 1993).

[13] The data for the GATT period disputes were generously provided by Marc Busch and Eric Reinhardt, and are described in their analysis (Busch and Reinhardt, 2003). The data for the WTO disputes are from the World Trade Law database summary of all WTO disputes available at http://www.worldtradelaw.net/.

on key economic variables were not available.[14] For these countries, low capacity represents a major obstacle for the use of trade adjudication. As beneficiaries of unilateral preferential market access offered to LDCs, they also have less need to invoke WTO rights. Special provisions in the WTO agreement for this group of members allow them exceptions to commitments. Only one least developed country, Bangladesh in a 2004 complaint against India, had filed a dispute during the period of analysis. Table 3.1 provides a list of the sample for analysis and shows the wide variation in their use of adjudication when comparing number of complaints filed during the GATT and WTO periods.

The EU is treated as a single state because of the common trade policy. In addition to establishing a common tariff and harmonized regulatory standards, trade policy is determined at the centralized decision process among members in the Council of Ministers and through delegation to the Commission (Meunier, 2005). Representatives of member governments in the Council have delegated to the Commission tasks to enhance foreign market access through negotiations and investigation of exporter complaints while maintaining mechanisms of control in a process that closely parallels delegation of tasks by Congress to the USTR (De Bievre and Dur, 2005). Although there are a handful of disputes initiated by a member state, even these disputes are coordinated closely with the EU trade officials. Both bilateral negotiations and WTO adjudication are conducted by EU officials acting on behalf of the membership. Therefore, after accession to the EU a state is removed from the sample and is included as part of the EU for subsequent years. Where possible, data for the EU represent the EU aggregate value (i.e., GDP is the total GDP for EU members as reported in international financial statistics). Democracy, partisan orientation, and rule of law, however, are measured only at the national level, and so I use the average of all members. Executive constraints are coded to approximate how EU institutional checks and balances would be coded if the EU were a state (as described below). I also test the results for coding EU checks as the average of EU members or excluding the EU from the sample.

---

[14] The definition of LDCs is based on the list of LDCs on the United Nations web site, June 22, 2004. Czechoslovakia, Cuba, Macao (China), Qatar, and Suriname are omitted due to lack of data. There are a handful of countries that had a short period between the end of GATT and their accession to the WTO. These states are omitted for the years in which the state is not a member.

CHAPTER 3

TABLE 3.1
Country List for GATT/WTO Dataset.

Country	Year	GATT	WTO	Country	Year	GATT	WTO
Argentina	1967	11	9	Kyrgyz Republic	1998		0
Armenia	2003		0	Latvia	1999		0
Australia	1948	14	7	Lithuania	2001		0
Austria	1951	1		Macedonia	2003		0
Bolivia	1990	0	0	Malaysia	1957	0	1
Botswana	1987	0	0	Mauritius	1970	0	0
Brazil	1948	17	21	Mexico	1986	5	12
Bulgaria	1996		0	Moldova	2001		0
Cameroon	1963	0	0	Morocco	1987	0	0
Canada	1948	26	26	Namibia	1992	0	0
Chile	1949	10	10	New Zealand	1948	7	6
China	2001		1	Nicaragua	1950	4	1
Colombia	1981	4	3	Nigeria	1960	0	0
Congo, Republic of	1963	0	0	Norway	1948	2	2
Costa Rica	1990	1	3	Oman	2000		0
Cote d'Ivoire	1963	1	0	Pakistan	1948	1	3
Croatia	2000		0	Panama	1997		1
Czech Republic	1993	1	1	Paraguay	1994	0	0
Dominican Republic	1950	1	0	Peru	1951	2	2
Ecuador	1996		3	Philippines	1979	3	4
Egypt	1970	0	0	Poland	1967	1	3
El Salvador	1991	1	0	Portugal	1962	1	
Estonia	1999		0	Romania	1971	0	0
European Community	1958*	49	68	Slovak Republic	1993	0	0
Finland	1950	5		Slovenia	1994	0	0
Gabon	1963	0	0	South Africa	1948	1	0
Georgia	2000		0	Spain	1963	1	
Ghana	1957	0	0	Sri Lanka	1948	0	1
Greece	1950	0		Swaziland	1993	0	0
Guatemala	1991	2	4	Sweden	1950	4	
Guyana	1966	0	0	Switzerland	1966	0	4
Honduras	1994	0	3	Thailand	1982	3	11
Hungary	1973	0	5	Trinidad and Tobago	1962	0	0
India	1948	4	16	Tunisia	1990	0	0
Indonesia	1950	0	3	Turkey	1951	0	2
Israel	1962	0	0	UAE	1994	0	0

TABLE 3.1
Continued.

Country	Year	GATT	WTO	Country	Year	GATT	WTO
Japan	1955	7	11	United States	1948	70	75
Jordan	2000		0	Uruguay	1953	2	1
Kenya	1964	0	0	Venezuela	1990	1	1
Korea, Republic of	1967	1	12	Zimbabwe	1948	1	0
Kuwait	1963	0	0				

Note: The initiations are the total count of GATT and WTO dispute case initiations during the period between 1975 to 2004. The accession year indicates when a country first joined the system. *The EC assumed de facto membership status. Upon EU membership, states are removed from sample.

Variation in Use of Adjudication

The dependent variable is the number of annual complaints initiated by a country.[15] In the sample the number of complaints ranges from zero to sixteen (the United States filed sixteen complaints in 1996 and the EU filed fifteen complaints in both 1997 and 1998), but most states do not file a complaint in any given year, so that the mean number of complaints is 0.27. Even among high-income states during the WTO period, the average remains at 0.86. Nonetheless, the United States is not the only country to have multiple disputes in a year. Brazil filed seven in 2000, and countries ranging from Chile to Thailand have filed more than three cases in a single year. Table 3.1 shows total filings by member.

In order to examine this variation, I use an event count model to estimate the conditions that increase the likelihood for states to file disputes. Ideally one wants a list of potential disputes that could be analyzed as a discrete binary choice model of whether a complaint was filed. This approach is followed in the subsequent two chapters that examine the influence of specific industry and trade partner characteristics to influence adjudication patterns of Japan and the United States using a dataset of potential disputes. Since it is difficult to generate a list of all possible cases for the full membership over thirty years, however, this chapter instead analyzes the underlying process that yields an annual count of complaints filed by each state. This assumes that in a year states face potential cases generated by an unobserved process that is conditioned

---

[15] Multiple filings for the same case are counted as a single initiation. For example, the two WTO complaints about Europe's banana import regime (DS16 and DS27) are treated as one complaint for each of the countries that filed. This is a necessary step to avoid double counting when the WTO has assigned two numbers to a dispute.

by the control variables in the analysis but would otherwise appear at random (i.e., the United States may face more potential cases because of the size of its economy with more large export industries). While it is not possible to observe the process creating potential cases, it is possible to observe the total number of decisions to file a complaint, or events, which are bound between zero and infinity. The negative binomial regression is a maximum likelihood method used to estimate the rate at which events occur when the count variable exhibits higher variance than its mean value (overdispersion).[16]

Democracy Measures

I will present five models to test different aspects of domestic political institution. First, model 1 tests a simple indicator variable coded 1 for democratic states and 0 for nondemocratic states. The indicator evaluates the "democratic difference" in adjudication. The Political Regime Characteristics and Transitions Polity IV Project by Monty Marshall and Keith Jaggers is a widely used measure of democracy that offers coverage for the countries and period of analysis. The central polity2 measure represents a scale index of authoritarian and democratic regime characteristics (-10 to 10) (competitiveness of political participation and executive recruitment as well as constraints on the chief executive). As is standard practice in studies of democracy in international relations, I treat 7 as the cutoff to code states as democracies.[17] Results are consistent whether using the full scale or the indicator variable. In a robustness test, I replace the polity measure with the Freedom House score, which is an alternative measure of democracy that combines a 7-point index of civil and political liberties.

Model 2 tests my hypothesis that increased constraints on executive autonomy lead to more adjudication when controlling for democracy. Constraints on executive autonomy vary considerably across government structures and in response to changing partisan balance. The Database of Political Institutions (DPI) developed as a World Bank research project provides a measure of the "checks" in government policy making.[18]

---

[16] A likelihood ratio test confirms the presence of overdispersion in the data that makes the negative binomial more appropriate than the Poisson model (King, 1989).

[17] Some studies use a lower threshold of 6, and the results here are consistent for either cutoff. The higher threshold for consolidated democracies is preferable given the focus on looking for behavior distinct to democratic states.

[18] Beck et al. (2001) describe the data. See Keefer and Stasavage (2003) for an application using the checks variable. I use the 2006 release. I make a small number of corrections to the checks coding for some countries, but the findings are not sensitive to these changes.

As an index that ranges from 1 to 18 (mean 3, standard deviation 1.7 in full sample), the measure increases by 1 for each of the following possible checks on executive autonomy: competitive elections, presidential system, and opposition party control over the legislature. In a parliamentary system, minority government is coded as an additional check with variation by the number of parties in the coalition and their ideological distance from the ruling party on economic policy. The variable is constructed to capture the number of actors who exercise an opposing force to executive leadership. I expect the level of checks would correspond with the likelihood of constraints on foreign economic policy, which could appear in the form of restrictions on negotiation mandate, reporting requirements, and more extensive consultation with the legislature and industry.

Authoritarian states such as China are coded as having the lowest value of 1, while the United States ranges from 4 to 5 depending on whether there is divided government.[19] In a parliamentary regime such as Japan, the ruling LDP enjoys substantial autonomy for a score of 3 when it holds a majority in the parliament, but faces more constraints for a score of 4 when it does not hold a majority even if the LDP retains ruling party status as the largest party. I follow the coding rules to assign values for the EU.[20] Since fragmented coalition governments can lead to a spike in the number of checks as a function of multiple parties opposing a minority government (i.e., Japan's score reached 11 in 1994 when seven parties formed a coalition government and India reached 18 in 1997), I take the log of the checks measure to smooth these extreme values for statistical analysis.

[19] For a presidential system, the coding rule adds one check for a chief executive, a second check for competitive selection of the executive, third and fourth checks for each chamber of the elected legislature, and a fifth check when the legislature is controlled by a different party from the executive.

[20] The EU is given 1 check for presence of a chief executive (the Commission) similar to a presidential system. A second check is allocated because the executive is selected through competitive selection. Although it is not a directly elected president, selection by the leaders of democratic EU member states can be treated as indirect democratic representation. The EU receives a third check for the Council of Ministers, which approximates a chamber of a legislature. The European Parliament is treated as a second chamber of a legislature for a fourth check beginning in 1993 when the EP gains the power of codecision. Partisan unity versus division is measured by the majority party of the member states—a fifth check for "divided" partisan rule is given when there is no party majority on the right/center/left scale among EU member states when coding the chief executive of each member. An extra "EU check" is added to reflect the special constraints on a supranational institution (i.e., the plural executive of the Commission, the de facto veto power of any member in Council voting). The checks measure for the EU ranges from 4 to 6 with a mean value of 5. On the dimension of checks and balances, one can treat the EU as equivalent to a state with highly developed accountability mechanisms comparable to the United States.

The electoral incentives of democratic government are tested in model 3. In addition to the democracy variable, the model includes an indicator for whether elections are by proportional representation. This variable is zero for states that either are not democratic or have a plurality system. Mixed systems (i.e., states like Japan, India, and Mexico that have some seats elected by plurality and some seats elected by proportional representation) are coded PR in the main analysis, and as a robustness check I switch these cases to zero. Although I am agnostic in my expectations for partisan effects on adjudication, they may have an indirect effect given partisan differences over support for free trade. Model 3 includes a variable measuring the left orientation of the executive, which is a three-level ordered scale from right, to center, to left. Both the PR and party variables are from the DPI database.

The WTO period is separately examined in model 4 with the subsample for 1995–2004. The status of rule of law at home captures democratic values for using judicial process to resolve conflicts. A World Bank dataset, Governance Matters, provides a variable that aggregates survey data about the perceptions of individuals and experts about whether the government upholds legal due process in the courts. This rule of law measure is added to model 3. Because it is available as a biannual variable starting in 1995, this variable is tested only in the WTO period, and missing years have been interpolated with the assumption of linearity.

Finally, in model 5 the separate dimensions for democratic constraints, electoral incentives, and values are included in the same model for a joint test of their influence on the initiation of GATT/WTO complaints. Since this model is trying to disaggregate democratic policy dimensions and includes the count of democratic years, the indicator variable for democracy is no longer included. Democratic values are measured by a variable that codes the years that a state has been democratic.[21] Those with more years since democratic transition will have had more consolidation of democratic values. Taking the log smooths the high values for old democracies such as the United States.

Control Variables

Economic size and trade dependence may influence use of adjudication through both the avenue of interest and capacity. Controlling for GDP and income takes into account the likelihood that a small economy would have fewer trade flows large enough to justify taking action against

---

[21] A Polity score of 7 represents the threshold for defining when a state became democratic, and the variable counts democratic regime duration from that date.

foreign violations and fewer resources ready to allocate for a costly trade strategy. States may also fear that their small market size weakens their potential retaliation threat such that even if they were to win a ruling the trade partner would not fully comply. Both the interest and capacity arguments imply that small and poor states would be less likely on average to use WTO adjudication. Taking the log of the GDP and per capita GDP measures smooths extreme values. [22]

The structure of trade relations also influences the position of a country within the global economy. The trade balance and share of exports in GDP are two measures of export orientation.[23] Those states with a larger surplus and export dependence have more interest in active export promotion strategies. Alternatively one could argue that trade deficits generate pressure for export promotion as one measure to redress the problem, which is the kind of rhetoric frequently heard in the United States where trade friction rises in step with the swings of the trade deficit. Trade surplus countries, which recognize that their surplus could cause political problems for trade partners, may not want to provoke further trade tensions with initiation of a dispute.

The type of trade also matters. In particular, it is important to control for the share of agricultural goods in total exports. The agricultural sector has long been the beneficiary of high protection levels, and this leads to many "potential cases" for agriculture exporters trying to crack these tough markets. Moreover the same factors that make farmers a powerful group for seeking protection also help them to gain government intervention against foreign trade barriers.

International trade institutions directly shape the options and cost of adjudication. First, the establishment of the WTO in 1995 brought a more legalized dispute settlement process. By removing the right of the defendant to block panels and rulings, the institutional change increased the range of cases that could be challenged. The expansion in the scope of matters covered by the trade agreement also substantially increased the number of potential cases. Second, states that have concluded preferential trade agreements (PTAs) have alternative venues to address their trade disputes (Busch, 2007). For example, U.S. and Canadian firms with an objection to the antidumping duty assessed against their industry can challenge the respective government decision directly through NAFTA Article 19. The intergovernmental dispute resolution procedures of NAFTA and many other PTAs are modeled closely on the WTO dispute process. PTAs may also reduce demand for adjudication to the extent

[22] GDP data are in purchasing power parity constant 2000 international dollars form the World Development Indicators (World Bank).
[23] Trade data are from the World Development Indicators.

that trade barriers with important partners are removed as part of the PTA negotiations. The variable for PTA represents a count of the number of PTA agreements that the country has in effect during the year.[24]

There may be concern about missing variables that make particular countries differ in their trade strategies. The analysis addresses this through three approaches. First, I include a variable that counts the previous complaints filed by the country over the past ten years. This is a kind of lagged dependent variable that would capture unobserved factors that make one country more litigious on average. Previous complaints also measures the role of experience itself to directly increase the capacity of a state to engage in future adjudication (Davis and Bermeo, 2009). Second, I compute heteroskedasticity-consistent robust standard errors by clustering on country to account for correlation among repeated observations for the same country that may persist even after controlling for the key observable economic and political variables. Finally, later in a robustness test, I will discuss the results for an alternative specification that uses fixed country effects to estimate the filing pattern when including indicator variables for each country.

Table 3.2 presents a snapshot of the top fifteen users of trade adjudication by the number of complaints filed between 1975 and 2005. To what extent do variables measuring domestic institutions account for these litigious states as compared with their income levels? More than half of the high filing states are democracies. Even some exceptions such as Korea hide the actual relationship since all but one of Korea's adjudication cases came after its democratic transition, yet the years of authoritarian rule bring down the average democracy score for the period. The measures of institutional checks and rule of law do not present a clear pattern. These variables have considerable variation over time that is not being captured here. More than half of the high filing states have above average income, but the ordering does not follow a ranking by income, and there are some surprising frequent filers with lower income levels. The next section will present the results of multivariate regression analysis, which can provide more attention to the variation over time and control for multiple variables.

Democratic Challengers

The estimates shown in table 3.3 support the hypothesis of democratic propensity to use adjudication. While controlling for the size of their

---

[24] Mike Tomz generously shared data on PTAs. See Goldstein, Rivers, and Tomz (2007) for a description.

TABLE 3.2
Top fifteen Users of Trade Adjudication.

Country	Complaints	Democracy	Checks	Rule of Law	Income
United States	145	10	4.6	1.7	28,058
EU	117	10	4.9	1.5	21,016
Canada	52	10	4.1	1.8	22,859
Brazil	38	4	3.3	−0.3	6,637
Australia	21	10	4.3	1.9	21,081
Argentina	20	4	3.0	−0.2	11,006
Chile	20	2	2.3	1.2	6,484
India	20	8	6.3	0.0	1,752
Japan	18	10	3.6	1.5	21,881
Mexico	17	3	3.2	−0.4	8,285
Thailand	14	6	5.2	0.3	5,253
Korea	13	1	2.7	0.7	10,411
New Zealand	13	10	3.1	2.0	17,793
Colombia	7	8	3.0	−0.7	5,649
Philippines	7	4	2.5	−0.4	3,830
Average of full sample	7	3	3.0	0.2	9,493

Note: "Complaints" lists all GATT and WTO complaints filed between 1975 to 2005. The variables for democracy (polity 2 score), checks, and income (per capita GDP in U.S. dollars) represent the mean value for the country over its years as a GATT/WTO member during the period of the sample (1975–2004). "Rule of Law" measures the average for the period 1995–2004. The full sample refers to the mean for members listed in table 3.1 during years following accession.

economy and structure of trade, democratic states are significantly more likely to file cases. Using estimates from model 1 with control variables set at their mean values, shifting the democracy indicator from 0 to 1 nearly doubles the predicted probability that a country files one or more cases in a given year from 0.09 to 0.17 (the first difference of 0.082 has a standard error of 0.028).[25]

Rather than democratic values or electoral incentives for free trade, the evidence is strong that political constraints are what pushes democracies into adjudication. In model 2, the democracy indicator is no longer

---

[25] I first simulate model parameters from their sampling distributions and compute the Monte Carlo estimates of predicted probability of one or more GATT/WTO dispute initiations. I repeat this by changing the value of a variable of interest while holding all other variables constant at their means, and then calculate the first difference between the two estimates. See Michael Tomz, Jason Wittenberg, and Gary King. 2003. CLARIFY: Software for Interpreting and Presenting Statistical Results (Version 2.1; Stanford University, University of Wisconsin, and Harvard University, 5 January 2003), available at http://gking.harvard.edu/.

TABLE 3.3
Estimated Coefficients of Negative Binomial Regression Models for Dispute Initiation.

Variables	Model 1	Model 2	Model 3	Model 4	Model 5
Democracy	0.736**	0.381	0.783**	0.927**	
	(0.290)	(0.312)	(0.324)	(0.448)	
Checks		0.416**			0.486**
		(0.179)			(0.133)
PR system			−0.445*		−0.415*
			(0.245)		(0.246)
Party			0.109*		0.109*
			(0.066)		(0.061)
Rule of law				0.203	
				(0.184)	
Dem. years					0.068
					(0.065)
Previous	0.016*	0.014*	0.006	0.004	0.004
initiations	(0.008)	(0.008)	(0.006)	(0.013)	(0.005)
PTAs	−0.022	−0.022	−0.004	−0.029	−0.002
	(0.018)	(0.018)	(0.016)	(0.019)	(0.018)
GDP	0.716**	0.697**	0.694**	0.903**	0.665**
	(0.091)	(0.087)	(0.087)	(0.113)	(0.087)
Per capita GDP	0.297**	0.330**	0.321**	0.025	0.352**
	(0.089)	(0.090)	(0.080)	(0.212)	(0.074)
Ag export %	0.026**	0.027**	0.025**	0.028**	0.026**
	(0.005)	(0.005)	(0.005)	(0.006)	(0.004)
Export % GDP	0.007	0.005	0.002	0.011	−0.001
	(0.007)	(0.007)	(0.007)	(0.007)	(0.008)
Trade balance	0.002**	0.002**	0.002**	0.001	0.002**
	(0.001)	(0.001)	(0.001)	(0.002)	(0.001)
WTO period	0.410**	0.399**	0.455**		0.470**
	(0.144)	(0.136)	(0.133)		(0.127)
Constant	−24.369**	−24.325**	−23.773**	−26.794**	−23.413*
	(2.885)	(2.815)	(2.658)	(4.053)	(2.638)
Dispersion	−0.703	−0.767	−0.824	−0.969	−0.873
Parameter	(0.216)	(0.217)	(0.262)	(0.362)	(0.271)
Countries	81	81	79	74	79
N	1,388	1,371	1,325	600	1,313

Note: Models 1–3 and 5 are for the full period 1975 to 2004. Model 4 is for the WTO period 1995–2004 when the rule of law indicator is available. The dispersion parameter is $\log \alpha$. *Significant at the 10 percent level. **Significant at the 5 percent level.

significant when also including the measure of checks and balances. The effect of executive constraints is highly significant and substantively important. Shifting the value of the checks measure by one standard deviation while holding the democracy variable constant at 1 and other variables at their mean values changes the predicted likelihood for a country filing one or more cases from 0.14 to 0.18 (first difference of 0.039 with standard error of 0.016), representing a 27 percent increase.[26]

The role of the electoral system also has an effect on initiation, but not in the expected direction. Model 3 shows that PR system governments tend to file *fewer* complaints. The role of proportional representation to broaden the average constituency size and support provision of public goods leads to an expectation that a PR system would correlate with free trade preferences that in turn would support active enforcement of trade agreements. The negative direction of the effect from a PR system fits with a view that WTO adjudication is a private good pursued for narrow interests rather than a public good. The narrow constituency of plurality systems is more responsive to private interests. When holding other variables at their mean value, a shift to a PR system reduces the likelihood of filing by 35 percent. This effect should be viewed with some caution, however, because it is weakly significant (first difference of 0.058 with standard error of 0.036) and depends on treating mixed PR systems as PR. Changing the coding of the mixed PR systems from PR to plurality rule makes the variable insignificant. Therefore I examined another variable that connects electoral incentives to free trade preferences. The argument by Bueno de Mesquita et al. (2003) that winning coalition size determines provision of public goods such as free trade is tested by running model 2 replacing the democracy dummy variable with the measures of winning coalition size and selectorate. The effect of the checks and balance measure remains strong while the coefficients for winning coalition and selectorate are insignificant (these results are not shown here). It would appear that trade enforcement does not occur as provision of a public good.

Model 3 tests the influence of partisan orientation of the executive. Although the business constituency and ideological views of conservative parties could be expected to be more favorable to free trade, which could lead them to support enforcement actions, the results show

---

[26] The estimated effect of executive constraints is slightly larger when omitting the indicator variable for democracy. Since the effect of executive constraints may be mixed in with the democracy measure, multicollinearity could reduce the apparent individual impact of each variable (correlation is 0.66). In a reestimation of model 2 without the democracy indicator, the checks variable coefficient increases to 0.542 (standard. error 0.162), and the shift of checks by one standard deviation leads to a 37 percent increase in the likelihood of filing one or more complaint.

the opposite: a left orientation encourages use of adjudication. This fits the pattern in the United States where the Democratic Party has advocated stronger enforcement of trade agreements.[27] The effect of left orientation to increase adjudication appears more evident for developing countries where the labor sector has greater gains from free trade, but an interaction term of income and party is not significant.

There is little evidence that democratic values are a key factor driving some states to be more litigious. Neither the rule of law measure in model 4 (tested on the WTO period given the limited availability of the data for this variable) nor the years of democratic rule tested in model 5 reach statistical significance. Model 5 shows that the role of checks remains strong when controlling jointly for the separate dimensions of democratic pressure for adjudication (note this model omits the democratic dummy variable because the democracy measure is operationalized as years since democratic transition). In this model there is an estimated 32 percent increase in the likelihood of filing when changing the checks level by one standard deviation and holding other variables constant.[28]

Other control variables generally perform as expected. Market size and income have large positive effects. A shift of GDP from the mean to one standard deviation above the mean more than doubles the likelihood of filing one or more complaints.[29] Agriculture exporters are significantly more likely to file frequent cases, which reflects the high mobilization of agricultural groups on both sides of the dispute.

The trade balance corresponds with greater adjudication activity, which suggests that states with a trade surplus file more frequently. The United States acts as an influential case, however, to determine this particular result. When excluding the United States from the sample, the variable becomes negative and insignificant. A quick look at the pattern of U.S. filing shows that the relatively lower trade deficits of the period from 1989 to 1997 were when the United States was extremely active in trade adjudication while there was a steady decline in U.S. cases thereafter just as the deficit reached historic high levels.

---

[27] The result is not entirely driven by the United States. When excluding the United States from the sample and reestimating model 3, the party variable changes to 0.118 with a standard error of 0.072 for a p-value of 0.100. Although no longer reaching conventional levels of statistical significance, the tendency for liberal governments to file more frequently remains apparent.

[28] The first difference estimate of 0.042 has a standard error of 0.013.

[29] I calculate this using the coefficient estimates from model 1 and setting all variables to their mean values and shifting GDP by an increase of one standard deviation above the mean value. This estimates a first difference of 0.25 (standard error 0.03). Simultaneously shifting the per capita GDP variable to one standard deviation above its mean adds an additional 0.04 increase in the probability of filing (standard error 0.01).

The WTO reforms for a strengthened dispute system opened the doors to a period with more cases being filed. No longer concerned that the defendant would block the panel or ruling, states could file on the basis of their own demand for redress against a violation. The expansion in the scope of the trade rules to include new issues also generated demand for adjudication. Based on model 5, the coefficient estimate for WTO period leads to a first difference of 0.06 (standard error 0.018) for the shift from the GATT to the WTO period, which represents an increase of the predicted probability for any state to file one or more complaints in a year by over 50 percent when holding other variables constant.

PTAs offer states another venue to resolve their trade disputes, but here they do not have a strong effect on the overall propensity to use WTO adjudication. We will see in dyadic analysis presented later in this chapter that the specific pair of states who share PTA membership is significantly less likely to take disputes to WTO adjudication.

There is a modest positive effect from prior initiations, which help to add experience and lower the start-up costs for each case. Yet as shown in other work, this effect is strongest for developing countries (Davis and Bermeo, 2009).

Robustness Tests

First I examine the sensitivity of the findings to modeling decisions. A key concern was the possibility of omitted variables related to country characteristics, and so I estimate a fixed effects model that includes all of the variables from the models in table 3.3, and country dummy variables.[30] Since all countries that have never filed a case are dropped from the sample for this analysis (the sample for this model as a result includes forty-four countries for 963 observations), it represents a conservative test of how well the changing level of checks over time within a country explains trade adjudication. The coefficient of checks remains positive and significant (0.316 with standard error 0.167). Next, for the full sample a zero-inflated negative binomial model allows me to estimate a two-stage specification that models a separate process in which income (per capita GDP) predicts the likelihood of zero filing values. This produces consistent results in which the checks variable has a positive significant effect on filing behavior in the second stage estimates.

---

[30] The loss of efficiency in fixed effects estimation reduces significance. When including multiple measures of domestic institutions, none are significant but direction is consistent. Results for the checks measure alone are significant.

I evaluate additional economic control variables including the concentration of trade (share of all trade by top three industries), rate of economic growth, and share of trade exported with PTA partners. None of these variables are significant. An indicator for presidential system as another control for political institutions is not significant when added to model 2. The variable checks is consistently positive and significant regardless of the inclusion of these additional control variables. Lagging explanatory variables by one period does not change the results.

Adjusting the sample shows support for the robustness of the key finding. The importance of checks and balances remains strong when omitting the United States from the sample, which allows me to reject the possibility that the United States is driving the overall findings. The results are also robust either to recoding the EU checks variable to include the average member values or when excluding the EU from the sample. Finally, one could be concerned that the political influence on adjudication matters for rich countries while developing country trade strategies would simply be a function of capacity and interest. The statistical analysis already controls for income as a variable and excludes the least developing countries that are limited by extreme capacity constraints and face different rules. To explore the point further, however, I examine the role of political constraints with separate regressions for the subsample of developing countries (listed as low or middle income by the World Bank) and developed countries (listed as high income by the World Bank). The magnitude and significance of the checks measure are much greater in the high income sample, but there is supportive evidence that even among developing countries political institutions are an important factor to explain the pattern of complaints.[31] It is more often going to be true in developing countries that they would sue a trade partner only when a major export interest is threatened in a way that would produce the same decision regardless of the balance of political forces. Nonetheless, some developing countries have emerged as frequent litigants that use adjudication for cases that reach beyond defense of a vital trade interest, and there is a strong correlation between democracy and use of trade litigation for developing countries.[32] Politicized trade strategies are not restricted to the United States and Europe.

[31] For the developing country sample replication of models 1–5 the results are consistently positive for the democracy and checks variables and retain statistical significance at the 10 percent level with the exception of model 2 where the checks and democracy variables are positive but not significant for developing country sample and model 4 where neither democracy nor rule of law is significant in developing or high income subsample analysis.

[32] See Davis and Bermeo (2009) for analysis of developing country patterns in use of WTO adjudication.

In a strong test that the result is not a by-product of the correlation between democratic regime type and the number of checks, I reestimate models 2 and 5 using the *subset of democratic states* in the sample (using polity 2 index score 7 or higher as the definition of democratic). The coefficient value of checks is positive and significant in the smaller sample of democratic states.[33]

Next I consider alternative measures of democracy and political constraints. Replacing the democracy indicator with either the polity 2 or Freedom House index does not change the strong positive relationship between democracy and trade complaints evident in model 1. The political constraints variable developed by Henisz (2000) offers an alternative measure of institutional veto players that constrain executive autonomy. Replacing the checks variable with the "polcon" variable yields consistent results with a positive coefficient, although less robust given that the constraints variable is significant only in isolation when omitting the control for democracy. The polcon measure, however, is less direct as a test of the argument given that the index makes little incremental change for the shift from majority to minority government.[34]

My focus on executive strength relative to the legislature suggests looking more closely at the partisan dimension of divided government. I disaggregate the data used to calculate the checks score for a more basic measure of executive-legislative relations focused on partisan balance (the checks variable combines both institutional and partisan sources of constraints). The share of the executive party in total seats in the legislature offers a continuous measure of executive strength. An executive whose party held a 38 percent share of seats would be more constrained than one with a 49 percent share even though both would receive the same checks score. My expectation would be that the former situation would give rise to more pressure for enforcement actions. When I reestimate model 2 replacing the checks measure with executive percentage of Lower House seats, the coefficient is in the expected negative direction and highly significant (−1.074 coefficient with 0.412

[33] For model 5, the coefficient is 0.52 with a standard error of 0.20 for a p-value of 0.011. Sample size is 773. The first difference is equivalent in magnitude to the full sample models with a predicted 0.042 increase in the probability of filing one or more disputes for a standard deviation increase of checks when other variables are held constant. This produces an 18 percent increase in the overall probability of filing, which is smaller than the full sample increase because baseline variables lead to a higher expectation of filing by the group of democratic states.

[34] For example, the shift from united control of Congress and presidency in 1994 to divided government with Republican control of Congress in 1995 corresponds to polcon moving from 0.389 to 0.398 (2 percent increase) relative to a shift of the logchecks variable from 1.386 to 1.609 (16 percent increase).

standard error). Based on these estimates, a shift of the executive party seat share from 50 percent to 75 percent would reduce the likelihood of a state filing complaints by 22 percent holding constant for democratic regime.[35] Executives who have more influence over the legislature are less likely to use courts for trade disputes than those facing legislative constraints.

Democratic Defendants

Looking at the defendant side of adjudication also sheds light on how democracies differ in their strategy for trade disputes. Doing so offers further testable implications for which dimension of democracy matters for trade policy. To the extent that democracies have stronger commitment to rule of law and high audience costs for violation of international agreements, they should on average be less likely to be challenged in WTO disputes because they would comply with the agreement. Likewise, to the extent that the large selectorate of democracies leads them to support free trade, democracies will impose fewer trade barriers for foreign states to challenge. Evidence strongly supports the view that democratization and level of democracy lead to more trade openness (Milner and Mukherjee, 2009). Thus both the normative and pro–free trade hypotheses for democratic trade policies would suggest that democracies would not appear often as defendants in WTO disputes.

In contrast, my argument about checks and balances suggests democracies would be more likely to stonewall in their own disputes until dragged into court by a legal challenge. Even if they had a lower overall number of trade barriers, the greater tendency to go to court in defense of each barrier would produce a large number of democratic defendants. Thus checks and balances would lead to democracies being more active as *both* complaints and defendants, whereas legal norms or free trade preferences suggest democracies would be active only as challengers while being less likely to appear as defendants. As noted earlier, checks and balances function to restrict executive autonomy. The relative strength of the executive versus the legislature is critical because the executive and legislature often hold different positions on trade policy. Similar to their willingness to advocate tough enforcement policies in response to demands from export industries, politicians in the

---

[35] The base probability when setting the democracy indicator to equal 1 and executive seat share at 50 percent is a 0.15 probability of filing. The first difference is −0.034 (standard error 0.011).

legislature are also ready to supply protectionist measures in response to demands from import-competing industries. In comparison, the greater weight given to aggregate gains from free trade and diplomatic relations makes the executive more cautious about imposing barriers that are inconsistent with multilateral trade rules. A vast literature in political economy has described how narrow interests can generate political demand for protection in democratic politics (e.g., Schattschneider, 1935; Grossman and Helpman, 1994; Kono, 2006). The long-term incentive to escape these incentives for protection has motivated delegation to the executive of trade policy authority. Yet this delegation has never been complete and varies considerably, as shown in studies of both U.S. and EU policy (Lohmann and O'Halloran, 1994; De Bievre and Dur, 2005). Rickard (2010) provides evidence that electoral institutions that reward narrow transfers are more prone to commit violations of trade rules and be challenged as defendants in WTO disputes. When the legislature restricts its delegation of authority to the executive, the result is likely to be more trade barriers and less flexibility for the executive in negotiations with trade partners who demand removal of the barriers.

Both channels lead to adjudication; first, new barriers increase the number of potential disputes, and, second, lower flexibility to reach settlements in bilateral negotiations means that each potential dispute will have a higher likelihood of leading to adjudication. The affected sector easily finds allies in the legislature willing to take up its cause to support adoption of a trade barrier and to defend it from foreign pressure. This makes it especially difficult for a government to resolve issues in bilateral negotiations. An official with the Korean Ministry of Foreign Affairs and Trade noted that for politically sensitive issues the government may go forward to defend a case in WTO adjudication even when it is certain to lose the case because otherwise it would be "blamed for not even trying."[36] Reinhardt (2003, p. 98) shows the importance of divided politics to explain defendant behavior in adjudication when legislatures raise trade barriers and "executives may seek to tie their hands with an adverse WTO ruling."[37] For many governments the needs to demonstrate commitment to the industry and buy time for adjustment

---

[36] Interview, Geneva June 26, 2008.

[37] See also Busch (2000), who presents a dyadic theory about how pairs of democracies interact in dispute settlement. He contends that democratic norms make democratic pairs of states prefer formal third-party settlement, but also confront lock-in from domestic pressure. He reveals two distinct patterns in GATT disputes: first, democratic pairs of states more frequently settle their disputes during the consultations that follow the formal legal complaint, and second when consultations fail, democratic pairs are more likely to escalate by continuing through the panel stage. My argument and findings complement the latter argument about democratic lock-in leading to escalation. In my analysis of why states

make it well worth the additional costs of legal fees and diplomatic friction. Checks on executive autonomy are expected to be the key source of variation as increased influence from actors in the legislature makes a state more likely to be a defendant.

This presents a simple test that can be implemented with a few modifications to the models of the previous section. Here the dependent variable is the number of annual complaints filed against a state, which measures the frequency of its appearance as a *defendant*. Some adjustments to control variables reflect the different context of defending a protectionist barrier. Trade dependence (exports plus imports as a share of GDP) and agriculture production as percentage of GDP replace the variables for export dependence and agriculture percentage of exports. Additional variables for unemployment, average tariff, and GDP growth were also evaluated but since they did not approach significance and had limitations on data availability (unemployment data for the sample are unavailable before 1980) they are not included in the models shown.

Table 3.4 shows strong support for the checks hypothesis. Democratic states are more likely to be challenged as a defendant. Controlling for democracy, states with more checks on executive autonomy are especially likely to have trade barriers challenged by legal complaints. Using the estimates from model 2 while holding democracy at 1 and shifting the level of checks by one standard deviation increases the predicted probability that a country will be a defendant by 78 percent. The findings hold up strongly for the same series of robustness tests conducted for the complainant model.[38] A PR electoral system reduces the likelihood of defending trade barriers in WTO adjudication.[39] Neither rule of law nor years of democratic governance corresponds to reduction of defendant cases, which counters the argument that democratic norms would lead states to avoid policies inconsistent with trade law. The previous complaints variable suggests that, if anything, frequent filing complainants deter others from targeting them.[40] While some disputes occur due to genuine uncertainty about the status of a policy and

---

seek adjudication, however, the failure of negotiations precedes the escalation to filing a complaint.

[38] The simulations estimate a first difference of 0.042 (standard error 0.009), which increases the probability of one or more cases as defendant from 0.054 to 0.10.

[39] This is consistent with the findings of Rickard (2010), who shows in addition that district size reduces the number of complaints filed against a country. As with the previous section, however, the result here is sensitive to the coding of mixed systems.

[40] As a cumulative count of complaints in previous ten years, this variable correlates with many factors that explain initiation including democracy and GDP. Since the correlation is below .60 and the results for the checks coefficient are robust to omission of the previous complainant variable, it is not a problem for inference to include this measure.

TABLE 3.4
Estimated Coefficients of Negative Binomial Regression Models for Being Targeted as Defendant.

Variables	Model 1	Model 2	Model 3	Model 4	Model 5
Democracy	0.872**	0.102	0.899**	0.570	
	(0.354)	(0.341)	(0.395)	(0.444)	
Checks		1.001**			1.032**
		(0.202)			(0.170)
PR system			−0.511**		−0.539**
			(0.210)		(0.203)
Party			0.056		0.042
			(0.074)		(0.064)
Rule of law				0.088	
				(0.286)	
Democratic years					−0.011
					(0.078)
Previous initiations	−0.002	−0.004	−0.011*	−0.002	−0.013**
	(0.009)	(0.007)	(0.006)	(0.012)	(0.005)
PTAs	0.027*	0.023	0.049**	0.043**	0.046**
	(0.016)	(0.015)	(0.014)	(0.020)	(0.013)
GDP	0.699**	0.655**	0.658**	0.614**	0.612**
	(0.077)	(0.072)	(0.071)	(0.101)	(0.064)
Per capita GDP	−0.138	−0.126	−0.022	−0.273	0.034
	(0.248)	(0.222)	(0.229)	(0.517)	(0.246)
Ag. % GDP	−0.073**	−0.083**	−0.067**	−0.053	−0.075**
	(0.024)	(0.022)	(0.024)	(0.035)	(0.022)
Trade % GDP	−0.004	−0.004	−0.008**	−0.010	−0.009**
	(0.004)	(0.004)	(0.004)	(0.005)	(0.004)
Trade balance	−0.001	−0.001*	−0.001	−0.002*	−0.001**
	(0.001)	(0.001)	(0.001)	(0.002)	(0.001)
WTO period	0.323	0.260	0.428**		0.395**
	(0.211)	(0.173)	(0.203)		(0.184)
Constant	−18.783**	−18.177**	−18.403**	−14.521**	−18.045**
	(3.384)	(3.075)	(3.081)	(5.190)	(3.122)
Dispersion parameter	−1.343	−1.799	−1.523	−1.512	−1.950
	(0.350)	(0.383)	(0.336)	(0.631)	(0.352)
Countries	80	80	78	74	78
N	1,466	1,450	1,415	637	1,404

Note: Models 1–3 and 5 are for the full period 1975 to 2004. Model 4 is for the WTO period 1995–2004 when the rule of law indicator is available. *Significant at the 10 percent level. **Significant at the 5 percent level.

interpretation of the agreement rather than deliberate violation of the agreement, one would not expect any difference by regime type in terms of legal uncertainty.

Without a measure of trade barriers and potential disputes, however, I cannot distinguish whether the defendant pattern reflects a difference in protection barriers or negotiation behavior. The literature has suggested that divided government is more likely to lead to protection, and my argument contends it would also restrict bargaining flexibility for negotiations and lead to more adjudication. This is the drawback to the study of defendant patterns where domestic political conditions influence both the level of trade barriers and the strategies taken in disputes.[41] The complainant choice to target a democracy may be based in part on an expectation that democratic states will comply with the ruling and not take retaliatory actions against a state for using the legal venue. In this scenario, democratic legal norms could be important through their effect on complainant expectations. Looking next at which pairs of countries have disputes will be helpful to shed light on such effects.

Alliances and Dyadic Dispute Patterns

Harm to diplomatic relations represents one component in the cost of trade enforcement. These costs lead a state to ignore some trade barriers when giving priority to diplomatic stakes over economic interests. In the argument of this book, distrust that the executive will choose to be too soft with trade partners out of concern for diplomacy represents a central reason for the legislature to impose constraints on delegation of trade policy. Governments attempt to balance the competing priorities through modification of their trade strategies. Using a legal dispute settlement mechanism appears less confrontational than unilateral enforcement. Nonetheless, even a complaint filed within the WTO dispute settlement process represents a public accusation of violating rules. In most cases the respondent tries to keep talks at the bilateral level, and the complainant forces the shift of venue. Indeed, it has become nearly a ritual for the defendant to issue a statement of regret when targeted in a complaint. Do considerations about diplomatic relations influence the pattern of trade enforcement actions?

---

[41] This endogeneity concern would not affect the enforcement analysis unless one believes that state A's decision to adopt a trade barrier as a potential defendant is influenced by the regime type of their trading partner B as a potential complainant.

To answer this question, I assess three alternative scenarios. First, trade enforcement may simply respond to domestic politics, economic interests, and legal interpretation of each case without any consideration for political relations between trade partners. Courts should depoliticize disputes by offering a neutral arena with third-party involvement. This expectation has been implicit in existing studies on WTO dispute settlement that have given little attention to the geopolitical context. For example, measures of alliance relations between states have not been included as a variable in research on WTO disputes (Reinhardt, 2001; Busch and Reinhardt, 2001; Busch, 2000, 2007; Bown, 2004b; Guzman and Simmons, 2005; Bown, 2005a; Kim, 2008; Davis and Bermeo, 2009; Rickard, 2010; Sattler and Bernauer, forthcoming).

But the international political economy literature offers strong evidence that political relations between states influence their pattern of trade flows and trade agreements (Gowa, 1994; Mansfield and Bronson, 1997). The next two scenarios explore opposing perspectives on whether states are more or less likely to target allies in trade disputes. States may be more eager to challenge cheating by adversaries, which would give rise to a pattern of "fighting with foes" in WTO disputes. To the extent that states consent to trade with nonallied governments they hope to at least attain the optimal trade outcome from reciprocal market opening rather than one-sided liberalization in which the other state reneges on its promise to provide access. Allies may win some deference in how to address the trade dispute given the cooperative relations developed through security cooperation.

In contrast, the desire to contain diplomatic costs while responding to economic interests could lead to "fighting with friends." Given the need to demonstrate tough enforcement policies in response to industry and legislature demands, the executive will prefer to target allies over adversaries. States can afford to take more aggressive trade action toward those states where strong diplomatic relations will prevent spillover. They must be more careful toward states where sensitive diplomatic relations could lead to a trade dispute acting as a spark to worsen problems in the overall relationship. This supports the expectation that trade disputes would be more frequent among allies. Since allies also are more likely to trade with each other in the first place and often favor allies when selecting PTAs (Gowa, 1994; Mansfield and Bronson, 1997), it is important to control for the level of bilateral trade in order to assess whether disputes are simply a function of trade levels. This scenario suggests that the higher level of liberalization with allies generates a disproportionate increase of trade disputes.

The large number of cases between the United States and European Union supports the notion that trade disputes are concentrated among friends. Japan too has largely focused its use of WTO dispute settlement on its only ally, the United States. Yet we also observe a rising number of WTO disputes between the United States and China. Are power rivalries contributing to trade disputes? Clearly in these relationships it is necessary to consider both the level of economic exchange and political relations.

The statistical analysis to address these questions involves a change in the research design to examine dyadic trade disputes for the period 1975 to 2004. Whereas the previous sections examined the propensity for each country to file complaints, here I look at the likelihood of a GATT/WTO dispute being initiated between a particular pair of member states. The outcome is a dichotomous indicator for whether there was a GATT/WTO complaint filed by country A against country B in a given year. Although multiple filings in a year for a given dyad occur, they are so infrequent that dichotomous treatment is justified. Indeed, with the dichotomous coding for dispute incidence, zero outcomes still dominate the sample of 82,613 observations with a mean value of 0.006 disputes. Even for the most active GATT/WTO member, the United States, the mean filing rate by the United States in all of its trade partner pairs is merely 0.045 as complainant and 0.059 as defendant. I use a rare events logistic regression model to estimate the likelihood of a complaint (King and Zeng, 2001).[42] Each dyad pair appears twice in each year to allow for the directional test of A to B and B to A in the pattern of adjudication. To adjust for the possible correlation within a particular dyad pair, the statistical model estimates standard errors clustered on dyad pair. A "tit-for-tat" variable takes into account possible strategic interaction of complaints within a dyad pair. The variable counts the number of complaints brought against country A in the past five years by country B, which could generate a countersuit incentive to increase the probability for A to file against B.

The focus of analysis here will be on the effect of alliances on trade disputes. I use data from the Alliance Treaty Obligations and Provisions data set to measure whether two GATT/WTO members had a current active alliance relationship.[43] Of the dyad observations in the sample 12 percent have an alliance relationship. A first look at the

---

[42] This statistical estimator corrects for the tendency to underestimate event probabilities in data with low frequency events. The findings are not dependent on this modeling choice, however, and are also supported by estimates from standard logistic regression or negative binomial regression using the full count of disputes within each dyad. A dyad fixed effects specification of model 1 also yields consistent results.

[43] The dataset is available at http://atop.rice.edu. I use the variable "active alliances," which includes those with any promise of active military support (e.g., defense or offense) by any alliance member. This omits the neutrality and nonaggression agreements (e.g.,

breakdown of adjudication patterns shows that for the 467 observations in which one or more complaint was filed between two states in a single year, 238 were allied partners and 229 were between nonallied states. Although this is nearly an equal split among observed disputes, the base category of nonallied pairs without any disputes relative to allied pairs without disputes is so much more numerous that this figure represents a statistically significant positive association between the frequency of disputes and alliance relations.[44] Table 3.5 shows the pattern for the ten countries that have filed the most complaints.[45] Six of these states filed a majority of their cases against allies, even considering that these form a small share of their total number of trade partners. Clearly those countries like the United States that have more alliances will have a greater number of potential cases for targeting allies than a country like Australia with only one ally, and India, which has no allies to target. But these figures alone are only indicative and may reflect the high trade volume among allies or other features. The next step is to examine the pattern of disputes in multivariate regression analysis.

Similar variables are included here as in the analysis presented earlier in the chapter with some modification to reflect the dyadic data structure and strategic interaction. In addition to the variables included in models shown in tables 3.3 and 3.4 with checks measured for both the prospective "complainant" and the prospective "defendant" in each pair, I also add some dyad-specific variables and adjust the coding of others to fit the dyadic context. Democratic pairs of states may interact differently in trade disputes following a logic similar to that used to characterize the democratic peace debate in security studies (Busch, 2000). An indicator for whether the dyad includes two democratic states tests this argument.[46] The PTA variable in this model measures whether there is a PTA between the specific pair of countries in the given year.[47]

India and Pakistan) while including nonreciprocal pledge of military support (e.g., U.S.-Japan alliance). The data end in 2003, and I have extended all values in the last year of data to be identical in 2004.

[44] Pearson chi2 = 711.24 for a p-value of .000.

[45] The total complaints filed in table 3.5 differ from those listed in table 3.2 because of counting dyadic disputes and because this table adds totals through 2004 rather than 2005. In a small number of cases a country will file a complaint on the same trade barrier against multiple defendant countries (e.g., the 1984 case of Chile filing against eight trade partners for their quota restrictions). This kind of case would be treated as a single dispute for the monadic analysis but is broken out as separate dyad pairs for the analysis here.

[46] The variable uses a polity score of 7 or higher as the threshold to code a state democratic, and results are consistent when using the lower threshold of 6.

[47] The data are from Goldstein, Rivers and Tomz (2007) and measure only reciprocal PTAs.

TABLE 3.5
Targeting Allies.

Country	Number of alliances	Complaints against ally	Total Complaints	Percentage
United States	42	127	145	0.88
EU	8	65	116	0.56
Canada	38	43	52	0.83
Brazil	31	26	38	0.68
Chile	31	11	27	0.41
Argentina	31	8	22	0.36
Australia	1	6	21	0.29
India	0	0	20	—
Japan	1	12	18	0.67
Mexico	31	14	17	0.82

Note: Active alliances in 2004 and the pattern for percentage of all GATT and WTO complaints filed between 1975 to 2004 that target an ally.

One would expect PTA partners to have fewer disputes in the multilateral forum to the extent that they have eliminated trade barriers in the process of concluding the PTA and because they have an alternative dispute resolution forum.[48] I include a control for the bilateral export value from A to B.[49] As noted above, the variable "tit-for-tat" tests for any pattern of countersuits in the use of trade litigation (Busch and Reinhardt, 2002).

Previous research on trade disputes by Bown (2004b, 2005a) highlights the role of retaliation capacity as an important condition for states to go forward with filing a complaint. States that import a large share of the exports from their trade partner will gain leverage for retaliation in the case that they win the dispute and receive authorization to retaliate through raising tariffs. The variable "retaliation capacity" measures the share of country B exports to country A as a share of country B total exports. This offers a general indicator for the degree of market dependence that could make the potential defendant (state B) vulnerable to retaliation by the potential complainant (state A). In addition, retaliation could occur through linkage to foreign aid. Fear that dispute escalation would lead to loss of aid flows could motivate an aid dependent state to back down early rather than let the dispute go

---

[48] But see Busch (2007) for analysis of when states may nonetheless choose multilateral setting for dispute with PTA partner.

[49] The data are from the IMF and have been adjusted to constant billion U.S. dollars. Taking the log smooths for extreme values.

all the way to adjudication.[50] I include bilateral aid flows as a control variable that is measured as the log of net ODA disbursements to the complainant from the defendant (constant million U.S. dollars, OECD data). A second variable measures the ODA to the defendant from the complainant. Aid dependence on either side could reduce the likelihood of a formal complaint by adding leverage for retaliation if the trade partner links the dispute to future aid policy decisions.

The results presented in table 3.6 confirm the importance of domestic institutional constraints in both the complainant and defendant that was highlighted in the earlier analysis of the aggregate propensity to file complaints. The strength of the results in the dyadic context controlling for the economic size of markets and export stakes in the specific relationship further increases confidence in the primary findings of this chapter. If one considers a hypothetical scenario of the U.S.-Japan dyad in the year 2000, and shifts the measure of checks for the United States moving to divided government (Republican control of presidency) and Japan moving to rule by a fragmented coalition (equivalent to the shifts from 1993 to 1994 when the LDP lost majority status to a coalition group of seven parties), the estimates predict a 43 percent increase in the predicted probability of a dispute by the United States against Japan.[51]

There is little indication of a dyadic interaction between democracies. If one estimates a model with only the interaction term for the democratic dyad, it would appear that democracies are more likely to have disputes with each other (not shown). But this specification would suffer bias from omitting the independent effect of democratic institutions. The previous section analyzed how domestic institutions influence the overall propensity to appear as complainant or defendant. Model 1 demonstrates that the democratic dyad interaction term is not significant in a model that includes the institutional checks variables for domestic constraints on the complainant side and on the defendant side. When looking within the subset sample of democratic states on the potential complainant side (model 2), these democracies are no more or less likely to choose a democratic trade partner when filing a complaint. Although 82 percent

---

[50] In analysis of fifty-four WTO disputes with well-defined import products that allow him to consider "potential disputes," Bown (2005a, p. 307) finds that exporters affected by the barrier are substantially less likely to file a complaint or join as third party when they rely on the respondent for bilateral aid. He also finds that disputes are less likely to lead to a complaint filing when the defendant receives aid from the exporter. His specification calculates the bilateral aid as a share of GDP. In my analysis, this was not statistically significant but was also in the expected negative direction.

[51] The base probability is 0.57, and the first difference is 0.24 (standard error 0.03). This predicted probability is estimated from the coefficients of model 1 in 3.6.

TABLE 3.6
Estimated Coefficients of Rare Events Logistic Regression Model for Dyadic Trade Disputes.

Dyadic variables	Model 1 Full Sample	Model 2 Democracies	Model 3 WTO Period
Democratic dyad	0.213	0.256	0.303
	(0.179)	(0.287)	(0.261)
Alliance	0.592**	0.546**	0.928**
	(0.150)	(0.155)	(0.189)
PTA	−0.438**	−0.392**	−0.118
	(0.173)	(0.186)	(0.205)
Bilateral exports	0.447**	0.459**	0.575**
	(0.086)	(0.095)	(0.097)
Retaliation capacity	−0.001	−0.002	−0.019**
	(0.005)	(0.005)	(0.007)
Tit-for-tat	0.066**	0.063**	0.053
	(0.032)	(0.031)	(0.050)
Complainant ODA	−0.03	−0.055	−0.111*
	(0.043)	(0.051)	(0.058)
Defendant ODA	−0.075*	−0.076*	0.032
	(0.044)	(0.046)	(0.051)
Complainant variables			
Checks	0.312**	0.573**	0.433**
	(0.134)	(0.197)	(0.181)
GDP	0.574**	0.578**	0.638**
	(0.052)	(0.059)	(0.060)
Per capita GDP	0.219**	0.160	−0.012
	(0.093)	(0.105)	(0.122)
Ag Export %	0.030**	0.030**	0.03**
	(0.003)	(0.004)	(0.005)
Defendant variables			
Checks	0.87**	0.801**	0.941**
	(0.143)	(0.183)	(0.183)
GDP	0.637**	0.644**	0.500**
	(0.053)	(0.057)	(0.057)
WTO period	0.01	0.073	
	(0.119)	(0.126)	
Constant	−42.096**	−42.182**	−38.458**
	(2.446)	(2.598)	(2.678)
N	82,613	51,536	43,901

Note: Dyadic variables describe the relationship of the two states. Complainant variables measure the characteristics of state A, which is in the position to be a "potential complainant." Defendant variables measure the characteristics of state B, which is in the position to be a "potential defendant." Model 1 estimates disputes between any pair of countries 1975–2004. Model 2 includes only dyads where state A potential complainant is a democracy. Model 3 includes all dyads for the period 1995–2004. *Significant at the 10 percent level. **Significant at the 5 percent level.

of observations with disputes consist of two democracies, this pattern arises from institutional constraints that influence the behavior of each state independently rather than through an interaction effect with the regime type of the trade partner.

Other variables generally yield the expected results as larger export stakes in the bilateral trade flow measure, higher income and market size, dependence on agricultural exports, and tit-for-tat filing increase the likelihood of a dispute. Further, as expected PTA partners are significantly less likely to take trade problems forward for adjudication at the GATT/WTO. The evidence for the role of retaliation capacity is mixed. In the first two models that estimate filing patterns for the period 1975 to 2004, there is no significant effect. Only in the WTO period does retaliation capacity become a significant variable, and then it is in a negative direction that suggests dependence by the respondent on the potential complainant for market access on average reduces the likelihood of a formal dispute. States may use their retaliation capacity to avert the need to file a legal complaint by extracting compromise from dependent trade partners. When enforcement would be easy given high retaliation capacity, states are less likely to invoke the dispute mechanism in the first place.[52] ODA appears to also reduce the incidence of disputes although the statistical relationship reaches statistical significance only for the defendant side. An additional variable for the bilateral trade balance had no effect and was not included for final models presented. Backlash over deficits may dominate U.S. headlines and prompt congressmen to call for aggressive enforcement, but there is no larger pattern among the membership. The increase in the average likelihood of a complaint during the WTO period that was observed in the analysis of complainants (table 3.3) does not appear in the dyadic setting.

The key finding for political relations between trade partners supports the scenario of adjudication as legal fights between friends. Allied pairs are significantly more likely to litigate trade disputes than those who lack security ties. In order to illustrate the substantive significance of the results, I estimate the effect of alliance on the predicted probability of a complaint being filed. When setting all values to their levels for the observation of the U.S.-Japan dyad in the year 2000 there is a probability

---

[52] This counters the results of Bown (2005a) who finds that respondent exports to the complainant as a percentage of total exports has a positive effect on filing. His data on potential litigants examine fifty-four disputes that were filed and the affected exporters who chose not to file for the case. While a major improvement on existing studies, the research design is unable to provide inference about the population of disputes for which no country decided to make a complaint.

of 0.59 that the United States would file a dispute. Changing the alliance variable from its observed value of 1 to 0 for the counterfactual scenario of a U.S.-Japan dyad that was identical except for an end to the alliance would reduce the predicted probability that the United States would file a complaint against Japan by 0.15 (standard error 0.04), which represents nearly a 25 percent decrease in the probability of a complaint. Of course for other countries, the base probability of filing a complaint would be much lower, but the alliance relationship nonetheless has a significant effect to change the probability relative to the baseline expectation.

Anecdotal evidence suggests that diplomatic concerns can also restrain trade disputes between allies. Shaffer (2003, p. 64) cites an administration official who acknowledged postponing the filing of the U.S. complaint against a European ban on genetically modified seeds in 2003 because "there is no point in testing the Europeans on food while they are being tested on Iraq." But the United States went ahead with its complaint the following year after completing the invasion of Iraq. The case study of the Boeing-Airbus dispute later in the book will show that this case also was delayed out of consideration for sensitive periods in the transatlantic alliance relationship. Between allies, diplomatic concerns may influence the timing of filing a complaint, but business interests cannot be deferred indefinitely. A steady stream of trade disputes represents the norm for close allies.

This section has shown that international politics also influence the choice of trade strategy. Far from law representing an apolitical act, the decision to file a legal complaint is charged with political implications. The positive impact at home from strong enforcement is offset by negative impact for bilateral political relations. Multilateral adjudication reduces the diplomatic cost relative to unilateral retaliation threats, but suing a business partner is nonetheless an aggressive action. For allies with strong relations, a trade complaint can be seen as routine business. But absent an alliance, states are wary of ripple effects from trade friction and avoid going to court.

Conclusion

Democracies use adjudication to solve their trade problems more than other states because the executive faces domestic constraints that encourage responsiveness to economic interests. Not only are democratic governments under pressure to intervene on behalf of industries, however, but constrained delegation in the domestic policy process places a premium on use of adjudication over informal means as the trade strategy of choice. This chapter has shown that a higher level of checks on executive autonomy leads to more frequent trade complaints when controlling for economic variables. The complementary fit between democratic governance and international legalization reflects the need for visible accountability. Filing a formal complaint offers an executive a way to look tough without starting a trade war. There is less evidence that democratic norms or public interest in free trade explain democratic involvement in trade adjudication.

The democratic propensity for strong enforcement means that international institutions will be more effective when they have a larger core of democratic members. Institutions promote cooperation by establishing mechanisms that make it costly for states to violate the agreement. Challenges from other members are the main enforcement path, and states have more incentive to abide by agreements given expectations that violations will be challenged. Thus the hawkish enforcement preferences of democratic governments will generate conflict in terms of disputes over violations but in the long term support a higher level of cooperation.

Responsiveness to economic interests also makes democracies more likely to appear as defendants in WTO adjudication. Legislatures tend to be sympathetic to the import-competing interests that seek protection, and greater constraints from the legislature make it harder for the executive to reach a bilateral settlement. Suffering the costs of being dragged to court serves the purpose to demonstrate to domestic audiences that their interests are taken seriously.

Counteracting the domestic political pressure for enforcement is the cost of litigation. The material cost of legal and administrative work is well documented, but diplomatic costs are also important. Governments need to be cautious that their tough talk on trade does not harm diplomatic relations. Litigation as an alternative to unilateral enforcement reduces the diplomatic cost of enforcement actions but cannot eliminate backlash. Targeting friends offers another way to contain risk of spillover. The final section of this chapter highlighted a pattern in which states target their allies, even after controlling for trade structure and regime type. Legal disputes arise as part of a balancing act responding to both domestic and international politics.

4

The Litigious State: U.S. Trade Policy

THE U.S. GOVERNMENT has taken the lead in the establishment and legalization of dispute settlement within the trade regime and has been the most frequent user of adjudication. Does the size of the U.S. economy explain this pattern? As one of the top exporters to world markets the United States holds a large stake in the support of trade rules. Yet the United States has also been active using bilateral venues to pressure its trade partners to provide more market access. Threats of unilateral retaliation offer powerful leverage over trade partners without the need for legal rulings. More so than any other country in the system, the United States has strong outside options for using sticks and carrots to achieve its foreign economic policy goals without the WTO. This makes it more compelling to examine U.S. motives to use international law as a tool in its trade policy. Could the litigious nature of American society and abundance of lawyers promote this behavior at the international level? The U.S. business sector has extensive experience with litigation, but this does not translate well into the realm of WTO law. While most of the top international trade law firms are located in the United States, other countries also avail themselves of the services of American law firms. Proactive engagement with international trade law by the United States does not simply represent an outgrowth of domestic litigation culture and national interest in free trade, although both conditions are certainly supportive of U.S. policy.

In addition to economic interest and legal capacity, the interaction between Congress and the executive encourages the use of legal strategies to enforce trade rules. In this chapter, I present evidence that domestic political interests play a substantial role in the selection of U.S. cases for WTO adjudication. Statistical analysis of foreign trade barriers harmful to U.S. exports shows that WTO cases are more likely for those barriers that affect industries making large political contributions. This supports a model of politicized litigation in which court cases are used to reward influential industries. Indicators measuring resistance by the trade partner to liberalization also increase the likelihood that the United States files a WTO complaint. As a result, the WTO dispute system confronts difficult cooperation problems where there are influential domestic interests at stake. On the one hand, this is a classic story of interest group influence on trade policy. On the other hand, the institutions at the international level function as tools for managing such domestic pressures. In particular, adjudication helps to maintain support for free trade in Congress and forestall unilateral retaliation.

This chapter uses the U.S. case to demonstrate the role of legislative constraints to encourage active enforcement measures by the executive on behalf of influential export industries. In the first section I discuss how the United States has taken a lead role to enforce trade rules. In the second section I describe how legislative constraints and interest group pressure operate in U.S. trade policy. The Kodak-Fuji WTO dispute between the United States and Japan is used to illustrate an example of politicized selection of a case for adjudication (third section). In the fourth section I describe data on U.S. complaints about market access barriers by leading trade partners. By identifying potential trade disputes, these data allow me to examine why some cases go forward to adjudication. The fifth section presents statistical analysis showing that industry political contributions increase the likelihood of a particular case being chosen for a WTO complaint. The next two sections more closely examine specific disputes. The first case study looks at the Boeing-Airbus challenge of government subsidies to civilian airline companies that went through decades of bilateral negotiations before entering a phase of tit-for-tat adjudication in the WTO. A second case study explores how the U.S. government has addressed intense congressional pressure for enforcement against China through both bilateral channels for negotiation and the initiation of a series of disputes in WTO adjudication.

The United States has pursued free trade through a domestic bargain that exchanges a commitment to open U.S. markets for the promise of access to foreign markets (Gilligan, 1997; Bailey, Goldstein, and Weingast, 1997). Most scholarly attention examines the first side of this bargain to explain the degree to which the United States has opened or protected its domestic market (e.g., Baldwin, 1985; O'Halloran, 1994; Busch and Reinhardt, 1999; Hiscox, 2002). This chapter instead turns to the question of how the United States has pursued market access. The role of export industries is important because they are a key actor to mobilize against protection (Destler and Odell, 1987; Milner, 1988; Davis, 2003). At the same time, U.S. exporters have also become a source of protection as they support efforts to promote exports by means of retaliatory threats to close the home market (e.g., Milner and Yoffie, 1989; Bhagwati and Patrick, 1990; Bayard and Elliott, 1994; Noland, 1997; Gawande and Hansen, 1999). The role of Congress emerges at the forefront of all trade policy debates in the United States as legislators demand protection for sensitive U.S. industries and tough action to compel trade partners to provide access for U.S. exports. These domestic pressures from industry and legislature confront the executive who conducts foreign economic policy. At the international level, WTO rules have restricted the aggressive unilateralism that characterized U.S. efforts to gain market access in the 1980s. States now possess an expanded array of trade strategy options including strengthened multilateral rules for dispute settlement as well as the proliferation of bilateral trade agreements. Therefore it is necessary to take a new look at how the United States utilizes this menu of options in its pursuit of free trade.

U.S. Role as Enforcer of Multilateral Trade Rules

The United States is an important case because it is the leading user of trade adjudication (see table 3.1). The litigious society of the United States supports this strategy by contributing to a large supply of lawyers and norms favorable to legal dispute settlement. Nevertheless, the United States has a complex relationship with international law that cautions against the argument that domestic legal culture translates into international adjudication across all courts. For example, the United States has been involved in 21 of 109 contentious cases filed before the International Court of Justice between 1946 and 2006, but only 10 cases were as applicant and all but 2 of those applicant cases date prior to 1980 (Murphy, 2009). After a controversial case, in 1985 the United States withdrew from ICJ compulsory jurisdiction. The U.S. government actively opposed the International Criminal Court. While a legal culture argument would suggest uniform support of legal dispute settlement, the U.S. ambivalence toward other international courts suggests looking further at the interaction of interests and process.

As it has the largest national economy the United States can afford to play the role of trade police to support its interest in free trade. Wealth and trade interests alone fail to account for U.S. dominance of trade adjudication, however, because these conditions also support alternative strategies. Large market size increases U.S. leverage in bilateral negotiations so that it should not need to use adjudication. Bayne (2007) argues that the United States prefers bilateralism in its foreign economic diplomacy because this style of negotiation is easier to control and favors the strong by cutting out the option for smaller states to act against its interests in a coalition. The temptation to rely on strength in bilateral negotiations creates ongoing tensions in the U.S. commitment to the multilateral trade regime.

History demonstrates that economic size alone is insufficient to account for the direction of U.S. trade policy. Since emerging as the dominant economy after WWI, the United States has in turn supported protection and free trade policies, and it has led the way to multilateral dispute settlement and engaged in vigilante-style enforcement. The United States famously turned away from free trade with its adoption of the Smoot-Hawley Tariff in 1930 and spurned efforts to achieve international coordination for trade and exchange rate policies at the 1933 World Economic Conference in London. The critical realignment toward free trade depended upon election of Democrats to control the presidency and Congress along with appointment of a free trade–supporting Secretary of State Cordell Hull who pushed for the Reciprocal Trade Agreement Act of 1934. This legislation delegated more authority to the executive for the setting of trade policy by authorizing negotiation of tariff reductions with trade partners. Periodic renewal of this authority requires close consultation with Congress to maintain support for the executive mandate, but this procedural change took Congress out of the business of setting tariffs line by line. It launched a period in which the United States began to open its own market as part of a conditional bargain with trade partners. The story of the RTAA shows that U.S. support for free trade relies upon whether economic interests for free trade are translated into political coalitions that implement an institutional framework conducive to maintain the commitment to liberalization.[1]

The shift toward negotiation of reciprocal trade agreements and support for free trade agreements by the United States did not lead automatically to the choice of judicial enforcement of disputes. The bilateral agreements negotiated under the RTAA did not include dispute settlement provisions. For example, the 1935 and 1938 agreements between the United States and Canada do not contain procedures for consultation, let alone third-party adjudication (Hart, 1991, p. 194). When the rules themselves were a straightforward application of tariff reductions and the government's role in the economy was low, there was seen to be little need to establish formal dispute mechanisms.

Emerging from WWII as the dominant economic power and with a government committed to pursue reciprocal trade liberalization, the United States took a leadership role in the creation of a multilateral trade regime. Bayne (2007) argues that the natural interest in bilateralism by the United States was overcome largely by the special circumstances arising from war devastation and onset of the struggle against the Soviet Union that led the United States to establish multilateral institutions that

---

[1] On RTAA, see Bailey, Goldstein, and Weingast (1997), Gilligan (1997) and Hiscox (1999).

it then supported as tools of its foreign policy interests. In 1946, the Truman administration submitted a draft proposal for creation of an International Trade Organization (ITO) as a formal body to regulate trade rules, and this draft was discussed in a series of multilateral meetings and finalized in 1948 as the Havana Charter. To avoid delaying trade liberalization during this process, the United States invited states to a round of negotiations in Geneva where they agreed to reduce tariffs and follow principles of nondiscrimination and national treatment in their trade relations in the provisional General Agreement on Tariffs and Trade. The agreement in many aspects simply codified the bilateral agreements the United States had negotiated in the past decade with its major trade partners (Barton et al., 2006, p. 34). It continued the reciprocal bargain for U.S. trade policy while spreading to the broader membership. Binding the United States to continue its free trade orientation was also a valuable policy to reassure smaller states that would be vulnerable to any reversal by the United States (Goldstein and Gowa, 2002).

Some within the U.S. government already saw the need for legalized enforcement of trade law. The U.S. government draft of the ITO charter would have allowed members to appeal decisions of the contracting parties regarding the interpretation of the Charter to the ICJ for a binding legal decision. Hull's successor as Secretary of State Dean Acheson wrote in a 1949 State Department Bulletin about the Charter that "[no] code of laws is worth very much without an authoritative body to interpret it and administer it" (Dunoff, 2009, p. 330). But this vision of legal enforcement through the ICJ never materialized. Skepticism from the Republican-controlled Congress and opposition from business associations including the Chamber of Commerce and National Association of Manufacturers combined with the onset of the Korean War to undermine administration efforts to promote the formal trade organization (Odell and Eichengreen, 1998, p. 200). As the United States failed to ratify the agreement, and other governments had not held as much enthusiasm in the first place, the ITO never went into effect. The provisional GATT had to serve as the main rule framework for multilateral trade until establishment of the WTO in 1995. Since it had been drafted under the premise that the ITO would come into being, dispute settlement provisions in GATT were merely three brief paragraphs with few details on formal procedures and no reference to a third-party adjudication body. GATT Article XXIII calls for members to make written claims about actions by trading partners that result in the "nullification or impairment" of expected benefits from the agreement, and the contracting parties "shall promptly investigate any matter so referred to them and shall make appropriate recommendations to the contracting parties which they consider to be concerned, or give a ruling on the matter, as appropriate." The panel procedure evolved as an ad hoc response to the rising number of disputes and greater complexity of issues.

The United States would only slowly take on its role as the chief prosecutor enforcing trade rules. Having helped to nullify the more formal ITO, the United States let the GATT go forward as a more efficient multilateral aggregation of its earlier move to negotiate bilateral reciprocal agreements. In the first decade of the GATT dispute experience in the 1950s, Hudec (1993, p. 296) shows that the United States filed 21 percent of all complaints (thirteen of sixty-two), well below European governments. Furthermore, the United States together with Europe contributed to the declining use of formal legal claims in the 1960s through creating an environment among members in which "legal claims were viewed as unfriendly actions" (Hudec, 1993, p. 13).

Far from enforcement leadership arising from a position of strength, it was the relative decline of the U.S. economic position that corresponded with a more aggressive enforcement role. Stagnant economic growth in the United States, the emergence of economic rivals in Europe and Japan, and a rising balance of payment deficits led the United States to reorient its postwar economic policies. The Nixon administration abandoned the gold standard in 1971 and responded to increasingly strident protectionist pressure from Congress with both concessions to protect domestic industries and a move to undertake more aggressive foreign economic policy. A new Council on International Economic Policy advised the president to place more emphasis on economic issues over diplomatic niceties (Pastor, 1980, p. 129). The administration remained committed to free trade, but Congress was unwilling to continue supporting open U.S. markets in the face of what was perceived to be blatant cheating by trade partners to close their own markets. From this tense standoff emerged the initiative to start a new multilateral trade round and passage of the Trade Act of 1974.

In the Tokyo Round, a major negotiation among GATT members to reform the trade framework that was held from 1973 to 1979, the United States pushed both substantive rules to restrict use of nontariff barriers and called for procedural improvements to enhance enforcement. In its call for stronger enforcement, the United States supported automatic panels with authority to review complaints over objections from the defendant. Resistance from Europe and others prevented realization of automatic panels until the WTO, but the Tokyo Round Understanding on Dispute Settlement introduced several measures to streamline practice in dispute settlement by reducing the room for delays by reluctant defendants (Hudec, 1993, pp. 54–55). By the 1980s, the United States doubled the frequency of its legal complaints from the previous decade.[2] The shift in attitude by the United States from antilegalist in the 1960s to active adjudication in the 1970s and 1980s also encouraged other members to increase their adjudication. The GATT established a legal office to assist panels with the increasing case load.

The U.S. turn toward enforcement in the 1980s, however, involved both GATT adjudication and actions outside of the rule framework. In several high profile cases, the United States chose to pursue free trade through threats of unilateral retaliation against trade partners. Some of these cases arose when GATT adjudication failed to produce the result desired by the United States, as in the retaliatory use of export subsidies to compete with European wheat subsidies and the retaliation imposed on European imports as punishment for its ban on U.S. beef (Davis, 2003, pp. 273, 327). In the former instance a GATT panel declared it could not rule on the substantive matter. In the latter, both parties could not agree on the appropriate composition of a panel to rule on the matter. Unable to make progress through adjudication, the United States resorted to unilateral measures in the form of counter-subsidies and retaliatory tariffs.

Other disputes were completely outside of the GATT regime. The most notorious example was the semiconductor dispute with Japan that led to a 1986 "voluntary import expansion" agreement in the semiconductor market. Japan had removed formal quotas and approval requirements in 1975, and there was no claim of GATT violation. But the U.S. market share had not increased as a result of formal liberalization, so the semiconductor association pressured the U.S. government to challenge Japan. Japanese informal government guidance was targeted as an unreasonable barrier to trade. The industry also demanded protection of the domestic market, which led the Reagan administration to use the credible threat of raising barriers against Japanese semiconductor exports to the United States as leverage to force the Japanese government to promise in a secret side letter to encourage a 20 percent market share for U.S. semiconductor exports to Japan. When the U.S. market share did not increase and the U.S. Senate passed a nonbinding resolution calling on the administration to enforce the market share target, in April 1987 President Reagan imposed 100 percent tariffs on $300 million worth of Japanese electronics. This led to a revised bilateral agreement that made public the commitment by the Japanese government to support a 20 percent market share for the U.S. industry, which was achieved by the 1992 deadline.[3]

---

[2] Hudec (1993, p. 296) shows that the United States filed thirty-nine complaints in the 1980s relative to sixteen filed in the 1970s.

[3] See Irwin (1998) for analysis of the case.

There were many other cases with a similar characteristic of unilateral U.S. demand for removal of foreign barriers backed up by the threat of denying access to the U.S. market.

Although often effective to lower trade barriers, unilateral enforcement was costly for diplomatic relations as other countries resented the United States taking on the role of judge, jury, and police. Many condemned aggressive unilateralism as just another form of protectionism (Bhagwati and Patrick, 1990). Pelc (2010) argues that U.S. trade partners offered fewer trade concessions in cases with unilateral demands relative to disputes taken forward to GATT adjudication because U.S. unilateralism lacked legitimacy. Even those who saw gains from use of trade threats called for channeling U.S. complaints through multilateral venues out of consideration for larger stakes (Bayard and Elliott, 1994).[4] The level of resistance to unilateralism contributed to the decision within the United States to support a stronger multilateral enforcement option as a replacement.

The U.S. government took a lead role in the legal reforms of dispute settlement procedures in the Uruguay Round (1986–1994), which was the next major trade round to revise GATT rules and establish the WTO. Unilateral enforcement had been justified as a response to the weakness of the GATT system that allowed defendants to block rulings they did not like. In the Uruguay Round, the United States challenged other states to address these weaknesses and establish a stronger and more legalized dispute process. Specifically, the United States championed the automatic adoption of panel reports, time limits, and the right to appeal to a new Appellate Body. Thompson (2007) argues that the United States was willing to accept the constraint on its power through legalization of the WTO dispute settlement as a recognition that its use of unilateral trade measures caused excessive harm to diplomatic relations. It may also have been wishful thinking to assume that the United States would be on the winning side given that it could shape the substantive rules to its liking (Barton et al., 2006, p. 71). Japan, Europe, and developing nations saw the strengthened dispute system as a restraint on U.S. unilateralism and fully embraced the move to legalization.

With the establishment of the WTO, the United States quickly surged to a dominant role filing complaints. The United States files a larger share of WTO disputes than would otherwise be explained by its share of world trade. Table 4.1 shows that the United States filed over 20 percent of all WTO disputes from 1995 to 2010. Yet in 2007 the United

---

[4] Bayard and Elliott (1994, p. 331) analyze seventy-two Section 301 cases and conclude that the policy was "reasonably successful in opening foreign markets."

TABLE 4.1
Annual Pattern of U.S. WTO Complaints.

Year	United States	All Members	U.S. Share
1995	6	25	24.0
1996	16	39	41.0
1997	15	50	30.0
1998	8	41	19.5
1999	9	30	30.0
2000	8	34	23.5
2001	1	23	4.3
2002	4	37	10.8
2003	3	26	11.5
2004	4	19	21.1
2005	1	12	8.3
2006	2	20	10.0
2007	4	13	30.8
2008	3	19	15.8
2009	2	14	14.3
2010	4	17	23.5
1995–2010	90	419	21.5

Note: The table lists the year when the United States filed a WTO complaint, and provides the total complaints filed by all members as a reference with the last column listing U.S. complaints as a percentage of total complaints.

States held an 11.3 percent share of world merchandise exports and 18.9 percent share of world commercial service exports.[5] Aggregate power measures provide little leverage to account for the variation over time. While the extremely high number of complaints in 1996 and 1997 can be partly attributed to the backlog of cases held up until establishment of the WTO, there remains considerable fluctuation year to year.

I argue that the overall level of U.S. adjudication and individual cases can be explained as a response to industry pressure that is magnified by legislative constraints on executive autonomy. The pressure to challenge barriers comes from export industries that are harmed by the trade barrier. Private lobbying is widely observed in WTO adjudication (Shaffer, 2003). Interest groups help to identify specific trade problems, urge governmental action, and use their resources to

[5] Tables I9 and I11 in WTO, "International Trade Statistics 2008," available at the WTO website stat.wto.org.

support the negotiation strategy.[6] Lobbying provides information to legislative representatives that shapes their view of constituent interests (Milner, 1997).

The United States is not unusual to have export industries with a stake in market access. But it does stand out for the tense relationship between the legislature and executive in management of trade policy. As a superpower with global foreign policy interests, the United States has at times seemed to place more attention on foreign policy over economic interest. Support for free trade by the executive has its roots in economic benefits, ideology, and geopolitical strategies to build up allies in the Cold War. Whether encouraging creation of the European Community or tolerating industrial policy measures by Japan, U.S. foreign economic policy did not always consist of placing first priority on demands of specific export industries. As a consequence, industries had strong reasons to suspect whether the executive would enforce trade partner promises to provide market access. Sharing these concerns, Congress has taken extensive measures to provide reassurance to industries. Indeed, Congress can at times go beyond industry with its calls for strong action. Checks and balances in the U.S. Constitution are readily apparent in trade policy. There are few trade decisions in which the executive is not negotiating in the shadow of Congress. The next section will address how legislative constraints in U.S. trade policy act to encourage adjudication.

Legislative Constraints in U.S. Trade Policy

The U.S. Constitution grants Congress the authority to regulate commerce, and the activist role of Congress in setting the tariff and shaping foreign economic policy is well known (e.g., Schattschneider, 1935; Pastor, 1980; O'Halloran, 1994; Destler, 2005). Not only do constraints from Congress matter for the level of U.S. trade barriers, but they also influence how U.S. negotiators choose to address foreign trade barriers. High constraints from the legislature on executive autonomy bias trade policy to place greater weight on responsiveness to export industries over diplomatic concerns. While the U.S. Congress is not deaf to the need to balance foreign policy goals and no U.S. president would ignore export interests, the two branches of government differ in their preference intensity across the two dimensions. In addition to the different incentives

---

[6] USTR officials instruct companies seeking help from the USTR to resolve trade disputes with foreign countries that companies are expected to commit resources by providing a detailed rationale for their complaint, hiring lawyers and economists to conduct relevant analyses, and lobbying of agencies and politicians (*Inside U.S. Trade*, February 3, 2006).

created by institutional structure, the frequent occurrence of divided partisan control of Congress and the presidency deepens the gap. As discussed in the previous chapters, such divisions influence the overall level of adjudication by the United States as the checks on executive autonomy lead to more frequent complaints.

U.S. trade policy is centralized under the authority of a single executive agency that takes the lead role for negotiation, implementation, and monitoring of U.S. trade policy. Starting with the Trade Expansion Act of 1962, Congress required the president to appoint a special representative for trade negotiations who was expected to coordinate the interagency process for trade policy as an advisor to the president who would also report to Congress. Following subsequent reforms to strengthen the position, the Office of the U.S. Trade Representative now is an agency with over two hundred staff members, and the special trade representative has cabinet member status. As a highly professionalized agency with a focused mission, USTR sets the agenda for U.S. trade policy. An interagency process is required to clear negotiation proposals as well as decisions to initiate WTO disputes. This process includes officials from the State Department, Commerce Department, and any other agencies relevant to a particular issue. Gridlock can occur here when agency priorities differ, and one State Department official commented that some say it can be harder to negotiate between agencies in the United States than with the host government.[7] The main constraint on USTR autonomy, however, is from Congress, which closely guards its constitutional authority to "regulate commerce with foreign nations." Congress provides the mandate for the USTR to lead trade negotiations and makes demands for enforcement actions.

While Congress delegated negotiating authority to the executive in the Reciprocal Trade Agreement Acts of 1934, it uses both informal requests and its formal authority to ratify trade agreements as leverage to push the executive to support an aggressive trade agenda against foreign trade barriers. Nearly every major piece of U.S. trade legislation since 1934 has included restrictions on how executive authority may be used and specific demands from Congress (Schwab, 1994, p. 32). Schwab (1994, p. 30) describes "stepped up attacks on foreign barriers" as one example of the kind of quid pro quo extracted from the executive by Congress in exchange for its approval of trade-liberalizing agreements. The need for periodic renewal of executive negotiating authority, the "fast track" procedure that requires an amendment-free vote up or down on trade agreements (renamed "trade promotion authority"), has

---

[7] Interview by author, Washington, D.C., April 9, 2010.

ensured that Congress retains considerable influence over trade policy. Destler (2005, p. 112) notes that "[i]f U.S. trade negotiators were to keep their mandate from Congress and product interests, they had to appear tough in advancing and defending specific U.S. commercial interests."

Legislative constraints on delegation occur through specific legislation and the empowerment of industry. In the 1970s, dissatisfaction with apparent passiveness by the executive branch in the face of spiraling trade deficits widely blamed on foreign protectionism led Congress to enact a new provision for aggressive export promotion, Section 301 of the Trade Act of 1974.[8] The measure calls for the executive to respond to industry petitions about foreign trade barriers by negotiating with foreign governments and enacting trade sanctions when the foreign government refuses to cooperate. Subsequent amendments added timetables and criteria for targeting foreign trade barriers. In what came to be termed "aggressive unilateralism" the United States used this policy tool extensively in the 1980s to pressure trade partners to increase market access (Bhagwati and Patrick, 1990).

Legislative provisions enhance transparency and participation by calling on the USTR to hold public hearings on investigations of industry petitions and publish a justification for the course of action taken to resolve the trade problem in the *Federal Register*. Congress also mandated in the Trade and Tariff Act of 1984 that the U.S. Trade Representative office submit to Congress annual reports listing foreign trade barriers and the status of U.S. efforts to address these problems. Industry groups gained a formal role in the decision process through the creation of Industry Sector Advisory Committees, which bring together industry representatives who are cleared to receive confidential information about the status of negotiations.

The ability of Congress to intervene in trade policy benefits from high expertise. First, individual politicians have large support staff that facilitate close contacts with industry and the capacity to follow up on requests. Susan Schwab brought experience as a trade policy officer in the U.S. embassy in Tokyo and as agricultural trade negotiator for USTR before serving as legislative director for Senator John Danforth in a position that allowed her to play a major role in the writing of the Omnibus Trade and Competitiveness Act of 1988 (she was later appointed as U.S. Trade Representative in 2006). Second, the relevant committees are staffed by officials with competence in trade policy. For example, Tim Reif, who served from 2001 to 2009 as the chief

---

[8] Although most economists agree that the trade deficits were largely the result of macroeconomic policies, foreign trade policies were in part responsible and were easier targets for criticism. See Bergsten and Noland (1993).

Democratic Trade Counsel for the House Committee on Ways and Means, had prior experience working for USTR and in private practice served on the legal team of Dewey Ballantine to represent Kodak in a Section 301 case and WTO dispute (Reif was later appointed general counsel for USTR in 2009). Third, those politicians with seniority on trade committees are well versed in the details of trade policy from long years of experience in which they have closely followed legislation and negotiations. Such expertise within Congress facilitates its ability to have input over a wide range of trade policy matters, even as the efficiency logic for delegation to the trade bureaucracy remains present. A legislature that lacks any understanding of trade policy would be forced to delegate completely to the trade professionals, but Congress holds sufficient expertise of its own to push back against the decisions of the bureaucracy.

In sum, U.S. trade policy exhibits classic features of conditional delegation described in principal-agent theories (McCubbins and Schwartz, 1984; McCubbins, Noll, and Weingast, 1987; Epstein and O'Halloran, 1999; Huber and Shipan, 2002). Congress as the principal delegates conditional authority to the executive for administration of trade policy. Specific legislation sets clear guidelines for behavior within a limited mandate. Ongoing oversight hard wires the trade agency to respond to the interests of Congress. Fire alarm monitoring by industry alerts Congress to poor performance. This policy structure encourages responsiveness of the executive branch to the priorities of Congress.

Although the United States has consistently faced more legislative constraints on trade policy than most other democracies, periods of divided government and declining trade consensus coincide with increasing levels of constraints. The Trade Act of 1974 that transformed enforcement policy with the establishment of Section 301 was passed by a Democratic Congress that expressed distrust of a Republican administration. Destler (2005) highlights two conditions that had supported high delegation of trade authority to the president until the 1970s: bipartisan free trade consensus and strong leadership in Congress. The decline of U.S. dominance of world markets and rise of chronic trade deficits set the stage for the unraveling of the free trade consensus. As U.S. industries suffered under the forces of global competition, "fair trade" demands gained prominence as a claim that U.S. industries could not compete because U.S. markets were more open than its trade partners. The shift of the Democratic Party toward protectionism gave rise to divergent interests on trade policy, and fragmentation of authority in Congress meant less control over the short-term incentives of individual representatives. The rise of divided government further reduced willingness in Congress to grant a free hand to the executive to manage the details of trade policy. By passing the 1974 Trade Act, Congress required that the administration more closely consult Congress on trade negotiations and called for actions against foreign trade barriers. In 1988, again during a period of divided government and rising trade deficits, Congress passed the Omnibus Trade and Competitiveness Act of 1988 that established "Super 301," which required that the USTR designate priority countries with unfair trade policies and established deadlines for the use of GATT dispute settlement. This heightened the aggressive approach toward enforcement.[9]

Starting as early as the Trade Expansion Act of 1962, the executive adopted a strategy to use legal complaints to build support for new trade agreements in Congress. Hudec (1980, p. 155) reports U.S. trade officials said in interviews that a flurry of lawsuits were planned as part of a strategy to promote passage of trade legislation (both the 1962 Act and the 1974 Trade Act) at a time when Congress was less willing to embrace liberalization and accused the executive of not doing enough to enforce agreements. The legislation then locked in the strategy through constraints on the executive to encourage ongoing enforcement efforts.

To a large extent one can view the pressure from Congress for aggressive enforcement against foreign trade barriers as "political theatre" (Hudec, 1993, p. 112). Economists agreed that the causes of U.S. trade deficit lay in macroeconomic forces related to the federal budget deficit and low savings rate. But Congress could not (or would not) address these problems. Putting on a show of action against foreign protection provided a better political response. Even if enforcement could not resolve the trade deficit, enforcement measures delivered real gains for specific industries while their high profile demonstrated tough action that appealed to the public. Bashing trade partners offered opportunities for credit claiming by politicians trying to address worries about loss of competitiveness. As politicians pursue a broad mandate for job creation and economic growth through promoting a tough trade policy, it can lead them to exceed even the demands of the affected export industry.

The congressional pressure for enforcement that had been focused on Section 301 cases in the 1980s has now turned to WTO adjudication (Dupont, Mariani, and Benavente, 2008). Unilateralism generated such resistance among trade partners that it was not effective (Schoppa, 1997; Pelc, 2010). Since 1995, the number of Section 301 cases filed

---

[9] See Bayard and Elliott (1994) for background on the evolution of Section 301 and analysis of its use.

by industries has steadily declined, and no unilateral sanctions have been implemented for a Section 301 case. While some in Congress still make calls for unilateral trade retaliation, those on trade committees who influence the policy process view WTO adjudication as the means to resolve disputes.[10]

This leaves WTO adjudication as the main tool to visibly demonstrate enforcement. A USTR official lamented the emphasis in Congress on the number of WTO cases brought by the United States because it has a tendency to encourage filing cases just to "rack up the numbers."[11] Nevertheless, the USTR maintains on its website a list of cases filed at the WTO and the USTR refers to the number of cases and win rate in speeches about trade policy achievements. There is no equivalent for actions addressed in bilateral negotiations. Former USTR Susan Schwab acknowledged, "We don't do a good enough job advertising the issues solved in bilateral talks. For Congress, their actions may appear more credible if there is a press release on a WTO case."[12]

Beyond explicit legislation, informal pressure and the threat of future legislative changes are also tools of congressional influence to encourage filing WTO complaints. A search of the *Congressional Record* reveals considerable attention to WTO dispute settlement with an average of forty speakers making a specific reference to WTO dispute settlement in a speech during a congressional session. Over the period 1995 to 2007, there were a total of 236 speeches with such reference.[13] Several of these speeches each year directly mention U.S. initiation of a WTO dispute for a specific issue. On the day that the United States filed a complaint against Argentina for duties on footwear and textiles, a representative of Massachusetts in the House of Representatives said, "The action taken by USTR will help those businesses who have been discriminated against because of the unfair trade practices of Argentina. In Massachusetts, Companies such as Reebok and thousands of Massachusetts employees, depend upon fair access to foreign consumer markets for their livelihoods. Once again, I congratulate Ambassador Barshefsky and offer my continuing support for firm steps to enforce our international

---

[10] USTR official, interview by author, July 11, 2007.

[11] Interview, Washington, D.C., August 16, 2007.

[12] Susan Schwab, former USTR in administration of President George W. Bush from 2006 to 2009, phone interview by author, April 19, 2010.

[13] I conducted the search for the term "WTO Dispute Settlement" in the daily *Congressional Record* using LexisNexis Congressional for the period 1995–2007. The figure for the average speakers in a single session of Congress (two-year period) includes references to cases initiated by the United States and those against the United States as well as broader discussion about WTO dispute settlement.

trade treaties to benefit U.S. interests."[14] Following China's accession to the WTO in 2001 it has become routine for there to be "Sense of Congress" statements that the president should initiate WTO disputes against China on a broad range of issues including exchange rate manipulation, denial of trading and distribution rights, insufficient intellectual property rights protection, objectionable labor standards, subsidization of exports, and forced technology appropriation. Such statements may be directed both at the USTR and as credit claiming with home district constituencies.

The decline of U.S.-initiated WTO cases under the Bush administration from 2001 met strong criticism from Congress. Every spring when the USTR releases its report on foreign trade barriers, the House Democratic leadership issues a press release and letter to the president listing specific cases that they believe should be challenged in WTO adjudication. Since 2006, legislation has been submitted in Congress calling for appointment of a "Congressional Trade Enforcer," whose role would be to instruct the USTR to begin dispute procedures for specific cases.[15] A staff person with the congressional trade committee said the goal was to have a Senate confirmed individual who would be responsive to Congress and encourage the USTR to focus on enforcement.[16]

In this context of highly constrained delegation, WTO adjudication can become a valuable tool. The decision to file a complaint for a specific case is open to political influence. The executive will try to accommodate pressure for enforcement actions through filing more cases and choosing those that will go the furthest to satisfy Congress. This is not the only criterion for case selection. In an interview, the U.S. ambassador to the WTO Peter Allgeier listed the following five criteria for selecting WTO cases: strength of legal case, commercial importance, progress in negotiations, ramifications for broader relationship with trade partner, and political pressure from Congress.[17] These criteria are similar to those described by officials from many other countries. On a case-by-case basis, the relative importance of any given criterion will change. My argument suggests, however, that constraints from the legislature in the United States will on average elevate the weight given to political pressure to increase the frequency of politicized case selection.

Political pressure focuses on the decision to file a complaint rather than micromanagement of litigation. Indeed, the litigation phase itself

---

[14] Richard Neal (October 3, 1996), "USTR Announcement on Argentinean Footwear," 104th Congress, 2nd session, 142 Cong Rec E 1912.

[15] *Inside U.S. Trade*, April 4, 2008.

[16] Interview, Washington, D.C., August 17, 2007.

[17] Interview, Geneva. October 26, 2007.

experiences reduced political attention. Former U.S. Trade Representative Susan Schwab said in an interview that Congress will hold hearings and make speeches as a way to express their concerns and apply pressure on an issue, but this is less likely to occur after a case has been filed. "When in court of law holding a hearing would be superfluous and might even undermine the case. It is not as sexy—what are you going to talk about if the issue is already in court? The Administration will say that the case is pending. It doesn't get CSPAN in a room."[18] The litigation phase offers a window for the case to move forward in the hands of lawyers in Geneva having temporarily satisfied Congress that action is being taken. Nonetheless, a stall in litigation or release of the ruling will once again bring a return of attention.

The Kodak-Fuji Film Dispute

The Kodak-Fuji film dispute provides an example of how strong political pressure can lead to a WTO dispute on an issue that would not otherwise appear to have been a likely case for adjudication. In many ways this case represents an outlier in WTO adjudication as one of the few where the defendant was found to have no violation, but I will argue it highlights political pressures that are present in other cases as well. The dispute began in spring 1995 when Kodak filed a petition under the provisions of Section 301 requesting that the U.S. government take action to address unfair barriers in the Japanese market that prevented access for U.S. film exports. Kodak argued that connections between retail stores and Fuji film and the structure of the distribution market were discriminatory. Fuji film denied the claims and hired a legal team to counter point by point every argument, while the Japanese trade minister Ryutarō Hashimoto declared at a press conference in July 1995 that this was a matter of private business actions and not an issue for government negotiation (Taniguchi, 2000, p. 119). Later as prime minister with the full support of METI, Hashimoto would continue to stonewall against negotiations under threat of Section 301 investigation.

Fundamentally the complaint was about competition policy, which could more directly be addressed by filing a complaint to the Japan Fair Trade Commission. But Kodak was skeptical that the JFTC would bring any meaningful change and wanted to see direct action by the U.S. government. After a year of getting nowhere in bilateral talks during the

---

[18] Susan Schwab, former USTR in administration of President George W. Bush from 2006 to 2009, phone interview by author, April 19, 2010.

Section 301 investigation, political pressure mounted. The Japanese side had made no concession, and the terms of Section 301 call for retaliation if a foreign trade partner is not taking actions to redress the complaint.[19] Having just finished the auto dispute with Japan in which the Japanese government challenged U.S. retaliation measures in a WTO case, USTR was reluctant to again threaten unilateral retaliation.

Pressure on the administration to "do something" grew as the dispute became increasingly politicized. During the four years of the dispute from 1995 to 1999, the Clinton administration faced a united Republican majority in Congress that was opposing the administration on every front from budget politics to management of trade policy. The point person in Congress to support Kodak was Senator Alfonse D'Amato, the Republican senator from New York where Kodak has its headquarters and also the nemesis of the Clinton family as the chair of the Senate Special Whitewater committee that investigated impropriety in their personal financial affairs. As the dispute continued in 1996 it became caught up in presidential campaign politics, with Republican candidate Robert Dole making a speech in the senate critical of the Clinton administration for being soft on trade policy listing the Kodak case as an example where the administration had failed to bring results (Durling, 2000, p. 330). During a congressional hearing in March 1996 on U.S.-Japan trade policy, Kodak CEO George Fisher was invited to present his case against Japan. The pressure from Congress was not limited to Republicans. Democratic and Republican representatives from New York gathered seventy-one signatures with bipartisan support for a letter in April 1996 urging the administration to push forward negotiations on the dispute. Kodak drew upon its political connections, and calls were made by congressional offices to USTR demanding action. Figure 4.1 shows the rise of political contributions during the lead-up and duration of the WTO dispute.[20] Both Kodak and Fuji waged aggressive public relations campaigns with paid ads presenting the position of the companies.

Despite concerns about a weak legal case, in June 1996 the USTR filed a WTO complaint against Japan (DS44). In a broad-ranging case the United States alleged laws and regulations in Japan were violations

[19] Section 301 specifies that when USTR determines after investigation that a foreign government engages in policies that violate agreements or represent an unjustifiable burden for U.S. commerce, the law requires retaliation. Several exceptions are allowed, however, including a nonviolation finding by a WTO panel as well as determination by the government that retaliation is not in U.S. interest.

[20] Data on soft money contributions from Kodak to all federal candidates and parties are from the Center for Responsive Politics (CRP) at http://www.crp.org/.

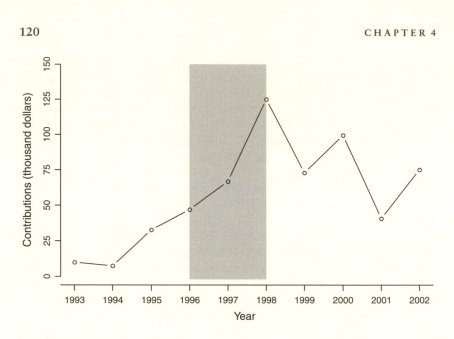

Figure 4.1. Political Contributions from Kodak. The figure shows total soft money contributions to both Democrats and Republicans. The shaded region indicates the period of WTO dispute settlement.

of GATT, GATS, and a 1960 GATT decision on restrictive business practices (Durling, 2000, pp. 382–387). The United States eventually withdrew the latter two claims and pursued only the GATT case, where it advanced complex legal arguments for "non-violation nullification and impairment." This argument implied that Kodak failure in the Japanese market resulted from a set of measures related to broad Japanese government intervention in the economy.

Shifting the dispute into the WTO allowed the administration to balance diplomacy, politics, and economic interest. An interagency process reviewed the USTR investigation of Kodak's Section 301 petition and made the decision to respond by filing a complaint at the WTO. In these discussions, the National Security Council position opposed confrontational action in which trade friction would hinder efforts to focus on critical issues facing the alliance, which was at a turning point with both sides reviewing defense arrangements for joint military cooperation and the U.S. bases in Okinawa (Durling, 2000, p. 340). Political advisors were also concerned about potential risk of harm in the upcoming November election if the administration rejected the Kodak petition or initiated a trade war with unilateral sanctions that could backfire like the auto parts case had the previous year. In the end, the hard-liner demands by those close to Kodak who wanted to use Section 301 for unilateral retaliation threats could not prevail over diplomatic concerns, but political support for Kodak was sufficient that the government could not simply reject its petition. The WTO option was attractive because it would defer resolution of the dispute until after the defense review and election were over. Much fanfare was made surrounding the decision to file the complaint as USTR officials announced the action flanked by congressional representatives and noting that nearly a hundred members of Congress had contacted their office along with demands from the Republican and Democratic Party leadership (Durling, 2000, p. 351).

The move to pursue legal action at the WTO was not the first choice for Kodak, which had hoped to see the U.S. government escalate bilateral pressure against Japan and compel concessions without the need to go to the WTO. All recognized that WTO rules did not cover many of the competition policy issues that Kodak identified as barriers to its success in the Japanese market. Indeed, during his March testimony before Congress, Fisher said "the Japanese government's toleration... of systematic anti-competitive activities that block market access for American and other imported products is simply not covered by WTO rules."[21] Furthermore, much of the evidence against Japanese government policies restricting the market was about actions taken in the 1970s, and Fuji had put forward extensive rebuttals of the factual case to demonstrate that the Japanese film market was open. This would not be an easy case to win in court. Nonetheless, for Kodak a WTO complaint represented a better outcome than a USTR decision to dismiss the Kodak petition, for the company could hope to gain influence in Washington as the government became the advocate for Kodak's position (Taniguchi, 2000, p. 116). Putting a good face on the outcome, Fisher said in an interview for the CNBC program 'Power Lunch' on June 13, 1996 that Kodak had "won about everything we were looking for" with the decision to file a WTO complaint (Durling, 2000, p. 358). There was extensive media coverage of the decision to file the WTO complaint in major newspapers and on television networks including CNN, CNBC, and PBS as well as local network affiliates (Durling, 2000, p. 361).

Similarly for the Japanese side, the WTO complaint represented a second best option. Japanese officials said from the beginning that this was a matter for the JFTC, which announced in February 1996 it would begin a survey of business practice in the photographic film market—an investigation that would begin in April timed to defuse the issue during the Clinton visit in April that would focus on the renewal of commitment

---

[21] *The Economist*, June 22, 1996, p. 98.

to security cooperation (Taniguchi, 2000, p. 117). At this time the government also suggested the OECD as an alternative venue for neutral fact finding about market openness in the photographic film sector (implicitly opening the record of U.S. market access for comparison with Japan given the widely noted fact that the Fuji film market share in the United States was the flip side of the Kodak market share in Japan). The United States vetoed the proposal for a fact-finding mission in the OECD meeting, which operates by consensus rules. Fearing the prospect of unilateral retaliation, the Japanese government welcomed the U.S. decision to file a WTO complaint. In his remarks following the complaint, MITI Minister Tsukahara criticized the United States for not waiting for the outcome of the JFTC investigation and denied the allegations of market barriers, but also affirmed "[W]e are confident that these misunderstandings can be resolved through the WTO rules" (Durling, 2000, p. 357).

Not many outside observers were surprised when two years later the United States lost the ruling.[22] Japan's policies were ruled consistent with WTO rules. Although most WTO rulings favor the plaintiff to find that the challenged measure contains a violation of the agreement, this case had been seen as pushing beyond WTO law from the beginning. The entire dispute had absorbed considerable resources for all sides involved and brought no change in the policy. Yet the use of adjudication finally convinced Kodak and its political backers that nothing further could be done and that the Japanese government would not back down under U.S. pressure. Statements from Kodak representatives and the New York congressional delegation as well as a *New York Times* editorial (December 10, 1997) criticized the WTO ruling, but none claimed the government had made insufficient effort or that it should undermine the WTO ruling. No more calls were issued for unilateral retaliation. Moreover, while contributions from Kodak declined after their high point in 1998, they remained well above the average level during the years before the dispute. Without delivering a market access result, the government escaped punishment by the firm since it had demonstrated strong commitment to export promotion. Even in this worst-case scenario with a difficult legal case, adjudication had served as the best response to political pressure.

The Kodak-Fuji dispute clearly illustrates the role of industry demands and congressional pressure to force the executive to give attention to a particular market access problem. It demonstrates that adjudication can emerge as the final strategy choice representing an alternative to

---

[22] The panel ruling was adopted by the Dispute Settlement Body on April 22, 1998.

both unilateral retaliation or continued negotiation. Nevertheless, this example may represent an outlier of politicized adjudication. It is unusual because it really was a battle between two companies and involved a complex range of nontariff barriers that could be seen to impede access. The case is one of the rare rulings in WTO adjudication to completely reject the legal claims of the complainant. More generally, is there a pattern of political influence on selection of WTO cases by the United States?

Foreign Trade Barrier Dataset

The hypothesis that case selection will reward politically influential industries will be evaluated with analysis of an original dataset of trade barriers. The dataset is based on coding government reports by the USTR that provide annual lists of trade barriers by U.S. trade partners that are harmful to the interests of U.S. exports. These data offer three major advantages that will contribute to the study of trade policy. First, the trade barriers that are listed in the government reports meet a minimum threshold of demand that makes them likely issues for a negotiation agenda. This facilitates analysis of politically relevant trade barriers, unlike studies that measure trade policy barriers as the residual for any product trade flow in a gravity model of trade.[23] The trade barriers in the dataset represent the set of *potential cases for WTO adjudication*. Second, the data include not only standard NTBs such as quotas or antidumping measures, but also regulations that affect the service industry, investment policies, and qualitative nontariff barriers related to technical standards and intellectual property rights protection. In contrast, the UNCTAD dataset that is the most frequent source in analysis of nontariff barriers does not include intellectual property policies. Datasets that examine antidumping measures miss large areas of trade disputes. For example, Japan very rarely applies antidumping duties so trade disputes against Japanese market closure are entirely missed by studies that focus on antidumping. Third, the data from the USTR reports reflect the U.S. perspective as a "victim" of the trade measures that has an interest in full disclosure of the barriers taken by other countries. In contrast, the UNCTAD dataset relies on official national reports of governments about their own trade policies, and as a consequence understates barriers where governments do not desire

---

[23] Such gravity model studies are subject to the critique that poor fit of the model would erroneously suggest that there are high trade barriers (Laird and Yeats, 1990, p. 35).

transparency (Laird and Yeats, 1990, p. 20). Finally, whereas most empirical studies of nontariff barriers focus on manufacturing industries, the data here include barriers affecting primary, manufacturing, and service sectors. In short, the data will allow me to examine the full range of trade protection whereas existing datasets focus on a small number of basic protection tools.

A brief background on the creation of the reports is necessary. They represent one tool by which Congress monitors the executive branch actions on trade policy. In the Trade Act of 1974, Congress mandated that every year the Office of the U.S. Trade Representative submit to the Senate Finance Committee, appropriate House committees, and the president 'The National Trade Estimate Report (NTE)' which should analyze market access barriers that adversely affect exports of U.S. goods and services. The report represents an inventory of trade barriers that was originally intended to help generate cases for the Section 301 process in which the U.S. Congress had mandated the government target particular foreign barriers for negotiation on a time schedule leading to possible economic sanctions. Noland (1997, p. 369) uses the report to measure U.S. government attention to bilateral trade problems.[24] The NTE is drafted in consultation with U.S. embassies abroad, trade policy advisors (academic and industry officials with formal clearance to participate in the trade policy process), USTR officials of the relevant area and policy specialties, and a public comment process in which industries make submissions.[25] Carmen Suro-Bredie, the assistant U.S. trade representative for policy coordination, confirmed that the NTE trade barriers represent the politically relevant trade barriers and said that briefing reports for U.S. officials going to a particular trade negotiation draw upon the information in the NTE.[26] Members of Congress have used the release of the report to urge more action by the administration to address specific foreign trade barriers.[27] This report is complemented by the "Annual Report on Trade Agreements Program and National Trade Policy Agenda" that provides information on the goals and reported actions and progress for specific trade agenda items.

[24] He counts the number of pages in the report devoted to each trade partner for a single number measuring the attention given to the aggregate trade problems with a specific trade partner. In contrast, my dataset codes the individual trade barriers.

[25] For example, there were thirty-nine new submissions for the 2006 NTE from associations such as the California Avocado Commission and the National Electrical Manufacturers Association as well as from companies such as PepsiCo and Walmart.

[26] Interview, Washington, D.C., May 11, 2006.

[27] Correspondence of House Ways and Means Subcommittee provided to author.

The data are coded in cross-section time series format with a trade barrier as the unit of analysis. First, a list of trade barriers was created from each annual NTE report. The annual lists were aggregated into panels of discrete trade barriers with start and end dates. Notes on government negotiation activities drawn from the NTE reports were confirmed against the USTR Annual Reports and the WTO dispute settlement website list of cases. A unit represents a distinct complaint about a specific policy measure with observations for every year in which the barrier continues to be mentioned in the NTE reports. Some industries are affected by multiple trade barriers stacked on top of each other, and each one is coded separately. For example, the NTE report on Korea lists discriminatory tax policies, standards, and anti-import bias generated by media campaigns as policies that adversely affect U.S. auto exports to Korea. These are coded as three barriers. This chapter analyzes the trade barriers that address a single industry that could be coded at the two-digit International Standard Industry Classification (ISIC) level (e.g., textiles or motor vehicles) and where data were available for key economic indicators and political contributions.[28] Other barriers that affect several industries such as general tax policies are not included for analysis in this chapter.

The data scope is U.S. complaints about trade barriers by nine top trade partners: Canada, EU, Japan, Korea, and Mexico represent the top five OECD trade partners. These trade partners are those with the highest trade volumes with the United States. Four additional countries, Brazil, India, Malaysia, and Singapore, were added to the sample as representative of top U.S. trade partners among developing countries that have also been WTO members since 1995 (note that while China is a major trade partner, it joined the WTO only in November 2001). In 2005, the value of U.S. exports to these nine countries represented 72 percent of all U.S. exports.[29] The time period begins with the establishment of the WTO in 1995 and continues to 2004, which is the most recent year for which industry-level data from the OECD are available. The complaints that are not specific to an industry are

[28] The two-digit level is used because this is the aggregation at which data are most consistently available for both political contributions and economic control variables. Some trade barriers are more narrow (e.g., dairy rather than agriculture or woolen coats rather than textiles). Data availability forces this aggregation, but one would also expect that lobbying influence draws upon the larger industry aggregation. For the following five industries for which data were consistently available, industry is coded at the four-digit level: pharmaceuticals, steel, aircraft, shipbuilding, and railroad transport equipment.

[29] WTO, International Trade Statistics 2006, table III.16, U.S. Merchandise Trade by Region.

excluded.[30] There are 403 barriers with data available on covariates for inclusion in the analysis. Each barrier has multiple observations for the years it continued to be reported in the NTE, with a range from one to ten years and an average of seven years total duration.

WTO DISPUTE

The initiation of a WTO dispute is the dependent variable for the models tested in the fifth section. The indicator variable is coded 1 for the year the U.S. files a WTO complaint, which is the first step to initiate formal adjudication of a trade dispute.[31] Of the 403 barriers 34 (8.44 percent) were raised in adjudication. The null values include years in which a barrier was negotiated in bilateral or multilateral settings or mentioned in the report without specific government action. Once the barrier has been subject to a dispute complaint it is dropped from the sample.

POLITICAL CONTRIBUTIONS

The selection argument suggests that the U.S. government will choose dispute adjudication as the negotiation strategy in response to demands from organized interest groups. Political contributions are a key indicator of industry political influence on trade policy (Grossman and Helpman, 1994; Hansen and Drope, 2004). Trade barriers that directly affect an industry with high political contributions would be the most likely to trigger the government choice to use WTO adjudication. I use contributions data provided by the Center for Responsive Politics (CRP), a nonpartisan research group that tracks money in U.S. politics.[32]

---

[30] For example, the quota restrictions by India across a range of products are listed in the NTE reports and led to the United States filing a WTO dispute in 1997 (DS90, "India Quantitative Restrictions on Imports of Agricultural, Textile and Industrial Products"). This case is dropped from the analysis because it is not possible to code industry-specific data for such an aggregation of goods. Limiting the sample to industry-specific complaints regarding policies of nine trade partners that are mentioned in the NTE reports means that not all WTO disputes are in the dataset—over this period the United States filed seventy-four complaints under the DSU and only thirty-four are in the sample. But since the same restriction applies to those NTE complaints that are not raised in adjudication it is not expected to introduce bias. The proportion of horizontal complaints that were too general for coding industry data was similar at 25 percent of the WTO cases and 25 percent of the complaints not brought to WTO.

[31] Although the WTO assigns multiple dispute numbers to some cases with repeat filings, these are aggregated in the dataset and treated as one complaint filed for a given trade barrier.

[32] The totals include contributions to all federal candidates and to parties. Data available at http://www.crp.org/.

The CRP collects the publicly listed data from the Federal Election Commission and summarizes the total contributions by individuals and PACs and soft money contributions according to industry category for over one hundred industries.[33] The main analysis sums contributions to all parties, but additional tests disaggregate contributions by party. The amount of contributions ranges from high levels of $99.8 million by the finance industry and $24.6 million by agricultural producers to lower values of $2.6 million by the auto industry and $859,000 by the TV production industry (these examples are from the 1996 election cycle).[34] The log of the U.S. dollar value is taken to smooth high values.

SECTION 301

Eighteen of the trade barriers in the data used for regression analysis are Section 301 cases. As described earlier, the U.S. Congress created a tool for export promotion in Section 301 of the U.S. Trade Act. The law mandates that the USTR investigate the complaints of industries that file petitions and initiate a Section 301 case for those evaluated to have sufficient merit. Congress also added provisions for the USTR to initiate Section 301 cases on its own without an industry petition when unfair trade policies by a trade partner called for such action.[35] Section 301 cases follow specific deadlines for government action to request negotiations with the foreign government. When met by continued resistance by the trade partner, the procedure calls for unilateral sanctions or initiation of a GATT/WTO dispute. Given the institutional constraint one would expect that Section 301 cases would be more likely to have an adjudication strategy chosen.

U.S. ECONOMIC INTEREST CONTROL VARIABLES

While my argument emphasizes political factors that influence the cost benefit calculation for a dispute, commercial stakes are also important. Although unable to measure the exact damage from a foreign trade

[33] Contributions are measured as the amount over the two-year election cycle leading up to the year of the observation. While contributions should vary in response to reward policy outcomes, studying the effect of trade strategies on political contributions is beyond the scope of this study. See Gawande (1997) for research showing that U.S. industry contributions increase as a function of NTB coverage. Mitra (1999) models lobby formation as a function of government willingness to offer policy outcomes for political contributions.

[34] The CRP industry categories have been adjusted when necessary to provide the closest match with the ISIC industry used for economic variables.

[35] See Bayard and Elliott (1994) for description of the use of Section 301.

barrier, I can proxy the commercial stakes through measurement of the industry and trade barrier characteristics. Industry size is an important control variable since larger industries are more likely to represent greater economic stakes. I use the production value of the U.S. industry affected by the foreign trade barrier.[36] Large export industries are more likely to present sufficient benefits to justify the cost of litigation.[37] I control for export interests using the world export value as reported by the OECD STAN Bilateral Trade Database (thousand U.S. dollars). It is important to use the world export value rather than bilateral exports because the latter are reduced by the trade barrier. For disputes that arise from a temporary defection from commitments, the lagged trade value could indicate market value for U.S. exporters, but many disputes represent incomplete implementation such that there is no accurate measure of expected trade flows available.[38] For the production and export values, the log is taken to smooth high values. Model 2 adds the annual trade balance with the trade partner for the given industry (billion U.S. dollars). Previous research highlights the importance of bilateral trade balance to influence the pattern of disputes and economic outcomes (Bayard and Elliott, 1994; Guzman and Simmons, 2005; Bown, 2004b). All economic control variables are converted to constant U.S. dollar values.

TRADE BARRIER CONTROL VARIABLES

To analyze the selection of disputes for adjudication, one wants to control for the legal strength of a potential complaint. Studies of the litigation behavior of administrative agencies contend that legal certainty pushes bureaucracies to prioritize their win rate over the actual economic gains per case (Posner, 1972). The observation that 90 percent of the rulings by WTO panels favor the plaintiff indicates that governments screen out weak legal cases before filing or in early settlement. Ideally, one would want a legal brief prepared to evaluate each trade barrier

---

[36] OECD STAN Database for Industrial Analysis. Others use these measures as the proxy for *political importance* (e.g., Lee and Swagel, 1997). This study is able to more directly measure political importance with data on political contributions. To the extent that larger industries will also have more resources to make political contributions, it is also necessary to control for this variable.

[37] Note however that the WTO does not require that a state have an industry interest in order to file a case, and there are examples such as the U.S. decision to file a complaint against the EU banana import regime even when the United States does not produce bananas.

[38] The research on dispute initiation that focuses on antidumping measures is more amenable to analysis using bilateral trade flows since there is a well-defined product and start date for the trade barrier. See research by Chad Bown (Bown, 2004a, 2005a, 2005b).

by a trade partner. Unfortunately this is rarely possible.[39] Evaluation
of the legal status of a trade barrier requires both extensive WTO legal
expertise and knowledge about the specific policy and its impact on trade;
even when governments conduct such internal analysis, they treat their
conclusions as private information. Coding legal status was not possible
for this project, which involves over four hundred distinct trade barriers.

I use a proxy variable for strong legal cases based on the nature of
the trade barrier as an import policy. A government looking for sure-
win cases is more likely to challenge trade barriers based on import
policies over other policy areas (e.g., standards, intellectual property
rights protection, services, or investment policies). Import policies have
always been at the core of the trade regime regulations, so there is a
large body of jurisprudence based on previous cases under both GATT
and the WTO that can help governments to build a legal case. In the
record of WTO jurisprudence, issues that directly limit imports, such as
antidumping measures or import quotas, have led to consistently strong
positive rulings.[40] There may also be higher certainty over prospects for
early settlement for import policy barriers. Guzman and Simmons (2002)
show that within the set of WTO disputes, those related to tariffs and
quotas are easier to resolve (and hence more likely to settle early) because
their "continuous" nature allows for compromise that cannot be made
on "all-or-nothing" regulations. Thus a bureaucrat trying to maximize
either early settlement or legal victory is more likely to choose cases
related to border measures affecting goods imports. The NTE divides the
report on each trade partner into sections for the type of trade barrier,
and I code an indicator variable for those included in the section on
import policies.

The level of trade distortion from the disputed barrier increases the
economic stakes and likelihood of a violation ruling, so one would
expect high-distortion trade barriers to be more likely to face challenge
by WTO dispute adjudication. I measure the distortionary burden
from the trade barrier with an indicator variable that codes cases that
involved substantial market closure resulting from policies such as high
quantitative restriction (ban, quota, or increase of tariff/duty by more

[39] Allee (2003) is one of the few studies to directly address this question. In his dataset of
antidumping duty cases he uses the criteria of WTO agreement for antidumping duties
to create a variable that evaluates whether the particular duty is likely to meet these
criteria. Busch and Reinhardt (2006) include variables on the legal merits of a case, but
this approach is possible only because their analysis focuses on those cases that have a
complaint filed that specifies the legal argument in public documents. For my analysis to
include the unfiled cases, I cannot construct such a variable.

[40] See Tarullo (2004) for a review of trends for positive rulings in antidumping cases.

than 10 percent), use of standards or rules of origin to implement a de facto ban on imports, violation of intellectual property rights, or subsidies provided to competitors. Of the barriers 51 percent involved such high-distortion policies. Other barriers coded as having a more moderate distortionary effect on trade included policies such as low-level quantitative restriction or burdensome procedures.

PROGRESS

The initiation of a WTO complaint is premised on the failure of earlier requests to remove the barrier. Controlling for progress toward resolving the trade complaint takes into account the status of policy response by the trade partner. In a year reporting substantial progress on the problem, the United States would be less likely to file a WTO complaint than when there has been no progress or even backward movement to worsen the trade distortion. This variable is measured annually on a 4-point scale that records the level of progress according to the information in the NTE reports about any policy changes undertaken by the trade partner. Further details on the coding of the variable are given later in chapter 6, which evaluates the effect of filing a complaint on the amount of progress reported for years after the complaint has been filed. I also control for the duration of the dispute, which counts for each observation the number of previous years that the barrier has been included in the NTE reports.

PARTNER INDUSTRY CONTROL VARIABLES

Finally, the economic and political conditions of the trade partner also influence choice of negotiation strategy. Ultimately the trade partner must agree to change its trade barrier to bring progress toward ending the complaint. On the one hand, the state seeking market access may be less likely to adopt costly adjudication strategies for cases where high trade partner resistance reduces the likelihood of success. Strategic restraint suggests that states would bother to file WTO cases only when they anticipate low trade partner resistance. This is the logic of skeptics who suggest that cooperation in institutional forums occurs for *easy issues* that are ripe for cooperation (Downs, Rocke, and Barsoom, 1996). On the other hand, the domestic commitment function of adjudication suggests that resistance by a trade partner pushes cases to WTO adjudication. Similar to governments that initiate a legal dispute to signal their willingness to take a high-cost negotiation strategy for their export industry, respondent states will refuse bilateral settlements and wait for a WTO ruling as a way to signal their willingness to accept high-cost adjudication in defense of their import industry. The two propositions offer opposite predictions about whether adjudication is more or less likely as a strategy against high trade partner resistance. This can be tested as an empirical question by controlling for the stakes to the partner industry.

The demand for protection in the trade partner from its industry influences whether the government will be more or less likely to remove the trade barrier. At the same time the expected market gain for the exporter influences the exporters' incentives to push for change. The import penetration ratio (share of imports in GDP) for the trade partner industry serves as a proxy for the market stakes to both sides.[41] The literature offers conflicting interpretations of whether import penetration increases demand for protection by threatening the domestic industry (Trefler, 1993) or reduces the supply of protection by increasing the cost to aggregate welfare (Grossman and Helpman, 1994). From the exporter perspective, a higher level of trade partner import penetration suggests a larger market. I also test for the impact of change in import penetration (growth from previous year).

Model 2 adds employment share and tariff rate, which are also common control variables in studies of nontariff barriers (e.g., Kono, 2006; Busch and Reinhardt, 1999; Lee and Swagel, 1997). Employment share of the industry in the trade partner proxies for the strength of demand for protection because industries that affect more voters have greater influence.[42] The tariff level is itself a product of past decisions that incorporate demands for protection.[43] I expect both high employment share and high tariff levels to increase the likelihood of adjudication as the trade partner resists settlement in other forums. For the trade partner as well, the high costs of adjudication signal government commitment to the industry.

[41] The data on import penetration ratios for Canada, the EU, Japan, Korea, and Mexico at the two-digit ISIC level are taken directly from the OECD STAN Indicators Database "MPEN" variable and represent imports as share of total market (imports plus domestic production minus exports). Since data on import penetration ratio were unavailable for the non-OECD countries, these observations are entered as zero, and any effect from the systematic nature of the missing data will be captured in the non-OECD indicator variable.

[42] The data on employment share by industry are from UNIDO's Industrial Statistics database for manufacturing employment and FAO's FAOstat database for agricultural employment, and total employment is from the ILO.

[43] Ray (1981) showed that there is little reverse feedback from the nontariff barrier to tariffs. Tariff rates are measured as the simple average MFN rate for the two-digit industry and are from the UNCTAD TRAINS dataset.

TRADE PARTNER FIXED EFFECTS

Including indicator variables for the trade partner imposing the trade barrier against U.S. exports controls for the possibility that other country-specific factors such as market size or preferential trade agreements influence the choice of strategy. States with larger markets promise greater potential gains from any market access improvement (Guzman and Simmons, 2005). The United States could be less likely to initiate disputes against Canada and Mexico because NAFTA provides an alternative venue.[44]

The distribution of trade complaints varies by trade partner. Of the trade barriers, 22 percent were EU measures, 18 percent were Korean, and 17 percent were Japanese. Canada and Mexico each had 9 percent of the barriers, Malaysia and India had 8 percent, Brazil 6 percent, and Singapore 3 percent.

Statistical Analysis of U.S. Forum Choice

I examine the selection of WTO complaints using logistic regression to analyze the decision to file a complaint for a particular barrier in a given year. Models 1 and 2 are population-averaged cross-section time series regression models including fixed effects for partner.[45] The first model is the base model for the analysis presenting the core variables. Model 2 includes additional controls for the trade partner's economic interests, which reduce the sample due to missing data on some of these covariates. In both models, I estimate standard errors clustered on the individual trade barrier in order to take into account possible correlation among observations over time for the same barrier. Another way to address this correlation is to directly model the panel-level variation as a random effect for each barrier. Model 3 uses a random-effects estimator that relaxes the equal-correlation assumption of the pooled estimator. The trade partner fixed effects are dropped here to improve efficiency. Results are consistent but the panel-level variance estimated in this model does not have a statistically significant effect.[46] Cross-section variation across

---

[44] Industries are empowered to initiate disputes directly under NAFTA Article 19. Indeed, the U.S. government has initiated only one NAFTA dispute under the Article 20 provision for government-to-government adjudication, while there have been over thirty Article 19 disputes initiated by U.S. companies against Mexico and Canada. The Article 20 dispute is included in the dataset as a bilateral negotiation, while Article 19 NAFTA cases initiated by companies are not mentioned in the NTE and are not included in the dataset.

[45] The group variable is the trade barrier.

[46] The likelihood ratio test for the variance is p-value > .498.

barriers rather than within-barrier variation over time provides the main power for estimating selection of WTO complaints. This reflects the fact that some important predictors related to the barrier itself such as the policy type and distortionary level do not change over time. Others that vary over time, such as political contributions, nonetheless have greater difference across sectors than by year. The generosity of the sector relative to other sectors determines political influence more than minor changes in funding year to year. It is the characteristics of the specific barrier and sector that shape choices over trade strategies.

The results shown in table 4.2 confirm that political pressure influences the choice of cases for WTO adjudication. Both political contributions by the industry and the Section 301 mechanism by which Congress applies pressure on the executive branch have a statistically significant positive effect on the likelihood that a complaint will be raised as a WTO dispute.

The substantive effect of political contributions is large, as can be seen through a comparison of how changing the variable influences the predicted probability for initiating a WTO dispute when all other variables are held constant.[47] I estimate the first difference for the quantity of interest based on the estimates from model 1 in table 4.2. Increasing the level of political contributions by one standard deviation above the mean while holding other variables constant more than doubles the predicted probability of WTO dispute initiation for a given barrier in a single year.[48] This is approximate to setting contributions to the level of the computer industry, which gave $5.8 million in the 1996 election cycle, with the probability of initiating a WTO dispute when setting the political contributions variable to the level of the agriculture industry, which gave $26.4 million in the 1996 election cycle.[49]

The effect of contributions does not appear to vary substantially by party recipient. When replacing the total contributions with the value of contributions to either the Republicans or the Democrats, the coefficient is positive and significant for each although slightly larger for

[47] Using the software Clarify, I simulate model parameters from their asymptotic sampling distribution and compute the Monte Carlo estimates of predicted probability of a WTO dispute initiation. See Michael Tomz, Jason Wittenberg, and Gary King, CLARIFY: Software for Interpreting and Presenting Statistical Results (Version 2.1; Stanford University, University of Wisconsin, and Harvard University 5 January 2003), available at http://gking.harvard.edu.

[48] The simulation estimates a first difference of 0.008 with a 95 percent confidence interval from 0.002 to 0.017 which increases from the base probability of 0.005.

[49] Note that the CRP data on contributions aggregate computer and software industries together, whereas in other economic control variables measured by the OECD these are separate.

TABLE 4.2
Logistic Regression Model of WTO Dispute Complaints.

Variables	Model 1		Model 2		Model 3	
Political contributions	0.724*	(0.258)	0.767*	(0.299)	0.912*	(0.459)
Section 301	3.002*	(0.534)	3.552*	(0.686)	3.272*	(0.517)
Production value	−0.536	(0.350)	−0.219	(0.491)	−0.130	(0.714)
Exports value	0.443	(0.236)	0.158	(0.521)	0.203	(0.596)
MPEN (partner)	0.015*	(0.007)	0.013	(0.010)	0.021*	(0.011)
MPEN growth			4.445*	(1.562)	4.749*	(1.713)
Empl. share (partner)			−0.00	(0.014)	0.004	(0.018)
Trade balance			0.274*	(0.103)	0.218*	(0.074)
MFN tariff rate			−0.00	(0.008)	−0.001	(0.012)
Import policy	1.069*	(0.388)	1.140*	(0.458)	0.979*	(0.448)
Distortion	1.217*	(0.506)	0.880	(0.561)	1.073*	(0.512)
Progress	−0.868*	(0.347)	−0.731*	(0.307)	−0.696*	(0.337)
Duration	−0.164	(0.096)	−0.038	(0.101)	−0.083	(0.094)
EU	1.168	(0.746)	0.560	(0.986)		
Japan	0.761	(0.818)	−0.654	(1.332)		
Mexico	0.897	(0.805)	1.227	(1.132)		
Korea	0.538	(0.775)	0.125	(1.046)		
Non-OECD	0.394	(0.770)	1.149	(0.916)		
Intercept	−15.984*	(5.807)	−18.087*	(5.296)	−11.590*	(54.685)
Wald chi-squared	82.62		122.61		68.82	
N	1,825		1,428		1,428	
Barriers	403		327		327	

Note: Data are trade barriers listed in the National Trade Estimate Reports during the period 1995 to 2004 that were industry specific. Models 1 and 2 are pooled time series with robust standard errors clustered by trade barrier shown in parentheses. Canada is the omitted comparison group for the trade partner indicator variables, and non-OECD groups the trade barriers of Brazil, India, Malaysia, and Singapore. Model 3 uses the random-effects estimator that incorporates panel-level variance for each trade barrier. Trade partner fixed effects are dropped in model 3. In models 2 and 3, an indicator variable for cases with missing data on employment share of partner was included but is not shown. *Significant at the 5 percent level.

Democratic contributions (results not shown). There is high correlation of .82 between Democratic and Republican contributions by industry.

An alternative measure of political influence that examines the level of organization within the industry also has a significant positive effect on the probability that a case will be raised in either WTO adjudication or multilateral negotiations. Organization is measured by a variable that counts the number of industry associations within the aggregate two-digit ISIC industry. For example, there was one industry association for ISIC 30 computer and office equipment, five associations for ISIC 34 motor vehicles, twenty-one associations for ISIC 17 textiles, and forty-two associations for ISIC 1 agriculture.[50] I expect that more associations corresponds with more lobbying activity. For industries with more associations there is a greater probability that any given trade barrier will affect exporters that have close ties with an industry association that will lobby for their interests. I use model 1 from table 4.2 and replace the political contributions measure with the organization measure. Whereas contributions vary by year, however, my measure of organization is time invariant. The coefficient for the associations variable in the WTO adjudication outcome estimates is positive and highly significant (results not presented here). This additional test shows that political influence is robust to measures of contributions or organization.

The effect of a trade measure being selected for Section 301 investigation is even larger. In the aggregate data used in the regression analysis, there are eighteen Section 301 cases, and twelve were raised as WTO disputes for adjudication. When using multivariate regression to control for other factors, the pattern for Section 301 to encourage WTO adjudication is even more stark. Moving the variable for Section 301 from zero to one increases the predicted probability of initiating a WTO dispute from 0.005 to 0.09.[51]

The characteristics of the partner industry also influence the decision to file a WTO complaint. Those industries with high import penetration are significantly more likely to be raised in WTO adjudication. A shift of trade partner import penetration ratio from 20 to 40 more than doubles the estimated predicted probability of dispute initiation.[52] Models 2 and 3 add growth of import penetration to show that the change component of import penetration is significant. Rather than avoiding WTO adjudication for cases with high stakes for the trade partner, it appears that governments are more likely to use WTO adjudication for

[50] I thank Wendy Hansen for sharing these data. I have aggregated her industry associations data from the four-digit NAICS level to two-digit ISIC by using the concordance provided by the U.S. Department of Commerce and summing the total number of four-digit NAICS industry associations that fall within the corresponding ISIC category. See Hansen, Mitchell, and Drope (2005) for the original data explanation.

[51] For model 1, The simulations estimate a first difference of 0.08 with a 95 percent confidence interval from 0.028 to 0.171.

[52] The mean import penetration ratio is 14, with a standard deviation of 65. Note that this variable was available only for OECD countries, and takes a zero value for the non-OECD partners. Results are robust to instead dropping the non-OECD partners from the sample. For model 1, the simulations estimate a first difference of 0.002 ($SE = 0.001$), which increases from the base probability of 0.005.

these tough cases. On the other hand, the control variables added in models 2 and 3 for employment share and tariff rates appear to have no substantial effect.

The variables measuring economic interests are useful to show that the effect of political contributions holds even when controlling for industry size and trade interests. They appear to have little independent influence on the filing decision. Only the trade balance with the partner in the affected industry is significant. The positive sign confirms that the United States is more likely to file where it has a positive trade balance indicating some comparative advantage for entry into the market. Neither is there a consistent pattern of partner selection as seen by the insignificant partner indicator variables. The option of another dispute resolution venue for NAFTA partners does not substantially reduce use of WTO adjudication with Canada and Mexico.[53]

The nature of the policy issues plays a large role in selection. Trade barriers that arise directly from import policies are the most likely trade measures to be targeted in WTO adjudication. Government agencies trying to maximize their win rate will prefer these measures as easy legal cases where WTO rules and jurisprudence offer more clarity about the legal standard compared with newer areas of trade regulations such as services, IPR, and technical standards. The data show a strong relationship between the distortionary effect of the barrier and the choice of WTO adjudication. As expected, barriers that are showing progress toward resolution of the complaint are significantly less likely to become the subject of WTO adjudication.

Further Robustness Tests

Several alternative model specifications reveal that the importance of political contributions is robust to changing the control variables or statistical estimation model. In additional analysis, I reestimate model 1 with variables for the U.S. industry employment share, industry concentration, and FDI outflows of the industry. In all of these specifications, the political contributions variable remains approximately the same magnitude and statistical significance.

The findings are also robust to choice of a different statistical model and subsets of the data. Results are similar when separating outcomes into categories of no negotiation, negotiation, and WTO adjudication

---

[53] The design of NAFTA may account in part for this pattern because the defendant can delay panel composition in NAFTA but not in the WTO. The WTO calls for the director general to establish a panel within twenty days of the request.

and using a multinomial logit regression model to estimate strategy choice for a single cross-section of the trade barrier dataset (contributions and control variables measured for the first year of the barrier). I also reestimate model 1 on the subset of barriers where some negotiation is mentioned in the report (dropping the cases that are not even subject to a negotiation). The political contributions coefficient is remarkably consistent even for this smaller sample of 249 barriers and 1,001 observations in time series analysis (model 1 estimates a coefficient 0.86 with standard error 0.28, significant to the 1 percent level).

In sum, there is a clear pattern in the selection of WTO cases that favors those industries that give more contributions. The United States is the most likely to choose adjudication for barriers that affect an industry that offers political contributions and when there is strong protectionist resistance by the trade partner due to high import penetration.

A final concern may be that there is bias in the generation of the cases in the dataset because they include only trade measures listed in the National Trade Estimate Report written by the USTR. It would be a problem for the central conclusions reported here only if industries that make more political contributions are *less likely* to have their trade problems reported in the NTE. Typically one would expect the opposite—those industries that offer political contributions are likely to have their trade problems overrepresented in the NTE reports. This direction of bias would imply that the results here, if anything, underestimate the role of political contributions in selection of WTO cases.

Looking closely at specific disputes will allow more attention to how political pressures influence trade strategies. When exporters encounter an obstacle to market access, there are multiple stages in the development of strategy that involve discussion among industry actors and government. Often the foreign trade measure remains contested for years as governments pursue a range of different trade strategies. What leads the parties to resort to adjudication for any given dispute at a particular time? Changing market pressures may determine incentives for the industry. Development of precedent through other cases contributes to new expectations about the legal status of a barrier. Empowerment of political representatives close to the affected industry or rising diplomatic tensions affect the tradeoff between legislative demand for action and executive restraint. Variables at this level of detail are not fully captured in the aggregate statistical analysis, and case studies will offer more leverage to compare the influence of such economic, legal, and political changes.

The next two sections will take different approaches to examine specific trade disputes. First, the case study on the Boeing-Airbus dispute focuses closely on a single trade issue, European subsidies for its civil aircraft industry, that will be studied over time following the past forty years of negotiations and adjudication. The case was chosen for its importance as the largest export industry in the United States. U.S. support for the industry is unquestioned, and it has consistently enjoyed high levels of access to government. This case study thus controls for industry influence. Even for this favored industry, however, considerable debate emerged over the best approach to address the equally strong commitment by Europe supporting development of its aircraft industry. This debate brought in calls from Congress for tough action and cautionary advice from diplomats. The industry itself voiced concerns about negative repercussions from challenging Europe on the matter. Only after decades of repeated negotiations and threats of adjudication did the case lead to a frontal assault with twin WTO complaints by the United States and Europe against each other's subsidy policies filed in 2004 that led to a pair of violation rulings and are widely expected to result in a negotiated settlement. Even for the leading export industry, adjudication played a role to demonstrate to Congress and Europe that the executive would no longer accept partial compromises.

The second case study section will discuss several trade issues with China in order to focus on how different strategies were adopted to address these barriers from China's accession to the WTO in December 2001 until the present. As the rising new export powerhouse, China drew the attention of Congress to become the most politically important trade problem. The China case section will examine the role of bilateral negotiations and WTO adjudication to help the executive manage tensions with Congress and achieve progress with China on currency policies, intellectual property protection, and industrial policy. Looking more broadly at one bilateral relationship highlights the connections across issues. From a perspective of legal argument or economic interest, U.S. demands for change in discriminatory policy against auto parts or semiconductor imports have little substantive connection with the criticism of China's undervalued currency. But as the executive faced a political problem to demonstrate tough enforcement policy, calibrating strategy across a set of issues helped to balance demands for action.

Boeing-Airbus Dispute

The first case examines one of the most important disputes taken to WTO adjudication that is seen as a test to the system itself. Boeing and Airbus represent premier export industries for the United States and EU. Civil aircraft is held up as the classic case for strategic trade policy in which imperfect competition, economies of scale, and spillover technology could justify active industrial policy by governments in support of their home industry.[54] Busch (1999, p. 60) describes how the willingness of the respective governments to contribute billions in subsidies to the companies leads them to remain on the "brink of a trade war" even as fear of such conflict encourages restraint and negotiated compromises. This study will consider the role of adjudication in helping states to achieve this delicate balance between support for a strategic industry and avoidance of full-scale trade conflict. Attention is given to market incentives for the industry, demands from Congress, and priorities of the executive. For a dispute that has been an ongoing issue for forty years, these shifts account for movement from an emphasis on negotiated agreements to legal action.

Setting the Stage: OECD and GATT Negotiations

Three U.S. firms dominated the market for civilian aircraft production in the 1970s when European governments decided to use subsidies to overcome the tremendous development costs that would otherwise have driven smaller European national firms out of the market entirely. The consortium led by France and Germany and later joined by Spain and the United Kingdom channeled subsidies to allow the market entry of Airbus in 1970 as a major new competitor with U.S. firms.[55] Forty years later, the smaller U.S. firms have left the market for civil aircraft (Lockheed) or merged with Boeing (McDonnell Douglas), and Airbus has grown to rival Boeing in sales volume. Why did the U.S. government not challenge the subsidies for Airbus *before* it seized market share from U.S. companies?

The United States could have engaged in several strategies to defend the interests of domestic aircraft producers. First, the United States could have offered equivalent subsidies to domestic aircraft producers in an attempt to outspend the European consortium. While Boeing has been the recipient of indirect subsidies through tax breaks from Washington

---

[54] See Krugman (1986) for discussion of academic and policy debate. Busch (1999) describes how strategic trade arguments influenced government policy toward civil aircraft industry and demonstrates the positive externalities internalized in both the U.S. and European economies from industry spillovers.

[55] Airbus Industrie began as a consortium that coordinated production among the leading European aerospace firms. Its historic launch was announced at the Paris Air Show in May 1969 as an agreement between France and Germany, and the first order was placed in 1970 by Air France. The consortium later expanded to include British and Spanish participation, and since 1998 the European Aeronautic Defence and Space Company has been the majority shareholder in Airbus as an integrated company.

State, defense procurement, and funds for research and development, the U.S. government refrained from following the European strategy to offer direct subsidies. Second, the United States could have used trade instruments to threaten Europe. One option would have been for the United States to impose countervailing duties against the subsidized Airbus sales. Boeing advised against this policy because it feared an escalating tit-for-tat response with retaliation from European governments (Waldmann and Culbert, 1998, p. 174). The company already had concerns about losses arising from directed procurement demands, and their major customers in Europe were national airline carriers that could readily be influenced by their government against Boeing purchases. Another option would have been to apply retaliatory measures closing off the U.S. market as a threat to coerce Europe to stop funding Airbus. None of these actions were pursued. From the beginning, the industry was unhappy with European support for Airbus but saw a trade war as the worst outcome for their interests.

Diplomatic stakes dictated against challenging Europe's decision to support the civilian aircraft industry. The issue had ramifications for national security given the close interdependence between civilian aircraft industries and defense industries. Asking Europe to allow the failure of their national aerospace industry was not simply about fair trade. U.S. geopolitical priorities at the time were focused on efforts to keep Europeans unified in opposition to the USSR in the Cold War. In 1966, France had withdrawn from NATO military command after several years of growing tensions with the United States that led to withdrawal of U.S. troops stationed in France. West Germany was also showing a more independent foreign policy as Chancellor Willy Brandt in 1970 espoused rapprochement with Eastern Bloc countries. Still mired in the Vietnam War, this was not a propitious time for the United States to pursue an aggressive trade policy toward Europe.

Rather, the United States took an accommodating approach that allowed Airbus to make its market entry but attempted to restrain the threat of competition. Using the OECD forum to discuss export financing and the ongoing GATT trade round to address trade and subsidies policies, the U.S. government negotiated new rules for the aircraft sector together with the European governments. Competitive use of export financing as a tool for export promotion was a problem for countries like the United States that had a mandate for their trade credit agency to operate close to market rates. In an early effort to address European support for Airbus, governments in 1975 concluded a "gentlemen's agreement" in the OECD setting limits on credit terms (Moravcsik, 1989). Despite this agreement, "predatory" export financing was accused of playing a critical role to win first sales by Airbus as favorable credit terms persuaded airlines to accept the new model A300 over Boeing's well-proven 747 model.[56] The Treasury Department responded to calls for "immediate action" from Congress with the pledge to renegotiate the OECD agreement.[57] Ultimately the move by the United States to match European financing terms led European states in 1985 to accept a new OECD agreement, the Large Aircraft Sector Understanding, which set minimum interest rates for export financing.[58]

Parallel to the multilateral negotiations of the Tokyo Round, the United States, European governments, and others negotiated a "pluri-lateral" agreement called "Agreement on Trade in Civil Aircraft" that was concluded in 1979. Initiative for the agreement came from efforts by U.S. industry leaders, which proposed in the Aerospace Industry Sector Advisory Committee that the U.S. government negotiate a sectoral agreement for the elimination of tariffs and discipline of subsidies (Waldmann and Culbert, 1998, p. 174). In negotiations, the Europeans sought to eliminate the 5 percent U.S. tariff on civil aircraft, and the United States sought to restrain European subsidies. The final agreement achieved the goals in terms of tariff elimination and endorsing that trade in civil aircraft would be subject to the regulations in the new Agreement on Subsidies and Countervailing Measures negotiated as part of the Tokyo Round. The general weakness of the subsidies agreement itself, however, meant this provision had little backbone. U.S. negotiators were unable to negotiate explicit limits on financial support, and had to be satisfied with a clause in the Aircraft Agreement requiring that civil aircraft prices reflect "reasonable expectation of recoupment of all costs," which they hoped would limit subsidies (Piper, 1980, p. 238). The U.S. aerospace industry representatives issued a favorable public report assessing the agreement and advocated its adoption when lobbying Congress (McGuire, 1997, p. 86).

The two agreements in the OECD and GATT reveal a willingness by the United States to back away from confrontation. Members of Congress called for tough action against a threat to a vital industry and used strong rhetoric to condemn unfair trade practices. But the industry

[56] Jack Pierce, treasurer of Boeing Co., testimony, Hearings Before the Subcommittee on Export-Import Bank Extensions, 97th Congress, 2nd session, 1978, pp. 465, 467.

[57] See exchange of correspondence between California Representative Mark Hannaford and Blumenthal recorded in Extensions of Remarks, Congressional Record, 95th Congress, 2nd session, 1978, 124, pt. 21: 28456.

[58] The Export-Import Bank took on such an active role to support Boeing sales that it become known as "the Boeing Bank" (McGuire, 1997, p. 57). McGuire (1997, pp. 60–61) also notes that in addition to European leaders' recognition that the United States could out-finance European terms, new practices to lease aircraft rendered export financing less central to aircraft sales.

itself urged against retaliatory threats to close off U.S. markets because they feared a trade war in which European governments retaliated against U.S. actions by discouraging purchase of American aircraft. Only in the area of export finance did industry concern point to direct action. Even here, however, tit-for-tat competition in export financing was capped before it could get out of hand. Given the rejection of unilateral strategies by industry, but faced with concerns in Congress, the administration chose to focus on negotiating rules to lay the groundwork for future actions within a rule bound framework. Against the backdrop of conflicting interests, the rules merely papered over underlying differences with vague terms such as "reasonable" that would give rise to ongoing disagreements about compliance. In the 1970s, adjudication was never broached as an option because existing rules did not regulate procurement, export financing, or subsidies. The Aircraft Agreement would set the stage for future legal action. Article 8 of the agreement established a committee to address disputes that would review and issue rulings on any matter raised by a member. Governments also retained their right to use the GATT dispute settlement process.

As the market leader Boeing may have underestimated the commercial threat from Airbus, and indeed its sales continued rising during the first years of Airbus. Milner and Yoffie (1989, p. 261) argue that export-dependent multinational firms switch from free trade preferences to support calls for government intervention against foreign competition only when they experience sharp profit declines, and so the continued profitability of U.S. civilian aircraft firms in the 1970s made them slower to call for government help. The first evidence that Airbus would cut into Boeing sales appeared in 1978, and this may well have increased its pressure on government to somehow restrain European subsidies. By the mid-1980s it was readily apparent that Boeing was steadily losing market share to Airbus and reporting lower profits, and this led to a renewed trade debate. The U.S. aircraft industry began to consider the possibility of using threats to restrict the U.S. market as leverage to change European policies.

Amidst a crisis of confidence about declining American competitiveness, political pressure from Congress urged the administration to take a stronger position against foreign trade barriers. Speaking in June 1985 during Senate confirmation hearings for the newly nominated USTR Clayton Yeutter, Republican Senator Robert Dole warned that while nobody wanted a trade war, "a point may soon be reached where economic arguments are replaced by political imperatives." Senator John Danforth pushed more directly to urge Yeutter: "Do you intend to address the intent of Congress seriously? Or do you intend to be dragged kicking and screaming into 301 enforcement?" (Dryden, 1995, p. 306). Criticism from Democrats was even stronger, and was backed by a legislative proposal to impose a 25 percent tariff increase on states with a large trade surplus. Although this debate was more focused on Japan than Europe, congressional ire over trade policy continued to set subsidies to Airbus as a priority. In response to pressure from Congress, Yeutter promised to take a "strong stance" against unfair trade practices. President Ronald Reagan gave a speech in September 1985 calling for pursuit of "fair trade" and shortly thereafter named European subsidies to Airbus as third on a list of foreign barriers harming U.S. exports (Tyson, 1992, p. 203). The next release of the USTR Report on foreign trade barriers added subsidies to Airbus as a prominent trade barrier.

In this heated trade climate, the USTR began to consider initiation of a Section 301 investigation against Airbus. The Trade and Tariff Act of 1984 had added a provision allowing USTR to self-initiate Section 301 investigations against foreign trade barriers (the earlier procedure required a petition from the harmed industry). Despite the political pressure from Congress, however, the shared concerns of diplomats and industry favored negotiation over threats or adjudication. During the December 4, 1985 meeting of the Reagan administration "strike force" established to address foreign trade barriers, Secretary of State George Shultz argued strongly against confronting the Europeans about Airbus saying that it would be a "threat to their manhood" (Dryden, 1995, p. 316). The commerce department also advised against filing a GATT complaint because it would be too confrontational, and only the USTR officials sought more specific action. The meeting ended with a decision to pursue informal negotiations with Europe, and not initiate a Section 301 petition or file a GATT complaint. This moderate approach pleased industry. Boeing did not want a Section 301 petition or any aggressive action that would risk harming relations with its best customers in Europe. As noted by Busch (1999, p. 50), "the tone in Washington has been more heated than in Seattle or St. Louis" as politicians called for tough action and even criticized the passive response to European gains by Boeing.

The victory of the Democrats in the congressional midterm election of November 1986 increased the pressure from Congress on the administration's trade policy. The Democrats regained control of the Senate from Republicans and reintroduced the 1986 trade legislation that included a mandate for retaliation against unfair trade partners and measures to "strengthen" USTR capacity to act against foreign trade barriers. This began an intense period of congressional-executive gamesmanship over who had authority to control trade policy as Reagan would label radical protectionist proposals from Congress for mandated actions against foreign trade partners "kamikaze legislation" and eventually veto one proposal in 1987 (Cohen, 2000, p. 220).

The market competition in the aircraft industry also heightened as Airbus launched another program for a pair of new models (Airbus 330/340) in 1987 to achieve its goal of a family of aircraft that could attract airline business through the complementarities across models. Airbus had only just showcased the first flight of the A320 model that same year and was already preparing for new planes that would extend its competition into the market for long-range aircraft. Tyson (1992, pp. 174, 190) argues that government subsidies to Airbus, which by the end of 1988 had grown to a total of $5.6 billion and held more than three times this value relative to corporate borrowing rates, allowed Airbus to "leapfrog both Boeing and McDonnell Douglas in technology, thereby gaining industry control over the pace of new product launch in the 1980s." The financial risk of new model development was so high in the aircraft industry that private companies were cautious while public launch aid for Airbus allowed it to be more aggressive as a quasi-government entity. The new models were forecast to compete with the latest McDonnell Douglas program (MD-11) and would shortly force Boeing to launch a new competitor itself (B777). Economic analysis shows that European subsidies to support Airbus market entry harmed welfare in the United States as production shifted to Europe, although technological innovation and lower consumer prices could partially offset these losses (Tyson, 1992, p. 194).

The European governments remained strongly committed to support for Airbus. They defended the legality of their subsidies, which served the GATT Aircraft Code goal to maintain a "competitive marketplace" by sustaining Airbus as a viable market competitor, and they noted European subsidies were matched by indirect subsidies in the United States through funding for aerospace-related military and space programs (McGuire, 1997, pp. 121–122). Beyond its value as a strategic industry, the Airbus project was also seen as an important showcase of successful European collaboration. Economic and political purposes strongly united behind support for Airbus.

Ongoing refusal by Europeans to restrain aircraft subsidies posed a political problem as the Reagan administration faced demands to "get tough" on trade partners from Congress. Bilateral discussions with British, French, and German officials in early February 1987 yielded no results. The British minister in charge of aerospace trade told U.S. negotiators in effect that they had no business meddling in the European aircraft industry, and French Premier Jacques Chirac went further to warn of counterretaliation against any U.S. restrictions on Airbus

(Dryden, 1995, pp. 331–332). Returning from these meetings determined to file a Section 301 case against Europe, USTR officials prepared proposals for action to be discussed at a February 13 meeting of the Economic Policy Council. Dryden (1995, p. 332) reports that the meeting instead ended with agreement to pursue GATT consultations after the chairman of McDonnell Douglas called Reagan administration cabinet members to oppose initiation of a 301 case—the company later admitted that European airlines had warned they would boycott McDonnell Douglas products if it backed strong action. State Department officials raised fears that relations with NATO allies would be strained by confronting Europe on Airbus subsidies (McGuire, 1997, p. 129). The decision to pursue GATT consultations represented a retreat from a Section 301 case that could lead to retaliatory trade war but was an effort to take negotiations to a new level.

Adjudication as Pressure on Negotiations

In the first foray into legal action for this dispute, the U.S. filed a GATT complaint February 25, 1987.[59] The legal arguments charged that the EC had violated the Aircraft Code of 1979 through offering prohibited subsidies and applying pressure on airlines to purchase Airbus. Challenging the subsidies by the Aircraft Code, which was a plurilateral agreement nested in the GATT regime, was seen as less confrontational toward the EC than it would have been to request a GATT dispute panel under GATT Article XXIII (McGuire, 1997, p. 120). Dispute resolution procedures under the Aircraft Code were more informal and the agreement acknowledged the role for government support of the aircraft industry. Within a month the United States withdrew its claims when clarification discussions in the special committee convened according to the procedures of the Aircraft Code showed little support for the U.S. position. It referred the issue to further negotiations to clarify rules in the Aircraft Code. The Aircraft Code provided a weak basis for a legal strategy to challenge Airbus because it contained vague clauses about restraint and avoiding adverse effects rather than specific prohibitions. Continued dominance of world markets by Boeing made it hard to demonstrate harm and made U.S. government officials fear losing a ruling should it try to push forward with further legal action (Tyson, 1992, p. 204).

In a move that would foreshadow future tit-for-tat litigation, the EC filed a GATT complaint against the United States in April 1987.

---

[59] See Hudec (1993, p. 544) for a description of the case (AIR/W/62).

The EC complaint focused on tax advantages to purchasers of aircraft produced in the United States, and was withdrawn the next month after clarification that the tax reform conferring such advantage had been allowed to expire.[60] Neither legal complaint was carried through, but negotiations continued in Geneva within the Aircraft Committee and through bilateral channels.

The administration used the ongoing negotiations to parry criticism during congressional hearings on the "Competitiveness of U.S. Commercial Aircraft Industry" held June 23, 1987. The chairman of the Subcommittee on Commerce, Consumer Protection, and Competitiveness, James Florio, launched the hearings with a statement declaring that Airbus subsidies violated GATT principles and threatened the U.S. industry and warning that "Congress cannot and will not ignore the failure of negotiations to produce an acceptable agreement."[61] Deputy USTR Michael Smith concurred that subsidized production by Airbus harmed U.S. industry and gave a detailed update on the GATT negotiations in which he affirmed that "clearly this is not a matter that the administration believes can, should or will drag out. It must address this question" (House Committee, 1987, p. 30; see note 61). Testimony from a Boeing representative affirmed that while skeptical of a positive outcome, the company believed that GATT discussions represented the "proper forum" that was preferred over using Section 301 action or countervailing duties (House Committee, 1987, pp. 64, 66). The chairman of the Aerospace Industries Association urged the representatives to wait for the GATT negotiations to conclude and stated it would be "premature to proceed in an alternative fashion" (House Committee, 1987, p. 86). Despite the ire expressed from congressmen who hinted at threatening Europe, the industry was satisfied with the administration approach to negotiate in GATT. This pattern repeated itself again the following year. Failure to close the differences in negotiations led to Airbus subsidies again being placed on the agenda of Economic Policy Council in May 1988 with another decision not to escalate (Dryden, 1995, p. 335).

A second legal complaint was necessary to push forward negotiations. In April 1989 the United States filed a legal complaint against the EC that challenged government financing of Airbus industrie. The specific issue was triggered by West German government payments to compensate exchange rate losses for firms involved in the privatization of Deutsche

[60] See Hudec (1993, p. 546) for a description of the case (L/6153).
[61] House Committee on Energy and Commerce, Competitiveness of U.S. Commercial Aircraft Industry: Hearing before the Subcommittee on Commerce, Consumer Protection, and Competitiveness, 100th Congress, 1st session, June 23, 1987.

Airbus, one of the partners in the Airbus consortium. The exchange rate guarantee was attacked by USTR Carla Hills as "[t]he most reprehensible type of subsidy. Much, much worse than the usual production subsidies" (Tyson, 1992, p. 206). Over EC objections, the United States insisted this time that the matter should be determined under the Subsidies Code by a GATT dispute panel, and not by the Aircraft Code (Hudec, 1993, p. 577). Claiming that the policy violated Article 9 of the Subsidies Code, which prohibited export subsidies, the United States used this as a wedge issue in a broader attack on the overall problem of government subsidies for Airbus. The legal case was set aside during periods of negotiations and revived again when negotiations reached an impasse. Finally a panel was convened in April 1991. The Europeans argued that GATT regulations did not apply to intra-EC trade and Deutsche Airbus was involved only in components production, but the United States countered that the program subsidized Airbus production, which clearly was exported. After presentations to the panel were completed in October, the panel issued its preliminary ruling against the EC in January, and in March it issued the public report finding that the EC exchange rate guarantee program constituted an export subsidy in violation of the Subsidy Code. As permitted under the GATT dispute procedures, the EC blocked adoption of the report. Yet at the same time it announced that the program would be terminated.

The ruling against the exchange rate scheme pushed the EC toward concluding negotiations on a far-reaching agreement to establish guidelines for subsidies. The Bilateral Large Civil Aircraft Agreement concluded in 1992 was hailed as having brought real concessions from Europe. It would cap direct subsidies to a maximum amount of one-third of development costs. Further measures limited indirect aid by regulating interest rates, military support, and sales inducements while also introducing greater transparency about government payments to their industry. In the assessment of Tyson (1992, p. 209), it was a "noteworthy accomplishment for both sides" that restrained rent-shifting subsidies while allowing beneficial development support. The United States also pushed Europe in the Uruguay Round negotiations to accept that aircraft subsidies would, with a few exceptions, fall within the purvey of the Agreement on Subsidies and Countervailing Measures, which updated the Tokyo Round Subsidies Code with stronger disciplines that are subject to enforcement by WTO dispute settlement. This established both the bilateral agreement and multilateral rules as complementary sets of rules to regulate subsidies, which had been a major objective of the industry (Waldmann and Culbert, 1998, p. 179).

Two factors helped bring these concessions from Europe. First, market changes were important. The Airbus consortium governments were more willing to compromise in 1992 when Airbus had clearly established itself as a success and could conceivably survive with less government support. Whereas the first Airbus plane had been fully funded by governments, later models were starting to repay some of the government funding and relied on a smaller share for total development costs (McGuire, 1997, p. 139). Yet this positive turn was already evident during the height of trade acrimony. In 1986 Airbus had received nearly one-fourth of all aircraft orders to edge out McDonnell Douglas as the second largest producer behind Boeing.[62] By 1987 it was already apparent that the A320 was selling briskly in what was a boom year for aircraft sales in both the United States and Europe, and there was growing interest among airlines for orders of the new A330/340 including a $2.5 billion commitment from Northwest Airlines. Nonetheless European negotiators then were defiant about their right to support the industry. The improving market position of Airbus would have supported agreement at an earlier date, but there was no crack in the resistance of European officials to U.S. demands.

A second factor to encourage a more conciliatory approach in Europe was the adjudication strategy, which demonstrated that the United States would no longer defer the issue. When the "Strike Force" decided not to initiate a Section 301 investigation to target Airbus subsidies in 1986, it revealed that the United States had no stomach for a trade war. Even the GATT complaint in 1987 represented a tentative move seeking consultations in the Aircraft Committee that were set aside when consensus did not emerge in the committee. This changed in 1991 as the United States pushed forward over EC objections to raise its GATT complaint for a panel ruling that policies violated the GATT Subsidies Code. Although the ruling was narrow and case specific, the United States had shown it would directly challenge the GATT consistency of Airbus subsidies. McGuire (1997, p. 168) notes about the ruling that "its crucial importance lay in the fact that the GATT panel ruled that the main GATT Subsidies Code could be used to hear aircraft cases; it was not necessary to refer only to the Aircraft Agreement of 1979." Rather than the ruling itself representing a breakthrough in legal interpretation, it was a watershed event to show the willingness of the U.S. government to use the stronger legal agreement. Alongside the complaint against the German exchange rate guarantee, the U.S. government in May 1991 had also begun consultations preliminary to filing a broader GATT complaint against all EC subsidies for Airbus

---

[62] *New York Times*, May 28, 1987.

(McGuire, 1997, p. 151).[63] The end of the Cold War in 1991 made it less likely that there would occur a repeat of events in 1985 where the secretary of state intervened to hold back U.S. trade demands. The more aggressive stance by the U.S. government was also backed by the private sector, which now saw Airbus competition cutting into profit margins. In a speech to the Council of Foreign Relations in January 1992, Boeing CEO Frank Schrontz said there was a strong case for taking retaliatory action against Airbus, and McDonnell Douglas launched its own offensive through exploratory talks with Taiwan for a possible joint venture that would promise substantial subsidies from the Taiwanese government as a counterweight to Airbus (Tyson, 1992, p. 210). EC officials were fearful the United States would continue its successful litigation strategy and this time challenge the entire subsidy regime backing the Airbus consortium. Dryden (1995, p. 373) attributes the new movements in GATT adjudication along with the fear of a subsidies war with prompting the Europeans to accept an agreement that capped their subsidies. This time it was the European side that feared trade friction was harming relations (McGuire, 1997, p. 145). The timing of the agreement in 1992 followed shifts in U.S. resolve that were communicated through changes to legal strategy.

The first phase of U.S.-EC trade friction over civilian aircraft illustrates a complex dynamic among domestic interests in the United States. Not only State Department officials concerned about diplomatic relations, but also the industry concerned about sales, voiced repeated calls for restraint from tough trade measures that could offend European governments. Avoiding a trade war was a shared priority of both the executive and industry. Yet the growing competitive threat from Airbus and pressure from Congress for unilateral action also led to the executive and industry backing the use of a strategy to combine adjudication and negotiation. As market stakes grew larger and with the use of even more egregious subsidy policies by Europe, the United States ratcheted up the level of pressure from "soft" litigation in the Aircraft committee to "hard" litigation in the Subsidies Code. This helped to convince European officials to negotiate a new agreement that met the main demands for restraint on overall subsidies and greater transparency. That agreement would hold the peace for a decade, before trade tensions again spiked as the release of new product models shook market stability.

[63] The 1992 agreement preempted this action so that the United States never formally filed its threatened complaint.

Tit-for-Tat WTO Adjudication

By 2000 it was clear that Airbus threatened not only profit margins for Boeing but even its status as market leader. In the next five years U.S. share of world aircraft deliveries fell 20 percent and Boeing revenues fell by 25 percent.[64] In 2003, Airbus placed more orders and delivered more aircraft than Boeing. Since then the companies have traded places as the top producer of civilian aircraft, with Airbus again edging into the lead in 2008. The two competitors were also facing off with release of new models as Boeing announced plans for development of the B787 "Dreamliner" at the end of 2003 and Airbus launched the A380 "Superjumbo" a year later.[65] Competing bids for a $40 billion U.S. military contract for aerial refueling tankers also loomed as a critical point of contention. These market conditions had both economic and political effects.

From the industry perspective, Boeing hoped to forestall further subsidies for the development of the A350, which would compete with its new B787 model. Boeing sought to paint Airbus as violating international law in order to tarnish its standing in the competition for procurement contracts. The fact that Boeing itself became embroiled in a major corruption scandal related to this procurement bid in 2003 only heightened incentives to launch accusations at Airbus. Both goals led Boeing to call for the government to take any action necessary to end subsidies for Airbus. This was a departure for the company that had in previous rounds of bilateral negotiations been cautious. In 1999, USTR Charlene Barshefsky met with Boeing CEO Phil Condit to ask whether he would support the U.S. government filing a WTO case against the EU subsidies to Airbus. His refusal to commit led to shelving plans for a case at that time.[66]

In Congress, headlines that the leading U.S. export industry had been surpassed by Airbus rallied support to Boeing's cause. House Democrats in a letter to President Bush on March 31, 2004 criticized the lack of action to enforce trade agreements and urged him to direct USTR to request immediate action to seek consultations under WTO dispute settlement for seven priority trade barriers including the EU subsidies to Airbus. Days before a critical negotiation meeting between U.S. and

---

[64] Figures cited in the opening statement of the U.S. submission to WTO panel, 15 November, 2006, available at http://www.ustr.gov/webfm_send/816.

[65] The two new models are not direct competitors given size differences. In the largest size market the A380 competes with the B747. In the midsize market the B787 competes with the A350, a new model updating the A330.

[66] *Financial Times*, October 8, 2004.

EU negotiators, Representative Norman Dicks, a senior Democrat from Washington State with long involvement with Boeing given its close ties to his district, spoke at length about the problem of subsidized Airbus competition harming Boeing and concluded that the United States should file a WTO case unless the EU would agree to end its subsidies.[67] Politicization extended to the presidential level in the midst of a heated election campaign in fall 2004 as Democratic candidate John Kerry criticized President Bush: "[F]or the last four years George Bush has been asleep at the wheel when it comes to enforcing existing trade agreements."[68] President Bush responded with a promise to bring a WTO complaint against the EU if it continued to subsidize Airbus.[69]

Given a green light from the industry leader and under pressure from Congress and the Kerry campaign, the government quickly took action. On October 6, 2004, USTR Robert Zoellick announced withdrawal from the Bilateral Aircraft Agreement and filed a complaint at the WTO requesting consultations under the dispute settlement procedures.[70] Charging that the Airbus had received $15 billion in subsidies for the development of new aircraft models (so-called "launch aid"), Zoellick said, "The EU and Airbus appear to want to buy more time for more subsidies for more planes. This isn't fair and it violates international trading rules."[71] European officials immediately countered by filing their own complaint at the WTO challenging that the U.S. indirect support to Boeing through subsidies for R&D, tax incentives, and military contracts has amounted to $23 billion in illegal subsidies in violation of WTO rules.[72]

The role of politics in the decision was a source of widespread media speculation. European officials said the United States had broken off bilateral talks because of election-year politics. In Washington, congressional Democrats welcomed the decision but were reported by

---

[67] *Congressional Record*—extensions, September 30, 2004, Cong Rec E 1757, vol. 150, no. 121.

[68] *Washington Post*, October 7, 2004

[69] *New York Times*, October 1, 2004.

[70] DS316 filed October 6, 2004, "European Communities Measures Affecting Trade in Large Civil Aircraft." The United States amended its legal claims in a second complaint (DS347) filed January 31, 2006, but the two complaints are treated as one dispute.

[71] *New York Times*, October 7, 2004. The largest share of subsidies consists of launch aid, but the U.S. complaint also targets subsidized infrastructure and other specific benefits conferred to Airbus by governments. Some public statements raise the figure of government subsidies to as much as $40 billion.

[72] DS317 filed October 6, 2004, "United States Measures Affecting Trade in Large Civil Aircraft." The EU amended its legal claims in a second complaint (DS353) filed June 27, 2005, but the two complaints are treated as one dispute.

the *New York Times* to be seeking credit for pushing the administration to take action as they tried to "prevent the Bush administration from scoring political points in the final three weeks of the campaign."[73]

Once the election was over, the Bush administration gave priority to patching up relations with Europe that had been damaged by disagreement over policies toward Iraq, and the WTO dispute was put on a back burner for several months. The dispute settlement timeline allowed the United States and EU to request formal panel review of their respective complaints at the end of January since the consultation period had ended without producing a mutual agreement, but they deferred in favor of continuing the bilateral talks for an agreement. Trade experts noted that President Bush had an upcoming trip to Europe aimed to deepen transatlantic cooperation, and a panel request would harm the atmosphere for talks on other issues.[74] Instead, both parties agreed to a "standstill" in litigation and pledged to refrain from new subsidies for three months. The EU trade commissioner welcomed the agreement and noted that a U.S. request for a panel in the dispute over Airbus subsidies "might have cast a pall over the president's visit."[75] Ambassador to the United States John Bruton said the decision to return to bilateral negotiations without further legal steps at the WTO "improves the atmosphere" for the coming summit meeting.[76]

But even as transatlantic diplomatic relations began to thaw, the aircraft subsidies negotiations remained unresolved. Despite both sides saying they preferred a negotiated agreement over going back to adjudication, neither would make concessions to break the impasse over how to define subsidies and whether to set a deadline for their elimination. EU Trade Commissioner Peter Mandelson and USTR Robert Zoellick broke off talks in March. Pressure from Congress increased with a unanimous Senate resolution in April calling for a hard line in the dispute. Senators Maria Cantwell and Patty Murray of Washington State, where thousands of Boeing workers are employed, endorsed the resolution and called for resolving the dispute at the WTO as they expressed frustration that U.S. efforts to negotiate were not taken seriously by Europe, which they said continued to pursue subsidy strategies to give Airbus a competitive advantage.[77] A letter from House Democrats to the president on March 31, 2005 criticized the January "standstill," warning that "flip flop trade policy sends a signal of weakness" and urging a

[73] *New York Times*, October 7, 2004.

[74] *Inside U.S. Trade*, January 7, 2005.

[75] *Financial Times*, January 12, 2005

[76] *New York Times*, January 12, 2005.

[77] *Congressional Record*—Senate, April 11, 2005, 151 Cong Rec S 3403 and S 3404.

return to the WTO dispute process unless bilateral agreement emerged within two weeks. WTO dispute settlement again became the central forum as both sides requested a panel May 31, 2005.

The Boeing-Airbus case confronted complex legal arguments and large economic stakes. It has stretched the calendar for regular dispute settlement—the parties could not agree on composition of the panel and the new WTO Director-General Pascal Lamy had to recuse himself so that the panel members were chosen by the deputy director of the WTO in October 2005. For the U.S. panel, members made submissions to the panel in November 2006 with the panel holding its first meeting in March 2007. Although the WTO calls for panels to complete their work within six months, the Boeing-Airbus panels would repeatedly request extensions noting the substantive and procedural complexities of the dispute. At several points during the legal process both parties have discussed a negotiated agreement that would forestall the need to proceed with further legal action. The lengthy litigation has been costly beyond legal fees as the two firms face ongoing uncertainty that affects their estimates about funding. Trade expert Gary Hufbauer of the Institute for International Economics has said that the market uncertainty induced by litigation may affect plane orders.[78] Both governments have made efforts to ensure that the trade dispute does not harm their broader relationship. For example, immediately after escalation of the dispute with request for a panel, the top U.S. and EU trade representatives issued a joint statement about their "determination that this dispute shall not affect our cooperation on wider bilateral and multilateral trade issues."[79]

Nearly six years later the WTO panel issued its decision on the U.S. complaint against Airbus in June 2010, which was followed later by a panel ruling on the EU complaint against Boeing in March 2011. Both of these rulings have been appealed, and the final outcome remains pending. The legal issues come down to conflicting views about what kinds of subsidies are allowed under WTO rules. The United States insists that grants and preferential loans from the government sponsors of Airbus represent illegal export subsidies that have had adverse effects on the U.S. industry to the extent that they nullify benefits to the United States under the GATT Agreement. Europe counters that governments received commercial rates of return on their investments since the loans are repaid by Airbus. The EU complaint against the United States contends subsidies for NASA and Department of Defense R&D along with local state tax preferences are contrary to the subsidy agreement and cause material

[78] *Inside U.S. Trade*, October 26, 2007.
[79] *Washington Post*, May 31, 2005.

injury to the EC industry. Lengthy accounting reports about financial transfers, economic analysis of market effects, and interpretation of the legal agreements constitute the body of the two cases. Yet from the beginning, both governments were expected to be found in violation for some aspects of their subsidy policies.[80] Two earlier WTO disputes on civil aircraft subsidies between Canada and Brazil foreshadow similar legal issues and culminated in a pair of violation rulings followed by further litigation over compliance.[81] Midway through the dispute process an Airbus spokesman noted that Airbus executives had looked at the Embraer and Bombardier experience in the Canada/Brazil aircraft cases and concluded that "at the end of the day both sides are likely to be found to be outside of the bounds of WTO rules somewhere down the line."[82] As predicted, while complex legal arguments were presented before the panels and the rulings offer hundreds of pages of legal analysis (1,049 pages and 850 pages for rulings against Airbus and Boeing, respectively), the final bottom line is that both sides were found in violation for providing large amounts of illegal subsidies. On the scope of claims, the United States has come out ahead given that $20 billion in European subsidies have been found in violation, whereas the ruling against Boeing calls for changes of subsidies worth only $2.7 billion. USTR Ron Kirk declared triumphantly:

> Today a WTO panel confirmed what we have been saying for the last 20 years—that the WTO-inconsistent subsidies that the Europeans gave to Airbus dwarf anything that the U.S. government has given to Boeing. ... This is an important victory for the United States, and particularly for American workers and businesses. It demonstrates the Obama Administration's dedication to using WTO dispute settlement to ensure a level playing field for American workers and businesses.[83]

Setting such proclamations aside, the rulings recommend removal of the specified subsidies after a reasonable period rather than an obligation to repay the amounts. Subsequent legal action would set amounts for authorized retaliation in case of noncompliance for removal of inconsistent subsidies.

---

[80] This was the prediction of Gary Hufbauer, a leading trade policy expert at Institute of International Economics. *Inside U.S. Trade*, August 5, 2009.

[81] DS46 filed by Canada, June 19, 1996, "Brazil Export Financing Programme for Aircraft"; DS70 filed by Brazil, March 10, 1997, "Canada Measures Affecting the Export of Civilian Aircraft."

[82] *Inside U.S. Trade*, October 26, 2007.

[83] USTR press release, "United States Prevails in WTO Dispute over Large Civil Aircraft," March 31, 2011.

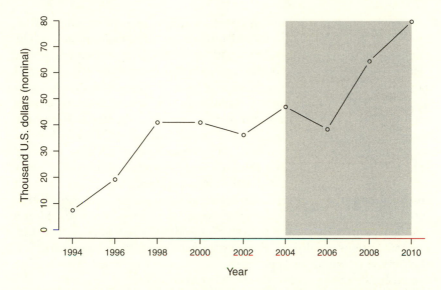

Figure 4.2. Boeing Corporation Political Contributions. The figure shows total contributions to members of the House Ways and Means Trade Subcommittee. The shaded region marks the period of WTO dispute settlement.

The Politics behind the Boeing Complaint

While final resolution of the dispute is pending, the key point for this chapter is the role of political factors to influence the escalation of a long bilateral dispute to legal adjudication. Industry preferences and a backdrop of strong political pressure pushed the United States to initiate legal action during the 1989 GATT dispute and 2004 WTO dispute. The industry favored negotiation settlement given fears that a public challenge of Airbus would produce such backlash in Europe that it would harm sales. Market uncertainty arising from litigation and the potential for government retaliation in the airline and procurement markets made U.S. aircraft companies extremely hesitant to go forward with a complaint. Only when the industry faced a new threat from Airbus models did it turn to WTO adjudication as a means to deter further funding. Not only governments but also firms worry about whether a lawsuit will offend foreign governments. The small number of market players and large role of the public sector in aircraft and airline decisions make this sector especially subject to these considerations. The reluctance of U.S. aircraft producers to directly challenge Europe accounts in part for the puzzle that the United States did not take a more aggressive approach to counter Airbus funding earlier.

Boeing represents a company with multiple sources of political influence. It can appeal to national interest as a strategic industry. The company employs more than 150,000 workers in the United States. It also participates in the political process through active lobbying and political contributions. Over the period from 1998 to 2009 Boeing spent $108,728,310 on lobbying activities, which placed it sixteenth among all lobby groups (both firms and organizations).[84] Figure 4.2 shows the contributions from Boeing to individual members of the House Ways and Means Trade Subcommittee.[85] The contributions are almost evenly split between Democrats and Republicans. This figure displays the funds most likely to be directed toward influencing trade policy (as opposed to procurement and other issues before Congress that are also of high interest to Boeing). The total contributions to all members of the House and Senate follow a similar pattern except there is less noticeable uptick in contributions in 2004 for the aggregate data, which fits an expectation that any extra contributions related to the move to WTO adjudication would be directed to the trade committee officials.

The executive branch officials showed concern at key junctures about potential spillover from the high-stakes trade dispute harming transatlantic diplomatic relations. These concerns, however, could delay but not forestall litigation. Resolutions in Congress, persistent lobbying from the Washington State congressional delegation, and even campaign rhetoric during the presidential election campaign made it imperative for the government to show its willingness to take an aggressive approach in the dispute. When negotiations failed to produce good outcomes, adjudication was the next step.

Evidence of close surveillance from Congress with specific demands for adjudication confirms that legal complaints can arise in response to domestic political demands. Analysis of congressional testimony offers one measure of attention to the dispute, although one must recognize that much congressional involvement in trade policy occurs through briefings and phone calls rather than public testimony. A search of congressional records for references in testimony to the Boeing-Airbus dispute reveals the pattern shown in figure 4.3.[86] The peaks in testimony coincide with three periods of adjudication. Seven speeches in 1987 criticized

[84] The data are from the Center for Responsive Politics list of top spenders for lobbying. http://www.opensecrets.org/lobby/top.php?indexType=s, accessed August 27, 2009.

[85] The data are from the Center for Responsive Politics available for each two-year election cycle, and the author's calculation sums the total for the list of current committee members for each period.

[86] The search of LexisNexis Congressional used the keyword terms "Boeing and Airbus and Trade," and every hit was read to confirm its relevance to the topic of subsidies. For example, testimony that related to the competing bids from Boeing and Airbus for

Airbus subsidies and included calls to investigate their legality. USTR
filed the complaint for an investigation in the Aircraft Committee in
February, however, and congressional attention does not arise until April
and over the summer. This was a period when the Aircraft Committee
had failed to reach consensus so that the USTR had withdrawn its
request and deferred from taking further legal action. There was little
attention to the Airbus subsidies issue in Congress during 1989 when
USTR filed another complaint, this time under the Subsidies Code
agreement of GATT. Congressional calls for further investigation of
legality of Airbus subsidies over the period 1991 to July 1992 may
have helped to push Europe to the negotiating table and preceded the
July bilateral agreement (ten speeches critical of Airbus subsidies were
made between September 1991 and April 1992, sixteen speeches in
April discussed bilateral trade negotiations and prospective agreement,
and one speech criticized illegal Airbus subsidies on July 9 immediately
after signing of the bilateral agreement). In 2004, three speeches and a
Senate resolution immediately preceded the filing of the WTO complaint
in October 2004 and four additional speeches were made in praise of
the complaint in the week after it was filed. The standstill in litigation
in early 2005 and March breakdown of bilateral talks prompted three
speeches and a unanimous Senate resolution in April 2005 calling for
the United States to renew efforts in WTO litigation, at which point the
United States requested a formal panel. Three more speeches endorsed
the WTO litigation later in 2005 and 2006 before a hiatus of no
prominent congressional speeches on the topic in three years 2007 and
2009.

Partisan differences are less obvious. In the data shown in figure 4.3,
forty-four speeches were made by Democrats and forty-seven speeches
were made by Republicans. The Senate resolution of March 2005 passed
with unanimous bipartisan support. While a surge of attention occurred
in 1992 when a Democratic Congress faced a Republican administration,
the pressure in 2004 and 2005 occurred under unified Republican control
of Congress and the executive. Democrats took the lead in their criticism
of the Bush administration for weak enforcement and in early calls for
WTO dispute settlement on the Airbus dispute, but Republicans also
voiced concerns about the issue. The large stakes of the Boeing-Airbus
dispute drew strong bipartisan demand for action to defend a critical
U.S. export industry.

Using the legal forum allowed the government to take action in
response to political pressure, and prompted tit-for-tat litigation with

an aircraft tanker procurement deal is excluded. I thank Mark Jia for his assistance with
the search and compilation of data.

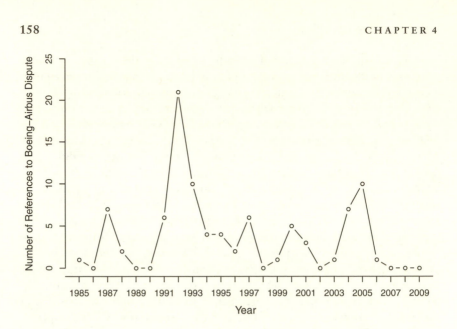

Figure 4.3. Congressional Testimony about Boeing-Airbus Dispute. The figure tallies the references to the trade dispute about subsidies to Airbus in congressional testimony in the House and Senate.

Europe instead of a trade war. The difficult question as both sides revise their subsidy policies and possibly face compliance challenges is this: Has the investment in costly litigation been sufficient to convince both sides that the other would retaliate against noncompliance? If so, they will reach a negotiated solution for politically acceptable revisions of their subsidy policies.

The China Problem

The Obama administration was quick to target China in the first WTO complaint filed under the new administration.[87] The complaint filed in June 2009 against Chinese export restraints on raw materials was featured prominently in USTR Ron Kirk's July 16 speech on the administration's plans to emphasize enforcement as a centerpiece of the trade agenda. Kirk spoke to mill workers at a U.S. steel plant in Pennsylvania that imports manganese from China as an important production input and has been harmed by the Chinese export restraints.[88] This was only

[87] DS394 filed June 24, 2009, "China Measures Related to the Exportation of Various Raw Materials."

[88] *Inside U.S. Trade*, July 17, 2009.

the most recent of many U.S. complaints against China that have been taken up within the context of WTO dispute settlement. Faced with relentless pressure from Congress to get tough with China, both the Bush administration and now the Obama administration have turned to WTO adjudication. Yet alongside each case that goes forward to adjudication are many more that are addressed in bilateral negotiations or ignored. This section will discuss how the legal forum has helped the executive to manage trade friction in the context of a sensitive diplomatic relationship.

Overview of U.S.-China Trade Relations

China has become one of the most important U.S. trade partners. In 2008, 12 percent of U.S. trade was with China, which formed the leading source of imports to the United States and the fourth largest export market after Canada, the EU, and Mexico.[89] The growing U.S. trade deficit has quickly brought U.S.-China trade friction to the forefront of political attention. In 2008 the trade deficit reached $268 billion. Figure 4.4 shows that the increase of U.S. exports to China has been outpaced by the growth of imports.

Trade with China has long attracted political attention in the United States. One might expect the governments as major powers that have often been strategic rivals, to limit economic interactions.[90] For years China held policies biased against trade during its period of isolationism. In 1979 it launched a remarkable reversal to open its markets to trade and investment (Shirk, 1994). The embrace of global markets has transformed China into an export powerhouse and production factory for leading multinational firms. This shift toward a high level of economic interdependence has not occurred without political problems. Suppression of citizen protests during the Tiananmen Square incident in 1989 heightened attention to the poor human rights conditions in China. Thereafter the U.S. Congress engaged in an annual debate about the status of trading relations with China.[91] In highly publicized debates, Democrats and Republicans in Congress threatened to raise tariffs on

---

[89] U.S. Census Foreign Trade Statistics, available at http://www.census.gov/foreign-trade/statistics/highlights/top/top0812yr.html, accessed September 14, 2009.

[90] For example, Gowa (1994) shows the theoretical basis for observed patterns that allies prefer trading with each other over adversaries.

[91] Following the Jackson-Vanik amendment to the 1974 trade act, nonmarket economies could be accorded normal trading rights (most-favored-nation status) only on an annual basis conditional on presidential approval that emigration rights were respected and U.S. national interest would benefit.

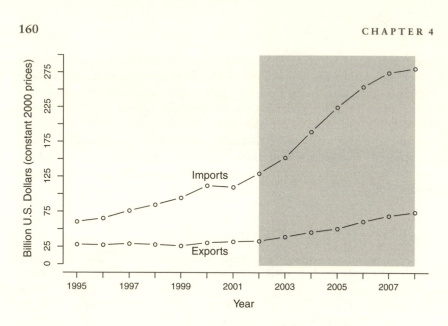

Figure 4.4. Bilateral Trade Flows with China. The shaded area indicates the period of WTO membership.

Chinese exports to the United States to protest Chinese policies on human rights, Taiwan, Tibet, missile sales, and any other controversy affecting U.S.-China relations.[92] Although every year the decision was made to continue to offer trade rights to China (in 1992 only a presidential veto stopped Congress from restricting trade), these debates added motivation for China to gain membership in the WTO, which it hoped would protect its trade from such arbitrary threats.

As part of the move to open the economy, in 1986 the Chinese government submitted an application for GATT membership.[93] GATT membership had been granted with few conditions for other states, but for China negotiations proved to be long and difficult as China needed time to complete the domestic reforms of its economy that were demanded by current members who feared the entry of a large low-cost producer with a state-controlled economy. A major step in this process was the vote by Congress in 2000 to grant China permanent normal trade status. As of December 11, 2001 China became a WTO member. In its accession protocol, China agreed to end its dual pricing system,

[92] *New York Times*, April 29, 1997.

[93] China had been an original signatory member of the GATT in 1948, but the Taiwanese government announced withdrawal after the revolution in 1949. For details on accession, see WTO, "History of China's Accession to the WTO," http://www.wto.org/english/news_e/pres01_e/pr243_e.htm, accessed September 25, 2009.

accorded imported goods national treatment, lowered tariffs across sectors, committed to implement the Agreement on Trade-Related Intellectual Property Rights (TRIPS), and agreed to allow foreign investment in the banking, insurance, and telecommunication service sectors. Unweighted average tariffs fell from 55.6 percent in 1982 to 12.3 percent in 2002.[94] The Chinese leadership recognized that this step would both lock in and accelerate reforms (Panitchpakdi and Clifford, 2002, p. 33). While current members expect to use the dispute settlement system as a means to enforce Chinese compliance, for China the dispute settlement process offers a tool to protect its market access rights under the agreement from unilateral restrictions that could threaten its export expansion.

There were soon signs of rising trade friction. The coverage of China in the National Trade Estimate Reports has been extensive relative to other major trade partners. This offers one indication of the attention given by USTR to a bilateral trade relationship (Noland, 1997). In 2004, the NTE included thirty-nine pages of coverage for China, compared with thirty-four pages each on the EU and Japan. By 2009 the NTE disparity had grown to the point that the NTE devoted fifty-six pages to covering trade barriers of China, while the section on the EU remained at thirty-four pages and the section on Japan had been reduced to twenty-two pages. There were eighty-four barriers against U.S. exports described in USTR National Trade Estimate Reports during the period 2002 to 2004, which were the first three years of China's WTO membership. Twenty-six barriers related to service market barriers (e.g., restrictions on the distribution of films). Nineteen barriers were import restrictions such as slow phasing out of import quotas, and twelve barriers consisted of problems with standards such as the encryption standards for Wi-Fi technology products. Ten barriers came under the heading of intellectual property rights issues, such as rampant piracy that harms the music and film industry as well as software. The remaining items included a range of topics from investment to government procurement. Thirty barriers indicated active negotiation efforts, and eleven of these items recorded some level of progress. Bilateral talks or pressure in multilateral committees may occur without specific mention in the reports, and listing in the reports itself acts as a moderate level of pressure. Of the fifty-eight barriers without reference to negotiation, nine indicated some level of progress. In the first two years of its membership there was an informal grace period in which trade complaints were put on hold to allow China time to adjust to the new commitments. Then in 2004, the United States

[94] IMF, *World Economic Outlook 2004*, p. 83.

filed the first complaint against China (this would be the only complaint filed against China until 2006).

During the confirmation hearings of Rob Portman as the USTR in April 2005, nearly all questions from members of the Senate Finance Committee focused on his intentions to take a more aggressive position toward the U.S. trade deficit with China and specific issues such as intellectual property rights protection. The pressure prompted a "Top-to-Bottom Review" released by the USTR in February 2006 titled "U.S.-China Trade Relations: Entering a New Phase of Greater Accountability and Enforcement." This document pledged new resources for enforcement such as appointing a chief counsel for China trade enforcement within USTR and posting a senior trade official at the U.S. embassy in Beijing to work alongside the economic section staff from the State Department. Several specific issues were highlighted as targets for new efforts on compliance as the report noted that the deadline for China to phase in its obligations had passed. The turn toward more active enforcement would draw on both WTO dispute process and bilateral channels that had been established prior to China's WTO accession.

In 1983 when trade between the countries remained at a low level, governments established the U.S.-China Joint Commission on Commerce and Trade (JCCT). The JCCT's role has been to promote trade and investment relations and resolve trade disputes. The United States has used the venue to push for stronger intellectual property protection and solutions to specific market barriers, while China has raised problems related to U.S. safeguards and antidumping policies. Between 1983 and 2000, the JCCT held thirteen conferences among officials and senior ministers representing China's Ministry of Foreign Trade and Economic Cooperation and the U.S. Commerce Department. As trade volumes grew after China's accession to the WTO, in 2002 governments established a new consultation mechanism within the JCCT framework, and meeting frequency increased to once or twice every year. The U.S. side also saw a shift to include USTR participation and occasional attendance by the Secretary of Agriculture.

The bilateral forum has been the favored choice of China for addressing trade friction. Officials have repeatedly emphasized the need for dialogue. Speaking to U.S. businessmen at a meeting in Seattle during his visit to the United States, Chinese President Hu Jintao referred to recent trade disputes with the comment, "We should properly address these problems through consultation and dialogue on an equal footing."[95] U.S. officials have been told by their Chinese counterparts that

---

[95] *Chinadaily.com*, April 21, 2006.

leaders would be unhappy if issues had to be taken to WTO adjudication. The Chinese commitment to take more action on IPR enforcement announced in the 2004 meeting came as part of a choreographed negotiation intended to show that both sides had made concessions on different issues.[96]

In 2005, both governments agreed to establish an additional venue for bilateral government-level talks, the Strategic Economic Dialogue. Intended to address more long-term strategies, these meetings have been led on the U.S. side by the treasury secretary and on the Chinese side by the vice premier. Adding the lead role for the Treasury Department opened the way for more attention to the currency issue. Whereas the JCCT has refrained from touching on the issue of currency value, this has been a priority within the Strategic Economic Dialogue talks. In an effort to increase attention to the security track of the talks, the Obama administration in 2009 renamed the venue to "Strategic *and* Economic Dialogue." Secretary of State Hillary Clinton joined the treasury secretary to lead the meeting in July.

Close-Up on Currency Issue

One of the most heated topics in U.S.-China trade relations has been Chinese currency policy and its effect on the bilateral trade balance. During the period 1995–2005, China held a currency peg that fixed the exchange rate of the renminbi (RMB) or yuan at 8.28 yuan to the dollar. While originally close to the market value, the extraordinary growth of the Chinese economy over this period would have increased the value of the currency under a free-floating exchange rate and has led to claims that the fixed rate is undervalued. In July 2005, China shifted its policy to a managed float that has allowed the RMB to gradually appreciate to a value of a 6.83 exchange rate with the dollar in April 2009, where it remained nearly fixed through April 2010 as the global financial crisis led China to repeg the RMB to the U.S. dollar. The 2005 reform did not end the claims that the Chinese government intervenes in currency markets to maintain an undervalued currency. Most economic studies agree that the currency is artificially below its market value, with estimates that the RMB is anywhere from 12 to 50 percent undervalued against the dollar.[97] Critics blame China's currency policies for its rapidly growing trade surplus by arguing that the undervalued currency acts as a subsidy for exports and tax on imports. While lowering the cost

---

[96] *New York Times*, April 20, 2004.
[97] *New York Times*, April 2, 2010.

of Chinese exports may undercut U.S. exporters, however, it benefits U.S. consumers who purchase goods made in China. The growth of foreign exchange reserves held by China from $403 billion in 2003 to $1.95 trillion in 2009, which includes purchases of $764 billion in U.S. Treasury securities, has helped to fund the U.S. federal budget deficit while maintaining low interest rates and a ready supply of capital for investment (Morrison and Labonte, 2009). These forces generate offsetting effects so that Chinese currency policy is unlikely to impact aggregate U.S. employment (ibid., p. 4). Nonetheless, the losses to some U.S. industries have mobilized political support in Congress.

Although China's undervalued currency can represent a barrier to U.S. exports, export industries have not mobilized strongly on the issue. In part this may reflect the benefits from the undervalued currency for the multinational companies that are invested in China. A large business coalition, which included multinational companies, export-oriented manufacturers, and agricultural interests that are among the largest donors of political contributions, backed the accession of China to the WTO and does not favor a trade war.[98] The coalition has acted as a force to hold back against tough demands for China to revalue its currency.

Industry pressure has been greatest from import-competing domestic industries and unions in the United States. The "China Currency Coalition" that organized to submit a Section 301 petition in 2004 includes major union organizations along with the textile, steel, and machinery industry associations. Subsequently replaced by the "Fair Currency Coalition," the organization has lobbied in support of legislation to pressure China to reform its currency.[99] In addition to the coalition, lobbying occurs from individual industry associations. For example, steel associations have sent letters to trade officials urging attention to the problem, which they argue provides artificial competitive advantage to Chinese steel makers.[100]

Several legislative proposals have demanded trade policy measures by the United States aimed to counter Chinese currency policy. Although the bills legislating specific actions have not been passed into law, they provide a focal point for congressional debate critical of China.[101]

---

[98] *Financial Times*, November 4, 2003.

[99] See www.chinacurrencycoalition.com and http://faircurrency.org.

[100] *Inside U.S. Trade*, June 11, 2010.

[101] Some resolutions with recommendations that China change its currency policy have been adopted, e.g., Senate Resolution 219 and House Resolution 414 in 2003. See Hufbauer, Wong, and Sheth (2006) for analysis of the series of legislative proposals related to U.S.-China trade disputes.

Threats to raise U.S. tariffs on Chinese imports have been a recurrent theme, with one bill introduced in 2003 calling for a 27.5 percent tariff on Chinese imports if China does not agree in negotiations to revalue its currency (S1586/HR3364). After having been put on hold to allow the administration to pursue negotiations, the bill was raised again in 2005. In 2006 the trade sanction bill was reported to have an unofficial tally of sixty-seven supporters in the Senate and was deferred only after a visit to China by the bill sponsor Senator Charles Schumer convinced him that the country was on the path to reform.[102] More moderate sanctions have since been put forward in other bills. Many of these legislative proposals urge the U.S. Treasury to name China as manipulating its currency (or set a lower threshold of "misalignment"), which would require the Treasury Department to negotiate with China on its exchange rate policy. Some bills would make currency undervaluation actionable under U.S. countervailing laws in the same way that other foreign government subsidies or dumping actions may be offset by duties on imports. Senator Schumer sponsored a proposal (S 1254) that calls for filing a WTO complaint against countries named by the Treasury Department as having misaligned currency. In June 2007, Senate Finance Committee Chairman Max Baucus and ranking Republican member Charles Grassley submitted further legislation aimed to pressure China on currency reform, which they advocated in an editorial with the following comments:

> A little pressure can go a long way to encouraging the right policies. If six months of consultations are fruitless, we propose that the US suspend federal purchases of the country's goods and services. Prolonged stalemates could trigger the filing of a WTO dispute settlement case and spark consideration of remedial intervention in currency markets to correct the misalignment.... The point of our bipartisan legislation is not to punish any one country, but to encourage all countries to follow international rules. When major trading partners intervene in the currency market to obtain unfair advantage, it hurts the US economy and undermines support for open international trade.[103]

These proposals met objections from USTR and the Treasury Department and threats of presidential veto. Treasury Secretary Henry Paulson urged that legislation was not the appropriate means to persuade China and progress would be forthcoming in negotiations.[104] Even within

---

[102] *New York Times*, March 23, 2006; *Washington Post*, April 18, 2006.
[103] *Financial Times*, July 6, 2007.
[104] *New York Times*, September 11, 2007.

TABLE 4.3
Congressional Testimony on Chinese Currency Reform.

Year	Democrat	Republican
2002	0	0
2003	10	14
2004	14	11
2005	40	36
2006	1	1
2007	9	0
2008	1	0
2009	1	0

Note: The two columns tally the number of speakers in each party who directly discuss the issue of Chinese currency reform in connection with the WTO during congressional testimony.

Congress, there was caution about going forward with the proposals. Business groups that represent multinational companies lobbied against the currency legislation.[105]

Members of Congress took the unusual step to file a Section 301 petition with the USTR over China's currency practices (Section 301 petitions are typically filed by the industry harmed or "self-initiated" by the USTR). In September 2004, in April 2005, and again in May 2007, Section 301 petitions from members of Congress urged that USTR immediately begin negotiations and proceed with a WTO complaint. In the annual letter to the president from House Democrats issued upon the release of the National Trade Estimate Report, currency manipulation is a prominent item in their petition requesting that USTR should file more WTO complaints against trade barriers. The letter, sent March 31, 2005, stated, "The Administration sought China's accession to the WTO on the premise that China could be held accountable under WTO rules. There is a growing consensus that China's currency practices violate at least three WTO provisions." The letter goes on to urge the administration to both accept the Section 301 petition and file a WTO complaint unless China agreed to a "Plaza-type accord" (a reference to the 1985 settlement with Japan that led to major revaluation of the yen).

Congressional attention can also be seen in testimony that refers directly to the issue of Chinese currency reform. Table 4.3 shows the surge of discussion connecting the currency issue with the WTO during the period that accompanied the legislation in 2003, and this attention

---

[105] *Inside U.S. Trade*, February 8, 2008.

continued through 2005.[106] Substantially more testimony discussed the problem in a broader context without reference to the WTO, such as the criticism of Treasury Department decisions against listing China as having manipulated its currency. This table shows only the testimony directly related to the currency issue in the context of the WTO. There is slightly more frequent commentary from Democratic members of Congress, but overall both parties express similar concerns. The July 2005 shift by China to adjust its exchange rate policy corresponds with a sharp decline in congressional focus on the issue, even while a core group of legislators continue to submit legislation calling for China to engage in more currency reform and House Democrats continue to list Chinese currency manipulation in their annual letter to the president to request additional WTO complaints.

During the 2004 presidential campaign, Senator John Kerry's campaign office released a report critical of the Bush administration record on trade policy. The report pointed out the decline of WTO complaints filed by the Bush administration and pledged to double the budget of the USTR to support more enforcement efforts. Kerry supporter Representative Sander M. Levin (D-MI) told reporters at a press conference that Kerry would "take a hard look" at the possibility of filing a WTO case against China on the currency issue.[107] Kerry's office released a written statement that "George Bush has made it clear that he wants to continue taking America in the wrong direction by refusing to enforce our trade agreements and continuing to allow China to manipulate its currency."[108]

Despite the claims from Congress about a consensus that China's currency policies violate WTO rules, there is uncertainty about the legal standard for currency manipulation as a trade barrier. In February 2004, USTR Robert Zoellick tried to deter industries from filing the Section 301 complaint, saying, "There's really no WTO obligation not to have a fixed exchange rate."[109] The WTO agreement (GATT 1994 Article XV:4), however, does contain a provision that "[c]ontracting parties shall not, by exchange action, frustrate the intent of the provisions of this Agreement." Others claim that currency manipulation violates the prohibition on export subsidies and represents nullification of expected U.S. benefits under the agreement. A survey of views from leading

---

[106] The search of LexisNexis Congressional used the keyword terms "China, WTO, and currency" to search the text of congressional testimony (floor speeches and documents, but not hearings). Every hit was read to confirm its relevance to the topic.

[107] *Washington Post*, April 27, 2004

[108] *New York Times*, September 10, 2004

[109] *New York Times*, February 27, 2004.

trade experts and legal counsel to trade law firms gathered by the Fair Currency Coalition shows mixed conclusions on the potential legal case against Chinese exchange rate misalignment.[110] Former chairman of the WTO Appellate Body James Bacchus reaches a negative conclusion with emphasis on the fact that the undervaluation is not a specific subsidy contingent on exporting goods or targeted to specific industries or regions in China, and only the Article XV:4 claim could provide legal basis for a case. Terence Stewart, a leading international trade lawyer for a law firm that often represents domestic firms seeking relief from imports, makes the argument that the currency misalignment could be found in violation of the agreement on subsidies and countervailing measures as a de facto export subsidy because the benefits are received when firms export. Hufbauer, Wong, and Sheth (2006, p. 17) contend that there is a plausible case for the subsidy argument (and not the argument based on Article XV:4), but it would most likely be rejected. In short, there is a potential case, but the WTO panel or Appellate Body could very possibly rule that there was no violation. In this sense, a case against Chinese currency policy would be similar to the Kodak case where the United States filed with full knowledge that it was pushing the boundary of where WTO rules apply. To the extent that complaints are more likely to be observed in the face of legal uncertainty this could be a case that would go forward if both sides had a sense of optimism about their case. But any government cautious about losing would steer clear of taking such a controversial matter before the court. Furthermore, many in the U.S. government may be reluctant to open the way for WTO rulings that push beyond straightforward interpretation of text given the greater impingement on national sovereignty.

On the Chinese side, experts emphasize that the United States would not win a WTO case against its currency policy. Speaking to the *China Daily* at the time of the first industry petition to USTR on the currency issue, Zhang Hanlin, director of the World Trade Research Institute of the Foreign Economic and Trade University, said that China never promised to end its exchange control system when joining the WTO and there was no violation.[111] He noted that having WTO dispute settlement for such conflicts was one reason why China had joined the WTO.

The administration has used both negotiations and public statements to apply pressure on China to adopt more flexibility in its exchange rate

---

[110] http:// faircurrency.org/ presscenter/ survey_of_views0407.pdf, accessed September 29, 2009.

[111] "Complaints to WTO about RMB: A Good Thing for China", www.chinaview.cn, October 23, 2003, article accessed from archives available at www.xinhuanet.com/ english.

policy. Early efforts occured through a technical cooperation program initiated in October 2003 as a bilateral forum to discuss financial system reforms (Morrison and Labonte, 2009, p. 7). By 2005 the pressure was of a higher profile with statements by Treasury Secretary John Snow at the G-7 summit of April 2005 critical of China's fixed exchange rate and hinted that the semiannual Treasury Department Report on exchange rates could cite China as having manipulated its currency. This was shortly followed by the Chinese government's announcement in July that it would shift toward a peg with a small window for fluctuation. Despite calls from Congress, however, the Bush administration did not name China as having manipulated its currency in the Treasury Department reports or initiate a WTO case. The consistent line from the executive branch has been that engagement in negotiations with China will be more effective (Hufbauer, Wong, and Sheth, 2006, pp. 13–14). USTR declined the Section 301 petition filed by the China Currency Coalition in 2004 and rejected similar petitions submitted by legislators in 2005 and 2007. When declining the 2005 petition, a spokesman said USTR officials do not think bringing a WTO complaint "is appropriate or a productive way" to persuade China to accept currency reform.[112]

The Bush administration in September 2006 convinced Schumer/Graham Currency Reform Bill sponsors to table their bill through making the commitment to address their concerns as part of the SED talks. The first SED meeting in December 2006 addressed the currency issue but reached no resolution. China offered a few concessions on currency timed to support the meetings. Prior to the first SED meeting, the Chinese currency appreciated in value slightly, and prior to the second meeting in May 2007 China announced it would widen the band within which the currency can float.[113]

Concern about foreign policy relations with China and the mixed interests for the United States regarding China's currency policy both contribute to reluctance by the executive to take stronger action. First, as a permanent member of the UN Security Council China held veto power over the UN resolutions that the United States sought to strengthen pressure on Saddam Hussein in 2002 and the failed effort to gain authorization for intervention. China also stands as the critical player in talks with North Korea toward ending its nuclear weapons program. In short, major strategic objectives for U.S. foreign policy have been contingent on cooperation from China. Fred Bergsten, director of the Institute for International Economics, wrote in an editorial to the

---

[112] *Washington Post*, May 28, 2005.
[113] *New York Times*, September 29, 2006; *Washington Post*, May 19, 2007.

Washington Post (September 10, 2003) that Treasury Secretary Snow was not pressuring China on its currency policies, which he cited as another example of how "short-term foreign policy concerns trumped U.S. economic interests within the administration." Second, many in the United States recognize the concerns of the Chinese government that rapid appreciation of the currency would destabilize the Chinese economy with its immature banking system and potentially spark a financial crisis that could spill over to harm the global economy. In 2004 testimony before the Senate, Federal Reserve Chairman Alan Greenspan advised against a floating exchange rate and an end to capital controls for China with warnings about risks to the Chinese economy (Hufbauer, Wong, and Sheth, 2006, p. 14). Furthermore, Chinese manipulation of currency markets maligned by critics also contributes to Chinese purchases of U.S. Treasury bonds, which is beneficial to the U.S. economy. These factors have led to a sharp contrast between restraint by the executive that reflects foreign policy jurisdiction and wider economic interests and calls for tough policies from Congress that express concerns about specific industries harmed by the currency policy.

It remains to be seen whether the many reasons for caution—mixed economic interests, unclear legal provisions, and delicate bilateral political relations—will continue to hold back against political pressure. The issue again became a headline item in March 2010 as 130 House members in a letter urged the Obama administration to impose tariffs on China in retaliation for the undervalued currency and several senators revived legislative proposals that contain threats of sanctions.[114] In hearings on the issue held before the House Ways and Means Committee on March 24, 2010, trade experts including Fred Bergsten of the Institute for International Economics recommended that the United States file a WTO complaint along with IMF consultation as part of a strategy to pressure China into agreeing to adjust its currency. Written statements from a range of groups including the chairman of the Congressional Steel Caucus and the Fair Currency Coalition urged unilateral action to restrict Chinese imports while statements submitted by the Cato Institute and national retail federation urged continued dialogue. Criticism mounted even as the administration announced on April 3 that it would delay the release of the Treasury Department report to Congress on exchange rates in order to allow time for negotiations in a series of upcoming meetings with Chinese leaders. Senator Chuck Grassley, the ranking member of the Senate Finance Committee, expressed his disappointment with the decision:

[114] *New York Times*, April 4, 2010.

Everyone knows China is manipulating the value of its currency to gain an unfair advantage in international trade. If we want the Chinese to take us seriously, we need to be willing to say so in public. The past few years have proven that denying the problem doesn't solve anything. The Treasury Department should cite China as a currency manipulator. I renew my call for the Administration to prepare a WTO case against China under Article XV of the General Agreement on Tariffs and Trade.[115]

Senate Finance Committee Chairman Max Baucus criticized the administration for giving short shrift to economic issues in deference to the current strategic policy priorities on getting cooperation from China on policies toward Iran and North Korea.[116] These sentiments have led to renewed efforts to use legislation on the issue. In September 2010, the House overwhelmingly voted to approve HR2378, which would authorize imposition of duties against imports from China to counter its currency policies. Similar legislation is under discussion for introduction in the Senate.[117] The administration faces deep skepticism in Congress that its negotiations are bringing results.

Adjudication with China

Unwilling to initiate a WTO complaint or take unilateral measures to pressure China on the currency issue, the administration has instead responded to pressure from Congress with actions on other trade barriers. It filed the first WTO complaint against China in 2004 against discriminatory tax policies (rebates on the value-added tax conferred to local producers) affecting the semiconductor industry. The U.S. semiconductor industry association had been requesting a WTO complaint for over a year with arguments that the 14 percent tax differential was an unfair burden for sales in the Chinese market, which are valued at $19 billion.[118] The VAT rebate policy had been adopted by China in 2000 and was viewed as an effort to promote foreign investment and local production over imports—indeed half of the companies to receive the rebates were local subsidiaries of multinational firms like Intel (Liang, 2007, p. 108). Experts agreed it was likely the Chinese policy would be

---

[115] Press release available at http://finance.senate.gov/newsroom/ranking/release/?id=d24a2af5-157c-4b2d-a69b-a90e3edecb53, accessed April 27, 2010.)
[116] *Inside U.S. Trade*, June 11, 2010.
[117] *Inside U.S. Trade*, February 17, 2011.
[118] *New York Times*, March 19, 2004.

found in violation of WTO rules. Talks at both industry and government levels over three years, however, had not brought agreement.

Within four months after filing the complaint, a settlement was reached during the consultation period with China agreeing to end the rebate system over nine months. Since the U.S. industry would continue paying the same tax rate, the change was a withdrawal of the benefit that had been conferred to a handful of Chinese and foreign companies. A spokesperson for China's largest semiconductor company told *China Daily* that ending the rebate would have little material impact on industry performance.[119] Liang (2007) explains that the Chinese semiconductor industry was consulted by the Chinese government and favored ending the rebate to replace it with other support policies that would be WTO consistent and more broadly help the domestic industry as a whole (only a small subset of firms had qualified for the rebate). USTR Robert Zoellick announced the outcome at a press conference standing in front of a banner declaring "real results" and claiming that the administration makes progress through negotiations but was not afraid to use litigation against China.[120] Having settled early before any legal ruling, the Chinese government was able to continue to insist its policy had not been a violation of WTO rules. The first U.S.-China WTO dispute was a victory for all as both industries were satisfied by the outcome, the USTR demonstrated to a home audience its willingness to "get tough" with China, and the Chinese government avoided the stigma of a violation ruling.

This was followed by several more complaints by the United States. In another complaint to target Chinese industrial policy, on March 30, 2006, the United States and EU (later followed by Canada) filed complaints against discriminatory tariff classification of imported auto parts that represented a de facto barrier against imports.[121] In its tariff schedule, China had agreed to charge a 25 percent tariff on imported vehicles and a 10 percent tariff on imported parts, but starting in 2005 it assessed the higher 25 percent duty on a manufacturer after assembly for the imported parts if they accounted for 60 percent of the total value of the complete vehicle. The dual tariff structure encouraged local assembly over imports of complete vehicles, and the new restriction on use of imported parts made it cheaper to purchase auto parts from domestic producers. The Chinese program for automobile import substitution

---

[119] "Agreement Ends Rebates for Chip Makers," www.chinaview.cn, July 10, 2004, accessed from the archives of Xinhua News at www.xinhuanet.com/english.

[120] *Washington Post*, July 9, 2004.

[121] See Wauters and Vandenbussche (2010) for detailed analysis of the case, DS342, "China—Measures Affecting Imports of Automobile Parts."

policies had been listed in National Trade Estimate Reports for many years and received some attention in congressional testimony with critical remarks about the trade deficit with China often singling out the auto tariff policy in addition to currency misalignment.[122] This was the first case against China that went through the full dispute process of panel and appeal stages with the final outcome in December 2008 upholding the main claims against China's policy. The legal outcome of violation ruling was characterized as "highly predictable" based on similarity with earlier cases (Wauters and Vandenbussche, 2010, p. 225). The filing of complaints met with wide acclaim beyond the specific affected industries: A spokesperson for the National Association of Manufacturers, which has taken a lead role in the industry pressure on China currency revaluation, stated it was "the first thing the administration has done to show it really means it when it says we have a new trade policy with China."[123] Following the violation ruling, the Chinese government announced it would end the discriminatory charges starting in September 2009, and it met this deadline to come into compliance with the ruling. By this time, however, most foreign firms had moved production to China. USTR Ron Kirk praised the case as an example of "the importance of enforcing our international trade agreement rights," but Kevin Wale, the president of General Motors China, said the policy change had little impact since GM now manufactures or purchases auto parts in China.[124] China had accomplished its infant industry strategy to foster inward foreign investment in the sector and witnessed spectacular growth in both domestic auto parts and vehicle production (Wauters and Vandenbussche, 2010, p. 234).

Filing a complaint against China for intellectual property rights challenged one of the core problems cited by U.S. business as a problem in the Chinese market. Counterfeit goods erode U.S. sales in the Chinese market and serve as low-cost import competition when such products are exported to the United States. Whether fake auto parts or illegal copies of software and music content, inadequate protection of copyrights, trademarks, and patents in China harms a wide range of U.S. industries. Even the conservative estimates of a Chinese government policy research institute state the value of pirated goods made in China as $19 to $24

---

[122] The search of Lexis Congressional testimony for the keywords *China*, *WTO*, and *automobile* for 2002–June 2009 shows that twenty-eight representatives made speeches that include reference to the auto tariff barriers of China (all speeches read to confirm relevance). The largest number was focused during the debate of HR414 in October 2003.
[123] *New York Times*, March 31, 2006.
[124] *New York Times*, August 31, 2009.

billion a year.[125] The International Intellectual Property Alliance (IIPA), a private-sector group of U.S.-based industry trade associations, reports that 79 percent of the PC software market is held by pirated goods, with higher levels of 90 to 95 percent pirated goods for audio-visual products.[126] In 2004 the U.S. Chamber of Commerce issued a report that praised considerable progress by China to comply with WTO obligations in most areas but warned that without further progress to improve IPR enforcement U.S. business would support a WTO case on this issue.[127] Notably, the Chamber had sided with the administration decision not to pursue WTO adjudication for the currency issue. In February 2005, the Chamber along with associations representing the movie and recording industries requested to USTR that it file a WTO complaint against China for weak IPR enforcement, which the business groups cited as costing American industry $200 billion a year.[128]

At this time, the USTR was reluctant to go forward with a WTO complaint, saying there had not been sufficient evidence of specific cases of illegal piracy harming U.S. business.[129] USTR lists China on the "Priority Watch List" of the annual USTR reports on the status of intellectual property right protection in trade partners.[130] Officials from USTR and the Department of Commerce continued to press China to improve the legal framework and prosecution record for IPR violations. Technical-level discussions also took place. The administration emphasized the need to engage with China on the bilateral level while making implicit threats of possible legal action should there be no progress in bilateral talks.[131]

Congress applied pressure on the administration to take stronger action against China on IPR issues. As early as 2002 when China had just joined the WTO, the congressionally appointed U.S.-China Economic and Security Review Commission produced a wide-ranging report that

[125] New York Times, January 14, 2005.

[126] International Intellectual Property Alliance, 2009 Special 301 Report on Copyright Protection and Enforcement: People's Republic of China, February 17, 2009, p. 94. Available at http://www.iipa.com/pdf/IIPAChinaTPSCwrittencomments092209.pdf. As noted by Mertha (2007, p. 61), however, these higher estimates make the unrealistic assumption that pirated goods substitute for the full-price product.

[127] Financial Times, September 23, 2004.

[128] New York Times, February 10, 2005.

[129] New York Times, April 29, 2005.

[130] The Super 301 reports were mandated by the 1988 Omnibus Trade Bill as annual reports monitoring the progress of trade partners to improve protection of intellectual property rights. The reports include categories for monitoring list, watch list, and a priority watch list. In the 2009 Super 301 report, twelve countries were included on the priority list and forty-six overall were noted in one of the categories for inadequate IPR.

[131] New York Times, January 14, 2005.

included among its many recommendations the call for Congress to pressure USTR to begin consultations toward a complaint against China for its poor enforcement of intellectual property rights.[132] Angered at the decision of the administration not to file a WTO case in response to the industry request, in April 2005 the Senate Finance Committee issued a written request for a WTO complaint against China on IPR policies. When the administration declined, Representative Benjamin L. Cardin of Maryland, who was the ranking Democrat on the House Ways and Means Trade Subcommittee, criticized the decision, stating that "[P]utting China on a watch list means nothing.... The administration has to understand that Congress is serious and wants action on China."[133] In July 2005, Congress debated legislation (HR6440, United States Trade Rights Enforcement Act) that called for more action against foreign trade barriers and gave considerable attention to the problem of Chinese IPR problems as one of the major enforcement issues that required greater attention from the U.S. government.[134] The level of congressional attention to the issue rose steadily over this period from a handful of speeches made in 2002 to fifty-five in 2005.

By June 2006, the USTR was in the midst of preparing its WTO case for a complaint against China on IPR. In testimony before the U.S.-China Economic Security Review Commission hearings on IPR policies in China on June 7, 2006, Michigan Senator Carl Levin accused the USTR of being a "paper tiger" for only warning China that it might pursue a WTO case and placing it on priority watch lists but taking no action.[135] The USTR official responded that USTR would establish a "China Enforcement Task Force" and was preparing to file a WTO complaint against China on IPR policies but needed more time for gathering the evidence to make a winnable case.[136] In October, USTR made a formal request through the WTO for China to provide detailed information on its enforcement of IPR.[137]

---

[132] Report available at http://www.uscc.gov/annual_report/2002/ch3_02.htm. The report was discussed by Representative Robert Byrd and read into the congressional record July 17, 2002, 107th Congress, 2nd session. Subsequent reports in 2004, 2005, and 2006 again called for Congress to urge the administration to file a complaint.

[133] *New York Times*, April 30, 2005.

[134] *Congressional Record*, July 26, 2005, 109th Congress, 1st session, 151 Cong. Rec. H 6440 vol. 151, no. 103.

[135] Hearing on Intellectual Property Rights Issues and Counterfeit Goods before the U.S.-China Economic and Security Review Commission, 109th Congress, 2nd session, June 7–8, 2006, p. 22.

[136] Ibid., pp. 41, 63.

[137] Article 63.3 of TRIPS allows parties to request information on judicial actions related to IPR enforcement.

The pledge to move forward with the filing of the WTO complaint appears to have held back congressional pressure. No further attention was given to Chinese IPR policies in floor testimony over the next three years. When USTR Robert Portman released a review of USTR policy toward China in February 2006 with new promises of aggressive enforcement against WTO violations, Representative Cardin complained that "the time for monitoring and bureaucracy has passed" but praised the hints of forthcoming WTO action against China on IPR and autos.[138]

IPR has been a frequent topic addressed in the JCCT venue. In 2004 China presented its action plan at the meeting with concrete proposals to reduce IPR infringement and increase penalties for those charged with piracy and counterfeiting. A new working group within the JCCT brought together trade, judicial, and law enforcement officials from the United States and China to consult on IPR-related policies.[139] The challenge for intellectual property rights enforcement is multilevel insofar as there are both specific points that call for changes of the laws and many more problems that are related to domestic implementation involving the police and courts. For example, one of the major accomplishments announced as part of the IPR action plan in 2004 was a decision by China's Supreme People's Court to release a new judicial interpretation about what would constitute an IPR violation for prosecution, which had been a frequent request from U.S. industry.[140] The following year JCCT also placed high attention on IPR with new pledges from the Chinese government to increase prosecutions and improve police coordination to investigate IPR crimes across the country. USTR Robert Portman praised the commitments from China but also warned that he expected results in terms of both prosecutions as well as outcomes for reduction of piracy and increased U.S. exports of software and media products.[141]

In early 2007 under the threat of an imminent WTO complaint, the Chinese government offered significant concessions with an announcement from China's Supreme Court that it would lower the threshold for criminal prosecution of copyright infringement in half and with highly publicized government raids to seize pirated goods.[142] Nonetheless, the United States went forward to file its complaint. Gary Hufbauer of the Institute for International Economics said, "The timing is clearly

---

[138] *Washington Post*, February 15, 2006.
[139] *Inside U.S. Trade*, April 21, 2004.
[140] *Inside U.S. Trade*, April 23, 2004.
[141] *Inside U.S. Trade*, July 11, 2005.
[142] *New York Times*, April 7, 2007.

[designed] to tell the Congress especially, but also to tell the Chinese: "We're going to thump you as a way of trying to head off congressional legislation."[143] While China viewed its concessions as substantial, the measures would have been insufficient to convince Congress after years of hearing promises that China would improve its protection of IPR. The decision to file a WTO complaint is typically made at the assistant USTR level after the interagency clearance process and meeting of the Trade Policy Staff Committee, but this case required clearance by the White House in light of the political and diplomatic significance. USTR had prepared to file the complaint and would not be stopped by last-minute concessions that only partly addressed its concerns. The United States filed a broad complaint against Chinese enforcement of IPR on April 10, 2007.[144] The case also held interest for many other WTO members with twelve countries joining later as third parties. Headlines in the U.S. media announced that "U.S. Toughens China Position," and congressional representatives praised the action while noting it was long overdue.[145]

In contrast to the earlier cases against industrial policy measures, IPR presented a more challenging area to prove violation. In the week before the United States filed its case, the *New York Times* reported that it was "unclear whether the WTO would agree with the United States."[146] The U.S. legal claims focused on issues related to high thresholds required before Chinese authorities would take criminal action against counterfeiting and piracy, the practice of releasing counterfeit goods confiscated at customs after removal of the unlawful trademark, and the denial of IPR protection for creative works that were not authorized for entry into China. The case proceeded slowly in light of the complex legal issues. The final ruling by the panel in January 2009 was mixed, with the United States losing on the first point that claimed Chinese law that calls for prosecution if "the amount of sales is huge" (implemented for pirated DVDs as five hundred copies at a value of about $7,000) violated the requirement of Article 61 of TRIPS to apply criminal penalties in cases of counterfeiting or copyright piracy "on a commercial scale." The ruling affirmed the U.S. claims that even products that

---

[143] *New York Times*, April 7, 2007.

[144] DS362, "China–Measures Affecting the Protection and Enforcement of Intellectual Property Rights." On the same day the United States filed a case against market access barriers for the distribution of media and publishing products (DS363). This is connected to the IPR case in substantive terms because restrictions on legal import of many products feed the demand for the pirated versions.

[145] *New York Times*, April 10, 2007.

[146] *New York Times*, April 7, 2007.

are not approved by "content review" (censorship) should receive IPR protection and counterfeit goods should not be sold at public auction. The USTR praised the ruling and noted that despite losing the legal decision on criminal thresholds, it had received concessions from China on this point in the lead-up before litigation and the ruling offered useful clarification of market-based standards for setting prosecution thresholds that should improve IPR enforcement in China.[147] The IIPA noted improved engagement from China on IPR issues in late 2008 while still calling for continued monitoring.[148]

WTO adjudication against China has delivered real policy concessions, but the direct economic gains may be surpassed by the political significance of bringing forward these cases. On IPR, the WTO case raised attention for the issue and brought the end to some egregious practices such as the resale of confiscated goods. Yet few think that there has been a dramatic change in the level of IPR infringement. To the extent that the problem reflects poor implementation that arises from local autonomy, changes in the rules or attention given by central government authority may not improve the problem on the ground. The auto parts case led to policy change insofar as China eliminated the tariffs found in violation in September 2009, but by this time most foreign firms had relocated to China. The economic impact of these cases on an individual basis may be relatively small in the scope of the overall bilateral relationship. But the cases loom large in the political relationship both as a warning to China that the United States takes seriously the provisions of the trade agreements and as a signal to industry and Congress that U.S. economic interests will be defended.

The Defensive Reaction in China

The Chinese response to U.S. WTO complaints has ranged from annoyance to anger. After the first case filed against China, officials said the move was "regrettable and hard to understand" because bilateral negotiations were ongoing and making progress.[149] The strongest reaction in China was sparked by the IPR complaint. A spokesman for the Chinese Ministry of Commerce said, "The decision [to file a WTO complaint] runs contrary to the consensus between the leaders of the

---

[147] USTR press release, "United States Wins WTO Dispute over Deficiencies in China's Intellectual Property Rights Laws," January 26, 2009. Available at http://www.ustr. gov/about-us/press-office/press-releases/2009/january.

[148] *Inside U.S. Trade*, February 20, 2009.

[149] "China Says US Semiconductor Trade Appeal to WTO Regrettable," Xinhua News Agency report supplied by BBC Worldwide Monitoring, March 19, 2004.

two nations about strengthening bilateral trade ties and properly solving trade disputes. It will seriously undermine the cooperative relations the two nations have established in the field and will adversely affect bilateral trade."[150] Officials also threatened that the U.S. move to adjudication would undermine cooperation on related issues in other negotiation forums.[151] The IIPA noted that as soon as the WTO complaint had been filed, all further bilateral engagement from China was terminated abruptly even as problems related to Internet piracy rapidly worsened.[152] Trade tensions had also escalated at this time with a protectionist move by the United States to impose duties on Chinese paper imports, but the Chinese government reaction to express "deep regret" over the WTO complaint was evaluated as more negative than its official statement of "dissatisfaction" with the duty increase.[153] Vice Premier Wu Yi, who led the Chinese trade delegation, was reported to have responded to the news of the IPR complaint with anger, stating the equivalent of "if you want a fight, let's fight."[154]

The negative reaction of the Chinese government is not only a concern for diplomats. Fear of angering the Chinese government makes industries hesitant to support filing WTO complaints. James Mendenhall, who served as general counsel in the USTR from 2005 to 2007 before moving into private practice for an international law firm, stated that "there is a palpable fear in the U.S. industry, and in industries around the world, of [Chinese] retribution."[155] While concerns about retribution are a factor with all countries, he considers the issue more substantial regarding China. Mentioning the possibility for rejection of an application for a license or some new regulatory barrier that would exclude market access, he said, "If you bring a case ... you have a strong sense that you will pay the price down the road." In particular, multinational firms are vulnerable because they often receive incentives offered by the central government to lure foreign investment, and since these policies are not covered by WTO commitments they may be expanded or reduced at the discretion of government officials. Gary Hufbauer of the Institute

---

[150] "China Expresses Regret, Dissatisfaction over U.S. Complaints at WTO", www.chinaview.cn, 10 April 2007, accessed from archives of Xinhua news at www.xinhuanet.com/english.

[151] "Vice Premier: U.S. Piracy Complaints Will Damage Co-op", www.chinaview.cn, April 24, 2007, accessed from archives of Xinhua News at www.xinhuanet.com/english.

[152] IIPA Written comments to the Trade Policy Staff Committee on China's WTO Compliance, September 22, 2009, p. 14. Available at http://www.iipa.com/pdf/IIPAChinaTPSCwrittencomments092209.pdf.

[153] *New York Times*, April 11, 2007.

[154] *New York Times*, May 19, 2007.

[155] *Inside U.S. Trade*, October 24, 2008, p. 26.

for International Economics said it was difficult to put together a case on the IPR issue because fear of offending Chinese officials and worsening the business environment in China made many companies "reluctant to provide facts that can be put into cases."[156] One expert witness providing testimony to the U.S.-China Economic and Security Review Commission noted that fear of retaliation was so great that a company like Microsoft would privately say it was losing $10 billion a year from IPR infringement in China but in public praise the Chinese government for improvements to IPR.[157] Mertha (2007) describes a systematic practice of "transnational trade deterrence" by which the threat that local-level officials will hinder business operations of foreign companies makes these companies reluctant to bring information about trade problems to their own government. A trade expert speaking about U.S. WTO cases against China said industries are often concerned about negative consequences if they are seen as supporting the case, but noted that "the government has been able to manage the cases so that in the end of the day there was not damage to U.S. industry."[158]

U.S. officials try to portray use of litigation as a nonconfrontational grievance procedure, but after meetings in the December 2007 Strategic Economic Dialogue, they admitted that the Chinese seem to view legal challenges as "personal insults."[159] Two years later, USTR Susan Schwab noted that with the buildup of experience as both defendant and complainant, China is finally beginning to take a more "business-like approach."[160] The WTO membership supported the appointment of a Chinese national to serve as a judge on the Appellate Body, which may help build support in China for the judicial process. China has also participated as a third party observing over sixty WTO disputes as a learning strategy (Bown, 2009b, p. 41).

In its early years of WTO membership China rarely used WTO adjudication even as it faced a wide range of trade barriers against its surge of exports. It joined the bandwagon complaint against U.S. steel safeguards in 2002 as its first case. It did not file again until 2007. Faced with the increasing number of antidumping duties applied against its exports, China has negotiated voluntary export restraints or simply tolerated the duties. In 2007 and 2008 China filed one WTO dispute

---

[156] *Washington Post*, April 18, 2006.
[157] Hearing on Intellectual Property Rights Issues and Counterfeit Goods before the U.S.-China Economic and Security Review Commission, 109th Congress, 2nd session, June 7–8, 2006, p. 208.
[158] Interview by author, April 16, 2010.
[159] *New York Times*, December 14, 2007.
[160] U.S. Asia Pacific Council, *Washington Report*, September 2009, p. 4.

complaint each year, which still represents low adjudication relative to other members and the expected number of potential cases for a major exporter. The theory of this book that states will seek bilateral settlements unless they face legislative constraints fits this pattern.

There are some elements of domestic pressure even within the context of authoritarian rule that have played out to encourage China to use WTO dispute settlement. As with other countries, countersuits may arise when governments are repeatedly on the defensive within dispute settlement. Bown (2009b, p. 34) describes China's initiation of cases as a "needed political counteroffensive to the repeated U.S. challenges" in addition to serving economic interests. Political pressure in China can also urge tough enforcement. In September 2009 the Obama administration approved a special safeguard measure that will impose a 35 percent tariff on Chinese tire imports. A *New York Times* article (September 14, 2009) noted that the government at first issued a "formulaic" response typical of past cases in which it has preferred to tolerate some foreign protectionism, but rising Internet pressure critical of the government was forcing its hand. The next day the Chinese government issued a statement that it would begin its own investigation of U.S. auto parts and chicken exports to China, in a move portrayed as retaliation. It also filed a formal complaint against the U.S. tire safeguard using the WTO dispute settlement process as another way to signal to domestic actors that it would "stand up" for its export interests. The Chinese mission to the WTO issued a statement upon filing the complaint: "China hopes that all sides will understand its determination to firmly fight against trade protectionism so as to commonly safeguard the multilateral trading system by respecting WTO Rules."[161] This was one of three WTO complaints filed by China in 2009. The Chinese government was concerned to fend off further protection moves by its trade partners and to quell domestic criticism.

Nonetheless, as discussed in chapter 1, China files far fewer cases than one would expect relative to its exports and the likely number of potential cases. As Chinese exports have surged, they have been met with a wide range of trade barriers. Bown and McCulloch (2009) document the rising number of antidumping disputes by the United States against China. The government has favored negotiation of voluntary export restraint agreements (VER), regardless of the fact that such agreements themselves are against WTO rules. Bilateral negotiation of a VER reduces the time of exclusion from the market and can facilitate rent seeking by

---

[161] World Trade Online Daily News, September 14, 2009. http://www.insidetrade .com.

firms to set prices. For the most part, the Chinese government has chosen this route over the option to challenge the antidumping duties in WTO dispute settlement, with the exception of a few cases. China is not on the sidelines any more, but neither has it taken the forefront as a litigious state.

Conclusion

The WTO disputes served an important role in the executive strategy to manage domestic pressure from Congress for a more aggressive policy against China. Multiple forces dictated caution for the executive in the approach toward trade friction with China. A trade war instigated by unilateral protection threatened in pending legislation in Congress could risk serious economic and diplomatic stakes. U.S. multinational firms would get caught in the crosshairs as their exports from China would be subject to any U.S. sanctions and their production in China could be targets of retaliatory measures from a hostile Chinese government. With financial markets closely watching two major economies with deep interdependence, none wanted to trigger a panic reaction. While both sides seemed eager to contain trade friction within the arena of trade policy, fear of spillover could not be neglected at a time when the United States was engaging with China over the North Korean situation as a critical partner in the six-party talks. Caught between the threat of protectionist legislation from Congress and Chinese demands to resolve trade problems through dialogue in bilateral discussion that could be framed as reciprocal concessions and mutual interest, WTO adjudication became the compromise tool. Filing complaints against China demonstrated to domestic actors the executive was taking action while representing a moderate response within agreed upon rules.

In both the China IPR and Boeing cases, Congress was if anything more aggressive than industry in its proposals. Reluctance to offend foreign actors can suppress demand for trade enforcement. Those industries engaged in multinational production are the most vulnerable to such concerns even as they have large stakes in the trade issue at hand. Consequently, the largest industry actors may be passive toward providing information and support for WTO action. To the extent that congressional pressure substitutes for direct industry demands it will counter this inhibition on the industry side. Politicians who hear private stories about problems can call for actions that no company dares to request. In governments with less active legislative intervention, fears by industry may eliminate many instances of enforcement action. The high level of congressional involvement in the United States was clearly a major factor pushing the USTR toward filing cases against China. Nevertheless, the USTR is not simply responding to every demand from Congress. Mixed interests for the U.S. economy, hostility from China to external pressure, and a questionable legal case all dictated restraint toward demands for a WTO complaint targeting China on its currency policy. Instead there have been more cases put forward on other matters to address the criticism that USTR is not tough enough against China.

The Kodak case study illustrates the political pressure behind WTO adjudication, but also reveals how adjudication represents the middle road between negotiation and unilateral retaliation. Far from a reluctant industry worried about offending the foreign government, Kodak actively called for retaliation against Japan. For most countries with smaller markets, unilateral retaliation is not a credible option. But U.S. trade legislation ensconced retaliation within the Section 301 provisions of trade law, and the United States had built a record of using retaliation. In the Kodak case the industry and its congressional backers preferred the retaliation option, and only later came to see adjudication as an acceptable alternative. For the executive the costs of unilateral retaliation were too high, and it was better to risk losing a WTO case than face another round of international criticism for unilateralism.

Alongside these cases that made headlines and drew attention from Congress, there are many others that went forward as low-profile affairs based on economic interests backed by a strong legal case. As with other countries, the United States responds to industry demands and seeks to advance cases that will win positive legal rulings. But on the margin among many potential disputes, the level of political influence for an industry helps to tip the balance to favor filing a complaint. The statistical analysis of U.S. complaints against foreign trade barriers revealed that those industries that are large sources of political contributions are also more likely to have their case raised for adjudication. The evidence from chapter 3 showed how governments with high domestic constraints file more frequently, and this chapter has demonstrated that the constraints also generate a politicized selection of cases.

A key point of this book is that international courts solve a domestic political problem. Filing a legal complaint offers governments a way to show they are making efforts for their home industry. The argument is supported by evidence that U.S. industries making larger political contributions are more likely to have a WTO complaint filed to challenge a foreign trade barrier that affects their exports. The channeling of aggressive unilateralism into WTO adjudication can also be seen from the high correlation between WTO adjudication and Section 301, which is a provision in U.S. trade law that triggers institutional constraints from Congress for the executive to take action against a foreign trade partner. In sum, when governments face political pressure to favor an industry, they often choose WTO adjudication. This dynamic works on both sides of the dispute. WTO adjudication is also more likely when the respondent state faces high resistance to liberalization, such as for industries with high import penetration and a large share of employment. Acting as a lightning rod for trade conflict, the WTO dispute system attracts politicized disputes, and then works to promote their resolution.

5

The Reluctant Litigant: Japanese Trade Policy

DESPITE BEING THE frequent target of protectionist measures, Japan has chosen to use adjudication only infrequently. A close government-business relationship in the context of political stability and centralized policy making have reduced the need for the government to undertake costly signals of commitment to industry interests. The government pursues a more selective adjudication strategy that reflects economic and bureaucratic interests more than lobbying politics. Negotiation emerges as the strategy of choice, which is used for a wide range of trade disputes.

Among democracies, Japan represents the counterpoint of unified government for comparison with the divided authority of government in the United States. First, as a parliamentary government, there is unity between the legislature and executive. Second, in what came to be known as the "1955 system," the Liberal Democratic Party (LDP) led as Japan's dominant party since 1955 with only one brief interruption of its ruling party status. Competitive elections produced uncertainty over the election of individual politicians, and the margin of LDP victory shifted from decisive to razor thin, but relative to other advanced industrial democracies, Japan has experienced high levels of political stability focused around the expectation of continued LDP rule. Several factors began to shake the foundations of LDP rule as voters grew disaffected by corruption scandals and the economic malaise of the 1990s, but with the exception of one year in 1993–94 the LDP maintained its ruling status by turning to smaller opposition parties as coalition partners. The election defeat in August 2009 brought an end to this long era of LDP rule, but for the period of this study LDP dominance was the political reality.

Against the backdrop of stable rule, the LDP granted wide discretion to the bureaucracy to manage public administration of economic policy. Indeed, the dominant presence of the bureaucracy in policy making during the postwar period of high economic growth led to the portrayal of Japan as an administrative state in which "the politicians reign, and the bureaucrats rule" (Johnson, 1982, p. 154). Yet the economic "miracle" that was produced under bureaucratic guidance also served the interests of the LDP. The observational equivalence of bureaucratic versus political control has led to debate in the literature on Japanese politics. Ramseyer and Rosenbluth (1993) argue that the LDP maintained effective tools to control the bureaucracy and were engaging in rational delegation of authority. In response to political needs, the LDP has intervened to change government spending priorities over time, and certain issues such as agricultural policy have been highly politicized (Calder, 1988; Mulgan, 2005). This chapter will bring the debate to bear on the area of foreign economic policy. How does the delegation of authority to the bureaucracy influence the choice of trade strategies by Japan?

The argument of the book contends that states with high levels of policy authority delegated from the legislature to the trade ministry engage in less adjudication. Administrative agencies are cautious about the use of adjudication, which brings a reduction of their control over outcomes by granting authority to a third party and raising the risk of public failure or harm to diplomatic relations. Industries may also be reluctant about a process fraught with uncertain outcomes, high legal fees, and potential for delays. The previous chapter has shown how in the United States intrusive supervision from Congress creates incentives for the USTR to favor adjudication as a visible form of enforcement action. Under conditions of divided authority, the executive must use adjudication as a costly signal to domestic and foreign audiences of commitment to an industry. In contrast, the lack of involvement by Japanese politicians in the details of trade policy gives bureaucrats a free hand to choose how they will promote Japan's export interests. They have chosen to do so largely by means of negotiation, while pursuing adjudication for a small number of cases that addressed major economic interests and policy areas with high precedent value.

This chapter will next outline the pattern of Japan's choice of trade strategies. The third section describes the influence of centralized government authority on the implementation of trade policy. First I explain why the structure of authority and interests in Japan for trade policy establish the conditions for high levels of delegation from the legislature to the trade ministry. Then I describe the trade policy process. The fourth section presents statistical analysis of a dataset of trade barriers that represent potential disputes. The results show little evidence of politicization in trade policy. The nature of the issue in terms of policy priorities and economic stakes influences selection more than the political contributions by the industry. The fifth section examines specific cases, looking first at the use of WTO adjudication to push back against the U.S. antidumping measures on Japanese steel exports. Then I look at alternative strategies taken with China where sensitive diplomatic relations dictated against filing a WTO dispute. These case studies allow close analysis of the nature of the legal status of the barrier, diplomatic relations with trade partners, industry demand, and political interests.

The cases further support the statistical evidence that political input on specific trade disputes is minimal in Japan. Industry demand and bureaucratic connections are more important than the political ties of the industry. In addition, the findings highlight that poor diplomatic relations make states more likely to resolve their trade disputes through negotiation while strong diplomatic relations are more supportive of trade conflict.

Defending Market Access for Japanese Exports

Access to foreign markets has been a critical underlying condition for Japan's postwar economic growth miracle. The support of the United States and the multilateral trading system acted as the guarantee for this access. Yet Japan has nonetheless experienced discrimination against its exports by foreign trade barriers. Overcoming such discrimination has been an important goal for Japanese trade strategy. Government policies to support the development of strategic industries through subsidies and regulatory policies were complemented by external trade policy that supported foreign market access through trade negotiations. Japan has used both multilateral and bilateral venues for negotiation while largely eschewing the use of adjudication to challenge discrimination against exports.

Japan's negotiations to join the GATT were long and difficult because many states feared a flood of cheap industrial goods from Japan. As soon as Japan regained its independence in 1952, it filed for accession to the GATT. Ending the discriminatory tariffs against Japanese tariffs was viewed as the first step toward rebuilding its economy, and membership would symbolize its return to the international community. The United States strongly backed Japan's accession, mostly out of concern to support its ally and strengthen the position of the conservative government in Japan. But the industrial concerns of European states led by Britain and Australia opposed Japanese accession. Only after repeated negotiations including high-level talks that appealed to common security interests could Japan gain consent for membership in 1955 (Akaneya, 1992). Even then, fourteen states applied the GATT Article 35 waiver that allowed them to not provide GATT MFN treatment to Japanese exports. Another decade of negotiations led to the eventual repeal of these waiver clauses so that Japan gained full rights of GATT membership.

The explosive growth of Japanese exports during its postwar economic boom created a surge of protectionism by trade partners. In particular, the United States began to threaten more conditional access to its markets. This led to the onset of almost ritualistic rounds of bilateral trade negotiations between the United States and Japan. The American Chamber of Commerce reported forty-five trade agreements between the United States and Japan during the period 1980 to 1996, and this does not include many of the informal disputes resolved through regular diplomatic channels (ACCJ, 1997). The United States accused Japan of unfair trade, while Japan tried to assuage U.S. concerns and minimize the risk of U.S. trade barriers cutting off market access. As noted by Campbell (1993), such negotiations were effective from a perspective of conflict management that preserved the bilateral relationship. Typically each negotiation ended with a compromise outcome that forestalled major protectionist legislation in the United States and brought some changes to open Japan's domestic market and restrain its exports. By the mid-1980s Japan had among the lowest levels of formal trade barriers in comparison with other OECD countries, although its regulatory policies and domestic market structure continued to be seen as a major source of nontariff protection (Bergsten and Noland, 1993, pp. 71–72). Japanese exports faced a broad range of trade barriers as both the United States and European governments used antidumping duties and other measures to protect their markets. The Japanese government and industry responded to such barriers by negotiating voluntary export restraints, which were seen as preferable to the direct barriers.

Some trade problems were resolved through comprehensive negotiations in the Tokyo Round and Uruguay Round. The multilateral trade rounds facilitated negotiations in which Japan made gains of new market access opportunities for its export sectors to offset the politically difficult liberalization of agriculture (Davis, 2003). The government has continued efforts to negotiate more restrictive rules for use of antidumping measures in the Uruguay Round and now the Doha Round multilateral negotiations. At the regional level Japan was active to promote the Asian Pacific Economic Cooperation, although it has favored using the forum for general improvement of the business environment rather than to negotiate specific market access gains (Krauss, 2004).

An alternative strategy for Japan instead of engaging in repeated bilateral negotiations would have been to wait for the United States to impose trade barriers and then challenge them as GATT violations by using the dispute settlement process. During the GATT period, however, Japan appeared reticent toward adjudication. Japan initiated only 8 cases under the GATT dispute settlement procedure, compared with 24 by Australia, 31 by Canada, and 109 by the United States.[1]

---

[1] I thank Eric Reinhardt and Marc Busch for sharing their data on GATT period disputes. See Busch and Reinhardt (2003) for a description of their data.

Japan shifted to take a more proactive position toward adjudication after the establishment of the WTO. The newly strengthened rules made adjudication more powerful as a tool with automatic rights to a panel and adoption of rulings. Japan supported the negotiation of the more legalized dispute system in the hopes that it would restrain U.S. unilateralism. Schoppa (1997) argues that a new social context of bilateral relations made Japan less willing to accept a hierarchical relationship with the United States. Pekkanen (2001) points to a change in the beliefs of METI bureaucrats about the utility of adjudication after Japan won a few critical cases. The government has initiated cases with much greater frequency under the WTO, having initiated twelve cases in the first fourteen years of WTO adjudication compared with the eight cases initiated during forty years of GATT membership. A majority of the cases have challenged antidumping and safeguard measures. Where once the government had responded to such measures by negotiating a voluntary export restraint, it now challenges them with adjudication.[2] Japan was not the only country to increase its frequency of adjudication as the strengthening of the dispute system under WTO rules contributed to a rapid increase in complaints filed by all countries.[3]

Despite having increased its use of adjudication relative to the GATT period, Japan initiates fewer WTO disputes than most advanced industrial democracies and developing countries such as Brazil, India, and Mexico (see table 3.2).[4] Existing studies on WTO dispute initiation contend that one should expect the level of exports to correlate with use of WTO adjudication because states with more exports will have more bilateral trade flows that could encounter a barrier that would justify initiation of a case (Horn, Mavroidis, and Nordstrom, 1999; Bown, 2005a; Sattler and Bernauer, forthcoming). This provides a benchmark for comparison of which countries file disputes. Over the years 1995 to 2008, the Japanese share of world exports ranged from 5 to 9 percent, but Japan initiated only 3 percent of WTO disputes. In comparison, over the same period the United States share of world exports ranged from

---

[2] The WTO Agreement on Safeguards made voluntary export restraints illegal. Nonetheless, countries continue to conclude voluntary export restraint agreements, and to the extent that both parties are satisfied it is unlikely to lead to any complaint of violation that would appear in the dispute settlement docket.

[3] Barton et al. (2006, p. 71) note that 535 complaints were filed during the forty-six-year GATT period compared to 269 complaints filed during the first eight years of the WTO period.

[4] Note that Japan filed one GATT complaint in 1960 that is not included in the table since the data are for the period 1975–2005. The counts exclude repeat filings on the same issue, e.g., Japan has two WTO dispute numbers assigned for complaints challenging Indonesia's national car program (DS55 and DS64), which is counted as one dispute.

8 to 11 percent, and it initiated 22 percent of all WTO disputes.[5] Even a smaller trading state such as Canada initiated more WTO disputes (8 percent) relative to its share of world exports (3.22 percent). Clearly Japan stands out for filing a small number of WTO cases relative to its high income and large manufacturing traded goods sector.

From the late 1990s, the government began a new form of bilateralism as it started to negotiate bilateral free trade agreements with other trade partners. Japan had long been a critic of such preferential trade agreements, but their proliferation in the 1990s led to discriminatory effects harmful to the interest of Japanese business groups.[6] The stalled Doha Round, which had removed investment from the agenda at the objection of developing countries, showed less realistic prospects of solving the concerns of Japanese business. As the Japanese business community called for the government to catch up with the global trend of FTAs and improve investment conditions, the Japanese government joined the bandwagon and began negotiations to conclude its first FTA with Singapore (2002), then Mexico (2004), followed by a series of Asian partners. Bilateral agreements offered the advantage of greater speed for negotiation and flexibility to shape agreements to meet political exigencies and economic needs (Urata, 2002; Pekkanen, Solis, and Katada, 2007). The agreements include dispute settlement procedures, but these have not yet been invoked.

In summary, Japan's choice of forum for trade disputes has largely been bilateral and multilateral negotiation. When Japanese exports have faced barriers, the government has responded by negotiating solutions. Only rarely has it challenged a trade partner in court.

Toward an Explanation for Infrequent Adjudication

What accounts for the pattern of Japanese trade policy to engage actively in negotiation while taking a very selective approach to adjudication? A survey of the literature on trade disputes would suggest looking at the role of trade flows, while studies of Japanese society would point to cultural and institutional barriers to litigation. A first answer lies in economic structure and Japan's trade surplus. Research on economic

---

[5] Japanese exports compose 8.6 percent of world exports, and U.S. exports constitute a 11.3 percent share. Those figures fell to 4.9 and 8.0 percent, respectively, in 2008. Data on merchandise trade (values basis) are from the WTO Statistics database time series on international trade. See tables 5.1 and 4.1 for the annual pattern of WTO complaints for both countries as a share of the total.

[6] In Japan PTAs are more commonly referred to as FTAs, for free trade agreements, or EPAs, for economic partnership agreements.

negotiations has shown that market size produces leverage for bargaining as a state can threaten to close access to its market (e.g., Bayard and Elliott, 1994; Bown, 2004b). The cross-national statistical analysis in the fifth section of chapter 3 did not show evidence that dependency in the bilateral trade relationship influences filing patterns, but it is possible that Japan is more sensitive. Japan's position as a country with a large trade surplus both made it vulnerable to foreign threats of market closure and weakened its own threat to close off its markets. In particular, Japan's asymmetric dependence on the United States for both market access and security defense may have made the government hesitate to challenge its "big brother." As a corollary, the protection of Japan's sensitive agricultural markets with measures that were vulnerable to legal challenge could have supported a cautious approach following the old adage that those in glass houses should not throw stones.

Yet this trade structure argument seems insufficient given that when Japan did file GATT complaints it contested barriers to the U.S. and EU markets even during the late 1980s when the trade imbalance had reached its highest. Moreover, Japan challenged U.S. sanctions in 1987 with a GATT case during the same year that it was engaged in a losing battle before a GATT panel against its agricultural quotas and when U.S. rice farmers had submitted a petition requesting that the United States initiate a GATT case against Japanese protection of its rice market.[7] Japan also initiated a case against European antidumping measures in 1988 when it was engaged in a defense against a European complaint about discriminatory tax measures on alcoholic beverages. If the trade surplus and glass house arguments were ever to restrain Japanese initiation of GATT disputes, they would have operated at their strongest in 1987–88. The decisions by Japan to initiate GATT cases against the United States and European Community in 1987 and 1988 when the trade surplus was at its peak and it was involved as a defendant in GATT disputes with both parties suggest that the trade balance and glass house arguments are insufficient, although certainly one cannot dismiss their overall relevance.

A second answer would point to the lack of a litigious culture and low legal capacity in Japan. One could argue that because Japanese are

---

[7] Japan initiated the case "Unilateral Measures on Imports of Certain Japanese Products (Semiconductor Retaliation)" in May 1987, which overlapped with the period of panel hearings for the case filed by the United States in 1986, "Restrictions on Certain Agricultural Products" (three panels were convened between March 1987 and the ruling in November 1987). The U.S. Rice Millers Association submitted its petition under Section 301 of the U.S. Trade Act in 1986 and again in 1988. See Davis (2003, pp. 161–162, 183).

less prone to use litigation in general, the government is also less likely to initiate international legal action for trade disputes. A noted Japanese legal scholar describes the Japanese "premodern" legal consciousness and view that private disputes should be resolved out of court (Kawashima, 1967, p. 127). In a series of case studies of famous litigation suits against pollution in Japan during the 1970s, Upham (1976, p. 597) describes the complex attitudes of the affected communities toward the litigation. He writes that the Japanese were unable to adopt the American model of litigation as a detached appeal to neutral rules and rather saw it as an assertion of individual rights akin to a violent action protesting abuse by authorities.[8] The preference for informal enforcement over litigation is also present in government. In his description of the power of MITI, Johnson (1982, pp. 40, 273) says government and industry find it convenient to enforce policies through informal administrative guidance and the threat of implicit authority to take punitive actions rather than by means of direct litigation and penalties.[9] Ramseyer (1985) contends that the bureaucracy has erected barriers to litigation in order to maintain a consensual myth supporting the legitimacy of bureaucratic authority. Product liability suits and antitrust actions were notably rare until the 1990s (Bergsten and Noland, 1993, pp. 73, 78). Specifically in the area of trade, Japan has not been a regular user of antidumping measures, which represent a frequent source of domestic litigation related to trade policy in many other countries.

Thus one might suspect that Japan finds it more costly to initiate trade complaints because it has a smaller supply of trained lawyers and is not accustomed to the practice of adversarial legal dispute settlement.[10] But a small supply of lawyers need not act as a constraint because states frequently hire international trade law firms to provide the legal support for WTO adjudication, a practice common for not only Japan but also other governments. The lack of domestic litigation experience has not impeded Japanese firms from gaining extensive experience with litigation as they have been targeted in product liability suits and antidumping investigations by foreign countries. Furthermore, Japanese government offices are staffed largely by officials who graduated from the law

---

[8] Despite the observation of low litigation levels in Japan, some scholars contest the notion of an antilitigation culture. Research shows that Japanese individuals respond to incentives—negotiating efficient out-of-court settlements or increasing their use of litigation when cost barriers are reduced (Ramseyer and Nakazato, 1989; West, 2001).

[9] See also Upham (1987, 1996) on bureaucratic informalism.

[10] The lower level of litigation in Japan is endogenous to the small number of lawyers, which are restricted by the low number of certification granted each year. Kelemen and Sibbitt (2002, p. 295) calculate that Japan in 2002 had one lawyer for every 7,000 residents, compared with one lawyer per 300 residents in the United States.

departments of prestigious universities. While not professional lawyers, such officials are well versed in law.

The empirical pattern of adjudication does not match the legal culture argument. First, if Japanese society and government have an aversion to litigation, one would not expect variation over time. Yet we observe that Japan increased its use of adjudication in the 1990s. Moreover, Japan's new willingness to use adjudication for trade disputes occured when the system became more legalistic with the establishment of WTO dispute settlement. GATT dispute settlement especially in the 1960s and 70s was largely a diplomatic affair with brief presentations by diplomats before a panel of diplomats. Nevertheless, the Japanese government advocated a more legalistic forum during the Uruguay Round. The addition of an Appellate Body of judges in WTO dispute settlement contributed to an increase of legalization, and WTO disputes involve presentation of lengthy formal legal briefs. Despite the greater legalization of WTO dispute settlement relative to GATT dispute settlement, Japan has engaged in the WTO dispute settlement at a higher frequency. Second, looking at the pattern over the WTO period there is little correlation between domestic legal changes and use of WTO adjudication. Japanese regulatory and judicial reforms beginning in the mid-1990s introduced more "American-style" law: policies to lower barriers to litigation have been accompanied by increased litigation across a range of areas, and the number of lawyers and use of formal contracts have gradually increased (Kelemen and Sibbitt, 2002). More recently, professional law schools and a jury system were introduced. The legal culture argument implies that these domestic legal reforms would have weakened restraints against litigation such that Japan would over time steadily increase its use of adjudication for trade disputes. In contrast, table 5.1 shows that Japan engaged in more frequent WTO adjudication during the first five years of the system (initiating seven cases in period 1995 and 1999). While Japanese society has become increasingly more litigious, the trend has been for Japan to initiate fewer rather than more WTO disputes (initiating two cases during the five years from 2006 and 2010).

In contrast with these economic and cultural explanations for Japan's trade strategy, I contend that one must look at the political context. Japan's centralized political authority and high delegation to the trade ministry are conducive to resolving trade disputes through negotiations. The trade ministry METI does not face monitoring pressures to show specific results and respond to individual industry requests like those constraining the USTR. Rather it is involved in a diffuse kind of exchange relationship with the ruling party to provide broad results of economic performance and support for critical national industries. The ministry has discretion to determine the appropriate means of delivering those results,

TABLE 5.1
Annual Pattern of Japan's WTO Complaints.

Year	Japan	All Members	Japanese Share
1995	1	25	4.0
1996	2	39	5.1
1997	1	50	2.0
1998	1	41	2.4
1999	2	30	6.7
2000	1	34	2.9
2001	0	23	0.0
2002	2	37	5.4
2003	0	26	0.0
2004	1	19	5.3
2005	0	12	0.0
2006	0	20	0.0
2007	0	13	0.0
2008	1	12	8.3
2009	0	19	0.0
2010	1	17	5.9
1995–2010	12	417	2.6

Note: The table lists the year when Japan filed a WTO complaint, and provides the total complaints filed by all members as a reference with the last column listing Japanese complaints as a percentage of total complaints.

in this case through choice of trade venue. The absence of direct political pressure accounts for Japan's less frequent use of adjudication relative to other states.

The shifts in political authority in Japan that occurred in the 1990s helped to change this dynamic and correspond with more active use of adjudication. As LDP rule was shaken and opposition parties came to have more voice in policy making, administrative reforms increased the pressures on the bureaucracy to demonstrate accountability. Although far from the level of U.S. government constraints on trade policy, there was an overall increase in the supervision of bureaucratic rule by politicians. This change was accompanied by a new ethos in the trade ministry to resist informal bilateral deals and instead use adjudication to defend Japan's trade interests. The period of increasing instability in Japanese politics from 1993 to 2000 correlates with the filing of nine GATT/WTO disputes (Japan filed one GATT dispute in 1993 against U.S. AD actions on steel), while only three disputes were filed during the 2001 to 2006 period when the popularity of the Koizumi administration strengthened the stability of LDP dominance once again.

Delegation in Japanese Trade Policy

Following the theoretical framework introduced in chapter 2, this section examines the motivation for high delegation in Japanese trade policy. By *delegation* I mean the conditional grant of authority from the legislature to the trade bureaucracy. A legislature can choose how tightly to constrain the bureaucratic agent through various means of supervision and control that determine the extent of delegated authority (e.g., McCubbins, Noll, and Weingast, 1987; Epstein and O'Halloran, 1999; Huber and Shipan, 2002). At lower levels of delegation, specific statutory instructions often accompany extensive monitoring and intervention by the legislature in bureaucratic decision making. This introduces politicization as politicians micromanage agency affairs.[11] At higher levels of delegation, the legislature uses less precise statutory language and minimal monitoring as it grants wide discretion to the administrative agent to achieve broad goals. Even high delegation that confers considerable bureaucratic autonomy does not imply that elected politicians are abdicating authority, as has been noted with reference to the Japanese case in the seminal work by Ramseyer and Rosenbluth (1993).

The central rationale for a legislature to delegate to an agency rather than explicitly legislate regulations is to reduce decision-making costs and improve outcomes. As the costs of decision making rise with issue complexity, the legislature finds it optimal to rely on agents who specialize and develop the necessary competence. Yet as noted by Moe (1990, p. 228), the legislature faces a tradeoff between the greater efficiency of allowing the bureaucracy to have flexibility and the desire to lock in behavior against either bureaucratic drift or future political intervention by opponents. When there is little political uncertainty regarding the preferences of the dominant legislative coalition in the next policy cycle, the legislature can afford the more efficient option of allowing greater autonomy. Leaving policy making in the hands of the bureaucracy is especially appealing when outcomes are unlikely to be popular, while politicians seek a more direct role in policies that offer opportunities for credit claiming.

This section will show that Japanese trade policy exemplifies the high delegation of policy-making authority from the legislature to an elite corps of bureaucrats in the executive. The classic study by Johnson (1982) describes MITI bureaucrats as exercising autonomous control

---

[11] McCubbins, Noll, and Weingast (1987) refer to ongoing oversight as "deck-stacking" agencies, which corresponds to what I describe as low delegation.

over a broad range of policy instruments to dictate the direction of Japanese industrial policy. Japan's experience has been viewed as a model followed by other states, with one of the core principles being a strong state role in export promotion.[12] The extensive research on industrial policies examines the role of government policies to support technology transfer and favor critical industries through allocation of subsidies and export credits. The success of these export industries relied upon continued access to foreign markets, and the Japanese bureaucracy also played the lead role in negotiations to maintain this access.

Several conditions support high delegation to the bureaucracy for the management of Japanese trade policy. First, the complexity of the issue area creates efficiency incentives for delegation. Japanese politicians lack the expertise to contribute to trade policy formation. Second, political stability and the absence of partisan differences in this issue area have reduced the political salience of trade policy. Third, Japan's defensive position in trade negotiations reduces opportunities for politicians to use trade policy for credit claiming. These three conditions will be explored in more depth below. I will also discuss how political changes in Japan during the 1990s have led to more political control with lower levels of delegation relative to the past.[13]

Each of the three dimensions that account for high delegation of trade policy in Japan contrasts with the evidence from the U.S. case study presented in chapter 4, which described conditions supporting low delegation of trade policy. The U.S. Congress was shown to tightly monitor trade policy because the combination of staff resources and close ties to industry allows representatives to achieve sufficient competence to intervene. Partisan divisions both in Congress and between Congress and the executive contribute to politicization of trade policy as Congress tries to lock in active enforcement policies. Finally, aggressive export promotion and calls for "fair trade" represent popular means for U.S. politicians to address constituent concerns about the trade deficit and globalization.

Issue Complexity and Bureaucratic Expertise

A common motivation for delegation is the need for policy expertise (Epstein and O'Halloran, 1999). Trade negotiations are highly complex.

---

[12] See for example Vogel (1979); World Bank (1993) and Leipziger (1997).

[13] One would expect additional variation in delegation to be observable across issue areas—for example, one observes low delegation in agricultural policy in Japan and most other democracies.

Multilateral talks address thousands of tariff lines across multiple sectors along with rules for subsidies and other policy areas. Even a narrow dispute about an antidumping duty applied to a single product will turn into a discussion of how to calculate the fair price of goods.

The requirement for policy expertise puts Japanese politicians in a marginal position because the Japanese political system has not promoted the development of independent expertise among politicians. The small staff of politicians and frequent rotation of senior leaders in cabinet posts mean that few politicians accumulate the kind of expertise to intervene in the details of policy. Even in the LDP Policy Affairs Research Council (PARC), which is the closest equivalent to congressional committees as a venue for politicians to influence policy, low staffing means that they rely upon ministry officials for information (Curtis, 1988, p. 113). The prime minister's office and cabinet secretariat also have inadequate staff to provide substantive policy guidance.[14] Trade ministers are appointed according to a seniority criterion and the balance of factional power within the LDP rather than for their expertise in trade policy, and one to two years is the average tenure for a trade minister. Consequently, few trade ministers take a hands-on approach to the management of trade policy.

Japanese politicians have increased their expertise and level of intervention in policy making relative to the period of the 1950s and 1960s described by Johnson (1982), but they remain disengaged from trade policy. So-called legislative tribes, *zoku*, emerged in the 1970s and 1980s among politicians who specialized in areas through LDP policy committees in PARC structured to parallel the bureaucratic organization (Inoguchi and Iwai, 1987). The zoku for industry and commerce is relatively large, while the foreign policy zoku is among the smallest.[15] Beginning with the oil shock of the 1970s and followed by the rising U.S.-Japan trade friction of the 1980s, globalization forced the politicization of foreign policy in the sense that foreign economic policy has direct consequences for local interests and creates incentives for politicians to "scapegoat" foreign actors for policy failures (Inoguchi and Iwai, 1987, p. 82). Politicians with close interest in industry could also turn to trade

---

[14] Calder (1997, p. 12) highlights the inadequate personnel resources for the prime minister by noting that Japan had only 11 staff directly advising the prime minister and a staff of 175 in the cabinet secretariat, which contrasts with the British prime minister having 70 direct staff and 400 employed in the cabinet office.

[15] There are different ways to count membership in these informal groups, but both the study by Inoguchi and Iwai (1987, p. 133) of members in 1986 and the study by Richardson (1997, p. 56) of members in 1990 show commerce as among the top three and foreign affairs as one of the smallest.

policy as part of representing constituency interests. Nevertheless, most politicians lack knowledge to address the specific questions of how to deal with foreign economic problems. For example, in a 1985 survey of politicians that asked their views on ways to address the U.S.-Japan trade imbalance, two-thirds of the politicians who responded to the survey gave no answer to this question even though the question allowed selection of three responses from a list of eleven policy options (Inoguchi and Iwai, 1987, p. 85).

Although interest groups can represent a source of information when industries lobby politicians about their concerns, this does not occur widely in Japanese trade policy. Japan's export industries have built such close contacts with bureaucracy that they have little incentive to seek intervention from their local representative.[16] With so many firms having headquarters in Tokyo, they do not require an intermediary at the capitol to represent their interests to the bureaucracy. An official of a private-sector trade organization commented that export industries do not even make the effort to lobby politicians on trade policy because they see politicians as lacking the influence to do anything for foreign trade policy.[17] This contrasts to active lobbying from import industries for changes of domestic trade policies where politicians frequently intervene to defend a tariff or subsidy protecting an industry in their home district. Most industry trade associations have a former METI official as their managing director, which facilitates close communication with the ministry. Thus in contrast to U.S. industry, Japanese industry does not rely upon politicians to mediate its relationship with the bureaucracy.

METI takes the lead role for trade policy as the ministry responsible for oversight of manufacturing and service sectors and trade policy. On the one hand, it is a relatively small ministry in comparison with other Japanese ministries and in comparison with the commerce departments of other countries. On the other hand, it gains strength from the broad scope of its jurisdiction and the legendary high quality of its staff (Okimoto, 1989, p. 113). The vaunted role of METI as the conductor for Japanese industrial policy has declined as liberalization of Japan's economy has taken away the tools for policy intervention. With few regulatory powers left, trade policy has remained an important function for METI (Sakakibara, 1991, p. 61).

Private actors are engaged through policy networks. The informal and formal groups that connect public and private actors augment

---

[16] Although see Naoi and Krauss (2009) for analysis of conditions that lead to variation over time in Japan for the level of contacts with politicians versus bureaucracy.

[17] Interview by author, Tokyo, January 11, 2008.

the effectiveness of METI across a range of policies (Okimoto, 1989, p. 152). The Industrial Structure Council, which is one such advisory body to METI, has a subcommittee on "Unfair Trade Policies and Measures" that is directly involved in the monitoring of Japan's market access agreements. Its members include representatives from industry and academia. One of their primary tasks is to advise METI on the drafting of its Report on the WTO Inconsistency of Trade Policies by Major Trading Partners (published since 1992), which is Japan's version of the National Trade Estimates Report produced by the USTR. Beginning in 2007, it started issuing reports on the compliance of trade partners with PTAs. The committee is parallel in some of its functions with the industry advisory system for the USTR and the Advisory Committee for Trade Policy and Negotiations, although it has a less extensive membership and more limited role in policy making.

Despite the high caliber of officials at METI, the relative lack of expertise on international trade law remains a constraint on use of WTO adjudication. Iida (2006) refers to "shallow legalization" in Japanese trade policy because of the lack of in-house legal expertise in the ministries. In contrast to the United States, EU, and Canada, which maintain from ten to forty lawyers for WTO adjudication, METI only has two or three professional trade lawyers. The private sector also has not specialized in trade law, with only a handful of lawyers who have experience in international trade litigation. In light of this supply constraint, Japan has hired American law firms to advise on WTO disputes and limited the number of cases it files. Of course, the decision not to invest in development of in-house legal expertise itself reflects lack of demand. If Japan had the demand for WTO adjudication seen in other countries, whether the United States or Brazil, it would likely have pushed for the development of more legal expertise. Yet no action was taken on a proposal in 2000 by the Council on the Promotion of Administrative and Fiscal Reform for establishing a committee of former negotiators and expert jurists to advise on WTO disputes (Iida, 2006, p. 42). There has been no substantial increase in the number of METI officials with international trade law expertise.

The Trade Consensus

Political stability is a second factor that supports high delegation to the bureaucracy in Japan. One-party dominance means that there has been continuity in the goals of Japanese trade policy with little need for frequent adjustment of policy orientation. The LDP traditionally counts in its core supporters both export industries as represented by the powerful business association Keidanren as well as weak sectors such as small business and farming. The tradeoff between these interests forces the LDP to perform a delicate balancing act as it seeks to maximize access for Japan's manufacturing exports while minimizing liberalization at home. Japan's mercantilist orientation toward trade policy has a long intellectual tradition as well as a strong political logic (Fallows, 1993).

The LDP position on trade policy is made easier by the agreement of the main opposition parties in support of similar goals. Across parties there is consensus that Japan is a "trading state" with strong interest in market access for its export sector. In the 1985 survey of politicians beliefs on trade policy mentioned above, partisan differences were evident to the extent that LDP politicians were slightly more inclined to favor concessions helpful for improving U.S.-Japan relations and policies for structural reform of the Japanese economy while opposition party politicians were more critical of the United States and supportive of government intervention and protection of the domestic economy (Inoguchi and Iwai, 1987, p. 89). But the left in Japan has not embraced protectionism in the way observed by some parties of the left in other countries. Unions are widely seen as weak and co-opted by the enterprise union structure that encourages members to identify with their company interest over broad class-based divisions (Weathers, 1997). Labor-based parties of the left have rarely had any input on economic policy (Okimoto, 1989, p. 123).

Even with the emergence of the Democratic Party of Japan (DPJ) as a strong opposition party since 1998 and ruling party in 2009, trade has not become a dimension with sharp partisan division. For example, examination of the issue positions listed on the official party websites shows that the LDP and DPJ both make similar statements endorsing cooperation with WTO negotiations and further expansion of FTAs as well as warning that liberalization must not undermine the domestic agricultural sector.[18] The concerns about adding labor or environmental provisions into trade agreements or outright calls for protectionism that divide party positions in the United States and Europe are not voiced in Japan. Across parties, the mercantilist consensus recognizes that Japan

---

[18] For the LDP 2005 Manifesto see http://www.jimin.jp/jimin/kouyaku/index.html; for the DPJ 2007 Manifesto see http://www.dpj.or.jp/special/manifesto2007/pdf/ manifesto_2007.pdf (accessed March 8, 2008). The Komeito 2005 Manifesto makes a statement similar to the LDP; see http://www.komei.or.jp/policy/policy/pdf/ manifest2005.pdf. The other opposition parties (Japan Communist Party, Social Democratic Party, and People's New Party) do not make any explicit reference to trade except for statements opposed to agricultural liberalization.

has a strong interest in supporting open markets and the multilateral trade system while also protecting its weak sectors.

As a consequence of political stability and consensus on goals, politicians have chosen to write vague legislative statutes on trade that provide considerable discretion to the bureaucracy. A party that fears it may be replaced in power by another that will change policy direction has incentives to use strict statutory measures to lock in policy direction.[19] U.S. legislation on trade enforcement fits this pattern—Section 301 of the Trade Act of 1974 mandates how USTR shall monitor and retaliate against foreign trade barriers including timelines to respond to industry complaints and conditions for when to take retaliatory measures. The EU Trade Barrier Regulation performs a similar function to mandate access for industry petitions and timelines for government response. In contrast, the two main laws for Japanese trade policy, the Customs Tariff Law (*Kanzei teiritsu hō*) and the Foreign Exchange and Foreign Trade Law (*Gaikoku Kawase oyobi gaikoku bōeki hō*) are much more general. For example, the clause that most directly relates to trade enforcement (Article 6 of Customs Tariff Law) states that the government may limit imports in order to achieve the purpose of the WTO Agreement and notes the circumstances of retaliation authorized by the Dispute Settlement Body or the Committee on Subsidies and Countervailing Measures or taken in response to discrimination against Japanese goods.[20] While establishing the legal basis for the government to issue a Cabinet Order that would impose retaliatory trade measures, the law does not contain a positive obligation for action or any provision regarding industry access or monitoring reports. This has in practice left it up to METI officials to respond at their own discretion when contacted by industries that suffer from a foreign trade barrier.

Blame Shifting and Credit Claiming

The logics of blame shifting/credit claiming are also given as common reasons for/against delegation. Where policies yield visible gains for constituents that can be attributed to the efforts of an individual politician, the incentives for credit claiming will dictate political intervention. Public works projects is the classic example. In the United States, hawkish trade policies have also been shown to be an area for credit claiming that

---

[19] See Huber and Shipan (2002) on the role of explicit versus vague statutes as different patterns of delegation dependent on political context.

[20] See the English translation of the law available at http://www.wipo.int/clea/en/details.jsp?id=2679&tab=2. Note the much more detailed provisions for antidumping measures or countervailing duties that raise tariffs in order to protect a Japanese industry.

encourages grandstanding by politicians. Japanese trade policy, however, is rarely an area for trumpeting success even when it achieves the main goal of continued access to foreign markets. Given its large trade surplus, Japanese external trade negotiations typically involve defensive actions. While the United States has been Japan's largest trade partner and ally, the power asymmetry of the relationship in both economic and diplomatic dimensions has dictated that at best Japan's trade disputes would end with a compromise involving concessions by Japan. Managing to forestall a 10 percent import surcharge threatened by Congress through negotiating a series of voluntary export restraints by Japan's leading export industries may be a relative gain for industry but hardly the kind of success for a politician to sell back home.

Political debate on trade policy is largely focused on implications for defensive interests in agricultural policy rather than promotion of opportunities for Japanese exports. This observation is generally supported by interviews with trade officials and politicians. In order to make a broader examination, however, I also look at the content of what politicians say in the Diet. The National Diet Library offers a searchable database of all Diet records, which allows textual analysis of the content of political deliberation.[21] As a shortcut to generalize about policy orientation, I examined the committee jurisdiction since comments issued in the agriculture and budget committees about trade are related to defensive interests, while more broad trade policy concerns typically would be raised in the foreign affairs committee and trade committee. A search of all speeches made in committee or plenary sessions of the Diet during 1995 showed that over half of the 526 speeches that made a reference to the WTO occurred in the agriculture or budget committees, and only 20 percent came up in the industry or foreign affairs committees. This pattern was even more sharp for a search of speeches in 2007, when only 16 percent of 382 speeches with reference to the WTO occurred in the industry or foreign affairs committees.[22] This skew in emphasis was only slightly less for the Diet debate over free trade agreements. A search of Diet speeches in 2007 shows that of the 579 speeches making reference to FTAs, 42 percent took place in the

---

[21] See Naoi (2009) for an analysis that uses Diet speeches to identify legislators' preferences on protection policies.

[22] See http://kokkai.ndl.go.jp. This search totals the number of speeches that made one or more reference to any of the following three terms: *gatto* (GATT), WTO, or *kokusai bōeki kikan* (World Trade Organization). This is a broad search and includes both floor and committee speeches. The search for specific reference to dispute settlement is discussed below and listed in comparison with a similar search of *Congressional Records* in chapter 4 and includes both floor and committee speeches.

agriculture or budget committees versus 27 percent in the industry or foreign affairs committees.[23]

Few politicians see gains from focusing their attention on foreign trade policy. Ken Matsumoto, a former director of the Japan Fair Trade Center, gave three reasons for the lack of politician's interest in trade: too complex, no money, and no votes.[24] Seiji Hagiwara, a former METI bureaucrat serving as an LDP elected representative in the Lower House of the Diet, noted that he followed trade issues only from personal concern and that his constituents would if anything find it odd for him to spend too much time on trade issues (he lost his seat in the 2009 election).[25] Given the many constraints on their time and resources, Japanese politicians do not want to invest in mastering the details of trade policy. Rather they have chosen to delegate these issues to the bureaucracy.

Trade Policy Process

The trade policy process in Japan centers upon the lead role of METI in coordination with other ministries and under guidance from the prime minister's office. Industry consultation occurs informally and almost entirely through contacts directly with METI and through policy networks established by the ministry rather than being mediated by political intervention.

Although I have described high delegation of trade policy to the *executive*, the prime minister's office and cabinet are typically not engaged in the agenda-setting process or direct conduct of negotiations. Neither the prime minister nor the cabinet has a formal role in the approval of a negotiating mandate for the trade round or in the selection of cases for dispute settlement. An exception has been the top-down process for negotiation of PTAs; Prime Minister Koizumi was an early advocate that the government should promote market access and improvement of the business environment for Japanese export and investment industries through negotiating free trade agreements. Filing a WTO complaint does not require cabinet discussion unless the case is seen to be especially sensitive or if a case reaches the stage of requesting WTO authorization for retaliation against a trade partner

---

[23] This search is more complicated because of the multiple terms of reference to economic integration. The use of the English abbreviation FTA, for free trade agreement, or EPA, for economic partnership agreement, is most common and provided the basis for the search cited here.

[24] Interview by author, Tokyo, January 11, 2008.

[25] Interview by author, Tokyo, January 29, 2008.

found noncompliant with implementation of ruling. A cabinet order is necessary to authorize the restriction of imports. Formal authority rests with the cabinet to submit any legislative changes and treaties, and so at the key junctures before the signing of an agreement and before its submission for ratification, trade issues will be directly discussed at cabinet meetings.[26] For most trade issues, however, officials within the bureaucracy are the lead actors in the executive branch.

The vertical bureaus of METI that oversee specific industries are typically the first contact point for an industry that encounters a foreign trade barrier. These problems are then forwarded to the horizontal trade policy bureau, which coordinates the multiple interests across Japan's industries to formulate a trade strategy. The trade policy bureau and its multilateral and regional trade cooperation sections draft proposals for trade rounds or PTA negotiations. The WTO dispute settlement section in the trade bureau addresses issues related to WTO adjudication.

Overlapping bureaucratic jurisdiction over trade can give rise to competition. METI supervises the industries affected by trade negotiations and takes the lead role in formulation of trade policy. Foreign economic policy also falls under the jurisdiction of the Ministry of Foreign Affairs (MOFA), which has authority over diplomacy and all matters regarding treaties. The Economic Bureau as well as the relevant regional sections take interest in trade negotiations, and MOFA has a WTO dispute settlement section. Yet a foreign ministry official in the international trade division acknowledged that METI starts the process by raising trade problems for discussion. He noted that because trade enforcement occurs on behalf of export interests, METI has the information and strong interest in pushing forward actions while MOFA assumes the coordinating role.[27] This coordinating role can be important when ministry interests conflict as METI pushes for liberalization for export industries and the Ministry of Agriculture resists due to the risk of liberalization for the weak agriculture sector. MOFA officials often participate in negotiations because of their staff at the embassies and delegation to the WTO in Geneva (METI assigns officials to serve abroad but at most has one or two at any given embassy). This overlapping jurisdiction has been given as an impediment to development of a more coherent trade strategy (e.g., Lincoln, 1999; Calder, 1988). Yet Japan is not unusual in requiring coordination between bureaucratic agencies for the conduct of trade policy. For example, in the United States trade policy authority is centralized in the hands of the USTR, but as described

---

[26] Foreign Ministry official, interview by author, Tokyo, January 24, 2008.
[27] MOFA official, interview by author, Tokyo, January 24, 2008.

in the previous chapter, the USTR engages in formal interdepartmental consultation with other departments before taking any actions for WTO dispute initiation or finalizing a proposal for the agenda of a trade negotiation.

The trade policy process does not involve frequent interaction with members of the legislature. Officials will brief the relevant trade committee to keep representatives abreast of the developments in negotiations, but such briefings are at most once a month.[28] WTO disputes themselves are not a topic of discussion except for an unusual situation such as the question of taking retaliatory measures against the United States after it has been noncompliant with a WTO ruling.

Politicians rarely express any interest in selection of cases for dispute settlement. Whereas U.S. trade officials acknowledge that political pressure has been present for many cases that the United States initiates at the WTO, Japanese trade officials remark that they do not encounter political pressure for initiation of a WTO dispute. Diet members rarely even mention dispute settlement. During the U.S.-Japan auto dispute in 1995 when Japan was engaged in its most controversial trade dispute that had huge stakes for its largest export industry, only fourteen Diet speeches referred to WTO dispute settlement. Speaking on May 10, 1995 at the foreign affairs committee of the Lower House, an LDP representative Iwao Matsuda urged Japan to initiate a WTO dispute if the United States implemented unilateral sanctions against Japan. The other Diet speeches about the auto dispute also encouraged Japanese use of dispute settlement for the case (five of the fourteen speeches making reference to the dispute, however, occurred *after* the government had already filed the complaint on May 17).[29] Yet this was an unusually high-profile trade problem for Japan. In most years questions about dispute settlement receive little to no attention in the Diet: over the period 1995 to 2007 only a total of 56 speeches made reference to WTO dispute settlement. In 2007, not a single politician made reference to WTO dispute settlement in a Diet speech. In contrast, over the same period there were 236 speakers in Congress who made reference to WTO dispute settlement. In 1995 the U.S. Congress held extensive oversight hearings on the U.S.-Japan Auto Parts Framework Negotiations as well as considering a legislative proposal that would have called for the USTR allowing industry to participate in WTO proceedings and appoint

[28] MOFA official, interview by author, Tokyo, January 24, 2008.

[29] Diet proceedings database available at http://kokkai.ndl.go.jp. The search used two phrases for WTO dispute settlement, *hunsō shori tetsuzuki* and *hunsō kaiketsu tetsuzuki*, and speech content was checked to confirm that the speaker statement was indeed about WTO dispute settlement.

a commission of judges to review WTO panel decisions.[30] Relative to the active attention to dispute settlement in Congress, Japanese politicians are at most passive cheerleaders of Japan's use of dispute settlement.

Thus while Japanese trade policy confronts fragmentation in terms of the division of authority between MOFA and METI, it benefits from a high degree of autonomy within the centralized political authority structure. The ruling party offers key policy direction, and ministers exercise the leadership to help conclude negotiations, while the bureaucracy engages in policy formulation and negotiation. At the level of deciding how to negotiate specific trade disputes, METI and MOFA have a relatively free hand compared with the constraints imposed on the USTR.

The differences in political intervention in trade policy between Japan and the United States contribute to the more aggressive market enforcement actions taken by the United States in WTO adjudication. But how well do they account for the variation over time as Japan has relatively increased its use of adjudication in the 1990s? I will turn to this question next and address how greater political contestation in Japanese politics has modified the logic for political delegation of authority to the bureaucracy and increased incentives for METI to take a more visible trade enforcement strategy through use of WTO adjudication.

Rising Constraints on Bureaucratic Authority?

The conditions for high delegation of trade policy discussed above have begun to shift along with the major changes in Japanese politics beginning in the early 1990s. First, institutional reforms have created incentives for politicians to develop more expertise and pressure the bureaucracy to provide greater accountability. Second, electoral competition has raised political uncertainty. And third, economic changes have created opportunities for politicians to use trade policy to gain popularity. Rising political competition has led to historic changes in electoral laws and administrative reform that were enacted with the explicit goal of encouraging policy-oriented political debate and a bureaucracy that would be more responsive to political guidance. These changes have increased the capacity for politicians to exert leadership in policy making. When the LDP fell from power in 1993, as the first

---

[30] Senate Finance Committee, May 10, 1995, hearing on the WTO Dispute Settlement Review Commission Act (S16).

non-LDP cabinet since 1955, the Hosokawa administration spearheaded the effort to bring fundamental change to the way of Japanese politics. The electoral reform adopted in 1994 replaced the multimember district system that had been blamed for the dominance of local pork barrel politics and personalism in Japanese politics with a hybrid system of single-member districts and proportional representation, which was intended to create incentives for politicians to focus on national-level policies and strengthen parties (Curtis, 1999, p. 138). Greater expertise among politicians was fostered by the addition of more political advisors for each ministry (parliamentary vice-ministers, *seimu jikan*). For the goal of furthering deregulation, the Hosokawa administration established a commission (the Hiraiwa commission) which was followed by a new Administrative Reform Committee (*gyōsei kaikaku iinkai*) in 1995. These bodies issued reports calling for cost-benefit analysis of regulations and asking ministries to justify positions publicly (Vogel, 2006, p. 99).

The reform initiative was carried on even after the LDP return to power as it sought to take over the issues advocated by the opposition and strengthen its position with the public. A series of laws beginning with the Administrative Procedures Act (1993), Information Disclosure Law (1999), and complete reorganization of the bureaucracy (the consolidation of ministries and agencies from twenty-three into thirteen was completed at the end of the year 2000) continued the pressure for greater accountability by the bureaucracy to political and societal input. From the perspective of delegation, these changes affected the first two conditions to the extent that they encouraged politicians to build policy expertise and increased partisan competition over policy issues.

At the same time, changes in the global context also increased the potential for trade negotiations to offer credit-claiming opportunities. The weakening of the Japanese economy along with the growth of China as a major export power shifted focus away from the Japanese trade surplus and reduced pressures for Japanese market opening. By the time Japan had accepted the Uruguay Round agreements in 1994, it had lower tariffs on industrial goods than the United States, had placed its agricultural protection into a WTO consistent policy framework, and was proactively engaged in a broad range of deregulation reforms long sought by foreign governments. In short, the change in Japan's economic and legal position in the global economy meant that trade negotiations did not have to be only about defensive reaction. As trade minister, Ryutarō Hashimoto won popularity at home during the U.S.-Japan auto dispute when he refused U.S. demands in a controversial negotiation breakdown in June 1995. His hawkish stance in trade talks was positively evaluated and helped propel him to selection as party leader and eventually prime minister.[31] The turn toward negotiating free trade agreements in the late 1990s followed a rise of political interest. These agreements could be concluded quickly and offered politicians something concrete to offer business groups—the business federation Keidanren positively evaluated the LDP conclusion of free trade agreements in its public "grading" of policy positions by parties.[32]

There are some signs that these political and economic changes have affected trade policy process. Naoi (2009) demonstrates that the 1994 electoral reforms led Japan to favor WTO-consistent forms of protection policies. There are also signs of more engagement to use rules for defending against foreign protection. As noted in the previous section, Japan has increased its use of adjudication since the establishment of the WTO. There are many factors including the change of multilateral rules for disputes that also contribute to this shift, but the rise corresponds with the period of increasing political contestation and pressure for higher bureaucratic accountability.

As one way to demonstrate its relevance in an era of restructuring, METI began to issue the annual reports on "WTO Consistency of Trade Policies by Major Trading Partners" in 1992.[33] These reports parallel in function the National Trade Estimate Reports that Congress mandated in the Trade Act of 1974 as part of its effort to encourage transparency. They publicize information about the trade barriers faced by Japanese industries and the actions of the trade ministry to address these problems. They are compiled after consultation with industry representatives. Yet, while consistent with monitoring of bureaucratic activity, the reports are prepared by the Industrial Structure Council, an advisory body to METI, and originated as an initiative from within METI. Thus the reports represent a form of self-monitoring more than supervision imposed by the Diet.

There was a proposal in 2000 from the Council on the Promotion of Administrative and Fiscal Reform that called for a committee on WTO disputes (Iida, 2006, p. 42). Since 2004, Keidanren has advocated a proposal for adopting legislative change to provide a formal institutional process by which industries could petition the government to receive assistance with foreign trade barriers.[34] METI opposed the proposals

---

[31] *New York Times*, August 29, 1995; *Financial Times*, July 19, 1996.

[32] The annual evaluations of the LDP and DPJ were initiated as a guideline to Keidanren members intended to advise them for allocation of political contributions.

[33] The title was changed in 2005 to "Report on the WTO Inconsistency of Trade Policies by Major Trading Partners" and again in 2007 to "Report on Compliance by Major Trading Trade Partners with Trade Agreements—WTO, FTA/EPA, BIT."

[34] The original proposal is available at https://www.keidanren.or.jp/english/policy/2004/016.html.

to establish a WTO committee or petition system with the justification that the ministry already responded quickly to industry concerns and a formal process was not necessary. Officials worried such reforms could gradually lead to establishing a USTR-style agency that would take over their role in economic negotiations. A former METI official who had been in a senior position at the time these proposals were raised commented in an interview that "METI thought that too much formalization would make it [WTO dispute settlement] more difficult to use."[35] He said that there would be backlash against cases selected through a formalized process noting that some politicians would request taking more cases to the WTO and others would say it is bad for relations with other countries. Mitsuo Matsushita, a leading scholar of Japanese trade law and former member of WTO Appellate Body, said that proposals to introduce a Section 301– style process in Japan were rejected because "METI and other bureaucracies want to keep a free hand. They don't want an automatic system that forces them to act."[36] With little interest from politicians, it was easy for the bureaucracy to resist such initiatives. As a consequence, METI continues to screen cases for those that it views best advance Japanese interests.

The election victory for the DPJ in the August 30, 2009 election augurs for further measures to instill accountability in the bureaucracy as the party platform included pledges to reduce dependence on the bureaucracy in policy making. This may lead to new attention to proposals such as the one discussed above that would reduce bureaucratic discretion. In terms of substantive policy direction, however, it is unclear that DPJ will differ in its approach to WTO dispute settlement. While questions related to new trade agreements arose in the election debates, the DPJ did not criticize the LDP on grounds of failing to defend exports from trade protection. One month before the election, a Ministry of Foreign Affairs official said that discussions with DPJ representatives about trade policy had not touched upon any issues related to enforcement and these would come up only when they had taken power and were presented with demands from industry for action.[37] There was little reason for the DPJ to attempt to micromanage trade policy in its first year, however, given that it enjoyed one-party dominance similar to the LDP. All indications are that the DPJ does not differ substantively from the LDP in its view of trade enforcement. The DPJ election platform called for market-opening efforts in terms of negotiations toward early conclusion of the WTO Doha Round and an FTA with the United States, but did not refer to

[35] Interview by author, Tokyo, July 14, 2009.
[36] Interview by author, Tokyo, January 9, 2009.
[37] Interview by author, Tokyo, July 1, 2009.

enforcement. A search of the *Asahi Shimbun*, which represents one of the leading national newspapers in Japan, shows that there were three articles about DPJ trade policy during the August campaign period and two articles during its first month in office, and no coverage of DPJ trade policy in the subsequent six months.[38] This small handful of articles focused on the policies toward the trade round and FTA policies, not enforcement or specific trade disputes.

In summary, overall there is a high level of delegation from the legislature to the executive in the conduct of trade policy in Japan. Changes in the 1990s increased incentives for greater political intervention. Nonetheless, one would still characterize Japanese trade policy, relative to that of the United States, as being shaped by high delegation.

Having provided the background for understanding Japanese trade policy decision making, it is next important to examine the actual strategy choices that have been taken to address foreign trade barriers. The nature of economic interests is a key factor left out of the above discussion. Indeed, Pekkanen (2008) suggests that the interests of trade-dominant industries largely determine the orientation of Japanese trade policy. Similarly, Iida (2006, p. 29) argues that large export industries have acted as the "enforcement constituency" that drives Japan's WTO litigation. Davis and Shirato (2007) emphasize the role of industry demand as a function of the business environment. This next section will use statistical analysis to test hypotheses about political pressure and bureaucratic interest while controlling for economic interests.

Statistical Analysis of Japanese Forum Choice

The goal of this section is to evaluate the pattern of selection for trade negotiation strategies. Japan on average files less than expected given its economic profile and in comparison with other WTO members. The analysis of this chapter examines the question of how Japan selects among its *potential disputes*. Although Japan has initiated a small number of disputes in adjudication, its trade policy has addressed many more foreign barriers in other forms of negotiations. Japan has now initiated twelve cases before the WTO, and the industry focus has been almost exclusively on steel and autos (see table 5.2). Through

---

[38] The search of the *Asahi Shimbun* online database of articles used the Japanese-language keywords for DPJ and WTO and covered the period January 2009 to April 2010. All hits were read for content to select only those with relevant content.

TABLE 5.2
Japan's WTO Complaints.

Industry	Date of Complaint	WTO Case	Short Title	Status to Date
Automobile	May 1995	DS6	US—Import Duties on Autos	Case settled before panel.
Automobile	July 1996	DS51	Brazil—Auto Investment Measures	Case settled before panel.
Automobile	Oct. 1996	DS55	Indonesia—Autos National Car Program	Appellate report adopted (July 1998).
Horizontal	July 1997	DS95	US—Procurement	Panel established, case settled before ruling.
Automobile	July 1998	DS139	Canada—Auto Pact	Appellate report adopted (June 2000).
Steel	Feb.	DS162	US—1916 Antidumping Act	Appellate report adopted (Sept. 2000), compliance arbitration.
Steel	Nov. 1999	DS184	US—Hot-Rolled Steel Antidumping Duties	Appellate report adopted (Aug. 2001).
Steel/ horizontal	Dec. 2000	DS217	US—Offset Act (Byrd Amendment)	Appellate report adopted (Jan. 2003).
Steel	Jan. 2002	DS244	US—Corrosion-Resistant Steel Sunset Review	Appellate report adopted (Jan. 2004).
Steel	Mar. 2002	DS249	US—Steel Safeguards	Appellate report adopted (Dec. 2003).
Ball bearings	Nov. 2004	DS322	US—Zeroing	Appellate report adopted (Jan. 2007).
IT products	May 2008	DS376	EU—Tariff Treatment	Panel report adopted (Sep. 2010).

Note: The table lists all WTO complaints filed by Japan through the end of 2008. The short title column lists the targeted trade partner and policy measure.

the analysis of why Japan initiated WTO disputes for some cases and not others, this section will highlight the importance of METI priorities and industry demand relative to a small role by political contributions from industry. In the absence of strong pressure from the legislature on trade enforcement, Japanese trade officials can feel free to both choose a smaller number of cases for adjudication and select the filed cases on the basis of their own criteria.

Data

I use an original dataset based on a sample of potential disputes coded from the annual METI Report on the WTO Consistency of Trade Policies by Major Trading Partners.[39] The reports were started in part as a response to the U.S. National Trade Estimate Reports that list trade barriers harmful to U.S. exports. The emphasis on evaluating the consistency of policies with WTO rules is in deliberate contrast to the NTE reports, which were viewed by Japan as unilateral U.S. criticism. METI officials compile a draft list of trade barriers primarily based on information from ministries and consultation with industry officials. They send questionnaires to industry associations and solicit both formal and informal comments. The Industrial Structure Council Committee on Unfair Trade Policies, a METI advisory body composed of scholars and industry representatives, suggests revisions, and there is a period for public comment. The stated goal of the report is to examine the trade policies of major trade partners from the perspective of their consistency with international law, and to urge trade partners to change those policies. According to a METI official, the report was specifically intended to provide a resource for finding areas in which the Japanese government should initiate WTO complaints.[40]

A single industry-specific barrier with a trade partner forms the unit of analysis. The dataset covers the period 1995 to 2004, coding all barriers mentioned in the reports for these years. Horizontal barriers that could not be classified as affecting a single industry are not included (one of Japan's eleven disputes filed during this period was on a horizontal policy and is not included in the dataset). The first year in which the barrier is mentioned in the reports is recorded as the start of the barrier. A duration variable controls for how many years the barrier remained an issue that continued to be listed in the reports. The data include ninety-four manufacturing sector trade barriers by Japan's major trade partners.[41] Japan's top fifteen trade

[39] The data were created together with Yuki Shirato. See Davis and Shirato (2007) for a description of the data.

[40] Author interviews with METI officials, Tokyo, June 3, 2003 and August 23, 2005.

[41] Although the report occasionally included references to the WTO inconsistent policies of trade partners in the agricultural sector, these are not included in the dataset because Japan has so few agricultural exports. Note that the WTO does not require that a country have exports of a good in order to file a dispute. The exclusion of agriculture rather follows from the logic of creating a set of relevant potential trade disputes. Japan is repeatedly on the defensive in WTO disputes regarding its agricultural protection policies and lacks any industry demand for a case, so that agriculture is not considered a realistic area for "potential disputes" by Japan.

TABLE 5.3
Forum Choice by Japan.

Negotiation Strategy	Frequency	Percentage
No action	25	26.60
Negotiation	59	62.77
WTO adjudication	10	10.64
Total cases	94	100.00

Note: Data on trade barriers harmful to Japanese exports are from METI reports on WTO Consistency of Trade Policies by Major Trading Partners (1995–2004).

partners were routinely included in the reports: Australia, Canada, China, EU, Hong Kong, India, Indonesia, Korea, Malaysia, Mexico, Philippines, Singapore, Taiwan, Thailand, and the United States. Trade barriers for Argentina and Brazil were mentioned oc-break casionally. The United States had the largest share of trade barriers with 31 percent (twenty-nine barriers), followed by the EU with 23 percent (twenty-two barriers).

DEPENDENT VARIABLE: FORUM CHOICE

The dependent variable is the selection of forum. In order to compare adjudication with alternative strategies, it is important to include those barriers that were raised in negotiation venues. Issues that were not explicitly addressed in either negotiation or adjudication fall into the category of no action. Table 5.3 shows the breakdown of barriers across these three categories.

The data show clearly that negotiation is the most frequent strategy used by Japan to address foreign trade barriers. Of trade barriers 63 percent were selected for negotiation, relative to only 11 percent raised in adjudication. Of the fifty-nine barriers addressed by negotiation, 44 percent were discussed in bilateral talks while the rest were addressed in WTO committees or other forums such as OECD or APEC groups.[42]

INDEPENDENT VARIABLES

This section will briefly describe the independent variables to be used in the estimation of forum choice. The key hypotheses regarding choice of forum examine the role of political pressure versus bureaucratic priorities. In my argument, WTO adjudication is chosen as a visible

---

[42] Frequently there was overlap among these negotiation venues as an issue would be raised in bilateral talks and mentioned at the WTO committee. This breakdown refers to bilateral as those that were mentioned only in a bilateral context.

and costly strategy of commitment to an industry. An executive facing legislative constraints would use WTO adjudication for politically influential industries. An executive with greater autonomy would adopt a technocratic approach that chooses cases according to bureaucratic policy priorities, economic importance, and the difficulty of the legal case. Following from the discussion on the high delegation of trade policy to the bureaucracy, Japan should fit the latter pattern. Japan's trade policy officials have a broad mandate to support Japan's prosperity with very little explicit guidance on the means by which they do so. Hence they can afford to treat WTO dispute settlement as merely one choice among several ways to address foreign trade barriers, rather than using it as a reward for politically influential industries. The following variables are used to operationalize these concepts for the statistical analysis:

POLITICAL CONTRIBUTIONS

I measure politicization by whether the level of political contributions by an industry influences the trade strategy selected to address the trade barriers in the industry. I expect that industries offering more contributions will be politically influential. In the politicized trade policy process seen in the United States (chapter 4), WTO disputes are initiated largely on behalf of politically influential industries. The parallel analysis of Japan's trade disputes will test whether a similar pattern is observed.

The contributions data represent the first attempt to test whether political contributions by industries in Japan correlate with policy outcomes. Despite the widely held perception that monetary politics are influential in Japan, few have examined the question with systematic empirical evidence. The larger question of how contributions influence policy should be addressed more comprehensively through analysis that examines disaggregated contributions data and different policy outcomes. I aim to achieve a more limited task of evaluating whether high levels of political donations make some industries receive greater government attention. As described in chapter 2, governments use the costs of WTO adjudication as a means to signal their commitment to an industry. Under conditions of low delegation from the legislature, I expect politicization of the trade strategy to be reflected in a correlation between industry contributions and WTO case selection such as observed in the United States. In contrast, for Japan where there is more delegation of trade policy, I expect less impact from political contributions.

The Japanese political contributions data measure the annual total contributions to the LDP by an industry using publicly reported totals from individual companies and industry associations. A summary below shows the totals for the period 1995 to 2002 by the leading industries.

TABLE 5.4
Political Contributions to LDP by Industry.

Industry	
Automobiles	2466.9
Electronics	2303.8
Steel	1564.3
Pharmaceuticals	897.1
Chemicals	288.9
Textiles	253.0
Heavy industry	225.2

Note: The figures are in million yen.

METI PRIORITY

It can be difficult to measure bureaucratic interest, but in this analysis I am able to rely on the statements of the ministry about its own priorities. As part of the reporting on foreign trade barriers, METI separately highlights in the preface and a press release "issues that METI deems to be a high priority in implementing trade policies."[43] Since Japan does not have a Section 301 process similar to the United States that creates a legal obligation for government action, the METI "priorities" are the closest equivalent of a public commitment to act on certain policies. Seven of the nineteen barriers that were identified as priority policies have been selected for WTO dispute initiation.

JAPANESE ECONOMIC INTEREST CONTROL VARIABLES

One would expect the government to be more willing to commit resources for larger industries that have a greater impact on the economy. I measure industry size as a production value using the OECD Stan Industrial data. Figures are adjusted to real values and are measured in log form to reduce the skew from extreme values.

High export value could similarly suggest greater economic stakes that would motivate government attention to a particular trade barrier. Pekkanen (2008) documents how trade-dominant firms have led the push for Japan to more actively engage in the use of international law to protect export interests. I measure the value of exports by the Japanese industry on a world basis in order to avoid the endogeneity of the bilateral trade flow with the presence of a trade barrier.[44] The data are

[43] This quote, taken from the 2006 report, appears in earlier reports in varying forms, although there was not explicit listing of priorities in the first years of reporting.
[44] See Trefler (1993) for an analysis of endogeneity in measurement of trade flows.

from the OECD bilateral trade dataset. Figures are adjusted to real values and are measured in log form to reduce the skew from extreme values.

The nature of industry demand for specific trade strategies depends on the opportunity costs from the given strategy. Those industries with fast product turnaround are more likely to cut their losses than invest in costly lobbying for trade adjudication that may take years to produce a result. In particular, Japan's high-technology electronics sector has shown less interest in requesting WTO disputes as a means to solve its trade barriers (Davis and Shirato, 2007). Therefore, I include a measure of the R&D intensity of the industry to control for the low demand for WTO adjudication by high-velocity industries with fast product turnaround.

TRADE BARRIER CONTROL VARIABLES

While ideally one would want a legal analysis to determine the strength of the potential legal case for every trade barrier, this is not feasible for a large dataset. Instead, I use the nature of the trade barrier as a proxy for those issues that are likely to be easier legal cases. Those barriers that represent direct barriers to imports, such as tariffs, quotas, and escape clause measures (antidumping duties and safeguard actions), represent strong legal cases for two reasons. First, the barriers are transparent and their damage to exports can be readily quantified. Second, import policies that are not consistent with WTO rules can typically be challenged on the basis of the main clauses of the GATT 1947 agreement regarding national treatment and nondiscrimination. The legal provisions are quite clear, and there is a substantial body of case precedent that can work to increase certainty of the likely ruling. In contrast to import policies, standards policies and intellectual property rights regulations represent areas that are less transparent as a trade barrier and have less previous litigation (especially for the agreements new to the WTO in 1995 such as TRIPS, TRIMS, and Services). One would expect states to prioritize import policy barriers because these policies offer more information to accurately estimate the likelihood of winning the legal case.

The economic stakes for a specific dispute are in part a function of how severely the trade barrier restricts trade. I measure the level of trade distortion from the barrier as a dichotomous indicator variable coded 1 for those barriers that are most distortionary, such as a de facto import ban, high duty (over 10 percent), or intellectual property rights violation. Other barriers coded as having lower distortion are nuisance policies such as cumbersome customs procedures and local purchase requirements. One would expect states to be more likely to target high-distortion barriers.

DURATION

I measure the duration of the dispute as the number of years that the barrier is mentioned in the METI reports. Controlling for the duration of the dispute takes into account the likelihood that states will have more time to take action on a dispute that has been simmering as a problem for many years. On the other hand, this variable could also correlate with lower significance problems from the perspective that the most serious trade barriers would have motivated action to bring a settlement sooner.

PARTNER CONTROL VARIABLES

There are many factors related to bilateral relations that influence choice of trade strategy. In particular, it is notable that Japan has close political relations with its ally the United States, which also serves as the largest market for its exports. An indicator variable for the United States allows me to control for the possibility that Japan is more or less likely to target the United States. An indicator variable for the set of developing country trade partners covered in the reports (Argentina, Brazil, China, India, Indonesia, Malaysia, Philippines, and Thailand) controls for the possibility that their lower level of development makes them less likely targets from a perspective of either diplomatic restraint or lower economic value (Guzman and Simmons, 2005). Separate indicators for all trade partners in a fixed effect model are not possible given that Japan has not initiated a WTO dispute against several of the trade partners included in the reports such that the indicator variables would be dropped.

Since trade disputes are a strategic interaction with another state, it is important to measure the resistance from the trade partner. One common indicator used for the demand for protection in an industry is the level of import penetration (ratio of imports to domestic output). The literature commonly suggests that higher import penetration brings stronger demand for protection (e.g., Kono, 2006; Trefler, 1993), although Grossman and Helpman (1994) offer the opposite expectation. Since it is likely that an import surge as measured by recent growth of import penetration presents the most critical demand for protection, I include both the import penetration ratio and the percentage change of import penetration (measured as growth from two years prior to the start of the trade barrier).

Tariff rates for the partner's industry affected by the trade barrier represent another measure of the latent protection demand by the partner industry. The barriers in the dataset are generally nontariff barriers, although a few of the barriers in the dataset are themselves directly related to tariffs. To the extent that tariffs and nontariff barriers are substitutes, one could expect a negative relationship as the high tariff reduces the need to maintain the nontariff barrier so that the partner would be more likely to make concessions in early talks without forcing a trade partner to file the WTO dispute. To the extent that the two kinds of protection represent complements, one would expect a positive relationship because a high tariff level would reflect the strength of the import-competing industry to gain government protection. Much of the empirical research on determinants of nontariff barriers includes tariff rates as a control variable (e.g., Kono, 2006; Busch and Reinhardt, 1999; Lee and Swagel, 1997).[45] Tariff rates are measured as the simple average MFN rate for the two-digit industry.[46]

LEGAL BANDWAGONING

Many WTO disputes involve complaints filed by more than one country. In some cases, such as the U.S. application of steel safeguards in 2002, eight countries including Japan filed WTO complaints against the United States. When another country files a WTO complaint against a foreign trade barrier that affects Japanese exports, it could produce a bandwagoning phenomenon to increase the likelihood of a Japanese government filing. The diplomatic risk is diffused through joint filing while compliance likelihood increases from the added leverage of other countries. Iida (2006, p. 30) argues that bandwagoning has been an important factor to shape Japan's WTO adjudication because "Japan is very reluctant to take the initiative on its own in the international community." On the other hand, a free-rider logic would suggest that when another country files a dispute against a barrier, Japan might choose not to file. Any policy change to correct the trade barrier resulting from dispute settlement would be generalized through MFN to benefit Japan's market access regardless of whether it actually filed a complaint. The variable is coded as a dichotomous indicator for whether another country has filed a complaint against the same barrier.

Results

Model 1 follows the same structure as the analysis of U.S. trade barriers in chapter 4. Using logistic regression, I estimate whether a complaint was filed in a given year for cross-section time series data on trade

---

[45] Ray (1981) showed that there is little reverse feedback from the nontariff barrier to tariffs.

[46] Data are from the UNCTAD Trade Analysis and Information System dataset.

TABLE 5.5
Logistic Regression Estimation Results: Model 1.

Variable	Coefficient	(Std. Err.)
Political contributions	0.008	(0.136)
Priority	3.013***	(0.914)
Production value	4.001**	(2.027)
Exports value	−0.739*	(0.445)
MPEN (partner)	−0.050**	(0.020)
Import policy	3.302*	(1.847)
Distortion	−0.426	(0.967)
Progress	0.844**	(0.398)
Duration	0.160	(0.128)
U.S.	−2.021	(1.332)
Non-OECD partner	−3.952**	(1.783)
Intercept	−30.731*	(16.105)
Wald chi-squared	89.93	
N	413	
Barriers	93	

Note: Data are manufacturing trade barriers listed in the Report on WTO Consistency of Trade Policies by Major Trade Partners. The table shows estimates for pooled time series with robust standard errors clustered by trade barrier shown in parentheses. *Significant at the 10 percent level. **Significant at the 5 percent level. ***Significant at the 1 percent level.

barriers.[47] All variables for model 1 in table 5.5 are parallel to those reported in model 1 of table 4.2. The indicator for METI priority has strong positive effect similar to the section 301 petition in the United States. The first difference for moving the priority variable from zero to one while all other variables are held constant at their mean is 0.10 ($SE = 0.13$), which is quite large relative to the low base probability of 0.006 for any barrier to be raised as a WTO complaint in a year if it has not been labeled a priority. The measure of political contributions from the industry that was important in the U.S. models, however, is insignificant in model 1 for Japan. Rather than contributions, the size of the industry as measured by its production value corresponds to greater likelihood of filing a WTO dispute by Japan. Production was insignificant in the analysis of U.S. barriers. Other factors such as the tendency to focus on import policies are the same in both countries. The positive sign

[47] Given the smaller sample size, however, I am unable to implement the fixed effects specification for the Japan data analysis and instead cluster standard errors on trade barrier. One trade barrier is missing data for covariates, so sample for analysis is ninety-three barriers.

TABLE 5.6
Multinomial Logistic Regression Estimation Results: Model 2.

Variable	WTO Initiation		No Action	
	Coefficient	(Std. Err.)	Coefficient	(Std. Err.)
Political contributions	0.537*	(0.315)	0.178	(0.263)
Priority	4.670**	(2.276)	−2.739**	(1.150)
Production value	10.596**	(4.139)	0.705	(0.619)
Exports value	−1.717***	(0.430)	−0.479**	(0.229)
Import policy	3.864***	(1.153)	0.114	(0.561)
Duration	−0.051	(0.074)	−0.200**	(0.083)
Distortion	0.653***	(0.233)	−0.134	(0.707)
U.S.	3.194**	(1.488)	0.481	(0.862)
Non-OECD partner	−2.815*	(1.547)	0.432	(1.514)
R&D	−0.999**	(0.475)	−0.033	(0.086)
MPEN (partner)	0.039**	(0.017)	0.001	(0.014)
MPEN growth	−7.884***	(2.155)	2.367	(1.819)
Intercept	−77.662**	(33.634)	−0.291	(5.306)

Note: The first set of columns presents coefficients and standard errors for the choice of WTO adjudication. The second set of columns presents coefficients and standard errors for the choice of no action. These two sets of coefficients are relative to the base category of negotiation in a bilateral or multilateral forum. *Significant at the 10 percent level. **Significant at the 5 percent level. ***Significant at the 1 percent level.

for the progress measure would suggest that Japan files after some partial compromise has been achieved in earlier negotiations, which contrasts with the U.S. pattern, as the United States is more likely to file when no progress was yet evident.[48]

Due to the small number of trade barriers raised for a WTO dispute in the sample, analyzing a wider range of outcomes and focusing on the cross-section analysis of trade barriers may be more informative than the time series analysis.[49]

I use multinomial logistic regression to estimate Japan's choice of forum among the three categories of adjudication, negotiation, or no

[48] The progress variable is coded by the same procedure as the variable described in chapter 4 as a four-point index. I also add the measures for MFN tariff rate, employment share of partner, and trade balance used in model 2 of the U.S. analysis. Since these variables are not significant and have no impact on the main findings, I do not display the results.

[49] The results for the key political variables (contributions and priority) are similar when estimating multinomial logistic regression of model 1 using the time series data and comparing the outcomes for filing a WTO complaint. The estimates for some of the other variables are sensitive to specification.

TABLE 5.7
Multinomial Logistic Regression Estimation Results: Model 3.

Variable	WTO Initiation		No Action	
	Coefficient	(Std. Err.)	Coefficient	(Std. Err.)
Political contributions	1.085	(0.714)	0.304	(0.273)
Priority	9.904***	(2.271)	−1.679**	(0.759)
Production value	13.689***	(3.136)	0.585	(0.599)
Exports value	−2.086***	(0.378)	−0.725*	(0.374)
Import policy	9.114***	(2.200)	0.107	(0.637)
Duration	−0.155	(0.456)	−0.174*	(0.101)
Distortion	1.091	(0.846)	−0.076	(0.699)
U.S.	4.662***	(1.411)	0.614	(0.418)
Non-OECD partner	−16.157***	(3.970)	−1.052	(0.919)
MFN tariff	0.450***	(0.081)	0.059**	(0.023)
Other country DS filing	3.382*	(1.739)	−1.311	(1.238)
Intercept	−115.871***	(32.220)	3.903	(3.742)

Note: The first set of columns presents coefficients and standard errors for the choice of WTO adjudication. The second set of columns presents coefficients and standard errors for the choice of no action. These two sets of coefficients are relative to the base category of negotiation in a bilateral or multilateral forum. *Significant at the 10 percent level. **Significant at the 5 percent level. ***Significant at the 1 percent level.

action. Given the relatively small number of observations (ninety-three), I restrict the number of independent variables used in any one model to avoid overparamaterizing the model. Model 1 (table 5.5) tests a base model with measures of the core variables for political and economic interests. Model 2 (table 5.6) adds to the base model variables for the business environment of the Japanese industry (R&D) and demand for protection by the partner (import penetration and its growth). Model 3 (table 5.7) adds variables for the tariff protection level of the trade partner as an alternative measure of partner demand for protection and also adds the indicator that another country has filed a WTO dispute. In each model, coefficients are estimated for the adjudication and no action categories relative to the base category of negotiation, which is the most frequent outcome. Robust standard errors are estimated with clustering by industry to account for unobserved correlation among cases from the same industry.

The effect of political contributions on the likelihood of WTO initiation is positive, but with marginal size and significance. The variable does not reach conventional levels of statistical significance in either model 1 or model 3, although it is significant to the 10 percent level in model 2. When testing a wide range of different model specifications, the variable is consistently positive but varies in its size and significance. In all models, the estimated effect of political contributions remains substantially smaller than METI priorities or industry size and import policy variables. As noted before, Japan initiates WTO disputes largely for the auto and steel industries. These are industries that make substantial contributions, but so does the electronics industry, which has had only one WTO dispute filed on its behalf. Overall it appears to be a relatively weak pattern of political selection in WTO disputes. This contrasts sharply with the evidence from the previous chapter showing that in the United States political contributions is one of the most important factors to influence which industries are selected for WTO adjudication. In the parallel statistical analysis of U.S. trade strategies, the political contributions variable had a larger effect than either economic variables or the preference for import policy barriers as easy legal targets.

The results show stronger evidence that bureaucratic interests shape strategy selection. The METI priority list increases the likelihood that the case will at least be negotiated (there is a significant negative coefficient for the no action estimates) and has a significant positive effect on the likelihood that the case will be selected for WTO adjudication. In addition, the government is more likely to file for the largest industries and those cases that are expected to be easy legal victories on import policies. Nobody benefits from losing a case, and Japan's bureaucracy does not face the strong political pressure that can lead other states to initiate marginal legal cases (the classic example is the Kodak-Fuji case, discussed in chapter 4, where political pressure led the USTR to initiate a WTO dispute against Japan with very little prospect of winning the legal ruling by the panel). Thus Japanese trade officials can select cases on the basis of ministry priorities and the cost-benefit analysis of helping larger industries and taking the strongest legal cases.

One surprise is the significant negative effect of exports value. The fact that the coefficient is negative for both the estimation of WTO initiation and no action indicates the underlying positive correlation with the choice of negotiation. Although I had expected the variable to be positive for WTO adjudication, the negative result could reflect use of negotiation to reach quicker settlements than would be likely through adjudication. Higher export dependence may also make firms more sensitive to the possibility that the publicity given to a WTO complaint, which appears aggressive as a lawsuit against a trade partner, would lead to discrimination by the partner government or hostility from consumers.[50] Thus trade-dominant firms may have a large stake in the multilateral trade system, and yet still favor low-profile negotiation of their disputes when possible.

As expected from earlier research, industries in a high-velocity business environment (measured by R&D ratio) have lower demand for WTO dispute adjudication (Davis and Shirato, 2007). For these industries, the need to invest in R&D to keep up with rapid product turnover increases the opportunity costs for the time and money of WTO dispute adjudication. Even while rampant piracy in Southeast Asia and China is a major concern for Japanese industries, they have not demanded WTO dispute cases. The United States has enacted an explicit measure to encourage the USTR to target the intellectual property violations that are frequent problems for such industries. Its "Special 301" of the Trade Act of 1974 instructs the USTR to investigate foreign practices that infringe on the IPR protection of U.S. firms. This U.S. institutional constraint works to counteract the general pattern among WTO members for lower initiation of WTO disputes for IPR as a policy issue and for the electronics industry. The United States has challenged China in the WTO with a complaint against its inadequate protection of intellectual property rights, but Japan chose the more low-profile role of third party in the dispute.[51]

The strategic dynamics with the partner merit further discussion. First, Japan is more likely to initiate disputes against the United States.[52] Even in an asymmetric relationship with dependence on the United States as both an export market and security guarantor, Japan is more likely to target the United States. One also observes the United States and Europe frequently engaged in trade disputes. Close interdependence gives rise to issues for dispute, and WTO adjudication has come to be seen as business as usual among these partners so that there is no need for deference toward friends. To the contrary, despite many serious concerns about Chinese trade policies that are inconsistent with the WTO, Japan has yet to file a case against China (Davis and Meunier, 2011). The high political

[50] The export dependence of a country did not have a significant relationship with its tendency to use adjudication according to the analysis presented in chapter 3, and the exports value of an industry did not have a significant effect on U.S. selection of WTO cases in the analysis presented in chapter 4.

[51] The case (DS362) was filed April 10, 2007. Third-party participation allows filing a brief to the panel but does not involve participation in all proceedings or require taking sides with regard to the dispute (i.e., sometimes a third party may side with the defendant or complainant depending on the issue).

[52] Although this measure is insignificant in model 1 and sensitive to specification in regressions, Japan initiated WTO complaints for 24 percent of disputes with the United states, relative to 5 percent of disputes with others.

tensions between the two countries encourage restraint in the WTO to avoid tipping relations in a negative direction.

Second, regarding the resistance by the partner industry, the results are mixed. The negative effect from rising import penetration in model 2 suggests deference to the trade partner in light of the tremendous pressure the government faces to uphold trade barriers. The Japanese government may fear that adjudication under these circumstances would fail either at the legal decision or through noncompliance. We see in model 3 that industries protected by higher tariffs are more likely to be targeted, and there is no consistent effect for the distortionary nature of the trade barrier. Japan appears more likely to engage in bandwagoning than free riding in its approach to WTO adjudication.

The results are generally consistent for a range of robustness checks. First, I found similar results when estimating model 1 using the subsample of 69 disputes that were raised in either negotiation or adjudication. Thus if one reframes the question to ask which disputes that the government negotiates are later raised for a WTO complaint, the findings are quite similar. I also find consistent results when using different economic control variables such as the employment share, FDI levels, and industry concentration.

The broad implications from the statistical analysis provide evidence that Japan's selection of trade forum follows a much weaker pattern of politicization than evident in the analysis of U.S. trade policy. Factors related to bureaucratic interest and economic stakes are more important than political contributions.

A closer examination of Japanese trade policy toward specific disputes will allow for more attention to context and process. In the following case studies, I will focus on whether the choice of trade strategy by the executive was influenced by domestic constraints in the form of industry pressure and intervention from the legislature (recall that in the Japanese context of a parliamentary regime, the executive consists of the prime minister's office, cabinet, and bureaucracy, with METI acting as the lead bureaucratic actor). I also investigate the role of diplomatic relations as a potential restraint on trade enforcement strategies. The pattern of events as well as evidence from interviews will shed light on why some cases are raised for adjudication and others are left at the bilateral level.

In my choice of cases, I compare Japanese trade policy toward the United States and China in order to maximize the variation in diplomatic relations. The domestic constraints theory predicts that Japan will give more attention to diplomacy because the executive has autonomy for dispute selection. This was a variable that could not be adequately measured in the statistical analysis of the previous section, however, and will therefore receive more attention in case studies. The United States is Japan's only formal ally and has a central position in Japanese foreign policy. The countries not only have a mutual dependence in security relations, with over thirty-thousand American troops based in Japan, but also coordinate policies broadly across a range of issues. Japanese prime ministers were long judged on the basis of their ability to manage U.S.-Japan relations. In contrast, Japan's relations with China are fraught with tensions lingering from historical legacy, ongoing territorial conflicts over islands in the East China Sea, and competition for regional leadership. Yet both countries are Japan's major trade partners, with China surpassing the United States as the leading destination for Japanese exports in 2004. The specific issues addressed in the case studies all meet the threshold for having industry harm and a legal argument for violation. This allows me to focus on the role of diplomatic concerns and bureaucratic priorities. The first case examines the strategy toward U.S. antidumping duties, which represents a priority issue for the Japanese trade ministry. The second case investigates how Japan has responded to noncompliance by China on tariffs and other policies. Across all cases, a common finding is the absence of strong political pressure from the legislature pushing either way on how the government should respond to the dispute. Instead, decision making largely reflected concerns within the bureaucracy about what would be the best strategy for the given issue. Variation in the perceived risk to diplomatic relations and importance of the policy precedent account for why Japan chose adjudication to challenge U.S. antidumping measures and negotiation to challenge Chinese tariff measures.

Active Adjudication Targeting U.S. Steel Protection

Japanese use of WTO adjudication has clearly been dominated by targeting the United States; eight of its twelve WTO disputes have been filed against the United States. Here I will examine the subset of the five cases in which Japan challenged U.S. antidumping duties imposed on Japanese steel exports and other related products. These cases address a trade issue with well-organized industries on both sides. Antidumping has also emerged as an area of WTO law in which there have been many rulings by WTO panels, and these rulings have had a consistently pro-plaintiff pattern (Tarullo, 2004). This suggests an area where there is less uncertainty over the law.

Demand for protection of the steel industry in the United States reached a new pitch in 1998 as the industry suffered from a sharp increase in imports. Steel firms and labor unions rallied a major campaign for government help that achieved wide support in Congress. Alongside efforts to pass legislation to impose quotas on steel imports, the industry sought administrative protection through petitions for antidumping duties. One complaint filed September 30, 1998 claimed that six Japanese steel firms were dumping hot-rolled steel products in the U.S. market. After nine months of investigation and court hearings, the final determination called for duties ranging in value from 19 to 67 percent.

Antidumping duties, which represent a duty applied on imports that are determined to have been sold in the home market at a price below normal value, have long served as a favorite tool for protectionism. Antidumping policies are defended as a tool against unfair trade practices, but the difficulty to objectively calculate margins for "below normal value" prices allows substantial room for arbitrary application of duties. The WTO Anti-Dumping Agreement provides rules intended to guide how governments determine whether dumping has taken place and whether there is evidence of injury to domestic industry to justify antidumping duties. Complaints against antidumping duties represent one of the most frequent sources of WTO disputes.

The Japanese government has long criticized antidumping policies and sought stricter regulation of their use. As Japanese exports surged, a wide range of products from steel to electronics and automobiles was threatened by antidumping duties. Over the years 1980 to 2008, there were 121 petitions for antidumping duties against Japanese products in the United States alone.[53] Between 1995 and 2008, Japanese industries were subjected to 105 antidumping measures from all countries.[54] At home, the government discouraged the use of antidumping by Japanese industries against imports with the result that there have been only seven antidumping measures by Japan on foreign imports to date.[55] Indeed, the three cases in the 1990s in which Japan imposed antidumping duties were used as an example of the strict procedures it was advocating others to follow (Yoshimatsu, 2003, p. 37). The business federation Keidanren complained that procedures were too complicated, and it took a year and a half to impose antidumping duties in Japan compared with less than a year in Europe and the United States.[56] Some reforms to facilitate use of antidumping measures by Japanese industries facing import competition went into effect beginning in 2009, but Japan remains a standout among all WTO members for its consistent opposition to antidumping measures

---

[53] Chad P. Bown "Global Antidumping Database" Version 5.0 Beta, June 9, 2009, available at www.brandeis.edu/~cbown/global_ad/, accessed July 2, 2009.

[54] *Nihon Keizai Shimbun*, November 23, 2008.

[55] *Nihon Keizai Shimbun*, November 23, 2008.

[56] *Nihon Keizai Shimbun*, November 23, 2008.

both at home and abroad. In multilateral negotiations, Japanese officials push antidumping as a priority negotiation item. During the final days of the failed Seattle Ministerial meeting in December 1999, the Japanese Prime Minister Keizo Obuchi directly refused an appeal from President Clinton that he withdraw a Japanese negotiation proposal to place antidumping on the agenda for a new WTO trade round (Iida, 2006, p. 214). Japan is a leading member of the negotiating group (oddly called "AD Friends") of sixteen states that seek to enhance disciplines of the antidumping rules as part of the Doha Round rules negotiations.

The Japanese steel industry and government share a common purpose in their efforts against U.S. antidumping measures. The steel industry is one of the most frequent victims of antidumping duties. By 1999 antidumping investigations affected 80 percent of Japanese steel exports to the United States (Pekkanen, 2008, p. 66). Industry representatives were angry because they knew there was strong demand for their products in the United States and they were losing the market directly as a result of the antidumping policies. In approaching METI, the industry said they would do whatever was necessary and wanted a WTO case.[57] The Japanese steel industry is only modest in size with iron and steel composing 2.7 percent of total manufacturing employment and 5.9 percent of the value of manufactured goods.[58] But it has long been one of the core industries in Japanese industrial policy and benefits from close relations with METI. Pekkanen (2008, p. 63) writes that steel has been "the single most consistently favored sector by the Japanese government over the postwar period," and affirms that this favoritism of the industry continues today. The industry gains influence through the activities of a strong industry association and the leadership role of Nippon Steel Corporation (NSC), which is among the top global producers of steel and one of the leading companies of the Japanese business federation Keidanren (three past Keidanren presidents have been NSC executives). The slow business environment and limited range of products that characterize the steel industry also increase incentives for the industry to adopt a long-term strategy and lobby against foreign protection (Davis and Shirato, 2007). Furthermore, the U.S. antidumping duties on Japanese steel products end up raising the costs for Japanese auto firms that have invested in the U.S. market but continue to prefer importing specialty Japanese steel for their inputs. Although the auto

---

[57] Interview of METI official, Tokyo, August 25, 2005.
[58] Figures from 2006 as reported in Statistics Bureau, Ministry of Internal Affairs and Communication, *Statistical Handbook of Japan 2008*, p. 67.

industry has not specifically lobbied the government for these cases, METI officials are aware of the broader ripple effects affecting industries beyond steel.[59]

In the hot-rolled steel case, the Japanese steel industry immediately rejected the charges of dumping and sought help from the Japanese government. With domestic demand down after years of economic malaise in Japan and cutbacks in public works projects, it was essential for the industry to defend its access to the U.S. market. As the case worked its way through the legal process, the Japanese ambassador to the United States Kunihiko Saito expressed concerns about the case to the top Department of Commerce (DOC) official involved in the case (Iida, 2006, p. 195). While the government was supporting the industry position and refraining from past practice to encourage a voluntary export restraint, Trade Minister Kaoru Yosano adopted a moderate approach to declare that "the Japanese Government was not taking a confrontational attitude toward the United States" in a speech the day before the DOC issued its preliminary ruling against the Japanese steelmakers (Iida, 2006, p. 201). This position hardened in response to demand from the industry. When the final U.S. International Trade Commission (ITC) ruling went against the Japanese companies in June 1999, NSC condemned the decision and said it would consider seeking a WTO case against the measures and increased its pressure on government (Iida, 2006, pp. 208, 211). An increasing number of petitions against other steel products had convinced the industry that strong action was necessary to deter future abuse of antidumping.

In September Trade Minister Yosano publicly stated the government was considering a WTO complaint, and on November 18, 1999 Japan formally filed the challenge (DS184, "United States—Anti-Dumping Measures on Certain Hot-Rolled Steel Products from Japan"). The Japanese steel industry paid the fees for the government to hire a top American law firm to represent the government for the case. The legal claims were based on charges that the ITC and DOC had used inappropriate data to reach the determination of domestic industry injury and sales price.

This was not an easy time for Japan to confront U.S. antidumping policies. As the U.S. geared up for a presidential election, steelworkers represented an important constituency for Vice President Al Gore. The administration had opposed the steel quota legislation at some considerable political cost, and so had to show strong support through other measures such as its "Steel Action Program" for negotiating

---

[59] Interview of METI official, Tokyo, January 30, 2008.

reduction of foreign government steel subsidies and greater use of antidumping policies.

On February 28, 2001 the WTO panel issued its report finding the U.S. antidumping measure inconsistent with WTO rules. Several points in the U.S. adoption of the specific AD measures were found to be problematic, such as the DOC decision to reject information submitted by the Japanese companies. More general DOC practices, in particular its selective use of information on home market sales defined as "arm's length" for the calculation of normal value, were found to be biased toward making a positive dumping finding. The ruling was upheld on appeal and adopted by the Dispute Settlement Body on August 23. Some of the legal claims advanced by the Japanese government were dismissed, but the principle finding concluded that the U.S. measure should be revised to bring it into conformity with WTO rules.[60]

Compliance for the United States would require both administrative change for the specific AD measure and legislative change to amend the process for DOC calculation of dumping margins. The former was easier, and the dumping margins on hot-rolled steel were immediately reduced by the DOC. Yet by this time the dumping measures had shrunk Japanese steel exports to the United States to less than one-third of their 1998 level, and they could not soon recover (Iida, 2006, p. 218). The necessary statutory changes have proven difficult as Congress has failed to pass new legislative proposals by the administration intended to rectify the statutory guidelines. METI continues to list incomplete implementation by the United States for this case as a priority trade barrier in its annual trade barrier report.[61] The government did not pursue a compliance panel or retaliation, and instead continues to raise the matter in bilateral regulatory negotiations and at meetings of the WTO Dispute Settlement Body while noting that it reserves its right to seek authorization for retaliation against the United States.

In four additional WTO disputes that were each taken through the final stage of litigation with Appellate Body rulings, Japan challenged U.S. antidumping procedures. In 2002, the government responded to a request from the Japan Iron and Steel Federation to lodge a WTO complaint (DS244) about the DOC refusal to end antidumping duties

---

[60] In particular, Japan lost on its charges that the U.S. ITC used the wrong definition of industry in its determination of injury, and Japan was unable to persuade the panel to offer specific guidance to the United States on its implementation for repayment of duties collected. See Pekkanen (2008, pp. 66–76) for a thorough discussion of the legal findings in this case.

[61] See the report at http://www.meti.go.jp/english/report/downloadfiles/2008 WTO/2008Priorities.pdf.

applied on corrosion-resistant steel sheets since 1993 (Iida, 2006, p. 221). The persistence of antidumping duties, which in several egregious cases have become de facto permanent measures still in place ten to thirty years after initiation, has been emphasized as a further grievance by Japan against U.S. policy (Matsumoto, 2009, p. 188). Losing this case was a surprise to the government. Subsequently the U.S. International Trade Commission revoked the duties, so that the Japanese industry gained relief from the barrier even if the government had not won on the legal points.

The government fared better to win the legal ruling for three complaints that challenged U.S. antidumping law "as such" in systemic criticism that U.S. laws were directly in violation of the antidumping agreement (rather than simply having been applied in ways that could be inconsistent for a particular measure). In 1999, shortly before the hot-rolled steel dispute, Japan followed up on a complaint filed the previous year by the EU against the U.S. Anti-dumping Act of 1916, which was a rarely used controversial law that provided for civil and criminal proceedings against foreign companies accused of selling their products at below normal prices. Panels for both the EU and Japanese complaints ruled against the United States, which repealed the law in 2004 after lengthy legislative battles in Congress.[62]

Japan also joined ten other WTO members to file a complaint in 2001 against the U.S. Continued Dumping and Offset Act of 2000, otherwise known as the "Byrd Amendment," which rewarded the companies that filed antidumping or countervailing duty petitions with a share of the revenue from collected duties. The law was seen as a red flag to other countries opposed to what they viewed as excessive use of antidumping by the United States that would only get worse with such new incentives for industries to file petitions. President Clinton had opposed the measure when it was passed by Congress as part of the farm bill, but strong resistance in Congress prevented compliance with the WTO ruling against the U.S. law until 2006, by which time Japan had joined other countries to impose retaliation ("suspension of concessions" in WTO jargon). This was the first time Japan imposed retaliatory measures against any country under WTO procedures, and it selected fifteen U.S. imports including steel and bearings as targets for a 15 percent tariff increase covering a trade value of over $50 million.[63] In the face of

---

[62] See Pekkanen (2008) for discussion of the unusual measures taken by Japan to threaten the Japanese affiliate of a U.S. company (Goss) as a way to seek compensation for the penalties that the U.S. parent company had sought to impose on a Japanese newspaper printing press company, TKS, in litigation based on the 1916 law before its repeal.

[63] *Nihon Keizai Shimbun*, August 1, 2005.

ongoing disagreement over U.S. implementation following the revisions of 2006, both Japan and the EU continue to impose their retaliatory measures and call for the United States to come into full compliance. In 2004 Japan initiated a case against the U.S. practice of "zeroing" in the calculation of dumping duties (DS322). The products cited in the complaint included both ball bearings and steel products. This was an issue where several other WTO complaints challenged similar practice and won the ruling, which increased the certainty for a legal victory. Again Japan won the legal ruling but has found the United States resists compliance. The Japanese government requested a compliance panel, which ruled that the United States remains in violation of the agreement. The Japanese government has been slow to pursue retaliation. In January 2008, Japan requested authorization for suspending tariff concessions in the amount of nearly $250 million, but then reached an agreement with the United States to wait for further U.S. revision of its rules. In 2010 the government was again considering whether to renew the process of seeking authorization for retaliation.[64]

Several broad points emerge from this litigation challenge mounted by Japan against U.S. antidumping policies. First, the decision to use litigation in these cases has been based on demand from an influential industry and a policy priority of METI officials. For the bureaucracy, active engagement in international negotiations and adjudication related to antidumping has been an important area for demonstrating action on behalf of industry interests. They have had a free hand in their choice of strategies for any particular case. Pressure from the legislature was virtually absent. One official involved in the most recent WTO dispute against U.S. antidumping policies (zeroing) said he was not aware of any pressure from Japanese parliamentarians in support of filing the case whether through phone calls or letters, and noted "AD policies don't attract their attention."[65] An official with the Center for Fair Trade and WTO Studies, a nongovernmental center that advises firms dealing with antidumping barriers and other trade problems, said that "there is almost zero interest by politicians in AD," and the only reason for an industry to contact a politician regarding a WTO dispute would be to ask him or her not to interfere.[66]

Nonetheless, there was increasing concern within the bureaucracy to demonstrate responsiveness to industry. Shortly after the Uruguay Round, a leading trade expert in the Foreign Ministry, Yoichi Suzuki, along with other officials suggested the need for Japan to establish a

[64] *Inside U.S. Trade*, January 22, 2010.
[65] Interview, Ministry of Foreign Affairs Official, Geneva, October 26, 2007.
[66] Interview, Tokyo January 11, 2008.

petition process for industries to seek government help with foreign trade barriers.[67] The idea never went far, largely because many in MOFA and METI feared loss of control over cases. In 1998, a senior METI official criticized the bland academic style of the reports on "WTO Inconsistency of Major Trading Partners." He pushed for a report that would be more visibly connected with policy priorities and show the specific government actions taken to address the trade barriers.[68] This pressure led to more attention on enforcement as the ministry issued its own press release with a "priority" list along with the report and clearly catalogued the status of each barrier. Proposals from the Council on the Promotion of Administrative and Fiscal Reform and from Keidanren to change the trade policy process encouraged METI to back up its claim that officials were already taking actions on behalf of industry. As stated by one METI official, "Bringing a case to the WTO is a way to show the presence of the trade bureau."[69] Selecting cases for its favored industry and policy area satisfied this requirement.

Second, there have been few signs of diplomatic restraint toward the United States. The two cases in 1998 came at a politically sensitive time in U.S. politics that might have suggested Japan would tolerate its protection as political expediency. The challenge to the U.S. Byrd Amendment was controversial given its prominent support in the U.S. Congress. A MOFA official commented that while typically the decision to file a complaint would not require approval from the minister level, the political sensitivity of this case meant some MOFA officials were concerned and consultation at the minister level led to approval for filing the complaint.[70] The fact that Japan was but one of many countries to file complaints against the United States on this issue may have lowered the diplomatic cost, and Trade Minister Takeo Hiranuma made sure to emphasize in his statement about the decision to file the complaint that the case had the largest number of co-complainants ever, and this showed the widespread opposition to the U.S. measure (Iida, 2006, p. 245). The two cases in 2002 came at a critical period for security cooperation as the United States rallied countries to its side for its counterattack against terrorism through the war in Afghanistan. One might have expected Japan, which was unable to join this military effort due to constitutional constraints on use of force abroad, to avoid trade friction. On the contrary, Japan's trade policy went forward unconnected to these

---

[67] Interview of Yōichi Suzuki, then serving as Boston consul general of Japan, Boston, May 16, 2008.

[68] Interview of former METI official, Tokyo, January 14, 2009.

[69] Interview, Tokyo, June 3, 2003.

[70] Interview of MOFA official, Geneva, May 5, 2003.

political and diplomatic events. The two allies have reached a point in their bilateral relationship where a moderate level of trade friction does not impinge upon political relations and trade officials are free to act based upon industry concerns. These conditions will be reversed in the approach toward China where Japan has rejected WTO adjudication as an option given low industry pressure and high diplomatic restraints.

Other Solutions for China

The Japanese approach toward market access problems with China has focused on bilateral negotiations and stands in sharp contrast to its active use of adjudication against the United States. Even as accession to the WTO opened China's market, there have been widespread compliance problems ranging from failure to implement tariff concessions to poor intellectual property rights protection. These barriers are important to Japanese firms, especially as China grew to become the largest trade partner for Japan, surpassing the United States in 2004. METI trade reports have dedicated an increasing number of pages to the discussion of Chinese trade policy. The "2009 Report on Compliance by Major Trading Partners with Trade Agreements—WTO, FTA/EPA, BIT," dedicates eighty-four pages to Chinese policies, compared with sixty-eight pages about U.S. policies, twenty about the EU, and a mere two pages for Korea.[71] Several of the barriers represent major impediments to trade that have strong legal cases, but none have led to Japan filing a complaint at the WTO.

The key factor for restraint is the sensitivity of diplomatic relations between Japan and China. The historical legacy of invasion and atrocities committed by Japan against China during the Pacific War and earlier humiliation of China in the Sino-Japanese War of 1894 continues to evoke strong emotions in the Chinese public. The communist regime relies on nationalism as a force for legitimacy that draws upon the antagonism toward Japan. Provocative statements by right-wing Japanese politicians and controversies over historical references in Japanese textbooks stoke these tensions. Territorial disputes over islands in the South China Sea, competition for energy resources, and U.S.-Japanese military cooperation all contribute to potential security rivalry. At a news conference in December 2005, Japanese foreign minister Tarō Aso said China was

---

[71] For the report see http://www.meti.go.jp/english/report/data/gCT09_1coe.html. In the 2002 report, fifty-two pages cover China compared to seventy-eight pages about the United States.

"becoming a considerable threat."[72] Incidents related to Chinese submarines entering disputed territorial waters have led to protests from Japan, while Japanese statements in support of Taiwan have brought fierce reactions from China. Although far from actual initiation of hostilities, there are clear indications of potential security rivalry.[73] It is widely acknowledged that Chinese opposition represents a major barrier to Japan's long-sought goal of a permanent seat on the UN Security Council. In 2005 Japan's bid to gain a permanent seat on the UN Security Council led to major street protests in China and vandalism of Japanese stores. Even while engaged in deepening economic interdependence, Japan and China have extremely delicate diplomatic relations.

Against this background, the Japanese government tries to refrain from policies that could spark tensions with China. Filing a complaint to challenge Chinese trade policy as a violation of WTO rules falls into the category of provocative actions to be avoided if at all possible. A senior foreign ministry official said "there is caution about provoking with litigation" and noted that it is difficult to gain consensus in the government because of uncertainty about how China would react.[74] While most decisions about whether to file a WTO complaint are made at the director level in the interministry process, filing a case against China would be considered controversial and require consultation with cabinet ministers and the prime minister. Veto players in the bureaucracy often reject the potential case even before it rises to that level—within MOFA the Economic Bureau may be proactive to go forward while the Asia Bureau urges restraint, and within METI the Trade Policy Bureau will want to initiate the case while the industry-level divisions are hesitant for fear of harming the business environment for Japanese firms in China.[75] There are concerns about official anger in China, street protests, and possible retaliatory measures either against Japanese companies with investments in China or as tit-for-tat WTO disputes filed to target sensitive Japanese products.

As in the Boeing-Airbus dispute, firms share the diplomat's reluctance to offend foreign governments because of their fear of retaliation on other issues. Very few Japanese companies bring information about unfair trade barriers in China to the government, and even when discussing problems with METI related to Chinese policies, they do not want their firm to be associated with any government action. A METI official said that the emotional reaction by China to WTO complaints "may

[72] *New York Times*, December 23, 2005.
[73] Kent Calder, Japan and China Simmering Rivalry, *Foreign Affairs*, March/April 2006.
[74] Interview by author, Tokyo, July 1, 2009.
[75] Former METI official, interview by author, Tokyo, January 14, 2009.

partially explain Japanese companies' cautiousness and why they do not ask us to file a WTO complaint against China."[76] Anticipating that the government would not take action out of concern for diplomatic relations also induces restraint among firms. Without demands from industry, the government will not go forward to file a case. One METI official noted that when the U.S. government filed its first WTO complaint against China's semiconductor policies, Japanese industry had an interest in the case but "the political relationship of Japan and China makes it impossible for Japan to raise a WTO case against China—both industry and government know this."[77]

As with trade enforcement in general, politicians have left the problem of Chinese protection to bureaucrats. There are some differences in approach among individual politicians that can shift the policy approach at the margins; for example, the change of trade ministers in 2005 from Shōichi Nakagawa, who was known to be hawkish toward China, and Toshihirō Nikai, who has been a long-time "China hand," led to a more dovish policy toward China. Nikai was able to use his good relations with Chinese leaders to help solve trade problems on a bilateral basis, and he was more likely to oppose challenging China in public by filing a WTO complaint. "China bashing" has not gathered political momentum in Japan in the way observed in the U.S. Congress. Even while Prime Minister Junichirō Koizumi sparked tensions in the relationship through his visits to a war memorial shrine, he countered China fears with speeches endorsing that China represented an "opportunity" and not a "threat" for Japan. Kōsuke Hori, serving as chairman of the Policy Affairs Research Council of the LDP, said the main economic concern regarding China was the potential impact on unemployment in Japan as more factories relocated to China, but he said that overall there was a view that the economic relationship was smooth.[78]

The most high profile Sino-Japanese trade dispute arose in 2001 when Japan imposed preliminary safeguard measures to protect three traditional primary-sector products (Japanese onions, mushrooms, and tatami) from Chinese imports, which followed several other cases of Japanese industries petitioning for safeguard measures to restrict imports. Strong political pressure backed the effort to protect influential agricultural and textile industries.[79] China responded by imposing 100 percent tariff hikes on Japanese autos, cell phones, and air conditioners. This controversy included accusations on both sides about violations

[76] Interview by author, July 14, 2009.
[77] Interview by author, Tokyo, August 22, 2005.
[78] Interview by author, Tokyo, January 14, 2009.
[79] See Pekkanen (2008) for detailed analysis of these cases.

of WTO rules, but China had not yet completed its accession to the WTO. Moreover, as Pekkanen (2008, p. 159) points out, the Japanese government was hoping all along to achieve a voluntary export restraint from China, which itself was a violation of WTO rules resisted by China on the grounds that it should not violate the rules on the eve of accession. The final resolution emerged with an agreement that private-sector cooperation would manage demand and supply (an informal VER) and Japan would not impose definitive safeguards.

At first, one could expect that this dispute would foreshadow future cases where China and Japan would go forward with WTO adjudication. Indeed, in 2002 after China's accession to the WTO, two records in Diet debate include a specific reference by politicians to the potential to use WTO dispute settlement against China now that it is a WTO member.[80] But this did not lead to sustained attention, and certainly not the escalation of demands from Congress for tough enforcement against China seen in the United States. There was no further mention of dispute settlement as a tool for addressing trade barriers with China in a search of Diet debate for each subsequent year through 2007. Even as major Japanese export industries suffer harm from weak intellectual property rights protection, frequent antidumping measures against Japanese exports, and a wide range of other barriers in the Chinese market, politicians are not calling for WTO cases against China.

An additional restraint for adjudication against China reflects that many of the barriers encountered in the Chinese market represent problems of implementation rather than laws that directly violate terms of the agreement. For example, in the area of antidumping METI describes duties applied by China against individual Japanese exports based on questionable calculation of dumping margins as a priority issue, but it is unlikely to file a WTO complaint because the formal procedures of China's antidumping legislation generally meet the requirements of the antidumping agreement. It is more difficult to prove that dumping margins are in violation when the claims arise from procedural lack of transparency rather than outright violation by the laws on the books.[81] Therefore many potential cases against China have a lower certainty for the legal outcome, and this alone could make risk-averse bureaucrats reluctant to proceed with legal action. Yet the case study below will take up an issue with clear legal violation to illustrate that even with a strong legal case, Japanese officials have been reluctant to choose adjudication against China.

---

[80] Lower House Foreign Affairs Committee session, May 29, 2002, Ryū shi Tsuchida (DPJ); Upper House Finance Committee session, March 20, 2002. Hidehisa Otsuji (LDP).

[81] Former METI official, interview by author, Tokyo, July 14, 2009.

With a consensus between industry and the government that litigation should be seen as a last resort in dealings with China, the government has pursued negotiations at the bilateral level and by filing as a third party in WTO disputes initiated by the United States. On the eve of China's accession to the WTO, Prime Minister Koizumi acknowledged that trade friction would grow between the countries and emphasized the need to resolve these problems through bilateral "dialogue" (Pekkanen, 2008, p. 117). The Japan-China Economic Partnership Consultation was established as a venue for such exchanges. WTO committee meetings and transitional review of China's accession as well as the various regional trade forums also provided opportunities for raising bilateral issues for wider discussion among members or as a meeting on the side among officials. The WTO rules and outside option of adjudication shaped these talks by setting expectations, but both sides sought to reach common understandings rather than public invocation of law with formal legal proceedings.

The use of alternative strategies to adjudication is discussed in this section with case studies of negotiations on barriers to Japanese exports of film and a brief overview of Japan's participation as a third party. [82]

Negotiating Chinese Compliance on Film Tariffs

The most basic commitment in the multilateral trade rules (GATT Article II) consists of the pledge to set tariffs according to the schedule negotiated. Therefore when China failed to apply tariffs on photographic film at the rates in its tariff schedule, Japan had an easy legal case for filing a WTO complaint. Although China's schedule set tariffs for 35 mm film at the equivalent of a 43 percent duty, the government was charging over a 100 percent duty. The Report on WTO Consistency of Trade Policies by Major Trading Partners refers briefly to the problem in 2002, and beginning in 2003 boldly stated that the measure "is clearly in violation of GATT Article II."[83] A senior official at METI stated, "The Chinese government has a clear intention to protect local firms."[84]

---

[82] The case studies include information based on interviews with private-sector and government representatives involved in the negotiations. Given the sensitivity and current nature of the disputes, all requested that the information be used on a background basis without source attribution.

[83] METI, 2003 Report on WTO Consistency of Trade Policies by Major Trading Partners, p. 84.

[84] *Nikkei Weekly*, April 15, 2002.

The government raised the problem in bilateral talks at the vice-minister level and in the context of other meetings including APEC and WTO committee meetings. The 2003 Report on WTO Consistency of Trade Policies explicitly raises the possibility of filing a WTO complaint. The report describes the issue in detail and concludes with the statement, "Japan will continue to urge the government of China to correct this problem in a timely manner, and will consider using WTO dispute settlement procedures if necessary."[85] The matter is labeled as a METI priority in the press release from METI that accompanies the annual trade reports in 2004, although without specific reference to WTO dispute settlement.

The industry involved had already demonstrated its willingness to back WTO adjudication. Fuji Film paid millions for its successful defense against charges initiated by Kodak that the Japanese film market was closed to imports, which eventually led to a WTO ruling in 1998 that rejected all of the claims presented by the U.S. government. Along with NSC in the steel industry, Fuji represents one of the few Japanese companies that has substantial legal experience with WTO adjudication. The economic stakes were large. Fuji had not yet established any FDI presence in China and had expected substantial exports once China completed its WTO accession. The barrier represented millions of dollars in lost trade. It was also a continuation of Fuji's battle with Kodak. Kodak had established an FDI presence in China through a 1998 deal with the Chinese government that promised major investment in China in exchange for a freeze on access to other foreign companies until 2002. In 2001 Kodak held a 50-percent market share in China, followed by Fuji with 30 percent and the local producer Lucky that had long received government support through failed development promotion plans.[86] Kodak and Lucky benefited from the tariff, while Fuji complained it was at a competitive disadvantage for development of sales in Chinese market.[87] As wealthy countries were moving to digital cameras and markets for film products dwindled, China was seen as a large market that would remain interested in film because it was not as wealthy — a market prediction that would later be proven incorrect as Chinese quickly jumped to digital photography.

Four years of bilateral negotiations led to minor revisions of the tariff, but there was still no sign that China would move to full compliance with

---

[85] METI, 2003 Report on WTO Consistency of Trade Policies by Major Trading Partners, p. 85. http://www.meti.go.jp/english/report/downloadfiles/gCT0303e.pdf.

[86] *National Post* (Canada), February 27, 2001; *South China Morning Post*, March 2, 2001.

[87] *Australian Financial Review*, July 8, 2002.

its tariff commitments. The Japanese government began preparation for a WTO complaint. It notified the Chinese government of its intentions to file a complaint on a Friday evening in January 2006, and the next week the Chinese government suddenly lowered the tariff to the accession rate. The Chinese government was just as reluctant as the Japanese government to see the two face off in a public trade dispute and chose to make a concession on the matter in order to preempt Japan from filing a complaint.

This kind of early settlement is one of the cases missed in most analyses of WTO disputes that examine complaints after they have been filed. It illustrates how the shadow of the law extends over all negotiations. But simply saying that the policy was a violation and that the government might pursue WTO dispute settlement was inadequate. The extra step to begin preparing legal briefs and announce a government decision to file the complaint brought the concession from China. With a high level of discretion over trade policy, METI could accept the concession without needing to go forward to file a complaint that would have chalked up a public victory.

Third-Party Filing for WTO Disputes

Whereas the Japanese government was on its own for the film dispute with China because the U.S. competitor benefited from China's trade barrier, in other trade issues it has been able to free ride on U.S. pressure on China. This is readily apparent in the pattern of Japan filing as a third party for five U.S. complaints against China. This contrasts with its willingness to file solo complaints or bandwagon as co-complainant for cases against the United States. Third-party participants may request to join the dispute settlement process at the consultation and/or panel stage. They have rights to receive the written submissions of both sides and present views to the first meeting of the panel. Third-party filing is less confrontational for bilateral relations since the third party may advance arguments in support of points made by either defendant or complainant.[88] The United States filed the first complaint of any member against China in March 2004 with a challenge that China's selective refund of value-added tax on semiconductors for some domestic

---

[88] In a study of 202 WTO disputes with 61 third parties, Busch and Reinhardt (2006, p. 461) find that 66 percent of the third parties present legal arguments in support of the complainant, while 27 percent support the defendants and 7 percent adopt a mixed position. Their analysis shows that third-party involvement reduces the likelihood of early settlement (Busch and Reinhardt, 2006).

companies represented discrimination against imports.[89] Japan joined as a third party along with several other countries. Similarly it joined as a third party for the U.S. complaint against Chinese regulations on auto part imports in 2006.[90] Japan was one of twelve members to file as a third party to the U.S. complaint against Chinese IPR protection in 2007, and in the same year joined as a third party in the U.S. complaint against audiovisual barriers.[91] It has also participated in the panel as a third party for the U.S. complaint against Chinese export restrictions for raw materials.[92]

In each of these cases there was sufficient industry interest and clear inconsistency of the policy to merit consideration of whether Japan would file as an independent complainant. Industries were reluctant, however, expressing concerns about whether filing a complaint would anger the Chinese government and lead to less favorable treatment for Japanese firms on other issues. There was considerable consternation when even filing as a third party and insisting that Japan did not share the same position as the United States still failed to avert Chinese anger. Following Japan's third-party filing for the U.S. complaint about Chinese IPR policies in 2007, Chinese officials suspended other negotiations on software and standards involving important interests for Japanese companies for several months.[93] Yet more typically, filing as a third party offers a middle route for Japan that avoids taking sides and still offers access to the minimum information about the case to avoid being left out of a settlement.

It is remarkable that the government chose the third-party option even for the case of inadequate protection of intellectual property rights in China, where Japanese companies arguably have more at stake than the United States given the higher integration of production networks by Japanese firms in China. Successful management of innovation strategies within the context of deep regional integration is critical for Japanese high-technology firms (McNamara, 2010). Japanese firms account for nearly one-fourth of all patents granted in China, but surveys of Japanese firms by METI and the Patent Office show high levels of infringement of intellectual property rights for Japanese affiliates in China and complaints about counterfeit products originating in China (McNamara,

[89] DS309, "China–Value-Added Tax on Integrated Circuits."

[90] DS340, "China–Measures Affecting Imports of Automobile Parts."

[91] DS362, "China–Measures Affecting the Protection and Enforcement of Intellectual Property Rights." DS363, "China Measures Affecting Trading Rights and Distribution Services for Certain Publications and Audiovisual Entertainment Products."

[92] DS394, "China–Measures Related to the Exportation of Various Raw Materials."

[93] Former METI official, interview by author, Tokyo, July 14, 2009.

2010, p. 6). The issue of China's treatment of counterfeit and pirated products has been an ongoing item in the list of METI priorities regarding WTO inconsistent trade barriers of major trading partners. McNamara describes how the Japanese approach to the problem has been active pursuit of dialogue in an example of public-private cooperation for bilateral negotiations. The chairman of Panasonic established a forum for firms to discuss their concerns regarding IPR in China through technical exchanges as well as delegations to China that involve meetings between Chinese government officials and leading executives of firms and Japanese government officials. These delegations have pressed for legislative reform and improved enforcement of IP protections in China. Alongside these efforts, government officials also raise their IPR concerns about Chinese policies in TRIPS Council meetings (Pekkanen, 2008, p. 203).

In short, the industry and government are not passive toward enforcement problems with China, but have preferred negotiation and third-party dispute participation over the more confrontational approach to directly file a complaint against China in WTO adjudication. The consent of the legislature to this decision can be inferred from the absence of Diet testimony, let alone resolutions urging initiation of WTO disputes. Officials involved in the relevant sections of METI and MOFA report no political pressure to launch more cases. The contrast with the legislative constraints on USTR regarding the U.S. trade policy approach toward China is readily apparent.

Conclusion

This chapter has examined Japanese trade policy to promote market access for its exports. Relatively low use of adjudication by Japan in comparison with other countries results from bureaucratic choice within the executive. The political context in Japan shaped by a parliamentary system with long-term rule by one party has supported high delegation of authority to the bureaucracy to determine foreign economic trade policy. Without the pressure from an interventionist legislature, there is no need for METI to use initiation of WTO disputes to demonstrate that it is taking action for Japanese export interests. Indeed, the trade barriers affecting high-export-value industries are the most likely to be negotiated. Since this may well be the preferred outcome for industry, METI is fulfilling its mandate. Even when the government did not initiate a single WTO dispute for almost four years between November 2004 and May 2008, there was no criticism in the Diet calling for more active enforcement of trade agreements. On the contrary, there were less frequent references to WTO dispute settlement in the Diet after 2004. This contrasts with the protests from Democrats against the Bush administration for initiating fewer cases than the Clinton administration and the proposal for new trade enforcement legislation. In Japan, the legislature has been content to leave the management of trade disputes in the hands of the able bureaucracy.

The comparison of the United States and Japan shows clearly the role of legislative constraints to push the United States toward more adjudication and absence of such constraints in Japan. Yet the U.S.-Japan comparison involves two extremes in the domestic society use of litigation, such that some may be inclined to attribute legal culture rather than bureaucratic autonomy as the explanation for low adjudication by Japan. The example of Korea offers an additional reference for comparison that is relevant to address this concern. On the one hand, Korea shares with Japan a legal culture at home with low litigation. On the other hand, following democratization in 1988 the Korean political system has been closer to the United States in terms of a presidential system with alternation of party control and high contestation of trade policy. Relative to its economic size (one-fifth of Japan), Korea stands out as an active user of WTO adjudication. Korea has filed thirteen cases since 1995 compared to Japan's twelve complaints.[94] An official of the Korean Ministry of Foreign Affairs and Trade acknowledged that Asian culture against litigation as a means of dispute settlement held back the government in the early years of the WTO, but said that eventually in 1997 the government felt "we need to show the public that we can take advantage of the system."[95] While less directly a result of pressure from the legislature, political contestation in Korea encouraged a focus on visible acts for the public such as WTO adjudication. This supports the argument of the book that incentives for public accountability influence how states view international adjudication. While legal culture may operate as a restraint, this alone does not explain the relatively infrequent use of adjudication by Japan. Korea has been able to overcome this same resistance factor. In Japan there has been less demand for use of adjudication as a public display of enforcement action than was true for Korea or the United States.

Furthermore, the societal argument that Japanese culture is averse to litigation provides a poor account for variation over time and across issues within Japan. Legal culture arguments suggest either a static view that Japan would be uniformly averse to adjudication or a more dynamic

[94] World Bank Development Indicators report 2008 GDP for Japan as $4.9 trillion and for Korea as $929 billion.

[95] Interview, Geneva June 26, 2008.

perspective that the shift toward reform of the legal system in Japan would contribute to increasing familiarity and acceptance of adjudication with the corresponding steady increase in complaints. Instead we observe that Japan has engaged in adjudication by fits and starts. Between 1995 and 2000, Japan filed one or two cases every year for the highest level of activity in its overall record from membership in GATT from 1956 to 2009. Thereafter its use has become more sporadic, with four years of no complaints. The period of heightened adjudication corresponds with heightened political competition and bureaucratic reform pressures. Pekkanen (2008) counters the notion that Japan is averse to using law to serve its trade interests with extensive evidence of areas in which the government uses legal arguments and courts for both offensive and defensive claims. The evidence in this chapter has highlighted how the government was eager to use WTO adjudication as a tool to address U.S. antidumping policies. The variation in when and how the government uses legal strategies suggests that there are more complex decision processes involved than a blanket aversion to litigation arising from culture.

Neither do trade interests provide a sufficient explanation for the pattern of Japanese adjudication. Although antidumping barriers have long been a severe problem for Japan's industries, they are declining in their significance as a problem even as the government has been taking more action to file WTO disputes on this issue. In contrast, serious trade interests have been affected by poor intellectual property rights protection in China, but the industry and government have agreed that negotiation would be the better approach. One has to understand how trade interests are filtered through the government decision process to account for the decisions on adjudication. Where the bureaucracy sees a policy priority without risk of diplomatic harm, adjudication is advocated as a solution to the industry problem. Other tactics are taken for issues that may represent an important economic problem but call for a more subtle approach. The key point is that the industry and bureaucracy can reach their decision on the optimal trade strategy for a given issue free from interference by political pressures that loom much stronger in other states.

6

Conflict Management: Evaluating the Effectiveness of Adjudication

THE PRECEDING CHAPTERS have demonstrated that legal action helps governments manage domestic political pressures. The portrayal of adjudication as political theater, however, does not mean it fails to resolve disputes. Taking legal action works both as a political tactic at home and to improve bargaining outcomes at the international level. Indeed, these dimensions are complementary. The noise generated by domestic political pressures could prevent resolution of disputes and instead is dampened during the process of dispute settlement. The argument presented in chapter 2 contends that states gain more information about each other's domestic political preferences through the decision to file complaints, and this allows them to more efficiently reach acceptable bargains at the international level. This chapter will present empirical analysis to assess the effectiveness of legal complaints to bring an end to the trade dispute.

Most studies that evaluate WTO dispute outcomes have been limited to the set of filed WTO disputes (Bown, 2004b; Busch and Reinhardt, 2002, 2003; Iida, 2004).[1] They have increased our understanding of the conditions within WTO disputes that encourage more liberalization, such as retaliatory capacity and a positive ruling. Overall, adjudication appears to produce good outcomes. The director of the WTO legal affairs division, Bruce Wilson, acclaims members for high compliance with rulings (Wilson, 2007). Busch and Reinhardt (2003, p. 725) find GATT/WTO disputes produce substantial concessions in 50 percent of cases, and partial concessions in another 20 percent of cases.

Assessing the outcomes from observed legal disputes, however, does not help us understand how WTO dispute settlement compares with *alternative strategies*. The fact that Brazil's WTO complaint against U.S. cotton subsidies took eight years to yield a satisfactory (and still temporary) agreement cannot be judged as success or failure without considering what Brazil could have achieved if it had continued

---

[1] Horn, Mavroidis, and Nordstrom (1999) and Bown (2005a) are two innovative studies that generate potential disputes in order to examine the choice of whether to initiate, but they do not take the next step to analyze outcomes.

negotiations without filing a legal complaint. Furthermore, since one would not expect cases raised for adjudication to be the same as those negotiated in other venues, research based on observed legal disputes is vulnerable to criticism about selection bias. This could give rise to a scenario in which WTO dispute settlement would appear effective only because states do not file cases where the stakes are high or compliance is unlikely.[2] Such restraint was clearly evident in the U.S. decision not to file a complaint against China for its currency policy. Yet WTO panels for trade adjudication confront a docket including many of the most difficult trade disputes. Government subsidies for aircraft development and agriculture production, regulations on food safety, and safeguards to limit textile and steel imports are just some of the issues with high economic and political stakes that have been addressed in WTO dispute settlement. In sum, research on the effectiveness of legal dispute settlement has long been troubled by the lack of evidence for the counterfactual: What if a similar case had not gone to court?

This chapter undertakes the task to compare alternative strategies and similar issues through use of the potential cases data and the theory about selection of disputes presented in the previous chapters. My argument about domestic pressure contends that the political demand for adjudication filters hard cases into the adjudication forum.[3] By *hard cases* I mean those where domestic constraints and influential domestic lobbies are involved on both sides of the trade dispute. Chapter 3 showed that democracies file more complaints because domestic constraints push them toward escalating disputes as both complainant and defendant. Chapter 4 found that the U.S. government is more likely to resort to adjudication when the complainant industry has political influence (measured by political contributions) and the defendant industry has strong resistance (measured by import penetration). The presence of domestic constraints and stakes for strong lobbies dictates against easy settlement of the dispute. Nevertheless, the analysis of this chapter will show that the choice of legal forum counteracts these negative factors to bring better outcomes for the dispute than could have been achieved by other strategies. After discussing the role of information and obligation to promote settlement, I will turn to empirical analysis of U.S. trade disputes to assess outcomes in terms of progress to remove the trade barrier and dispute duration.

---

[2] A central critique of research about international institutions contends that the selection of easy issues for cooperation in institutions biases findings about their effectiveness (Mearsheimer, 1994–95; Downs, Rocke, and Barsoom, 1996; Simmons, 2010).

[3] Guzman and Simmons (2002) reach a similar conclusion in an analysis of which cases escalate from complaint to panel stage within the adjudication process.

Solving Hard Cases

Rather than coercing cooperation through retaliation threats, I argue that dispute settlement works because it provides information and shifts domestic political balance toward cooperation. Screening for cases that are priorities for the government is an important function of the legal process. Exporters may charge that they face unfair barriers in a foreign market while the trade partners defend that their policy is reasonable. Both sides have incentives to dissemble about their willingness to compromise over a range of possible negotiated outcomes, which makes it harder to reach any agreement. As discussed in chapter 2, entering the dispute process raises a moderate cost for both complainant or defendant. Bearing these costs sends a credible signal of government resolve. The formal procedures for making the complaint, engaging in consultations, requesting a panel, and responding to the ruling all structure the interaction between both parties. As argued by Morrow (1994, p. 389), an institutional forum can "alter the players expectations about one another's actions by creating the opportunity to exchange meaningful messages." Such information facilitates more efficient bargaining over a settlement.

In addition to providing information about resolve, legal framing of a negotiation changes the stakes by adding obligation and reputation concerns to the existing disagreement over economic interests. When there is a ruling, it attains a status of legitimacy to pull states toward compliance (Franck, 1990). Most states are reluctant to be seen as violating agreed upon rules. As they are engaged in repeat interactions across a range of issues, it becomes worthwhile to play by the rules for any given case. Several different strands of institutional theory offer explanations for why states comply.[4] Socialization within the institution encourages norm-compliant behavior (Johnston, 2001). The public and leaders may hold a preference for compliance with international law (Gaubatz, 1996; Tomz, 2008). Interest in upholding the overall credibility of the rules system leads countries to comply with rulings (Kovenock and Thursby, 1992; Jackson, 1997; Hudec, 2002).

Yet it is important to note the limitations of legal rulings as the determinant of dispute outcomes. First, compliance with a ruling is a second order compliance problem that follows an original decision to implement policies that are inconsistent with the agreement. Second, a majority of WTO complaints are resolved *before* a ruling has been issued. Finally, for those with a ruling there is still considerable leeway

---

[4] See Raustiala and Slaughter (2002) and Simmons (2010) for reviews of the literature.

for negotiation over the policy change. A ruling determines whether the current policy is in violation but rarely specifies the new policy that should be adopted. Even the adjustment of a policy to achieve technical compliance with the law may not resolve the dispute if the other party remains unsatisfied. The negotiations after a ruling may quickly resolve the issue or involve tough bargaining. In a small number of cases, protracted disagreement over compliance leads to another round of litigation, as seen in the well-known dispute over the EU restrictions on the import of bananas. More than the content of the legal interpretation, it is the process of going through adjudication that helps states coordinate on an agreed outcome. Dispute settlement can be judged to have been effective if it helps to end a dispute, which may be achieved with or without a legal ruling.

The dispute process works as a communication tool *between states* and also *within states*. Governments are often driven to make extreme commitments to support a powerful domestic industry. Such public statements may push negotiators into a corner by reducing bargaining range and flexibility even in the face of potential overlap in agreements that both governments would be willing to accept (Leventoglu and Tarar, 2005). With the moderate step to escalate a dispute in the legal venue, leaders respond to demands from domestic audience and gain space to work out a solution in the international negotiation. After filing the legal complaint, in consultations the officials can explore whether a settlement could be reached if they became more flexible without the risk that they appear to have voluntarily offered a concession. Adjudication makes it possible to simultaneously send a signal of tough action and open new talks.

Likewise, reputation and obligation offer leverage for domestic bargaining. The third-party role of an international court offers political cover for leaders who must back down from their earlier commitments if an agreement is reached. The same compromise that would have appeared as a sign of weakness when offered in negotiations to an opponent can now be portrayed as cooperation that will reap future benefits (Simmons, 2002; Allee and Huth, 2006). Research has shown that legal proceedings can shift interest group mobilization against protectionist interests to make compliance possible (Davis, 2003; Goldstein and Steinberg, 2009). Leaders need a justification to give their domestic regulatory agency and lobby groups before they can change policies that were adopted to protect sensitive sectors. This argument supports the expectation that disputes brought to adjudication will be more likely to be resolved than those in negotiations.

In contrast, to the extent that coercive power drives outcomes there should be little independent effect from adjudication. Within the trade regime, the legal steps of dispute settlement if anything restrain rather than augment retaliation. There are no provisions for collective punishment, and authorization of retaliation remains limited to suspending concessions at a level determined to be equivalent to lost trade (Lawrence, 2003). Going to court may facilitate credible retaliation through information about resolve following the logic outlined above, but it does not change the capacity to retaliate. Indeed, this is often noted by developing countries that fear they will be unable to enforce rules. From the perspective of power dynamics, the venue itself will have little effect after conditioning on the capacity of actors and stakes that influence the decision to bring the issue into the legal forum.

Analysis of Progress to Remove Barrier

In this section, I evaluate WTO dispute effectiveness using the subset of my U.S. trade barrier data for the trade barriers that were either negotiated or raised in WTO dispute adjudication (see chapter 4 for a description of the data and key variables). This allows me to compare the effectiveness of dispute settlement relative to the alternative of negotiation in a different forum.

Evaluating the effectiveness of negotiation strategies poses a significant measurement challenge. One way would be to look at the change in trade flows after settlement. Bown (2004b) uses this approach in his analysis of the economic outcomes of GATT/WTO disputes. However, as Bown himself notes, GATT/WTO do not call for an increase of trade flows as the measure of compliance, and "better measures of economic success would thus include detailed information on the change in the tariff or non-tariff measure under dispute" (p. 814). Along this line, a second way to evaluate outcomes requires direct evaluation of the policy change. Busch and Reinhardt (2003) use this latter approach to classify the outcomes of GATT/WTO disputes on an ordered scale. Bayard and Elliott (1994) also evaluate the outcomes of Section 301 cases in terms of a categorical variable for policy change.

I measure effectiveness by evaluating the progress in resolving the trade complaint recorded in the National Trade Estimate Reports. I code a dichotomous indicator variable for whether the report mentions specific policy improvement for the trade barrier. The advantage of this approach from a theoretical perspective is that it is closer to the goals of the WTO agreement. It also maintains consistency with the underlying data without introducing measurement error that would come with using a trade flow measure (i.e., product trade flows and period would only loosely correlate with the specific items in dispute and expected period of implementation).[5] The disadvantage is the risk of bias in the reports if the USTR tends to be more positive about outcomes for those disputes raised in WTO adjudication (uniform bragging about results achieved across venues would not bias my findings). This seems unlikely, however, since industry actors know whether their problem has been solved and will inform Congress. Overly positive commentary would also undermine the role of the reports to inform foreign governments that the United States is concerned about an issue. The reports reveal variation in description of policy reforms with both positive and negative assessment.

The following illustrates a comparison of the coding for three cases that were all WTO disputes. For the WTO dispute about Canadian restrictions on U.S. periodicals (DS31), the report states, "In June 1999, the United States and Canada announced an agreement under which U.S. publications would be allowed gradually improved access to this market."[6] For the WTO dispute challenging EU export subsidies for processed cheese (DS104 against Belgium), it states that the United States filed a complaint in 1997 and held initial consultations that November, while noting that "the United States is considering next steps."[7] No further mention of the dispute is made again in the reports and no settlement was disclosed to the WTO. A search of the widely used trade briefing report *Inside Trade* shows that in 1999, U.S. agricultural industry sources complained about EU circumvention of export subsidies while specifically noting the example of "inward processing" for cheese.[8] For the WTO dispute filed against Mexico for antidumping duties on high-fructose corn syrup (DS132), the 2000 report states that Mexico will have to comply with the ruling adopted by the Dispute Settlement Body, but the 2001 report notes that the Mexican corn industry is considering filing a new antidumping petition and the 2002 report says that the Mexican Congress passed a consumption tax on beverages including high-fructose corn syrup, which is described as "a major barrier to a settlement of broader sweetener disputes between the United States and Mexico."[9] The first case on Canadian periodicals was coded as having progress, and the second and third cases about European cheese

---

[5] Progress is measured as the policy change observed in the years after the filing of a complaint or start of a negotiation without a fixed evaluation period. The next section will analyze the time to removal of the barrier.

[6] NTE 2001, p. 31.

[7] NTE 1999, p. 120.

[8] "Agriculture Coalition Sets priorities for WTO, Sidesteps Radical Reform," *Inside U.S. Trade*, May 21, 1999.

[9] NTE 2002, p. 293.

TABLE 6.1
Measuring Dispute Outcomes.

Dispute Outcome	WTO DS	Negotiation	All Cases
No progress	10	134	144
(percentage)	(24.39)	(46.69)	(43.90)
Progress	31	153	184
(percentage)	(75.61)	(53.31)	(56.10)
Total cases	41	287	328

Note: The data represent industry-specific trade barrier cases coded from the National Trade Estimate Reports of the USTR from 1995 to 2004. The first column describes progress toward resolving the U.S. complaint for trade barriers that were initiated for WTO dispute settlement, and the second column describes those that were negotiated.

export subsidies and Mexico's barriers against high-fructose corn syrup were coded as having no progress.

As a first look at the problem, I examine the measure of progress in the aggregate data for the 328 cases coded for trade complaints with the nine trade partners that were negotiated or raised in WTO dispute settlement (table 6.1). Of the WTO disputes 76 percent (31 of 41 cases) recorded progress. This suggests that the WTO dispute system achieves better outcomes than negotiation. Before drawing any *causal* conclusions from such *descriptive* inference, however, one needs to consider the selection mechanism that sends cases to the adjudication forum.

One may be concerned that the cases going forward for dispute adjudication differ from those that are only being negotiated. Statistical techniques of matching offer a means to bring the observational data closer to a comparison of cases that are similar in all but the treatment (e.g., Rubin, 1973, 1979). Here, the treatment group is those barriers raised for WTO dispute settlement and the control group is those barriers that are only negotiated. The pre-processing of data involves removing from the sample observations that lack common support in terms of overlapping covariate distribution for the treatment and control groups. Creating a smaller sample of more similar units by "pruning" outlier observations in this manner allows for less model-dependent and more robust causal inference (Ho et al., 2007).

I conduct three-to-one nearest neighbor matching with exact restrictions on trade partner.[10] The propensity score, which represents a single

___

[10] I implement matching procedures using the MatchIt software available at http://gking.harvard.edu/matchit. For observations with missing data for production and export control variables, I recode missing values to zero and add control indicators for the analysis (not shown).

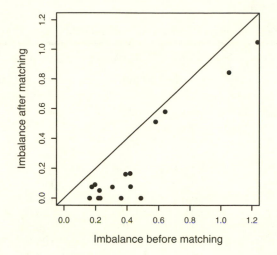

Figure 6.1. Imbalance Before and After Matching. Each circle represents a variable, and its coordinates indicate the level of imbalance before and after matching. The level of imbalance is measured in terms of standardized mean difference. See table 6.2 for a description of the results summarized here in the figure.

measure summarizing variables that estimates the probability of a unit receiving treatment (in this case, WTO dispute settlement), is estimated based on logistic regression with the covariates from model 1 in table 4.2 (excluding progress covariate). Exact matching on trade partner means that for each dispute case filed against a specific trade partner, the matching procedure will select control cases from within the group of negotiation cases with that same trade partner (the four developing countries are grouped together). I find that this improves the balance on other covariates. The choice to exact match on partner also addresses the concern that bilateral relations are shaped by an economic and political structure specific to the trading pair.

Figure 6.1 shows the imbalance between the control group and treatment group before and after matching. The horizontal axis represents the standardized mean difference (i.e., mean differences measured in terms of standard deviation units) between the treatment and control groups for a variable before matching, and the vertical axis represents the remaining imbalance after matching. The forty-five-degree line indicates where values would lie if there were no change, and variables with improvement of balance fall underneath the line. The figure shows that the remaining imbalance after matching is smaller than the imbalance before matching for all control variables. Table 6.2 describes the percentage balance

TABLE 6.2
Percentage Improvement in Covariate Balance after Matching.

	Mean Diff.	eQQ Med	eQQ Mean	eQQ Max
Contributions	58.9	64.7	51.2	11.0
Section 301	9.4	0.0	8.3	0.0
Production (log)	53.9	95.4	88.6	91.7
Exports (log)	81.7	88.3	73.4	14.1
MPEN (partner)	77.2	78.9	16.1	22.0
Import policy	60.6	0.0	62.5	0.0
Distortion	19.9	0.0	17.6	0.0
EU	100.0	0.0	100.0	100.0
Japan	100.0	0.0	100.0	100.0
Korea	100.0	0.0	100.0	100.0
Mexico	100.0	0.0	100.0	100.0
Non-OECD	100.0	0.0	100.0	100.0
Duration	11.8	0.0	9.4	20.0
Propensity score	15.2	7.9	13.8	12.5

Note: Each column shows the percentage improvement in covariate balance in terms of mean difference and the median, mean, and maximum values of differences in empirical quantile functions. The table shows that matching substantially improves covariate balance across all variables.

improvement for each covariate through a comparison of the mean difference and quantile breakdown. The exact restrictions on trade partners are reflected by improvements of 100. The table shows that matching substantially improves balance across all variables in terms of various balance measures.

I use logistic regression to estimate the effect of dispute settlement on progress using the smaller sample of matched data. The propensity score is included as an additional variable. The results in table 6.3 show dispute settlement is effective to increase the likelihood of progress toward removal of the trade barrier. Dispute settlement increases the predicted probability of progress resolving the complaint by 28 percentage points.[11] The model correctly predicts progress 70 percent of the time.[12] In a robustness check, I find similar results when using ordered logit to estimate a four-category variable measuring progress. In sum, WTO adjudication makes a substantively important contribution toward policy reform of trade barriers, and this is not because states are sending

[11] The first difference of 0.28 (95 percent confidence interval from 0.11 to 0.44) is calculated from 1,000 simulations using the estimates of table 6.3.

[12] This calculation follows a cutoff rule to compare predictions with 0.50 or higher probability of progress to those in the data that actually report progress.

TABLE 6.3
Matched Sample Logistic Regression Model of WTO DSU Effectiveness.

Variable	Coefficient	(Std. Err.)
WTO DS	1.546**	(0.568)
Contributions	−0.365	(0.203)
Section 301	4.179**	(1.173)
Production (log)	0.317	(0.516)
Exports (log)	0.262	(0.390)
MPEN (partner)	0.001	(0.007)
Import policy	0.952	(0.673)
Distortion	0.995*	(0.586)
EU	0.060	(0.657)
Japan	−0.548	(0.687)
Mexico	−0.062	(0.357)
Korea	0.316	(0.744)
Non-OECD	−0.527	(0.954)
Duration	0.459**	(0.221)
Propensity score	−6.836**	(2.808)
Intercept	0.710	(8.478)
Pseudo R-squared	0.112	
N	160	

Note: The coefficients estimate the likelihood that the NTE reports describe progress toward trade barrier removal. Robust standard errors (clustered on industry) are in parentheses. Canada is the omitted comparison group for the trade partner indicator variables, and non-OECD is an indicator for barriers of Brazil, India, Malaysia, and Singapore. *Significant at the 10 percent level. **Significant at the 5 percent level.

only *easy* issues to the forum. On the contrary, when controlling for the process that sends cases with strong interests on both sides into the dispute settlement mechanism, WTO adjudication is effective relative to negotiation.

Analysis of Trade Dispute Duration

Another measure of the effectiveness of adjudication as a conflict resolution mechanism is the speed with which the process ends a dispute about a trade barrier. The delays of the GATT dispute process were long blamed as a flaw in the institutional design such that a major goal of reforms establishing the WTO dispute settlement system was to streamline the process. Nonetheless, even with the automated adjudication of the WTO, foot dragging is possible, and many criticize the process as being too slow. The Boeing-Airbus dispute discussed in chapter 4 has lasted seven years and still not reached its conclusion. The average duration when looking across all cases, however, appears better. Cases settled during consultations often end within one year, and the median time for disputes filed prior to 2002 that went through the formal panel process was thirty-four months (Davey, 2005). The delays in WTO adjudication have made it less attractive for dynamic industries that face rapidly changing market conditions (Davis and Shirato, 2007). Yet from the perspective of evaluating the effectiveness of WTO adjudication, it is necessary to compare dispute duration with cases that were not raised for WTO adjudication. There have also been many issues that have experienced prolonged stalemates in bilateral negotiations — indeed European subsidies to Airbus had been the subject of talks in various other negotiation venues for three decades prior to the WTO dispute. The goal of this section is to use my trade barrier dataset to evaluate whether WTO adjudication ends disputes more quickly than other strategies.

The outcome of interest here is the duration of the trade dispute. I measure a dispute by whether the NTE reports continue to include the trade barrier as a problem for U.S. exports (note this is distinct from the duration of the dispute in the WTO process). There may be some cases in which the exporting industry loses interest and the complaint is removed from the NTE reports even though the barrier was not fully removed. For example, in the Kodak complaint about Japanese market closure the barrier is reported from 1996 to 2001. After the United States lost the ruling in the WTO dispute in 1998 and Japan made some partial changes to deregulate distribution policies, the USTR and Kodak no longer pushed the issue even though Japan had not changed many of the structural policies that were central to the complaint. This would be recorded as the end of a dispute even if not the complete liberalization of the concerned measures. While conceivably a barrier could be removed from the NTE reports and later reappear, in the dataset there are no such cases. My research into the final outcome of the cases suggests that most often removal of the complaint from the NTE reports corresponds with the removal of the trade barrier.

I use the Cox proportional hazards regression to model the "risk" that a dispute will end in a given year. The data are a cross-section of the trade barriers listing the start and end dates for their inclusion in the NTE reports. The key variable of interest, WTO dispute settlement, is measured as a time-varying covariate with one observation for the years prior to filing a complaint and a second observation for years after filing a complaint. All other control variables are measured at the year the

TABLE 6.4
Cox Proportional Hazards Regression for Duration of Dispute.

	Coefficient	Std. Err.	Exp(Coef)	Lower .95	Upper .95
WTO DS	0.38*	(0.22)	1.47	0.95	2.27
Contributions	−0.24**	(0.12)	0.79	0.62	0.99
Section 301	0.13	(0.29)	1.14	0.65	2.02
Production (log)	0.29	(0.23)	1.34	0.85	2.10
Exports (log)	−0.04	(0.08)	0.97	0.83	1.12
MPEN (partner)	0.00	(0.00)	1.00	0.99	1.01
Import Policy	0.49**	(0.19)	1.64	1.12	2.39
Distortion	−0.32**	(0.12)	0.73	0.57	0.93
EU	0.13	(0.43)	1.13	0.49	2.64
Japan	−0.74	(0.58)	0.47	0.15	1.47
Mexico	0.35	(0.36)	1.42	0.70	2.90
Korea	−0.03	(0.37)	0.97	0.47	1.98
Non-OECD	−0.83*	(0.50)	0.44	0.16	1.15
Likelihood ratio test	32.2				
$p = 0.002$					
N	261				

Note: Robust standard errors (clustered on industry) are in parentheses. Canada is the omitted comparison group for the trade partner indicator variables, and non-OECD is an indicator for barriers of Brazil, India, Malaysia, and Singapore. *Significant at the 10 percent level. **Significant at the 5 percent level.

trade barrier is first listed in the reports. I estimate robust standard errors clustered on industry to take into account possible correlations across barriers within the same industry. In order to avoid the problem of left censoring, I include only the cases that are first reported after 1995 (I lack the necessary duration information for barriers listed in 1995 because my dataset does not include earlier years). The right censoring is handled in the usual manner within the Cox proportional hazards model. The event status is coded 1 for the end of the dispute when the barrier is no longer included in the report. The covariates are the same as those in the previous section with the exception that I no longer control for the duration of the barrier since this is explicitly modeled.

The results of table 6.4 show the positive effect of filing a WTO complaint to reduce dispute duration. The exponential coefficients shown in the third column of the table are the clearest for interpretation and represent the multiplicative change in risk. The exponential coefficient of dispute settlement indicates that filing a WTO complaint is associated with a 1.5-fold increase in the risk that the trade dispute will end compared with other disputes where a complaint has not been filed. The 95 percent confidence interval ranges from 0.95 to 2.27, and the variable is weakly significant (p-value<0.087). Given the widely held view that adjudication is a lengthy process, the positive effect to shorten duration of a dispute is itself an important finding.

This result highlights that while adjudication is slow, it may nonetheless be the fastest way to end disputes when controlling for the factors that influence selection of cases. Disputes that involve industries with large political contributions and highly distortionary trade barriers are at risk for longer duration, and yet these were also variables important in the decision to file a WTO complaint. For dynamic industries or heavily trade-dependent small countries the adjudication process may take too long, but it still is likely to be more effective than alternatives.

Conclusion

This chapter has shown evidence supporting the role of international institutions as a conflict resolution mechanism. Based on evidence from U.S. trade policy, WTO dispute settlement is effective to bring progress to change the trade barrier and shorten the duration of the dispute. Given that politicized cases are channeled into the WTO forum, it is remarkable that the dispute system has been relatively successful to resolve trade disputes.

Underlying the effectiveness of legal action is its role to defuse pressure from stake-holders at the domestic level. These mechanisms were not tested in the aggregate analysis of this chapter but were clearly evident in the case studies of chapters 4 and 5. First we observed that filing the complaint created a period with less intense domestic pressure. Whether it was congressional complaints about Chinese intellectual property rights or Japanese steel industry demands for help against U.S. antidumping policies, government initiation of the complaint put a hold on further demands. Second, the settlement that came after legal action was accepted. Even in the worst-case scenario of the Kodak dispute where the United States lost the ruling, domestic backers stopped demanding further action.

There may also be additional mechanisms by which dispute adjudication plays a role to maintain an open trade system. In particular, any legal system has as the fundamental goal the *deterrence* of violations. Thus any one WTO adjudication case may have ramifications beyond the change of the single barrier by one country that is in contention. Although rulings do not formally represent legal precedent, there has been a de facto evolution of jurisprudence building on earlier cases. Jackson (2001, p. 209) credits the high-quality jurisprudence from WTO panels as one standard of institutional effectiveness. Each ruling clarifies ambiguities in the agreement, and in response other states may decide not to adopt similar barriers. The record of strong enforcement may lead more generally to higher compliance. In this sense, each ruling has a broader trade value that cannot readily be measured. The deterrent effect of a WTO ruling is cited by industry representatives as a reason they seek WTO adjudication (Davis and Shirato, 2007). Busch (2007) argues that the desire for multilateral precedent vis-á-vis other states not party to a dispute accounts for why NAFTA parties often use WTO adjudication with each other even when NAFTA provides an equivalent dispute mechanism. In an analysis of preferential trade agreements, Kono (2007) shows that having a dispute settlement mechanism increases trade liberalization by promoting compliance. The broader deterrence effects of adjudication to improve compliance across members and over time would be on top of the directly observed effects for specific disputes analyzed in this chapter.

The evidence in this chapter has been from U.S. trade policy. Can other states with less power also use adjudication to resolve disputes and protect their access to foreign markets? Some have argued that developing countries gain less from WTO dispute settlement than developed country members (Busch and Reinhardt, 2003; Bown, 2004a). Yet the key point is the need to compare outcomes in WTO dispute settlement relative to negotiation. Market size and trade dependence would be even more important outside of the legal setting that favors rule orientation over power orientation (Jackson, 1997). Indeed, given the relative power of the United States to use side payments or threats in the informal setting of negotiations, one would expect the differential in outcomes to be the *smallest* for the United States. The effectiveness of dispute settlement relative to alternative strategies would be even greater for other countries that lack the market power to enforce agreements by other means. This will be the topic of the next chapter.

7

Level Playing Field? Adjudication by Developing Countries

THE PREVIOUS CHAPTER has shown effectiveness of adjudication to resolve disputes involving the United States as the enforcer, but one may wonder about the effectiveness of adjudication as a tool for smaller countries. Are they able to use adjudication to improve outcomes? Smaller market size makes it ineffective for developing countries to use threats of retaliation in order to combat discrimination against their goods. In contrast, retaliation measures taken by larger economies can easily cause severe damage to a smaller economy. This leaves developing countries vulnerable to discriminatory trade policies adopted by their major trade partners. For developing countries, the dispute mechanism offers an alternative recourse when bilateral negotiations fail to resolve a trade problem. While the United States and EU have unilateral policy options, developing countries often lack outside options. Without the framework provided by the dispute settlement process, a developing country is likely to encounter refusal to negotiate by powerful countries, arbitrary standards, limited interest from third countries in their trade problem, and lack of leverage to bargain for concessions.[1]

While the earlier sections of the book have focused on the decision that leads to the choice of trade strategy, this chapter complements chapter 6 to assess the effectiveness of WTO dispute settlement. Here the focus will be on comparing dispute settlement with alternative strategies in the context of asymmetrical bargaining between a small state and a larger trading partner. Two case studies provide evidence that adjudication can also be effective for small states. Although less attention is given to domestic politics of the complainant state in this chapter, the cases will reveal how adjudication adds leverage to overcome domestic resistance against removal of a protection barrier in the defendant state.

Simply getting a wealthy trade partner to agree to talk about its protectionist trade barriers is difficult for a developing country. Clearly,

---

[1] This chapter represents a slightly modified text based on an earlier publication. See Davis (2006).

developed countries will have the upper hand in a negotiation that resorts to retaliation and counterretaliation and can use side payments to bribe weaker countries to overlook their use of unfair trade barriers for their sensitive products. Most often, they may simply stonewall to ignore demands by small developing countries. Filing a complaint helps in this situation because it obligates the two sides to engage in bilateral consultations, and the DSU guarantees WTO members the right to a panel.

Once initiated, adjudication offers several advantages important for developing countries, especially when they are engaged in asymmetric bargaining. The adjudication process forces both sides to make a consistent argument based on existing law. This prevents the kind of moving target that occurs when there is no agreed upon standard for evaluating different arguments. Since developing countries lack the power to issue threats and side payments or to unilaterally determine the standard of evaluation, in practice this constraint binds the developed country more than the developing country. The role of legal framing to raise stakes for obligation and reputation adds new leverage that does not depend on market size—even small states are able to use rules to shame bigger states. International law provides political cover for making difficult policy reversals. Refusal to change the policy would damage a rules system that brings gains from free trade for many other sectors while compliance with the ruling represents fulfillment of international obligation to support the international trade system.

On the other hand, some aspects of the dispute process disadvantage developing states. Many have pointed out that developing countries lack representation in Geneva and legal resources to adjudicate cases. The increasing number of legal reviews under the strengthened procedures of the new WTO dispute rules places a "premium on sophisticated legal argumentation" that may work against developing countries (Busch and Reinhardt, 2002, p. 467). Even U.S. and EC trade authorities rely on extensive private-sector support for trade disputes that is unlikely to be available in developing countries (Shaffer, 2003; Bown, 2009b). The comparative advantage in legal skills held by countries such as the United States augments the power disparity.

The expense and difficulty of managing a complicated legal case clearly inhibit many developing countries from even filing a complaint. It is notable that the least developed countries have initiated very few WTO disputes. Yet the more advanced developing countries such as India and Brazil have been frequent users of the dispute system. Developing countries compose 40 percent of the countries filing WTO complaints, and there have been ninety-six complaints filed by a developing country against a high-income member.[2] Some have relied on their own legal counsel while others have hired leading international law firms. Since 2001, developing countries have also had the option to receive legal training or hire legal counsel from the Advisory Centre on WTO Law, which was established to provide discounted legal services for developing countries. A report by the Mexican delegation to the WTO on the problems of the DSU for developing countries concluded that "financial aspects of engaging in a WTO dispute do not seem to be at the core of the problem." The report cited the availability of low-cost legal assistance from the Advisory Centre on WTO Law and the relative insignificance of legal fees relative to the value of export losses from a trade barrier.[3] While legal costs may reduce the number of cases initiated by developing countries, they are not insurmountable for many governments. More important is whether the government overcomes the initial barriers to participation related to using international adjudication to gain experience in the process (Davis and Bermeo, 2009).

The historical record provides mixed evidence about whether developing countries have fared better or worse in legalized disputes than other countries. Some find that economic asymmetry has not been a major factor influencing the conduct of dispute settlement (Horn, Mavroidis, and Nordstrom, 1999; Goldstein and Martin, 2000; Guzman and Simmons, 2002). Others emphasize that larger states gain better trade outcomes in dispute settlement through the leverage they gain from their market size (Bown, 2004b). Busch and Reinhardt show that there is a gap in the ability of developing countries to gain positive outcomes compared to developed countries (Busch and Reinhardt, 2003). In an evaluation of 380 GATT/WTO dispute outcomes from 1980 to 2000, Busch and Reinhardt show that developing country complainants were able to gain partial or full concessions for 63 percent of their complaints, in comparison with developed countries, which gained partial or full concessions for 72 percent of their complaints (Busch and Reinhardt, 2003, p. 725). This is a disturbing sign that the playing field is not entirely level, yet also indicates that developing countries do surprisingly well to hold their own despite their weaker economic position. More importantly, Busch and Reinhardt argue that developing countries do poorly during the early consultation period, rather than because of bias in rulings or difficulty to get concessions after a favorable ruling. Their statistical analysis shows that once a panel has been established, income

[2] Calculated by the author based on tables of WTO disputes filed between 1995 and May 2010 available at http://www.worldtradelaw.net/dsc/database/classificationcount.asp, accessed May 20, 2010.

[3] "Diagnosis of the Problems Facing the Dispute Settlement Mechanism: Some Ideas by Mexico," proposal presented to the WTO DSU Body, Geneva, November 2003, pp. 5–7.

does not have a significant effect on outcomes. If developing countries are in a weaker position in the informal negotiations that precede establishment of a panel, then one must wonder how they fare in their bilateral negotiations outside of the dispute settlement process. Looking more closely at the negotiation process will help to reveal whether and how GATT/WTO dispute settlement improves outcomes for developing countries relative to the alternative of negotiations outside the WTO.

This chapter will explore the question by comparing the experience of Peru and Vietnam to challenge labeling policies that hindered their fish exports to major trade partners. The two cases were selected as a controlled comparison where both disputes involve asymmetric power and similar trade barrier. The key difference is that Peru as a WTO member had the option to file a complaint in the WTO while Vietnam in this period had not completed its accession negotiations and could negotiate only on the basis of a bilateral trade agreement. While WTO membership is not randomly determined, the different membership status of the two countries means that for reasons independent of the specific dispute at hand Peru used WTO adjudication and Vietnam relied only on bilateral negotiation. Taking as given the choice of trade strategy, the analysis will focus on effectiveness for dispute outcomes. To preview the final result, Peru won reform of EU labeling policies for sardine imports from Peru while Vietnam was unable to change U.S. labeling policies for catfish imports from Vietnam. The case analysis will assess the role of adjudication to provide additional bargaining leverage for developing countries relative to their weak position in a bilateral negotiation outside of the institution.

The labeling cases raised similar strategies pursued by the United States and EC to protect against fish imports that threatened influential producer groups. Of course, there are important differences between the two pairs of negotiating countries. The economic interests and political institutions of the United States and EC are likely to influence their negotiating behavior. Nevertheless, there is little reason to expect that the EC is substantially more favorable to free trade or more supportive of the WTO than the United States—both represent major trade powers that have a large stake in the multilateral trade system, and both have adopted policies that could be challenged as violations of the WTO rules. One could also question whether Peru and Vietnam are comparable. Politically Peru shifted from dictatorship to democracy in 2001 with the election of President Alejandro Toledo, while Vietnam has remained in the hands of the communist leadership even as the government has loosened state control over some sectors of the domestic economy. Such differences in the domestic institutional context could influence the strategy to seek negotiation or adjudication, but this chapter will take as exogenous the choice of adjudication versus negotiation strategy and instead focus on the outcomes both parties achieve.

The cases are comparable examples of asymmetric bargaining. Vietnam and Peru are both poor countries, although Vietnam at $430 per capita income is ranked by the World Bank as a low-income country while Peru at $2,050 per capita income is ranked as a lower-middle-income country.[4] Yet both clearly lack the market power to counterbalance the United States or Europe and are dependent on access to these valuable markets for their goods. Looking at power alone would lead one to expect that Peru and Vietnam would be unable to prevail over the EC or United States, which were determined to protect their domestic producer interests.

The examination of labeling policy is important because internal nontariff regulations are among the most problematic trade barriers. Food labeling in particular has become controversial. A new set of agricultural trade disputes has arisen regarding the use of geographical indications to recognize regional specialties as distinct products. Trade talks about genetically modified products and food safety have also come down to a debate over appropriate labeling policies.

Peru Challenges European Food Labeling

Governments frequently regulate labeling policies for the sake of providing the consumer with accurate information. For example, regulations may require specification of contents and product names or the addition of health warnings. The challenge for international trade law is to distinguish between policies that legitimately regulate labeling policies and those that act as trade barriers. The legal framework for labeling policies relates generally to the GATT principles of nondiscrimination and national treatment (Articles 1 and 3 of GATT 1994). These rules stipulate that the products of one state shall not be treated less favorably than the products of another state or than domestic products. More specific rules for such regulations are found in the Agreement on Technical Barriers to Trade (TBT).[5] Too many standards or arbitrary procedures for setting standards would indirectly or directly impede trade. Labeling policies represent one kind of nontariff barrier that could be used to discriminate, such as by reserving the common marketable name

---

[4] World Bank, "Gross National Income per capita 2002 (Atlas Method, U.S. Dollars)," http://www.worldbank.org/data/databytopic/GNIPC.pdf, accessed July 28, 2003.

[5] First established in the 1973–79 Tokyo Round, the TBT was extended and clarified in the Uruguay Round.

for domestic products. The TBT Agreement stipulates that technical regulations should not have the effect of creating unnecessary obstacles to international trade (Article 2.2) and encourages members to use relevant international standards as a basis for their technical regulations whenever possible (Article 2.4). For example, the Codex Alimentarius Commission establishes guidelines that are accepted as the benchmarks for international standards on food regulations. Its standards are based on recommendations from scientific committees that are approved by members. However, since the TBT Agreement recognizes national governments' right to choose higher levels of protection for legitimate objectives to protect public welfare and the environment, there is much room for interpretation.

When changes in the application of regulations regarding labeling standards harmed Peru's exports to the EC market, it used the above rules framework to demand that the EC change its regulations.[6] The EC Regulation (Council Regulation 2136/89) adopted June 21, 1989 forbid marketing of fish under the name "sardine," unless it was the species common to Sardinia and found in the Atlantic Ocean and Mediterranean Sea (*Sardina pilchardus Walbaum*). The regulation had not been enforced, and Peru had developed a market niche in Germany for its sardines under the label of "Pacific sardines." The trade problem arose in 1999, when the European Commission began to enforce the regulation by refusing to allow the import of the Peruvian fish under that label. EC officials suggested that the species from Peru (*Sardinops sagax sagax*) should instead be marketed as "pilchards" or "sprats," in order to protect consumers and avoid confusion.[7] Peru declared that this was simply a disguised effort by Europe to protect its local fishermen. Unable to reach agreement through bilateral negotiations, Peru formally filed a complaint to the WTO and requested consultations. This forced the EC to the negotiating table.

Peru had a strong legal basis for its complaint because the Codex Alimentarius Commission has a standard for canned sardines and sardine-type products that clearly lists the Peruvian species among several others in its definition of sardines. This standard, which had been adopted in 1978, called for the European species to be called by the name "sardines" alone, while other species should be labeled "X sardines" with the modifier indicating the country, geographic area, species, or

---

[6] Since the Community Pillar has authority for economic policies, following WTO practice I will refer to the European Community (EC) when referring specifically to trade policies.

[7] *Financial Times*. June 17, 2002.

common name of species in country where sold.[8] In its request for consultations filed with the WTO, Peru referred to this standard to claim that the European regulation represented an unjustified barrier to trade.[9] An official of the WTO Secretariat said, "From the beginning, it was clear what direction this case would take—the EC regulation was a trade barrier. I am surprised it went to a panel."[10]

An official of the EC delegation agreed that the sardines issue seemed like a case that should have been settled early. He said, "The threat of a panel clearly gives impetus to find a solution," but also commented that it depends on the political reality in the Community whether the threat of a panel will be sufficient.[11] In this case, fisheries represent a sensitive sector, and among members, Spain, France, and Portugal had sardine producers that compete with Peru and could be expected to oppose the change. The original policy was a Council regulation, so member approval would be necessary to change the policy. Moreover, the major exporter of sardines to EC markets that competed with Peru was Morocco. Morocco stands as a beneficiary of special economic relations with the EC, already holding an association agreement with the EC that lowers trade barriers and having nearly completed the process of concluding a free trade agreement.[12] As a result of the political difficulty to compromise on these interests, the EC continued to uphold its position that the name "sardines" must be reserved for the one species.

Peru was at a disadvantage because it lacked experience and trade law expertise. One of the lead negotiators for Peru said, "We are a small delegation and this was my first case. It is hard because we are competing in an unfair situation—they have cases all year long and have specialists on every aspect of trade law."[13] Fortunately, Peru's delegation received the help of the Advisory Centre on WTO Law, which had been established in 2001 as an independent intergovernmental organization to provide a low-cost alternative for developing countries that need legal expertise in order to participate in the dispute settlement system. For a membership fee, developing countries gain access to low-cost legal services rather than paying the fees of a private law firm, which in 2002

---

[8] Codex Standard for Canned Sardines and Sardine-Type Products (CODEX STAN 94-181 Rev. 1995), www.codexalimentarius.net/standard_list.asp, accessed July 25, 2003.

[9] Request for consultations by Peru, "European Communities—Trade Description of Sardines," WT/DS231/1, April 23, 2001.

[10] WTO official, interview by author, Geneva, May 7, 2003.

[11] Official of EU delegation in Geneva, interview by author, Geneva, May 5, 2003.

[12] http://europa.eu.int/comm/trade/issues/bilateral/regions/euromed/index_en.htm, accessed July 31, 2003.

[13] Official of Peru's delegation in Geneva, telephone interview by author, July 30, 2003.

could exceed \$300,000 for a WTO case.[14] Fees to the Centre are based on income of the member, so that Peru was charged only \$100 an hour for legal services.[15] Peru's legal counsel admitted that without these services, they would not have been able to manage the case on their own (Shaffer and Mosoti, 2002, p. 15).

Peru also benefited from the contribution of interested third parties. Although Peru was the only country to file a complaint, Canada, Chile, Colombia, Ecuador, Venezuela, and the United States all participated in the process as third parties. The United States presented an oral statement that supported Peru's argument that the EC measure violated TBT Article 2.4: "There is ample evidence indicating that the EC measure, if anything, undermines the EC's objectives, since European consumers have in fact come to know the Peruvian product as a form of sardine, and will likely be confused by the use of other names. Indeed, the use of a proper descriptor prior to the term 'sardine,' as provided for in the international standard, appears to be a very effective means of assuring transparency and protecting the consumer."[16] The U.S. official also responded to questions from the panel that several sardine species were sold by U.S. fishermen to many parts of the world but were not exported to the EC because of the restrictive labeling requirements, and that these same fish could be sold in the United States under the name "sardines."[17] Finally, meeting later before the Appellate Body review of the panel decision, USTR Associate General Counsel Dan Mullaney neatly rebutted a central claim of the EC legal defense: "The EC claims that its Sardine Regulation is based on this international standard, because it adopts the first part of the standard, even though it contradicts the second part. If the EC's assertion is correct, then a regulation that permits *only non*-European species to be marketed as kinds of sardines—and prohibits European sardines from being marketed as sardines at all—would also be based on the international standard. Even the EC would presumably agree that this would be the incorrect result."[18]

---

[14] *Financial Times*, October 24, 2002. See Davis and Bermeo (2009) and Bown (2009b) for evidence that ACWL has been an important tool to increase the capacity of developing countries in WTO adjudication.

[15] The rates range from \$25 for least developed countries to \$200 for the highest income developing country members. http://www.acwl.ch/, accessed January 20, 2004.

[16] USTR, Oral Statement of the United States at the Third Party Session with the Panel (November 28, 2001), "European Communities—Trade Description of Sardines" (DS231), http://www.ustr.gov/enforcement/2001-11-28_USoral.pdf, accessed July 31, 2003.

[17] USTR, Responses of the United States to Questions from the Panel from the Third Party Session (December 7, 2001), "European Communities—Trade Description of Sardines" (DS231), http://www.ustr.gov/enforcement/2001-12-07_QA.pdf, accessed July 31, 2003.

[18] USTR, Statement of the United States at the Oral Hearing (August 13, 2002), "European Communities—Trade Description of Sardines" (DS231), http://www.ustr.gov/enforcement/2002-08-13-eusardines-oralst8.pdf, accessed July 31, 2003.

The panel released its ruling May 29, 2002. The report found the EC regulation inconsistent with Article 2.4 of the TBT Agreement and recommended that the Dispute Settlement Body request the EC to bring its measure into conformity with the TBT Agreement. The EC decided, however, to appeal the panel ruling. After further legal proceedings, the judges of the Appellate Body released their ruling on September 26, 2002. The Appellate Body ruling upheld Peru's arguments on every major point, with a few exceptions that had no substantive impact for the case.[19]

The public release of the ruling helped EC trade officials to justify to the Fisheries Commission that the regulation would have to be changed.[20] Where the difficulty to reach an internal agreement in the sardines case prevented the EC from offering an early settlement, following the negative ruling they overcame opposition to changing the policy. Now talks focused on reaching a mutually acceptable agreement with Peru. In the months that followed, officials negotiated everything from whether the name "sardines" would be followed or preceded by the country name or the scientific name to the size of type to be used on the labels. The original deadline for EC compliance came in April, but a request for an extension until July was granted. Peru's officials were satisfied when the EC officials offered a proposal that would allow the use of the name "sardines," followed by the scientific name of the species in small italics.[21] The Commission published the new regulation (EC 1181/2003), which would allow those species recognized by the Codex standard to be labeled as sardines joined together with the scientific name of the species.[22]

Peru's officials said that the ruling had provided the basis for their ability to get a good outcome from the EC. "We have to have a panel ruling or we get nothing. Winning the panel ruling opens space for negotiation and strengthens our position."[23] Officials were confident that the market gains would easily recoup the financial cost of pursuing the WTO case. The Advisory Centre on WTO Law clearly played an important role to reduce legal costs and to manage the case. Peru appears not to have suffered from any adverse political costs. During the dispute

---

[19] The Appellate Body allowed the submission of *amicus curiae* briefs from an individual and from Morocco, although declaring that the contents were not necessary for deciding the appeal. This latter decision has been viewed as controversial for members, and was protested by Peru during the proceedings and by many others afterward.

[20] Official of EU delegation in Geneva, interview by author, Geneva, May 5, 2003.

[21] Official of Peru's delegation in Geneva, interview by author, Geneva, May 5, 2003.

[22] European Commission, OJ L165, July 3, 2003, pp. 17–18.

[23] Official of Peru's delegation in Geneva, interview by author, Geneva, May 5, 2003.

there were no threats of significance issued against Peru, and officials did not feel that there had been any damage to bilateral relations.[24] While many developing country officials express fear that they will suffer negative consequences, such instances may be rare in occurrence.

Peru was able to win a major case and bring about compliance by the EC. The case serves as an example to other developing countries that the dispute system can help a small country get a fair hearing and reach a satisfactory outcome. The legal process was necessary to convince European governments that they could not stonewall on the issue. Although the EC regulation for labeling of sardines was a clear violation of WTO rules, resistance to change prevented settlement until faced with the public challenge of a lawsuit.

Vietnam and the Catfish Dispute

In order to consider the counterfactual of a developing country that faces a similar problem but cannot choose a strategy of WTO adjudication, I next examine a negotiation by a non-WTO member, Vietnam, against the United States.[25] This case highlights the disadvantages faced by developing countries that do not have recourse to WTO adjudication when facing discrimination against their exports. The dispute revolved around unilateral policies by the United States taken against imports of Vietnamese catfish.

The institutional framework for U.S.-Vietnam trade relations is based on a bilateral treaty concluded as part of the process of normalization in diplomatic relations between the two countries. Until 1994, the United States and Vietnam did not have any trade relations due to the trade embargo imposed since the end of the Vietnam War. The lifting of the embargo by President Clinton opened the way for only a trickle of bilateral trade. Since Vietnam still lacked most-favored-nation status, goods from Vietnam faced substantially higher tariffs than those from other countries.[26] The path to full normalization of relations involved lengthy negotiations for a bilateral trade agreement. Concerns about full accounting for prisoners of war and human rights in Vietnam made the

[24] Official of Peru's delegation in Geneva, telephone interview by author, July 30, 2003.

[25] Vietnam became a WTO member January 11, 2007. During the period of this case study it was still in the accession process and did not have the right of dispute settlement.

[26] The Trade Agreements Extension Act of 1951 suspended MFN treatment for communist countries. By the time that the United States granted MFN status to Vietnam starting in 1998 (on a provisional basis with the need for annual renewal of the Jackson-Vanik waiver), only six countries did not receive MFN treatment.

return to normalization politically sensitive in the United States, while it was also a major step in the market-oriented *doi moi* reforms being undertaken by the Vietnamese communist leadership.

The U.S.-Vietnam Bilateral Trade Agreement (BTA), signed July 13, 2000 and entering into effect in 2001, was a comprehensive agreement that brought far-reaching internal reforms in Vietnam and produced a doubling of bilateral trade in its first year. With MFN recognition, Vietnam gained access to U.S. markets on the same terms as WTO members. Average U.S. tariffs on imports from Vietnam fell from around 40 percent to around 3–4 percent. In exchange, Vietnam agreed to lower its own trade barriers by 25–50 percent on goods, grant market access for services, and provide regulations to protect intellectual property rights. This involved a major overhaul of domestic policies and the legal system and decisions that would expose weak sectors such as banking and telecommunication industries to competition. An official of the Vietnamese embassy in Washington, D.C., described the reforms as a revolution and said that the prospective gains from the agreement had been important to overcome opposition from those who would lose out.[27] The U.S. negotiators saw the rising economic potential of Vietnam and demanded these comprehensive reforms with the view that this moment was "the best leverage we'll ever have" and could be used to get Vietnam to open their market.[28] At the same time, supporters of the agreement in both the United States and Vietnam could sell the liberalizing policies as a stepping stone toward Vietnamese accession to the WTO.

The BTA is closely modeled on the WTO agreements. Many sections such as those on national treatment and intellectual property protection are directly taken from the relevant passages in the WTO agreements. Most importantly for the questions that later arose regarding labeling policy for catfish, the text from TBT Article 2.2 is adopted in Article 2:6b of the BTA text.[29] The United States and Vietnam committed not to have regulations that would create unnecessary obstacles to trade.

One major exception to the parallel structure of the BTA and WTO agreements, however, is the lack of a formal dispute settlement mechanism. While the WTO and even some regional agreements such as NAFTA provide for adjudication of trade disputes, the BTA simply

[27] Official of the Vietnamese embassy to the United States, interview by author, Washington, D.C., July 11, 2003.

[28] Former USTR official, interview by author, Washington, D.C., July 15, 2003.

[29] Agreement Between the United States of American and the Socialist Republic of Vietnam on Trade Relations, mimeograph available at the USTR Reading Room, 1724 F St., N.W., Washington, D.C.

establishes a "Joint Committee on Development of Economic and Trade Relations" that is given a mandate to serve as a forum for consultations over problems regarding implementation of the agreement (Chapter VII Article 5).

Therefore, when in the first months after the start of the agreement Vietnam faced an unexpected protectionist measure by the United States against its catfish exports, there was nowhere for Vietnam to turn for third-party mediation. The BTA reduction of tariffs and the growth of a promising industry for Vietnam resulted in a surge of Vietnamese catfish into U.S. markets—increasing from five million pounds of frozen fillets in 1999 to thirty-four million pounds in 2002, and capturing 20 percent of the U.S. market.[30] Declining prices intensified the difficulties for U.S. producers, who in 2001 experienced a 30 percent drop in the average earnings from a kilogram of catfish.[31] The U.S. Association of Catfish Farmers of America (CFA), representing the catfish farmers concentrated in a few southern states of the United States, soon lobbied for measures to restrict the import of Vietnamese catfish. Although the U.S. catfish market is a mere $590 million, in both countries the dispute over catfish exports has taken on larger political significance and influenced how both sides view the bilateral trade relationship.

The Labeling Dispute

The first stage of the "catfish war" involved a U.S. decision to change a labeling policy and its refusal to negotiate any compromise of that regulation. The U.S. industry had invested in developing high-quality, farm-raised catfish and dramatically increased sales through a skillful marketing campaign. When Vietnamese catfish began making inroads into the U.S. market, with some being sold as "Cajun Delight Catfish" or other such names, the domestic industry struck back with its own advertising campaign against the Vietnamese fish. They claimed that the Vietnamese fish were lower quality because they were raised in "Third World rivers." Representative Marion Berry from Arkansas even referred to the danger that Vietnamese catfish were contaminated by lingering Agent Orange sprayed by the United States during the war.[32] Such xenophobic advertising did not prevent 30 percent of U.S. seafood restaurants from serving Vietnamese catfish.[33]

[30] *Washington Post*, July 13, 2003.
[31] *Far Eastern Economic Review*, December 6, 2001.
[32] *New York Times*, November 5, 2002.
[33] *Far Eastern Economic Review*, December 6, 2001.

When the labeling issue first arose, USTR officials went to technical experts at the Food and Drug Administration (FDA) for advice. The FDA officials said that they could not revoke the right for Vietnam to use the catfish label with a modifier such as "Vietnamese catfish," since the Vietnamese product was a kind of catfish. At the time, "The Seafood List, FDA's Guide to Acceptable Market Names for Seafood Sold in Interstate Commerce 1993" listed twenty different kinds of fish including the Vietnamese species as eligible for marketing with a label including the word "catfish." Vietnam had readily agreed to any labeling policy requiring it to identify country of origin and/or use "Mekong Catfish" on labels.[34] FDA inspectors who visited Vietnam confirmed that quality standards complied with FDA requirements, and the U.S. embassy in Vietnam reported that it had found "little or no evidence that the U.S. industry or health of the consuming public is facing a threat from Vietnam's emerging catfish export industry."[35] The matter would have ended there if it had been up to the USTR and FDA.

Determined to maintain their hold on the domestic market, the CFA engaged southern politicians to legislate a change in U.S. regulations to prevent Vietnam from being able to sell its fish as catfish. Their central claim held that the basa and tra catfish (*Pangasius bocourti* and *Pangasius hypothalmus*) from Vietnam were a different product from the U.S. channel catfish (*Ictaluridae*). There was not a specific international standard regarding the labeling of catfish. The *Saigon Times Weekly* (January 26, 2002) quotes Carl Ferraris, a researcher from the California Academy of Sciences, to support the Vietnamese claim that the basa and tra fish are catfish—among over twenty-five hundred kinds of catfish around the world known by that name. The fish database of the International Center for Living Aquatic Resources Management with sponsorship from the FAO lists over seven hundred fish species with "catfish" in the name.[36] The CFA and its supporters, however, argued that only the one species, *Ictaluridae*, should be called catfish.

---

[34] Indeed, the marketing controversy was less the result of Vietnam's exporters than about the American wholesale retailers and supermarkets that were adding labels they thought would make the product sell better. Former USTR official, interview by author, Washington, D.C., July 15, 2003.

[35] U.S. embassy report cited in Senate debates. Agriculture, Conservation, and Rural Enhancement Act of 2001, Senate debate, December 18, 2001 (S13427).

[36] http://www.fishbase.org, accessed July 28, 2003. Specific references for entries on *Pangasius bocourti* and *hypophthalmus* are from T. R. Roberts and C. Vidthayanon, "Systematic Revision of the Asian Catfish Family Pangasiidae, with Biological Observations and Descriptions of Three New Species," (Proceedings of the Academy of Natural Sciences, Philadelphia, 1991), 143: 97–144.

In the closing days of debate on an appropriations bill, southern representatives inserted an amendment to change the FDA regulation. The amendment would prevent the FDA from processing fish labeled as catfish unless it was of the species *Ictaluridae*. One Vietnamese negotiator who had tried to urge reconsideration, said the issue was decided "purely by domestic politics—we have no leverage."[37] Their best effort was to contact the congressmen who had helped to support the BTA and the normalization of U.S.-Vietnam relations, such as Senators John McCain and Phil Gramm. These senators spoke out strongly against the measure when the bill came up before the Senate. McCain condemned the amendment and the process by which it had been passed:

> In fact, of the 2,500 species of catfish on Earth, this amendment allows the FDA to process only a certain type raised in North America—specifically, those that grow in six Southern States. The program's effect is to restrict all catfish imports into our country by requiring that they be labeled as something other than catfish, an underhanded way for catfish producers to shut out the competition. With a clever trick of Latin phraseology and without even a ceremonial nod to the vast body of trade laws and practices we rigorously observe, this damaging amendment ... literally bans Federal officials from processing any and all catfish imports labeled as they are—catfish.... It patently violates our solemn trade agreement with Vietnam, the very same trade agreement the Senate ratified by a vote of 88 to 12 only 2 months ago. The ink was not dry on that agreement when the catfish lobby and its congressional allies slipped the catfish amendment into a must-pass appropriations bill.[38]

Despite such impassioned speeches, the measure was adopted as part of the 2002 Farm Act.[39]

There was some effort by the senators who opposed the amendment to use the WTO cases on labeling to strengthen their argument. The Peru-EC sardine dispute was mentioned as a similar labeling restriction that the United States had opposed when it was European policies harming U.S. producers. The southern representatives claimed that the difference between the fish species at hand was much greater than the related WTO

---

[37] Official of the Vietnamese embassy to the United States, interview by author, Washington, D.C., July 11, 2003.

[38] Agriculture, Conservation, and Rural Enhancement Act of 2001, Senate debate December 18, 2001 (S13426).

[39] The provisional measure became permanent in Section 10806 of the 2002 U.S. Farm Act, which became law May 13, 2002 (Pub. L. No. 107-171).

cases.[40] Examples were given that the U.S. and Vietnamese fish were as different as a yak and a cow. Unlike Peru, however, Vietnam could not file a complaint to the WTO and have a more neutral source decide what should count as a catfish. Given no choice but to accept the measure, Vietnamese exporters labeled their fish as basa and tra.

The Antidumping Determination

When the food labeling barrier did not restrain imports, the U.S. catfish industry switched tactics to file a petition in June 2002 requesting antidumping measures against the imports from Vietnam. The CFA petition claimed that Vietnam was selling its fish in U.S. markets at prices below the cost of production with injurious effects on the U.S. industry.

Dumping is considered a threat to fair trade conditions and competitive markets when exporters sell goods at a higher price in their home market while disposing of surplus capacity in foreign markets at lower prices. Domestic laws to counter dumping predate international trade rules and have been recognized by the GATT and now the WTO rules.[41] The United States accepts petitions from industries that claim to suffer from foreign dumping of like products and undertakes two parallel investigations before making a final determination. The first investigation is supervised by the International Trade Administration within the Department of Commerce (DOC), which evaluates the normal price of the foreign product in order to determine whether it has been sold below price in U.S. markets. The ruling of dumping, however, must also be accompanied by a finding of injury. The International Trade Commission hears evidence from both sides on whether the imports have caused damage to the domestic industry. Positive findings in both investigations result in the application of antidumping duties on the foreign product.

Problems arise, however, when antidumping policies become an alternative form of protection for weak import-competing industries. Given that the investigation of dumping and industry damage occur under the auspices of domestic law and national administrative officials serve as the judge in a dispute between a national and foreign industry, there is the possibility for bias in favor of the home industry. The initiation of an investigation alone can help the domestic industry and

---

[40] Agriculture, Conservation, and Rural Enhancement Act of 2001, Senate debate, December 18, 2001 (S13429).

[41] GATT Article 6 allows use of antidumping duties when there is evidence that dumping causes material injury to competing domestic industries.

harm the exporter by creating market uncertainty about future trade (when imposed, duties are retroactive such that importers may become hesitant to buy from an exporter under investigation) (Palmeter, 1996, p. 279). Cooperation with the investigation also imposes considerable administrative costs on the export firms that must provide detailed information about their business operations.

After having declared that the Vietnamese product was fundamentally different from U.S. catfish, now the antidumping suit depended upon defining the same fish to be a like product. According to U.S. law, an antidumping petition must be initiated by a domestic industry that produces a like product with the imported good subject to investigation. This determination of like product, however, is made on a case-by-case basis when the petition is first accepted and again later when officials evaluate the injury to domestic industry from imports. As such, the definition of like product is often a matter of disagreement (Palmeter, 1996, p. 268). The president of the American Seafood Distributors Association said during a hearing about the antidumping case that "changing the name of Vietnamese catfish to basa should have been sufficient grounds to protect the market name of the domestic catfish producers and thus give them the product differentiation that should have ruled out the need to pile on with a dumping suit as well. The fact that we are here today to perform the alchemy of turning basa back into catfish strikes me and the organization that I lead as nothing short of a convoluted action to serve only one master. It's protectionism."[42]

After the CFA filed their petition, Vietnamese officials tried to prevent initiation of an investigation. Contacts with the U.S. government were pursued at all levels. The DOC, however, was obligated by law to initiate the investigation so long as the CFA petition met their checklist as a valid claim (e.g., petitioners account for more than 50 percent of production of domestic like product, present evidence of injury from imports with data for calculation of estimated dumping margin, and follow necessary procedures). The petition from the CFA, which estimated that there should be a finding for a 144–190 percent dumping margin on the Vietnamese fish, was found to meet these standards.[43] Neither requests from Vietnam's officials nor letters from senators expressing concerns about broader relations could be taken into consideration at this stage.[44]

---

[42] U.S. International Trade Commission, "Hearing Report for Investigation no. 731-TA-1012 in the Matter of Certain Frozen Fish Fillets from Vietnam," June 17, 2003.

[43] Department of Commerce, "Initiation of Anti-dumping Duty Investigation: Certain Frozen Fish Fillets from the Socialist Republic of Vietnam," *Federal Register* vol. 67, no. 142 (July 24, 2002): 4837–40.

[44] Department of Commerce official, interview by author, Washington, D.C., July 11, 2003.

The DOC approved the start of an investigation, referring to the case as concerning "certain frozen fish fillets from Vietnam" in light of the naming controversy.

The first hurdle for Vietnam was to try and prove that prices in Vietnam should be used in the calculation of normal prices. The CFA requested that Vietnam should be considered a nonmarket economy, which would mean that a surrogate country would be used for pricing calculation under the assumption that real prices could not be estimated in a state-controlled economy. This judgment was made on an economy-wide basis rather than through examination of the specific sector.[45] As a result, even though the catfish producers in Vietnam are a group of companies and small-scale farmers that generally operate by market principles, and there was no evidence to show they had received government subsidies or price directives, the economy was judged to be a nonmarket economy.[46] The nonmarket finding pushed the investigation into the realm of hypotheticals—Brink Lindsey of the Cato Institute condemned the process for determining nonmarket economy prices: "Basically, you can come up with any dang number you want to."[47] In the case of Vietnam, prices from Bangladesh were used to estimate what it would cost to produce fish in Vietnam if it operated on market principles.

Vietnam found itself forced to wage a legal fight in U.S. trade courts. This being the first antidumping case for Vietnam, Vietnamese officials were completely lacking in expertise. DOC officials had weekly meetings with officials from the Vietnamese embassy and traveled to Vietnam to offer a seminar to help the companies that were required to submit extensive surveys on their business operations. The complexity of antidumping procedures, however, required legal expertise. The Vietnamese government hired a U.S. law firm to represent their interests in consultations regarding the case, while the Vietnamese exporters represented by the Vietnam Association of Seafood Producers (VASEP) hired another law firm to present their case before the DOC and ITC.

Proceedings went forward as an administrative investigation run strictly according to U.S. antidumping laws. The DOC made its preliminary determination for dumping duties in January 2003. Based on the DOC calculations, which drew on a regression wage rate for Vietnam's labor costs and Bangladeshi prices for inputs and pricing of fish, the DOC

---

[45] The DOC antidumping manual lists provisions regarding a market-oriented industry that might have been appropriate for the case. Vietnam unsuccessfully tried to prove the more general claim that the entire economy was market based.

[46] Official of trade industry association, interview by author, Washington, D.C., June 11, 2003.

[47] *Washington Post*, July 13, 2003.

determined that 38–64 percent antidumping tariffs should be applied.[48] The lower rate would apply to the large companies that had cooperated with the investigation by providing information, while the higher "Vietnam wide" rate would apply to all of the small Vietnamese catfish producers that had lacked the information or resources to participate in the investigation. These smaller producers, who compose 40 percent of all those employed in the catfish industry in Vietnam, are the most market driven and least likely to be able to afford selling products below price.[49]

The next phase opened a window for negotiation. Vietnam requested to negotiate a suspension agreement, which is an effort by the government of the industry that is charged with dumping to reach a settlement with the DOC. Although infrequent, such agreements have been reached by means of fixing import prices to an agreed level and/or administering a quota similar to a voluntary export restraint. The DOC then would suspend the dumping investigation and not issue a final determination on dumping. In this case, the officials from the Vietnamese delegation and the DOC could not reach a mutually acceptable agreement on the price level and quota size. An official from the Vietnamese side said that the DOC took an inflexible approach, starting off with a high price and low quota and agreeing to increase the quota only if the price was also increased. The Vietnamese side had begun with a request for a relatively low price and high quota, and then came back having modified their own offer slightly to include a higher price. After another failure to reach agreement, the Vietnamese came back with a more substantial concession from their original proposal. DOC officials, however, had hardly changed their original position and agreed that the first offer had been the final offer. Since the Vietnamese side estimated that the DOC offer would be equivalent to 60–80 percent tariffs, they rejected it and let the antidumping investigation continue.[50]

DOC officials said that the negotiations for a suspension agreement were undertaken in good faith and that the legal obligations of U.S. antitrust law require that any suspension agreement must stop the undermining of prices that causes the domestic industry damage. They must also worry about a suspension agreement that leaves the petitioning domestic industry dissatisfied, because then it could launch an appeal.

---

[48] Department of Commerce, "Notice of Preliminary Determination of Sales at Less Than Fair Value," 68 FR 4986 (January 31, 2003).

[49] Official of trade industry association, interview by author, Washington, D.C., June 11, 2003.

[50] Official of the Vietnamese embassy to the United States, interview by author, Washington, D.C., July 11, 2003. Official of trade industry association, interview by author, Washington, D.C., June 11, 2003.

An earlier suspension agreement with Russia on hot-rolled steel was appealed by the domestic industry. In that case, the DOC agreement was upheld. If an agreement were overturned, however, it would be a bureaucratic nightmare to roll back the provisions of an agreement that had already entered implementation. Fear of an appeal from domestic industry restrained the DOC from considering any concessions. In the end, there was no overlap between their offer and what Vietnam was willing to accept.[51]

In contrast, a U.S. antidumping investigation against imports of fresh tomatoes from Mexico provides an example of a successful negotiation to reach a suspension agreement. After the DOC initiated the investigation April 18, 1996, Mexico filed a request for consultations under the WTO dispute settlement procedures with a complaint that the U.S. investigation violated its WTO commitments.[52] The WTO case never advanced to the panel stage, however, since Mexico and the United States reached a suspension agreement three months later.[53] This agreement provided for reference prices and was accepted by the Mexican exporters. The right to file a WTO complaint represents one tactic that may be useful to challenge dumping charges with a weak factual basis and even to gain leverage during negotiation of a suspension agreement.

Vietnam considered using threats to gain leverage in the dispute. The *Economist* reported that Vietnam was threatening to launch an antidumping suit of its own against the subsidized imports of U.S. soybeans.[54] In the end, however, threats were rejected as not serving Vietnam's own interests—there seemed little point in harming industries such as Cargill when the government was trying to encourage more investment by such companies. Moreover, it was unlikely that the United States would be moved by threats from a small country. In 2002, U.S. exports to Vietnam had a total value of $580 million, which is tiny relative to U.S. total exports of $693 billion and relative to its exports to other countries in the region (U.S. exports to China that same year were $22 billion, and its exports to Thailand were $4.9 billion).[55]

The DOC and ITC issued their final positive findings of dumping and injury after further hearings to evaluate the arguments presented by

[51] Officials of the Department of Commerce, interview by author, Washington, D.C., July 11, 2003.

[52] Request for Consultations by Mexico, "United States—Anti-dumping Investigation Regarding Imports of Fresh or Chilled Tomatoes from Mexico, WT/DS49/1 (July 8, 1996).

[53] *Federal Register* (61) 56617 [A-201-820] (November 1, 1996).

[54] December 14, 2002.

[55] Foreign Trade Division, http://www.census.gov/foreign-trade/balance/, accessed July 30, 2003.

both sides. In its defense against the dumping charges, the Vietnamese side tried to use the earlier congressional debate to argue that basa and tra fish were indeed different products from U.S. catfish and were not any more responsible for the troubles of the catfish industry than were exports of other fish species like sole. Statistical evidence was presented to show that imports of Vietnamese catfish did not influence U.S. catfish prices. This was countered by the CFA legal team, which argued that the labeling policy had not prevented basa and tra from competing with U.S catfish, and offered its own statistical analysis to show that imported Vietnamese fish did have an impact on domestic catfish prices.[56] The final determination issued in July 2003 called for dumping duties of 37–64 percent.[57]

Vietnam's government protested the outcome, saying the case against it had been groundless.[58] They contended the DOC price calculations had ignored the efficiency gains from an integrated production process that allowed them to sell the fish at a lower price. Press reports in both Vietnam and the United States mocked the notion that Vietnamese catfish farmers or the Vietnamese government had the money to engage in dumping its fish below cost.[59] A U.S. trade expert who had followed the case said it was unfathomable that Vietnam was dumping fish in the U.S. markets, but that the determination was possible because "reality was thrown out" when the DOC constructs prices for nonmarket economies.[60] The use of figures from Bangladesh that were calculated with different years according to data availability and the use of data from India when there were inadequate data from Bangladesh contributed to the sense that the dumping margins had been determined arbitrarily.

After the preliminary duties were imposed in January, the export of Vietnamese catfish to the United States was down 30–40 percent, and the announcement that these duties would now be permanent dealt a further blow.[61] One study that analyzes income surveys conducted in Vietnam before and after the imposition of duties concludes that the producers in

[56] U.S. International Trade Commission, "Hearing Report for Investigation no. 731-TA-1012 in the Matter of Certain Frozen Fish Fillets from Vietnam," June 17, 2003.

[57] Department of Commerce, "Notice of Final Anti-dumping Duty Determination of Sales at Less Than Fair Value and Affirmative Critical Circumstances: Certain Frozen Fish Fillets from the Socialist Republic of Vietnam," FR 68, no. 120 (June 23, 2003): 37116–121.

[58] *Financial Times*, July 24, 2003.

[59] *New York Times*, July 22 and 25, 2003; *Vietnam News Agency*, July 10, 2002, http://www.vietnamembassy-usa.org/news/newsitem.php3?datestamp=20020710154153.

[60] Former USTR official, interview by author, July 15, 2003.

[61] *Financial Times*, July 24, 2003.

the fishing industry in Vietnam experienced significant losses of income as a result of the U.S. duties (Brambilla, Porto, and Tarozzi, 2010). Yet with a price differential of almost one dollar per pound of fish that tastes the same as the U.S. variety, despite the labeling policy and antidumping duties, basa and tra exports from Vietnam to the U.S. recovered after several years of decline.[62]

Release of the final determination was the end of the case from the perspective of U.S. law, and there was no opening for Vietnam to negotiate the outcome. It could file an appeal for review by the Court of International Trade, but this remains a U.S. Court that places the burden of proof on the challenging party to show the determination is not based on substantial evidence—the court will not overturn the agency's statutory interpretation so long as it can be conceived of as a permissible construction of the law (Palmeter, 1996, p. 277). For Vietnam, further legal bills with little hope for a change in the regulation made the option of appeal unattractive.

This contrasts with the option for WTO members to file a complaint and force the government that has applied antidumping duties to defend its decision as meeting WTO standards. The Anti-Dumping Agreement specifies rules and procedures for application of antidumping duties, such as what facts are necessary to make a finding of dumping and injury (Jackson, 1997, pp. 255–257). Dispute settlement has been used to challenge cases where the methodology to calculate dumping or injury was questioned. Between 1995 and 2004, there were over fifty complaints regarding antidumping.[63] Indeed, the same day that the determination was made on Vietnam's catfish, the ITC also approved antidumping duties on semiconductors from Korea. The Korean government immediately announced it would appeal the decision to the WTO.[64] While antidumping laws are legal under international trade law, states can also be held accountable to justify the application of its procedures in any given case. Dispute panels have often ruled against antidumping policies where rules of thumb used by administrative authorities in calculating margins fail to hold up before an international standard of review (Hudec, 1993, p. 345).

One consequence of this case was a renewed urgency in Vietnam to join the WTO. Demetrios Marantis, then serving as chief legal adviser to

[62] *Washington Post*, February 16, 2010. USDA, "Catfish and Basa Imports Continue to Increase Despite Confirmed Antidumping," *Market News* (May 2007).

[63] This total represents requests for consultations under the Anti-Dumping Protocol listed at http://www.wto.org/english/tratop_e/adp_e/adp_e.htm, accessed January 23, 2004.

[64] *Financial Times,* July 24, 2003.

the U.S. Vietnam Trade Council in Hanoi, said that the government had accelerated its effort to join the WTO after this case in the hope that it would receive more favorable outcomes in the future from multilateral settlement of trade disputes.[65] After joining the WTO in 2007, Vietnam filed its first WTO complaint February 2010 against U.S. antidumping duties on shrimp (DS404).

Conclusion

The first hurdle for a developing country is to persuade a larger trade partner to engage in negotiation. There is little a small country can do when requests to discuss a trade problem are ignored as happened to Vietnam when the United States refused to negotiate about its unilateral change of labeling policy. In contrast, the WTO adjudication process mandates at least an effort at negotiation during the consultation phase and guarantees the right of members to a panel judgment on their complaint. Thus even when the EC refused to offer any concessions during bilateral talks and during the DSU consultation phase, it had to face Peru in court.

The second challenge is to shape the terms of agreement to conform with common rules rather than the will of the more powerful. Peru could use the WTO adjudication process to force the EC to engage it in a negotiation based on the standard of WTO policies for labeling. Vietnam should have been able to use a legal standard for leverage because the BTA and TBT Agreement include the same text prohibiting regulations that serve as unnecessary obstacles to trade. Lacking access to formal dispute settlement, however, Vietnam could not hold the United States accountable to its commitments, or even insist that the legal text of the BTA should serve as the basis for negotiation over trade disputes. Outside of an institutional context with established standards and procedures, more powerful countries can pick and choose any standard to justify the policy they prefer. U.S. policy could first declare Vietnamese basa and tra fish to be completely different from catfish and next insist they were a like product with catfish.

Trade barriers arise with the support of vested interests, and small states have little hope to offer either carrots or threats that would shift the domestic balance for protection in the defendant state. Adjudication, however, adds leverage to the demand for removal. The sardines case study showed the importance of adjudication to persuade domestic actors in Europe that the barrier should be reformed.

[65] *Business Week*, November 24, 2003.

Many fear that legal costs transfer the power asymmetry of bilateral negotiations into WTO disputes. Developing countries suffer from their lack of comparative advantage in international trade lawyers and are unable to afford to hire a U.S. law firm for every case. Discounted legal services offered by the Advisory Centre on WTO Law, however, are an important step that reduces this problem. Moreover, as developing countries build experience using the DSU, they can begin to improve their skills and join the ranks of repeat players (Davis and Bermeo, 2009).

The WTO adds to the tactical tool kit available to a developing country. Filing a complaint forces the other side to listen to this demand for a unilateral policy change and establishes a neutral standard to settle the dispute. The multilateral setting increases the opportunity to find allies and adds to the bargaining table the obligation and reputational interests in favor of compliance. A strong country may offer concessions to a weak state in order to support the rules system. Although the legal resources required for adjudication are an obstacle for using legal tactics, the alternative of a bilateral negotiation leaves developing countries in a situation with a far worse outlook for ending the discrimination against their goods by a developed country. With more progress in the area of legal assistance for developing countries, the WTO rules for dispute settlement can help to establish a level playing field.

For issues that are outside of existing WTO commitments, however, adjudication will not be relevant. New trade issues can be negotiated only through bilateral agreements or in trade rounds to expand on existing rules. In addition, cases with questionable legal interpretation will be more difficult. Developing countries lack the legal capacity to manage the more complicated legal cases and are less likely to find allies to support their case when their interpretation involves stretching existing legal commitments. Disputed rulings that raise legal controversy among members exert less compliance pull. While unable to solve all trade problems, adjudication offers developing countries an effective tactic against trade barriers that represent a clear violation of existing commitments.

8

Conclusion

LEGALIZATION OF INTERNATIONAL affairs poses a fundamental challenge to our understanding of how states cooperate. Rather than informal and temporary bargains, states are creating lasting rules with formal enforcement by courts. Hiring lawyers and presenting arguments before third-party judges now is a standard approach to resolve international disputes over territory or trade. Despite the absence of a police force to impose the ruling, court decisions are in most cases respected by participant states.

The goals of this book have been twofold. First, I set out to explain why states use adjudication for trade disputes. I have shown that domestic political pressure influences when trade rules will be enforced through legal strategies. The filing pattern of GATT/WTO members over thirty years shows that states with constraints on executive autonomy are the most litigious. Case studies of the policy process revealed how the interventionist role of the U.S. Congress pushes trade disagreements toward adjudication while the autonomy of the bureaucracy in Japan supports an emphasis on negotiation. Second, I have examined the effectiveness of adjudication as a conflict resolution mechanism. When comparing the outcomes for equivalent trade barriers that were negotiated versus those that were adjudicated, evidence from the United States supports the effectiveness of adjudication to bring progress toward reforming the trade barrier and shortening dispute duration. Developing countries can also use the dispute process to gain better outcomes than would be possible in bilateral settings.

The Political Role of Adjudication

In chapter 2, I presented a theory about how the need for accountability within domestic institutions increases the demand for law at the international level. Without domestic constraints, the executive would prefer to make informal settlements where it would have flexibility to balance economic and diplomatic priorities. This holds true for both powerful and weak states. The former have a full range of tools for leverage outside of the legal setting and should not need to appeal to third parties. The latter have fewer options outside of court, but their leaders are also more fearful of negative diplomatic repercussions from making public complaints. Executives across a wide range of states would prefer to get the best deal possible in negotiations. Legislatures, and especially opposition parties, however, distrust informal bargains. Responsiveness to industry makes the legislature demand tough enforcement and criticize the executive if it appears to neglect commercial interests for the sake of foreign policy. Therefore, states with stronger legislative checks on executive autonomy are more likely to pursue active enforcement. Adjudication offers a strategy for an executive to meet calls at home for enforcement of international agreements with public action that both signals commitment to domestic industries and minimizes the harm to diplomatic relations.

Recognizing the role of adjudication as a signal to domestic groups does not deny its importance to resolve disputes. On the contrary, the information about enforcement preferences that comes with filing a legal complaint improves bargaining efficiency at the international level. Disagreements can persist when states are uncertain about resolve, and the presence of a costly mechanism allows states to screen for challengers with high resolve and adjust their response accordingly. Defendants may need to engage in their own theater for domestic groups. Both sides learn from the willingness to bear litigation costs and take the case into the public arena that their trade partner takes the issue seriously. States will find it easier to coordinate on an agreement and convince their domestic audience to accept the compromise when they can point to the litigation process as evidence of resolve. Facing a legal challenge to a trade barrier, in most cases the defendant offers concessions to reform the policy. Outcomes still result from negotiation, whether in early consultations or after a ruling. But legal action helps to convince a skeptical legislature that the government has done its best to fight for the domestic industry at the highest level.

Key Findings

Evidence supporting the argument is found at multiple levels: cross-national adjudication patterns, trade policy, selection of complaints, and dispute outcomes. The dominance of democratic states in the use of WTO adjudication is readily apparent. Statistical analysis showed that democratic states were more than twice as likely to file complaints. There could be many reasons for this pattern. My argument emphasizes constraints on executive autonomy, but democratic support for free trade or values in favor of legal process could produce the same outcome. The analysis in chapter 3 about which states file more complaints for adjudication tested alternative democratic mechanisms favoring adjudication. The strong relationship between the measure of checks and balances confirmed that legislative constraints increase adjudication. Those countries with an institutional structure and partisan division that grants less executive autonomy are among the highest users of adjudication. Variation over time in the level of constraints within a country also corresponds with changing use of adjudication. The proportional representation electoral system associated with free trade preferences and public good provision has a negative correlation with adjudication. This supports my argument that courts are used in response to pressure group politics from industry and legislature. The majoritarian electoral system that magnifies responsiveness to private interests also encourages adjudication. Sources of democratic values measured by rule of law and years since democratic transition did not appear to influence trade enforcement strategies.

Close examination of the United States and Japan in chapters 4 and 5 showed how legislative constraints shaped trade policy and selection of enforcement strategies. In the United States, Congress provides conditional delegation of authority to the executive for the negotiation and enforcement of trade agreements. Because Congress wants high enforcement levels and suspects the executive may not share its preferences, however, it tightly constrains the autonomy of USTR as the agency that implements U.S. trade policy. Detailed provisions of legislation require the USTR to respond to industry complaints and closely report on trade barriers and enforcement activities so that Congress can easily monitor whether the bureaucracy fulfills its mandate. As a result of these limits on executive autonomy, demands from industry and Congress push forward adjudication choices. Not only does the United States initiate more disputes, but the variation in timing and selection of cases closely follows a political logic. Periods of divided government witness higher levels of adjudication. An embattled executive branch can point to legal complaints against foreign trade barriers as one response to criticism from leaders in Congress that the executive is too soft on trade partners. Using new data on potential disputes, I am able to demonstrate that even after controlling for industry size, trade partner, and the trade distortion of the barrier, the size of political contributions from the industry substantially increases the likelihood that the government files a complaint. Relentless pressure by industry and backers in Congress pushed the government to raise particular cases for adjudication such as the Kodak-Fuji film dispute and China IPR case. Whereas the USTR sought to handle these issues in bilateral negotiations that would offer more flexibility for complex legal and political problems, congressional representatives vocally criticized negotiations as inadequate and demanded stronger action. The executive chose to file legal complaints as a way to forestall retaliation while still taking an action that would signal tough enforcement. Even as the government resisted demands for a WTO dispute against China's currency policy, it used a string of other cases to fend off accusations from Congress that the executive was weak on enforcement with China.

The trade policy dynamic in Japan offers a contrast within the spectrum of democratic states. With a strong consensus on trade policy and many years of stable rule by one party, the Diet has delegated authority to the executive that offers the bureaucracy wide discretion to manage trade policy. Trade legislation lacks detailed provisions for enforcement, and politicians rarely give attention to problems regarding foreign trade barriers. Absent oversight or pressure from the legislature, trade officials in Japan have typically addressed foreign trade barriers through their preferred route of bilateral settlement. Interministry struggles between METI and MOFA increase the tendency to delay or defer legal complaints out of diplomatic restraint, and bureaucratic officials are reluctant to risk public defeat. Consequently Japan files legal complaints for only a small number of cases, and these tend to support bureaucratic priorities about important industries (steel) and policies (antidumping). Nonetheless, while Japanese trade officials face fewer constraints from the legislature than their counterparts in the USTR, rising political competition in the 1990s generated new incentives for the bureaucracy to show its ability to serve industry interests. In a political context shaped by calls for administrative reform and politicians declaring that Japan would stand up against U.S. bullying on trade policy, METI began reporting on foreign trade barriers and initiated a series of high-profile WTO disputes. Most of these cases focused on U.S. antidumping measures against Japanese steel and a handful of important barriers to Japanese auto investment. The absence of direct complaints against China goes unquestioned by Japanese politicians or industry. There is no reason to take the risk that public action would cause a backlash in China when there is willingness to accept the compromises reached in negotiation.

Adjudication works because it both addresses domestic problems and improves international bargaining. First, filing a legal complaint signals to the domestic audience, which includes the export industry and attentive representatives in the legislature, that the executive is willing to defend market access. Each case brought for adjudication builds support of industry and legislature for liberalization as part of a long-term commitment strategy. Although not all trade disputes will be resolved in favor of U.S. interests, by demonstrating willingness to enforce agreements the executive upholds the belief that on average industry can expect market access gains from trade agreements and fair treatment in disputes. The Kodak petition for U.S. intervention to address a broad range of informal barriers in the Japanese market showed the utility of WTO adjudication as a response to domestic pressure. While they were unable to bring reform of the Japanese policies, losing the ruling by a WTO panel finally convinced Kodak and its influential backers in Congress that no more could be done. Japan's bureaucracy has defended the steel industry with repeated disputes filed against U.S. antidumping policies. Poor compliance by the United States has meant the cases brought few market gains, but they offered METI an opportunity to show its efforts for a core industry.

Second, filing a complaint sends a signal to the trade partner of serious resolve. For many cases, this brings a better solution than could have been achieved in bilateral negotiations for a similar issue. The analysis of chapter 6 indicates that across all disputes negotiated by the United States, those raised in adjudication were more likely to have progress to reform the trade barrier and a higher rate of barrier removal. This effectiveness to resolve disputes is all the more surprising given that entrenched interests on both sides account for which cases are selected for adjudication. The domestic pressure for enforcement can perversely reduce the prospects of bilateral settlements because tough talk on a wide range of issues makes it difficult for trade partners to discern where to offer concessions. Costly adjudication offers a screening mechanism for defendants to learn whether they face a serious challenge. A majority of adjudication cases are resolved before legal ruling, because the information conveyed by the act of filing alone is sufficient for many parties to reach agreement without the need for actual third-party legal interpretation. For those cases in which defendant state resistance delays settlement until the end of the adjudication process, resolution most often occurs without retaliation. Chapter 7 illustrated the system can be effective even for smaller states. Poor countries harmed by the trade barriers of major trading partners have little recourse absent multilateral rules. A small country like Peru could use a WTO complaint to bring Europe to the table and force agreement on a mutually acceptable labeling standard. Even without a credible threat of retaliation, Peru demonstrated its resolve within the legal system to raise the stakes in a public dispute. Doing so helped to mobilize norms of international obligation and reputation as leverage for compliance.

The adjudication mechanism has been sufficiently robust to obviate the need for states to resort to stronger action. Unilateral retaliation can impose quicker and higher sanctions to force removal of trade barriers but also risks trade wars and harm to the multilateral system. Following the strengthening of enforcement capacity in WTO dispute settlement, the United States has not implemented trade retaliation unless it has received authorization from a WTO panel. Neither has Japan responded to antidumping protectionism with similar measures of its own. By making retaliation conditional on legal rulings, retaliation has become a rare occurrence. States continue to engage in trade conflict, but they manage the conflict within accepted rules.

Contribution to Literature

TRADE ENFORCEMENT THEORY

The study of WTO dispute settlement has attracted growing attention in academic and policy circles. This book offers new insights about how political incentives influence enforcement of trade rules. Trade adjudication is fundamentally different from domestic courts because of the role of the state as gatekeeper. Governments may set aside legal principles and economic criteria in order to gain support from influential interest groups and achieve diplomatic goals. The pattern of who files legal complaints and the use of adjudication for particular industries and trade barriers is highly contingent on the way that political institutions shape the sensitivity of the government to private interests and diplomatic concerns.

Existing research on WTO adjudication has largely focused on analysis of observed cases. An important finding about escalation within the litigation process shows that the early informal consultation phase yields more concessions than the disputes that go further in the legal process to bring in a third-party legal ruling (Reinhardt, 2001; Busch, 2000). The gains achieved during informal consultations prior to panel hearings, however, depend upon the challenging state having already revealed its serious intent by filing a complaint. Relative to negotiations conducted without any formal complaint, adjudication is more likely to bring policy reform. In other words, the key escalation phase to promote settlement of a dispute occurs when states decide whether or not to use the legal system. This helps to explain the observation that changes in the binding nature of legal constraints for implementation of rulings do not affect outcomes.[1]

The leading economic explanation for why states establish multilateral trade rules fails to explain the role of adjudication. Bagwell and Staiger

---

[1] Busch and Reinhardt (2002) argue that the improvements to the GATT dispute settlement procedures that ended the veto right of defendants had little impact. Kono (2007) shows that the impact of PTA dispute settlement mechanisms is not sensitive to variation in the degree of binding constraint.

(2002) argue that trade rules help states escape from a terms-of-trade-driven prisoners' dilemma through introduction of a repeated games framework for "self-enforcement." This implies that one should rarely observe adjudication. Yet there have been over four hundred trade disputes since 1995 that involved a formal legal complaint against noncompliance. A commitment to repeated interaction is not enough for self-enforcement.

Neither do market power and retaliation capacity explain the choice of adjudication. Certainly law can become a tool for the powerful to coerce the weak. Large states have been the most frequent users of WTO adjudication, and research has suggested that they gain better economic outcomes from WTO disputes (Bown, 2004b). But power-based arguments fail to account for why the states with the most market power such as the United States and EU nonetheless have to resort to adjudication when their credible retaliation threat should bring concessions during negotiations without the need for adjudication. Asymmetric disputes in which rich states use adjudication against the weak or in which developing countries challenge U.S. or EU protectionism are puzzling from the perspective of power-based explanations. Yet asymmetric power balance between opposing litigants is a common occurrence in WTO disputes—high income states have filed ninety-one complaints against developing country members, and there have been ninety-seven complaints by developing country members against high-income states.[2]

The political role of adjudication described in this book challenges the conventional view that courts are primarily necessary to interpret the law.[3] Most disputes do not arise from misunderstandings over the terms of the agreement. The agreements are sufficiently clear, and meetings in bilateral talks or multilateral committees offer opportunities to discuss and correct the disagreements over implementation. Yet many potential disputes with inconsistent barriers remain as states defend trade barriers protecting important industries. Economic shocks and political changes that occur after states sign an agreement can lead them to later choose to renege on their promises. Of panel rulings 90 percent have found a violation in the policy that was the subject of the complaint.

---

[2] A summary of complaints by income is available at http://www.worldtradelaw.net/dsc/database/classificationcount.asp, accessed June 8, 2010.

[3] Legal scholars from the managerial school perspective emphasize inadvertent violations that are best resolved through more information about legal obligations (Chayes and Chayes, 1993), while legal scholars from a contract theory perspective emphasize that the GATT and WTO agreements represent incomplete contracts and courts are used to fill the gaps (Schwartz and Sykes, 2002).

Interpretation of the law is an important function of courts, but it is far from their only role in the settlement of disputes.

Furthermore, to the extent that commitment to rule of law norms promotes compliance, democratic states should be more likely to comply with their WTO commitments and have fewer WTO inconsistent trade barriers. The evidence in chapter 3, however, showed that democracies were instead more likely to be targeted as defendants in trade adjudication than other states even when controlling for economic characteristics. *Democratic states both choose temporary noncompliance themselves and vigorously prosecute the noncompliance of their trade partners.* The pattern of democratic challengers and defendants in WTO adjudication is consistent with their responsiveness to interest group pressure in a context of high domestic constraints on the executive by the legislature. The legitimacy of legal rulings by a third party is important within a domestic constraints perspective because it provides political cover to leaders (Allee and Huth, 2006). Yet this can be only a partial explanation because more than half of the disputes settle early without a legal ruling. Moreover, it is unclear why democratic states responsive to domestic audiences that favor abiding by international law would adopt a WTO inconsistent trade barrier in the first place. Domestic constraints rather than norms of compliance account for why democracies appear on both sides of disputes.

INSTITUTIONAL THEORY

I show that courts promote dispute settlement not through mechanisms based on power or norms but rather through information. The costs of legal procedures convey information about serious resolve that promotes settlement. The argument highlights the dual role of international institutions as commitment and signaling devices. States agree to rules regulating their trade policies and establish an enforcement system to increase the credibility of their commitment. States can then use legal complaints in the dispute settlement mechanism to signal their willingness to defend export interests. Domestic divisions of authority increase the need for such signaling because legislatures seek aggressive enforcement but executives prefer restraint. Only through taking the costly action of suing a foreign state can the executive convince domestic and international actors that they will enforce agreements.

My conclusions highlight the domestic origins of demand for institutions. Existing theories of international institutions focus on the need to lower transaction costs at the international level and solve bargaining problems that arise because states are uncertain about the actions of other states and have short-term incentives to defect. I show that bargaining problems also occur when governments cannot make domestic commitments. If the legislature does not believe the executive will enforce agreements, it will not go forward with more liberalization agreements. Such domestic pressure could push states to escalate conflicts. Adjudication offers a middle course letting the executive signal to domestic audiences that it takes serious enforcement action without having to threaten more extreme actions such as unilateral retaliation.

The selection dynamic highlighted here counters the "selection/endogeneity" critique of theories about international institutions. The claim is that institutions appear effective only because states use them for easy issues where they already want to cooperate (Mearsheimer, 1994–95; Downs, Rocke, and Barsoom, 1996; Von Stein, 2005). I show that in the area of trade adjudication, the selection bias is in the *opposite* direction. Domestic pressures produce a tendency to send the most difficult cases that have entrenched political interests on both sides into the institutional venue. One sees a similar pattern in other issue areas. For example, Fortna (2004, p. 149) shows that strong cease-fire agreements are implemented when peace is more fragile rather than when it will be easily achieved. In analysis of human rights treaties, Simmons (2009) finds that transition democracies that have domestic audiences that are concerned the state will violate human rights are the most likely to ratify the human rights treaties. Observing that use of a particular institution correlates with factors that would otherwise make cooperation difficult increases confidence in the findings that show positive effects from the institution. In contrast to the critique that selection bias renders institutions epiphenomenal, inadequate attention to the selection process may have led research on international institutions to underestimate the effect of some institutions to promote cooperation. Scholars need to pay careful attention to how issues arrive in a venue as the first step to examining the effectiveness of the institution to change policies.

COMPARATIVE FOREIGN POLICY

The democratic difference in foreign and trade policies has been the focus of much scholarly debate. Research points to the role of distinct democratic preferences, norms, or domestic constraints. Looking at the question of rule enforcement, I conclude that democracies are more likely to use legal strategies such as trade adjudication because their domestic constraints privilege visible accountability mechanisms. This provides a more compelling explanation for the pattern of democratic challengers and defendants than either free trade preferences or law-abiding norms.

The bargaining literature on two-level games has debated whether tied hands from domestic constraints increase bargaining power (e.g., Schelling, 1960; Putnam, 1988; Iida, 1993; Tarar, 2001). I argue that in trade disputes, democracies are less effective at bargaining. Otherwise they would not have to go to court to get what they want. In democracies, domestic pressure creates incentives to bluff with strong demands for enforcement so democratic governments have to escalate further by going to court in order to convince a trade partner they are serious. The bargaining problem is especially high in democracies like the United States where trade policy has been politicized, and less severe in democracies like Japan where the bureaucracy retains substantial autonomy. As argued by Milner (1997), domestic constraints in democracies make them less likely to cooperate. Adjudication alleviates this problem because while democracies are more likely to fail in bilateral talks, they can cooperate after taking the issue to adjudication. Legal action often brings a concession from the trade partner and, in the absence of such a concession, still is sufficient to restrain the pressure from domestic industry without retaliation.

This book is one of few studies to engage in systematic comparison of trade policy making across a range of countries including both cross-national comparison and detailed process tracing of two leading economies. The analysis examined the underpinnings of a political model of U.S. trade policy and a bureaucratic model of Japanese trade policy. In the United States, divided interests between legislature and executive create incentives for the legislature to place tight conditions on its delegation of authority to the executive for the negotiation and enforcement of trade agreements. Politicized trade policy for enforcement encourages the trade bureaucracy to closely monitor foreign barriers, submit frequent legal complaints against potential violations, and select adjudication cases according to political influence. In contrast, the shared interests in Japan fostered by one-party rule in a parliamentary system have long supported extensive delegation to the bureaucracy. Consequently, bureaucrats can choose when and how to use the tools of trade policy like WTO adjudication and focus enforcement efforts on those policies and industries the bureaucracy deems important. Consistent with the expectations of Ramseyer and Rosenbluth (1993), Japan's trade bureaucrats are responsive to industry demands and operate within the larger mandate for export promotion from the legislature. But the bureaucratic dominance model of Johnson (1982) remains relevant today as bureaucratic control over policy implementation continues to exert systematic influence over outcomes.

Implications for the Reform of Dispute Settlement Process

The theory of adjudication presented in this book accounts for several puzzling features in the design of dispute settlement rules for trade. The fundamental weakness of penalties in the WTO dispute settlement system appears strange from a perspective of retaliation. Rather than large punitive penalties for deterrence, WTO panels issue a call only for removal of the barrier within a reasonable period of time after the legal ruling. This is equivalent to a court ruling that an individual found guilty of stealing a car two years ago must simply return the car to its owner within a year and not steal again. Such weak enforcement measures are consistent with a notion of efficient breach in which some level of violations may be acceptable, but it does not represent punishment (Schwartz and Sykes, 2002; Lawrence, 2003). Even rebalancing the bargaining quid pro quo would call for tougher measures. WTO dispute settlement allows the defendant to buy up to two and a half years of noncompliance while the challenging state loses market access for that period and bears the costs of enforcement just to regain the original expected payoffs. The U.S. application of safeguards for its steel industry in 2002 is the classic example. The United States chose to break its commitments for a politically influential industry prior to an election and promptly withdrew the measure when it was ruled a violation. This best-case scenario for compliance with a ruling still shows that the exporting states had no compensation for the two years of lost market access and cost of challenging the U.S. measure. Yet this design serves the need to balance responsiveness to industry with diplomatic concerns. The government filing a complaint shows their industry they are taking action while giving a "pass" to their trade partner for limited noncompliance during the adjudication process.

This understanding of the design of dispute settlement suggests that some current reform proposals may have unintended consequences that create new imbalances. First, many calls for reform of the DSU focus on increasing penalties.[4] Several prominent scholars of dispute settlement have endorsed retroactive damages as a necessary step to prevent foot dragging by defendants to buy time for their industry (Busch and Reinhardt, 2003; Mavroidis, 2000). Such moves to raise the costs of violation neglect the important role of temporary noncompliance for systemic stability that has been highlighted by Rosendorff (2005). Not only the defendants but also their trade partners may prefer a delayed

---

[4] See for example the suggestion to have collective retaliation in the LDC Group proposal to the Doha Round, "Negotiations on the Dispute Settlement Understanding" (TN/DS/W/17, October 9, 2002).

and moderate penalty against cheating. As noted by Lawrence (2003, p. 83), raising penalties would risk "creating a momentum for conflict escalation rather than containment." Fear of such a scenario could induce states sensitive to diplomatic concerns to be even more reluctant to file complaints. As only the most politicized cases go forward, compliance could fall despite heightened penalties.

A second common theme in reform proposals emphasizes the need to reduce the barriers to filing complaints. Legal aid provisions are widely supported. Hoekman and Mavroidis (2000) call for use of a "special prosecutor" to multilateralize the act of filing complaints. While efforts to lower the imbalance between developed and developing countries in their capacity to file cases are worthwhile, measures to eliminate the costs of filing would undermine the signaling function of adjudication. If trade disputes were only about clarification of legal principles, then appointment of a special prosecutor to administer justice would advance the smooth functioning of the system. But the record suggests that few cases involve substantial legal uncertainty.

Tradable retaliation was put forward by Mexico in the Doha Round negotiations about DSU reforms and has been prominently discussed by economists.[5] The concern of developing countries has been that their small market size prevents them from offering a credible threat of retaliation to enforce a legal victory. In two cases, WTO panels authorized small countries to implement countermeasures through the suspension of other agreements (i.e., agreements covering intellectual property rights or services). Tradable retaliation offers one tool by which a small country authorized to implement countermeasures against noncompliance could borrow the power of another state, which would raise its tariffs against the violating country as a measure to induce compliance. The proposal is promising as a way to address the fears of developing countries that they lack the capacity to enforce agreements. But it does nothing to address the prior problem that many developing countries choose not to file cases because they are sensitive to diplomatic relations and do not wish to risk antagonizing a trade partner by challenging its trade barriers in court.

In order to preserve the role of adjudication as a moderate-cost signal, it is important that reforms not go too far in the direction of either increasing retaliatory measures or lowering transaction costs. Adding more teeth to enforcement will further screen out cases by countries sensitive to diplomatic relations or industries with less leverage over their

---

[5] WTO, Proposal by Mexico, TN/DS/W23, November 4, 2002. Bagwell, Mavroidis, and Staiger (2007) formalize the proposal with a model of auctioning countermeasures.

government. Making it too easy to file cases reduces the information about preferences revealed by the decision to file.

Conflict and Cooperation

Disputes among Friends

The pressure for legalization in society often arises from an increasing number of actors, making the practice of market exchange on the basis of personal trust impossible. In the classic story about the rise of institutions for trade, the expansion of trade in medieval Europe beyond the village to large fairs where merchants would conduct business with strangers led to the breakdown of the old way of business and the growing need for a third party to uphold reputation (Milgrom, North, and Weingast, 1990). The assumption is that legal dispute resolution is necessary among strangers and not friends. Yet for international adjudication, law is used even in a small community of states (current WTO membership is 153), and the most frequent users are those who have the closest political relations. The states most frequently involved in WTO adjudication with each other are the United States, EU, Canada, and Japan. Chapter 3 presented evidence from analysis of dyadic data that any particular bilateral pair of countries is more likely to have a trade dispute when they hold an alliance relationship. How does my theory account for this puzzle of legalized conflict among friends?

The answer is twofold. First, adjudication patterns reflect trade patterns. Because friends trade more with each other they also encounter more potential disputes as a function of high trade volumes.[6] Nonetheless, many states engage in extensive trade without the basis of an alliance relationship. China's large trade volume with both the United States and Japan offers an important example. These states encounter conflict over trade but are less likely to use adjudication to resolve this conflict.

A second answer lies in the tradeoff for enforcement between responsiveness to industry interests in tough enforcement and sensitivity to diplomatic relations that may be harmed by enforcement action. On the one hand, domestic constraints tip the balance toward responsiveness to industry and more frequent adjudication. On the other hand, executives continue to care about diplomatic relations and seek to manage trade policy in ways that will not interfere with foreign policy goals. This

---

[6] See Gowa (1994) on why security externalities motivate allies to trade more with each other. Mansfield and Bronson (1997) show that allies are also more likely to share preferential trade agreements.

leads them to use adjudication rather than unilateral enforcement and to focus their enforcement actions on "friends." For states with a broadly positive relationship there is less risk that escalation of a trade dispute through a public lawsuit will jeopardize overall relations. As noted by Snyder (1984, p. 485) in his classic study of alliances, "allies are free to disagree" so long as their security dependence on the alliance remains stable. Moreover, these states are repeatedly engaging each other in trade adjudication to the point where it has become business as usual. When diplomatic relations are more sensitive, filing a trade complaint would be a provocative action that could have unacceptable repercussions across issues. Addressing trade problems in a bilateral negotiation allows more flexibility to accommodate concessions and keep the dispute at a lower profile.

The case studies related to trade disputes with China revealed that both the United States and Japan have shown restraint toward using adjudication against China. During the first years of China's membership in the WTO, USTR refrained from filing complaints even while it continued to highlight ongoing compliance problems in China. The National Trade Estimate Report on China quickly outgrew even the sections on the EU and Japan as the concern about Chinese trade barriers skyrocketed. In 2004, as the end of an implicit "grace period" following accession and in response to inexorable pressure from Congress, USTR initiated the first WTO complaint against China. Since then it has initiated more cases against China. Although other countries have bandwagoned to join the United States for many of these cases, no other WTO member had initiated a complaint against China acting alone as of January 2010. Japan stands out as a major exporter with very large trade interests damaged by Chinese noncompliance on a range of issues from failure to apply tariff commitments to inadequate protection of intellectual property rights. Yet despite a large number of WTO-inconsistent policies reported in the METI reports, the government has declined to file an independent complaint. Third-party filing offers a low-profile option for Japan to free ride on the U.S. complaints. For issues such as the film tariffs that primarily affected Japanese exports and did not bring any U.S. pressure, the government patiently pursued the matter in four years of bilateral negotiations.

The cost to diplomatic relations from adjudication can be subtle. Chilling the environment for a summit meeting or ongoing talks about related trade issues is more likely than outright issue linkage between a trade dispute and security cooperation. In addition, this cost is not a concern only to diplomats. The case studies highlighted that U.S. aircraft manufacturers were more worried than the administration about the business spillover from offending the European governments that held sway over airline purchasing decisions. The hesitation to file complaints against China is held by firms that fear any association with public accusation against the Chinese government would lead to loss of other benefits or a hostile business environment.

One of the key features of international adjudication is the role of states as gatekeeper. Courts are intended to reduce the diplomatic harm of trade disputes, but this does not eliminate consideration of broader relations. Surprisingly little attention has been given to this point in studies of trade disputes. I find that cooperative political relations are permissive to conflict over economic issues, while political tensions may suppress trade conflict. Suing friends in a small community of states makes sense for a leader who faces domestic pressure to do something and diplomatic restraint against actions that could destabilize political relations.

Feedback between Rule Making and Adjudication

What is the relationship between enforcing rules and negotiating new rules? This study has focused on trade disputes that arise when states experience conflict over existing agreements. They can choose to resolve these disagreements through negotiations or adjudication. But some trade problems require *new* agreements. Adjudication cannot be used for lowering tariffs below current commitments or expanding commitments to new areas. To create new rules, governments face the choice of negotiating bilateral or regional free trade agreements or negotiating changes to the multilateral agreements in a trade round. Explaining such efforts to further liberalize trade is outside the scope of my argument about enforcement. Nonetheless, the feedback between enforcement and negotiation is an important dynamic for understanding the role of adjudication.

Expectations about the ability to enforce agreements shape willingness to commit to liberalize. Consequently, using legal enforcement to challenge foreign trade barriers can pave the way for future liberalization. The legislature is more likely to commit to a new agreement when it is convinced that the executive is a hawk on enforcement. Chapter 4 showed that the U.S. executive initiates a surge of adjudication cases in the lead-up to major trade legislation as part of a strategy to build support in Congress. Criticism about poor enforcement and the low number of WTO disputes initiated by the Bush administration accompanied resistance in Congress to ratification of free trade agreements signed by the administration. In an effort to get out ahead of the problem, the administration of Barack Obama has emphasized enforcement as a keyword central in its trade policy (although not yet launching a surge of WTO complaints). When President Obama announced his national export initiative in his January 27, 2010 State of the Union Address to Congress, he spoke of the need to sign trade deals and enforce them: "We have to seek new markets aggressively, just as our competitors are. If America sits on the sidelines while other nations sign trade deals, we will lose the chance to create jobs on our shores. But realizing those benefits also means enforcing those agreements so our trading partners play by the rules."[7] The process of building confidence among constituency groups and Congress for new agreements depends on convincing them that the promised gains from reciprocity will be achieved. The actions taken to enforce past agreements inform the legislature's assessment of what they can expect from future agreements.

Evidence shows states are more likely to abide by those commitments when they believe their partners will challenge violations. The presence of a strong adjudication record has a broader deterrent effect (Blonigen and Bown, 2003). Mansfield and Reinhardt (2008, p. 627) contend that restraint of arbitrary protection can be observed in terms of how the regime reduces volatility in trade flows among its members. Empirical support for the connection between enforcement mechanism and liberalization is given by Kono (2007), who finds that preferential trade agreements with a dispute settlement mechanism liberalize trade volumes more than preferential trade agreements that do not have a dispute settlement mechanism.

Specific trade disputes can also push forward negotiations on new rules. Disagreements about interpretation of rules can highlight areas where the rules need improvement. The prospect of being targeted by legal complaints in adjudication may encourage a state to offer concessions in rules negotiations. Faced with a choice between having to unilaterally withdraw its inconsistent policies after a violation ruling or reform the policy as a concession in quid pro quo negotiations within a large package deal, many leaders would prefer the latter. This dynamic has been clearly evident in the area of agricultural policy where adjudication of agricultural disputes has led to renewed efforts to negotiate reductions of agricultural protection in trade rounds. In the 1980s, the United States led a frontal assault targeting key pillars of agricultural subsidies and quota policies used by the EU and Japan to shelter their agricultural markets. Threats outside of the rules framework and adjudication both motivated willingness to agree to negotiate agriculture in the Uruguay Round and eventually accept the

---

[7] The full speech transcript is posted at http://www.whitehouse.gov/the-press-office/remarks-president-state-union-address.

Agriculture Agreement. More recently Brazil tried to use its challenge of U.S. and EU agricultural subsidies in WTO adjudication cases as leverage to demand concessions in the Doha Round, with mixed results to date. Regulation of aircraft subsidies has also gone back and forth between negotiation and adjudication. In chapter 4, the case study revealed that Europeans chose to negotiate a bilateral agreement for restraint of aircraft subsidies in 1992 rather than risk the likely prospect that the United States would go forward with further adjudication challenging the entire subsidy program. Europe would have tried a similar strategy in 2004, but neither Boeing nor the U.S. Congress was interested in repeating the past deals. Without burnishing its reputation for enforcement, the executive could not gain confidence from the legislature for new rules. Mansfield and Reinhardt (2003, p. 840) find that engaging in WTO disputes also increases the likelihood for a state to enter preferential trade agreements. They contend states pursue the PTA "as a way of bypassing the dispute process." Conflict at one level may drive states toward more cooperation at another level.

Deadlock on negotiations, however, will push states back into the realm of adjudication. The long-stalled Doha Round negotiations mean that some issues that could have been resolved through negotiations are instead working their way through the dispute settlement process. Chapter 5 discussed the Japanese emphasis on bringing change to U.S. antidumping rules with a twin strategy of negotiation and adjudication. As the United States refuses to negotiate its antidumping policies in the trade round, it has left Japan and others little choice but to focus on repeated use of adjudication where jurisprudence has been accumulating against the U.S. interpretation of the rules on antidumping as applied to a range of related issues. Eventually, however, there is the risk that excess use of courts will raise fears of judicial activism. States must find the balance where ongoing adjudication on related issues will lead them back to the negotiating table.

Toward a Broader Theory of Legalization

This book has argued that domestic constraints generate demand for using trade adjudication. Similar dynamics shape many areas of economic regulations. The reforms undertaken to open capital markets or pursue regional integration are premised on reciprocity, which raises the enforcement dilemma seen in trade. Will states allow each other discretion or demand rigid compliance? States face a tradeoff between representing affected interest groups and preserving diplomatic relations. In order to manage the tension, democracies will favor the adoption of

legal dispute mechanisms and lead in their use. Indeed, third-party mediation of disputes is a common feature of preferential trade agreements,
bilateral investment agreements, and regional integration agreements.

The role of democratic checks and balances to push forward legalization should be explored as a more general pattern in international
affairs. Goldstein (1996) shows that the U.S. executive supported dispute
settlement procedures in NAFTA as a way to strengthen its position
relative to the legislature. Looking beyond trade also holds promise.
Lipson (1991) attributes "the rise of democratic states with principles
of public accountability and some powers of legislative oversight" as the
cause for the decline of secret treaties. He notes that in the United States,
Congress has attempted to rein in the use of informal agreements and
increase oversight (p. 517). Martin (2000) presents a general theory of
how legislative participation in bargaining is a key condition to promote
credible commitments for international cooperation.

There is already recognition that democratization leads states to
join international organizations (Mansfield and Pevehouse, 2006), and
another step would be to examine the *form* of organizations that they
enter. A quick look at regional integration supports a correlation between
democracy levels and legalization in regional institutions. Regional
cooperation in Europe where all members are democracies has achieved
the highest level of legalization, and Latin American regional institutions (Mercosur and the Andean Pact) have active courts in a largely
democratic region. In contrast, the Gulf Cooperation Council among
Arab states with low levels of democracy and East Asian regionalism
(ASEAN and APEC) among a widely heterogeneous set of regimes have
been characterized by informal norms and avoidance of legal dispute
resolution mechanisms. Future research in this area could test whether
accountability requirements of democratic governments lie behind these
choices of institutional design.

While states have tightly guarded their role as gatekeeper of trade disputes in the multilateral system, some PTAs, investment agreements, and
regional courts allow individuals and firms to file complaints. Keohane,
Moravcsik, and Slaughter (2000) highlight how this difference in access
distinguishes between interstate and transnational dispute resolution.
Transnational dispute resolution provides individuals standing before the
court. This increases the scope of filed cases since individuals may lodge
a complaint at an international court against their own government's
actions. They may also file against a foreign government when their
government would have declined to file. The logic of the argument in
this book suggests states will be reluctant to cede their role as gatekeeper
for filing complaints. Only against a background of common interests
would states undertake deep integration and delegate to nonstate actors

the decision of when to adjudicate (Downs, Rocke, and Barsoom, 1996; Moravcsik, 2000). Careful selection of membership makes it less likely that heightened enforcement levels from direct access would jeopardize political relations. For example, based on close regional ties, Canada, Mexico, and the United States agreed to provisions in NAFTA that allow their respective firms to directly challenge the administrative decisions regarding unfair trade practices and abide by the judicial review of binational panels.[8] The highest levels of legalization occur in the ECJ where the transnational court both provides access to nonstate actors and embeds the decisions within domestic judicial processes. Notably this development has been confined to European states with shared democratic values, economic union, and alliance interests.

How do democratic constraints affect state behavior in other inter-state tribunals outside of economic issues? Using adjudication to signal responsiveness to domestic audiences could also apply to some territorial disputes. As public backing for a grievance over a territorial claim rises, deadlocked negotiations may be met by demands within a state for taking more extreme actions. Even when leaders prefer a compromise deal over militarized conflict, they fear to appear weak by backing down. Taking the issue to a tribunal offers a middle course. There is evidence of an im-portant role for domestic constraints to explain patterns of adjudication for territorial disputes. Allee and Huth (2006) find that states are more likely to submit territorial disputes to adjudication/arbitration when the executive faces strong domestic opposition.

Human rights presents a different dynamic because the victims of noncompliance actions lie within the state violating the agreement. As noted above, transnational dispute resolution that provides standing to individuals to file complaints will not generate the kind of signaling dynamic central to my argument about how states use courts as a response to domestic constraints. Even for interstate dispute settlement of human-rights-related issues, there would not be the same dynamic of domestic accountability that arises when stakeholders in one state demand changes of the policies in another state. In the area of human rights, more complex strategies must emerge in which victims ally with transnational groups and mobilize around treaty commitments to apply pressure against their own government (Keck and Sikkink, 1998; Simmons, 2009). Nonetheless, it is possible that governments will see court action as a way to condemn abusive behavior by another state in response to the moral outrage of domestic constituents. Future research

---

[8] Goldstein (1996) persuasively shows that the U.S. executive favored delegation to binational panels because of incentives based on domestic constraints similar to those discussed in this book.

should explore the conditions under which states choose legal strategies versus informal efforts at moral persuasion or sanction strategies.

Concluding Remarks

The rise of international courts has been an important development for international affairs. With increasing frequency, states resolve disputes in the realm of lawyers and judges rather than in back-room deals by diplomats. International adjudication, however, is not simply a technocratic enterprise of interpreting legal provisions and resolving problems on the basis of compliance norms. This book has demonstrated how the constraints of diplomacy and interest group politics remain very prominent even in an issue area like trade that is regulated by rules and third-party dispute settlement. Few international courts allow individuals access to file complaints or provide for a public prosecutor. In their role as gatekeeper, states retain control over which cases are filed for adjudication. Choices over when to use adjudication versus alternative strategies reflect political calculations that weigh the tradeoffs between multiple interests. Some states will overlook violations, while others will take on the role of police and prosecutor. This difference in litigiousness among states will be as much a function of their political system as a function of their bargaining power. Domestic constraints encourage litigation as public action that signals responsiveness to domestic interests. States with less need to engage in political theater can avoid court action and resolve their disputes through informal settlements.

Far from eliminating anarchy by imposing outcomes, courts represent an alternative bargaining forum in which states defend their interests. Third-party rulings from a court offer a standard for interpretation of the law and make retaliation appear more legitimate. But much of the value added from courts occurs simply as an institutional venue that facilitates state actions to provide information about their preferences. The costs of taking recourse to legal action are sufficient to signal resolve in a dispute without having to actually implement retaliation. At the international level, adjudication makes it more likely states can calibrate their concessions to reach a mutually acceptable level of enforcement. At home, giving local victims their day in court helps states to uphold the domestic bargain supporting the international agreement.

Bibliography

Abbott, Kenneth W., Robert Keohane, Andrew Moravcsik, Anne-Marie Slaughter, and Duncan Snidal. 2000. "The Concept of Legalization." *International Organization* 54:401–419.

ACCJ (American Chamber of Commerce in Japan). 1997. *Making Trade Talks Work: Lessons from Recent History*. Tokyo: American Chamber of Commerce in Japan.

Akaneya, Tatsuo. 1992. *Nihon no gatto kanyū mondai* (Japan's GATT Accession Problem). Tokyo: Tokyo University Press.

Allee, Todd. 2003. "Going to Geneva? Trade Protection and Dispute Resolution under the GATT and WTO." PhD thesis, University of Michigan.

Allee, Todd, and Paul Huth. 2006. "Legitimizing Dispute Settlement: International Legal Rulings as Domestic Political Cover." *American Political Science Review* 100:219–234.

Alt, James, Jeffrey Frieden, Michael Gilligan, Dani Rodrik, and Ronald Rogowski. 1996. "The Political Economy of International Trade: Enduring Puzzles and an Agenda for Inquiry." *Comparative Political Studies* 29:689–717.

Alter, Karen. 2003. "Resolving or Exacerbating Disputes? The WTO's New Dispute Resolution System." *International Affairs* 79:783–800.

Axelrod, Robert, and Robert Keohane. 1986. *Cooperation under Anarchy*. Princeton, NJ: Princeton University Press.

Bagwell, Kyle, Petros Mavroidis, and Robert Staiger. 2007. "Auctioning Countermeasures in the WTO." *Journal of International Economics* 73:309–332.

Bagwell, Kyle, and Robert Staiger. 2002. *The Economics of the World Trading System*. Cambridge, MA: MIT Press.

Bailey, Michael, Judith Goldstein, and Barry Weingast. 1997. "The Institutional Roots of American Trade Policy: Politics, Coalitions, and International Trade." *World Politics* 49:309–338.

Baldwin, Robert. 1985. *The Political Economy of U.S. Import Policy*. Cambridge, MA: MIT Press.

Baldwin, Robert. 1998. "U.S. Trade Policies: The Role of the Executive Branch." In *Constituent Interests and U.S. Trade Policies*, ed. Alan Deardorff and Robert Stern. Ann Arbor: University of Michigan Press, 65–87.

Barton, John, Judith Goldstein, Timothy Josling, and Richard Steinberg. 2006. *The Evolution of the Trade Regime: Politics, Law, and Economics of the GATT and the WTO*. Princeton, NJ: Princeton University Press.

Battigalli, Pierpaolo, and Giovanni Maggi. 2002. "Rigidity, Discretion, and the Costs of Writing Contracts." *American Economic Review* 92:798–817.

Bayard, Thomas, and Kimberly Ann Elliott. 1994. *Reciprocity and Retaliation in U.S. Trade Policy*. Washington, DC: Institute for International Economics.

Bayne, Nicholas. 2007. *The New Economic Diplomacy: Decision-Making and Negotiation in International Economic Relations.* Hampshire, UK: Ashgate.

Beck, Thorsten, George Clarke, Alberto Groff, Philip Keefer, and Patrick Walsh. 2001. "New Tools in Comparative Political Economy: The Database of Political Institutions." *World Bank Economic Review* 15:165–176.

Bendor, Jonathan, Amihai Glazer and Thomas Hammond. 2001. "Theories of Delegation." *Annual Review of Political Science* 4:235–269.

Bergsten, Fred and Marcus Noland. 1993. *Reconcilable Differences? United States-Japan Economic Conflict.* Washington, DC: Institute for International Economics.

Bernstein, Ann and Peter L. Berger. 1997. *Business and Democracy: Cohabitation or Contradiction?* London: Pinter.

Bhagwati, Jagdish and Hugh T. Patrick, eds. 1990. *Aggressive Unilateralism: America's 301 Trade Policy and the World Trading System.* Ann Arbor: University of Michigan Press.

Blonigen, Bruce and Chad Bown. 2003. "Antidumping and Retaliation Threats." *Journal of International Economics* 60:249–273.

Bown, Chad. 2004a. "Developing Countries as Plaintiffs and Defendants in GATT/WTO Trade Disputes." *World Economy* 27:59–80.

Bown, Chad. 2004b. "On the Economic Success of GATT/WTO Dispute Settlement." *Review of Economics and Statistics* 86:811–823.

Bown, Chad. 2004c. "Trade Disputes and Implementation of Protection under GATT: An Empirical Assessment." *Journal of International Economics* 62:263–294.

Bown, Chad. 2005a. "Participation in WTO Dispute Settlement: Complainants, Interested Parties and Free Riders." *World Bank Economic Review* 19: 287–310.

Bown, Chad. 2005b. "Trade Remedies and World Trade Organization Dispute Settlement: Why Are So Few Challenged?" *Journal of Legal Studies* 34: 515–555.

Bown, Chad. 2009a. *Self-Enforcing Trade: Developing Countries and WTO Dispute Settlement.* Washington, DC: Brookings.

Bown, Chad. 2009b. "U.S.-China Trade Conflicts and the Future of the WTO." *Fletcher Forum of World Affairs* 33:27–48.

Bown, Chad. 2010. "Taking Stock of Antidumping, Safeguards, and Countervailing Duties, 1990-2009". Policy Research Working Paper No. 5436. World Bank.

Bown, Chad and Rachel McCulloch. 2009. "U.S.-Japan and U.S.-China Trade Conflict: Export Growth, Reciprocity, and the International Trading System." *Journal of Asian Economics* 20:669–687.

Brambilla, Irene, Guido Porto, and Alessandro Tarozzi. 2010. "Adjusting to Trade Policy: Evidence from U.S. Antidumping Duties on Vietnamese Catfish." Forthcoming in *Review of Economics and Statistics*, posted online 8 December 2010.

Bueno de Mesquita, Bruce, Alastair Smith, Randolph Siverson, and James Morrow. 2003. *The Logic of Political Survival.* Cambridge, MA: MIT Press.

Busch, Marc. 1999. *Trade Warriors: States, Firms, and Strategic-Trade Policy in High-Technology Competition*. Cambridge, UK: Cambridge University Press.

Busch, Marc. 2000. "Democracy, Consultation, and the Paneling of Disputes under GATT." *Journal of Conflict Resolution* 44:425–446.

Busch, Marc. 2007. "Overlapping Institutions, Forum Shopping, and Dispute Settlement in International Trade." *International Organization* 61:735–761.

Busch, Marc and Eric Reinhardt. 1999. "Industrial Location and Protection: The Political and Economic Geography of U.S. Nontariff Barriers." *American Journal of Political Science* 43:1028–1050.

Busch, Marc and Eric Reinhardt. 2001. "Bargaining in the Shadow of the Law: Early Settlement in GATT/WTO Disputes." *Fordham International Law Journal* 24:158–172.

Busch, Marc and Eric Reinhardt. 2002. "Testing International Trade Law: Empirical Studies of GATT/WTO Dispute Settlement." In *The Political Economy of International Trade Law: Essays in Honor of Robert E. Hudec*, ed. Daniel Kennedy and James Southwick. Cambridge, UK: Cambridge University Press, 457–481.

Busch, Marc and Eric Reinhardt. 2003. "Developing Countries and GATT/WTO Dispute Settlement." *Journal of World Trade* 37:719–735.

Busch, Marc and Eric Reinhardt. 2006. "Three's a Crowd: Third Parties and WTO Dispute Settlement." *World Politics* 58:446–477.

Butler, Monika and Heinz Hauser. 2000. "The WTO Dispute Settlement System: A First Assessment from an Economic Perspective." *Journal of Law, Economics, & Organization* 16:503–533.

Calder, Kent. 1988. *Crisis and Compensation*. Princeton, NS: Princeton University Press.

Calder, Kent. 1997. "The Institutions of Japanese Foreign Policy." In *The Process of Japanese Foreign Policy*, ed. Richard Grant. London: Royal Institute of International Affairs, pp. 1–24.

Calvert, Randall, Mathew McCubbins, and Barry Weingast. 1989. "A Theory of Political Control and Agency Discretion." *American Journal of Political Science* 33:588–611.

Campbell, John. 1993. *Japan's Foreign Policy*. Armonk, NY: M.E. Sharpe.

Chaudoin, Stephen. 2011. "Information Transmission and Dispute Settlement in International Institutions." PhD thesis, Princeton University.

Chayes, Abram and Antonia Handler Chayes. 1993. "On Compliance." *International Organization* 47:175–205.

Chayes, Abram and Antonia Handler Chayes. 1995. *The New Sovereignty: Compliance with International Regulatory Agreements*. Cambridge, MA: Harvard University Press.

Cohen, Stephen. 2000. *The Making of United States International Economic Policy: Principles, Problems, and Proposals for Reform*. Westport, CT: Greenwood.

Cooter, Robert, Stephen Marks, and Robert Mnookin. 1982. "Bargaining in the Shadow of the Law: A Testable Model of Strategic Behavior." *Journal of Legal Studies* 11:225–251.

Curtis, Gerald. 1988. *The Japanese Way of Politics*. New York: Columbia University Press.

Curtis, Gerald. 1999. *The Logic of Japanese Politics: Leaders, Institutions, and the Limits of Change*. New York: Columbia University Press.

Dai, Xinyuan. 2002. "Information Systems in Treaty Regimes." *World Politics* 54:405–436.

Dai, Xinyuan. 2007. *International Institutions and National Policies*. Cambridge, UK: Cambridge University Press.

Dam, Kenneth W. 1970. *The GATT: Law and International Economic Organization*. Chicago: University of Chicago Press.

Dam, Kenneth W. 2001. *The Rules of the Global Game: A New Look at U.S. International Economic Policymaking*. Chicago: University of Chicago Press.

Davey, William. 2005. "Evaluating WTO Dispute Settlement: What Results Have Been Achieved through Consultations and Implementation of Panel Reports?" Working paper, University of Illinois.

Davis, Christina. 2003. *Food Fights over Free Trade: How International Institutions Promote Agricultural Trade Liberalization*. Princeton, NJ: Princeton University Press.

Davis, Christina. 2006. "Do WTO Rules Create a Level Playing Field for Developing Countries? Lessons from Peru and Vietnam." In *Negotiating Trade: Developing Countries in the WTO and NAFTA*, ed. John Odell. Cambridge, UK: Cambridge University Press, pp. 219–256.

Davis, Christina. 2009. "Overlapping Institutions in Trade Policy." *Perspectives on Politics* 7:25–31.

Davis, Christina and Sarah Blodgett Bermeo. 2009. "Who Files? Developing Country Participation in WTO Adjudication." *Journal of Politics* 71: 1033–1049.

Davis, Christina and Sophie Meunier. 2011. "Business as Usual? Economic Responses to Political Tensions." *American Journal of Political Science* 55: 628–646.

Davis, Christina and Yuki Shirato. 2007. "Firms, Governments, and WTO Adjudication: Japan's Selection of WTO Disputes." *World Politics* 59: 274–313.

De Bievre, Dirk and Andreas Dur. 2005. "Constituency Interests and Delegation in European and American Trade Policy." *Comparative Political Studies* 38:1271–1296.

Deardorff, Alan and Robert Stern. 1998. "An Overview of the Modeling of the Choices and Consequences of U.S. Trade Policies." In *Constituent Interests and U.S. Trade Policies*, ed. Alan Deardorff and Robert Stern. Ann Arbor: University of Michigan Press, pp. 29–55.

Destler, I. M. 2005. *American Trade Politics*. Washington, DC: Institute for International Economics.

Destler, I. M. and John Odell. 1987. "Anti-Protection: Changing Forces in United States Trade Politics." *Policy Analyses in International Economics* 21. Washington, DC: Institute For International Economics.

Dixon, William. 1994. "Democracy and the Peaceful Settlement of International Conflict." *American Political Science Review* 88:14–32.

Downs, George and David M. Rocke. 1995. *Optimal Imperfection? Domestic Uncertainty and Institutions in International Relations*. Princeton, NJ: Princeton University Press.

Downs, George, David Rocke, and Peter Barsoom. 1996. "Is the Good News about Compliance Good News about Cooperation?" *International Organization* 50:379–406.

Doyle, Michael. 1986. "Liberalism and World Politics." *American Political Science Review* 80:1151–1169.

Dryden, Steve. 1995. *Trade Warriors: USTR and the American Crusade for Free Trade*. Oxford: Oxford University Press.

Dunoff, Jeffrey. 2009. "Does the U.S. Support International Tribunals? The Case of the Multilateral Trade System." In *The Sword and the Scales: The United States and International Courts and Tribunals*, ed. Cesare Romano. Cambridge, UK: Cambridge University Press, pp. 322–355.

Dupont, Cedric, Renato Mariani, and Daniela Benavente. 2008. "Taming the Eagle: Constraining Effects of the WTO on USTR Section 301 Investigations." Paper presented at the annual meeting of the International Study Association, San Francisco.

Durling, James. 2000. *Anatomy of a Trade Dispute: A Documentary History of the Kodak-Fuji Film Dispute*. London: Cameron May.

Dutt, Pushan and Devashish Mitra. 2005. "Political Ideology and Endogenous Trade Policy: An Empirical Investigation." *Review of Economics and Statistics* 87:59–72.

Ehrlich, Sean. 2007. "Access to Protection: Domestic Institutions and Trade Policy in Democracies." *International Organization* 61:571–605.

Eisenberg, Theodore. 1990. "Testing the Selection Effect: A New Theoretical Framework with Empirical Tests." *Journal of Legal Studies* 19:337–358.

Epstein, David and Sharyn O'Halloran. 1999. *Delegating Powers: A Transaction Cost Politics Approach to Policy Making under Separate Powers*. Cambridge, UK: Cambridge University Press.

Evans, Peter, Harold Jacobson, and Robert Putnam, eds. 1993. *Double-Edged Diplomacy: International Bargaining and Domestic Politics*. Berkeley: University of California Press.

Fallows, James. 1993. "How the World Works." *Atlantic Monthly*, December, pp. 61–87.

Farber, Henry and Michelle White. 1994. "A Comparison of Formal and Informal Dispute Resolution in Medical Malpractice." *Journal of Legal Studies* 23:777–806.

Fearon, James D. 1994. "Domestic Political Audiences and the Escalation of International Disputes." *American Political Science Review* 88:577–92.

Fearon, James D. 1995. "Rationalist Explanations for War." *International Organization* 49:379–414.

Fearon, James D. 1997. "Signaling Foreign Policy Interests: Tying Hands versus Sinking Costs." *Journal of Conflict Resolution* 41:68–90.

Fearon, James D. 1998. "Bargaining, Enforcement, and International Cooperation." *International Organization* 52:269–306.

Fey, Mark and Kristopher Ramsay. 2007. "Mutual Optimism and War." *American Journal of Political Science* 51:738–754.

Fortna, Page. 2004. *Peace Time: Cease-Fire Agreements and the Durability of Peace.* Princeton, NJ: Princeton University Press.

Franck, Thomas. 1990. *The Power of Legitimacy among Nations.* Oxford: Oxford University Press.

Galanter, Marc. 1975. "Afterword: Explaining Litigation." *Law and Society Review* 9:347–368.

Gaubatz, Kurt. 1996. "Democratic States and Commitment in International Relations." *International Organization* 50:109–139.

Gawande, Kishore. 1997. "U.S. Non-Tariff Barriers as Privately Provided Public Goods." *Journal of Public Economics* 64:61–81.

Gawande, Kishore and Wendy Hansen. 1999. "Retaliation, Bargaining, and the Pursuit of 'Free and Fair' Trade." *International Organization* 53:117–159.

Gibbons, Robert. 1992. *Game Theory for Applied Economists.* Princeton, NJ: Princeton University Press.

Giles, Micheal W. and Thomas D. Lancaster. 1989. "Political Transition, Social Development, and Legal Mobilization in Spain." *American Political Science Review* 83:817–833.

Gilligan, Michael. 1997. *Empowering Exporters: Reciprocity, Delegation, and Collective Action in American Trade Policy.* Ann Arbor: University of Michigan Press.

Gilpin, Robert. 1981. *War and Change in World Politics.* Cambridge, UK: Cambridge University Press.

Goldstein, Judith. 1996. "International Law and Domestic Institutions: Reconciling North American 'Unfair' Trade Laws." *International Organization* 50:541–564.

Goldstein, Judith and Joanne Gowa. 2002. "U.S. National Power and the Post-War Trading Regime." *World Trade Review* 1:153–170.

Goldstein, Judith, Miles Kahler, Robert O. Keohane, and Anne-Marie Slaughter. 2000. "Introduction: Legalization and World Politics." *International Organization* 54:385–399.

Goldstein, Judith and Lisa L. Martin. 2000. "Legalization, Trade Liberalization, and Domestic Politics: A Cautionary Note." *International Organization* 54:603–632.

Goldstein, Judith, Douglas Rivers, and Michael Tomz. 2007. "Institutions in International Relations: Understanding the Effects of the GATT and the WTO on World Trade." *International Organization* 61:37–67.

Goldstein, Judith and Richard Steinberg. 2009. *The Politics of Global Regulation.* Princeton, NJ: Princeton University Press.

Goodhart, Lucy. 2006. "Political Geography and Trade Restriction Bias." Paper presented at the 2006 Annual General Meeting of the Midwest Political Science Association, Chicago.

Gowa, Joanne. 1994. *Allies, Adversaries, and International Trade.* Princeton, NJ: Princeton University Press.

Gowa, Joanne and Soo Yeon Kim. 2005. "An Exclusive Country Club: The Effects of GATT 1950–94." *World Politics* 57:453–478.

Grossman, Gene M. and Elhanan Helpman. 1994. "Protection for Sale." *American Economic Review* 84:833–850.

Grossman, Gene M. and Elhanan Helpman. 2002. *Interest Groups and Trade Policy*. Princeton, NJ: Princeton University Press.

Grossman, Gene M. and Michael Katz. 1983. "Plea Bargaining and Social Welfare." *American Economic Review* 73:749–757.

Grossman, Gene M. and Giovanni Maggi. 1998. *Global Competition and Integration*. Dordrecht: Kluwer.

Guzman, Andrew. 2002. "The Political Economy of Litigation and Settlement at the WTO". Public Law and Legal Theory Research Paper No. 98, University of California, Berkeley School of Law.

Guzman, Andrew and Beth Simmons. 2002. "To Settle or Empanel? An Empirical Analysis of Litigation and Settlement at the World Trade Organization." *Journal of Legal Studies* 31:205–235.

Guzman, Andrew and Beth Simmons. 2005. "Power Plays and Capacity Constraints: The Selection of Defendants in WTO Disputes." *Journal of Legal Studies* 34:557–598.

Haggard, Stephan and Robert Kaufman. 1995. *The Political Economy of Democratic Transitions*. Princeton, NJ: Princeton University Press.

Hansen, Wendy and Jeffrey Drope. 2004. "Purchasing Protection? The Effect of Political Spending on U.S. Trade Policy." *Political Research Quarterly* 57:27–37.

Hansen, Wendy, Neil Mitchell, and Jeffrey Drope. 2005. "The Logic of Private and Collective Action." *American Journal of Political Science* 49:150–167.

Hart, Michael. 1991. "A Lower Temperature: The Dispute Settlement Experience under the Canada-United States Free Trade Agreement." *American Review of Canadian Studies* 21:193–205.

Henisz, Witold. 2000. "Political Institutions and Policy Volatility." *Economics and Politics* 16:1–27.

Hiscox, Michael. 1999. "The Magic Bullet? RTAA, Institutional Reform, and Trade Liberalization." *International Organization* 53:669–698.

Hiscox, Michael. 2002. *International Trade and Political Conflict: Commerce, Coalitions, and Mobility*. Princeton, NJ: Princeton University Press.

Ho, Daniel, Kosuke Imai, Gary King, and Elizabeth Stuart. 2007. "Matching as Nonparametric Preprocessing for Reducing Model Dependence in Parametric Causal Inference." *Political Analysis* 15:199–236.

Hoda, Anwarul. 2002. *Tariff Negotiations and Renegotiations under the GATT and the WTO*. Cambridge, UK: Cambridge University Press.

Hoekman, Bernard and Petros Mavroidis. 2000. "WTO Dispute Settlement, Transparency and Surveillance." *World Economy* 23:527–542.

Horn, Henrik and Petros Mavroidis. 2008. "The WTO Dispute Settlement System 1995–2006 Dataset Descriptive Statistics Overview." Technical report, World Bank.

Horn, Henrik, Petros Mavroidis, and Hakan Nordstrom. 1999. "Is the Use of the WTO Dispute Settlement System Biased?" Discussion Paper 2340, Center for Economic Policy Research.

Horn, Henrik, Petros Mavroidis, and Hakan Nordstrom. 2005. *The WTO and International Trade Law/Dispute Settlement*. Cheltenham, UK: Edward Elgar.

Huber, John and Charles Shipan. 2002. *Deliberate Discretion? The Institutional Foundations of Bureaucratic Autonomy*. Cambridge, UK: Cambridge University Press.

Hudec, Robert. 1980. "GATT Dispute Settlement after the Tokyo Round." *Cornell International Law Journal* 13:145–203.

Hudec, Robert. 1987. "'Transcending the Ostensible': Some Reflections on the Nature of Litigation between Governments." *Minnesota Law Review* 72:211–226.

Hudec, Robert. 1993. *Enforcing International Trade Law: The Evolution of the Modern GATT Legal System*. Salem, NH: Butterworth.

Hudec, Robert. 2002. "The Adequacy of WTO Dispute Settlement Remedies: A Developing Country Perspective." In *Development, Trade, and the WTO*, ed. Bernard Hoekman, Aaditya Mattoo, and Philip English. Washington, DC: World Bank, pp. 81–91.

Hufbauer, Gary Clyde, Yee Wong, and Ketki Sheth. 2006. *U.S.-China Trade Disputes: Rising Tide, Rising Stakes*. Washington, DC: Institute for International Economics.

Hussain, Turab. 2005. "Victory in Principle: Pakistan's Dispute Settlement Case on Combed Cotton Yarn Exports to the United States." In *Managing the Challenges of WTO Participation: 45 Case Studies*, ed. Peter Gallagher, Patrick Low, and Andrew Stoler. Cambridge, UK: Cambridge University Press, pp. 459–472.

Hylton, Keith. 1993. "Asymmetric Information and the Selection of Disputes for Litigation." *Journal of Legal Studies* 22:187–210.

Iida, Keisuke. 1993. "When and How Do Domestic Constraints Matter? Two-Level Games with Uncertainty." *Journal of Conflict Resolution* 37:403–426.

Iida, Keisuke. 2003. "Why Does the World Trade Organization Appear Neoliberal? The Puzzle of the High Incidence of Guilty Verdicts in WTO Adjudication." *Journal of Public Policy* 23:1–21.

Iida, Keisuke. 2004. "Is WTO Dispute Settlement Effective?" *Global Governance* 10:207–225.

Iida, Keisuke. 2006. *Legalization and Japan: The Politics of WTO Dispute Settlement*. London: Cameron May.

Inoguchi, Takashi and Tomoaki Iwai. 1987. *Zoku giin no kenkyū* (A Study of Legislative Tribes). Tokyo: Nihon Keizai Shimbun.

Irwin, Douglas. 1998. "U.S. Semiconductor Trade Policy." In *Constituent Interests and U.S. Trade Policies*, ed. Alan Deardorff and Robert Stern. Ann Arbor: University of Michigan Press, pp. 161–172.

Jackson, John H. 1997. *The World Trading System: Law and Policy of International Economic Relations*. 2nd ed. Cambridge, MA: MIT Press.

Jackson, John H. 2001. "The Role and Effectiveness of the WTO Dispute Settlement Mechanism." In *Brookings Trade Forum 2000*. Washington, DC: Brookings Institution, pp. 179–219.

Johnson, Chalmers. 1982. *MITI and the Japanese Miracle*. Stanford, CA: Stanford University Press.

Johnston, Alastair Iain. 2001. "Treating International Institutions as Social Environments." *International Studies Quarterly* 45:487–515.

Karol, David. 2000. "Divided Government and U.S. Trade Policy: Much Ado about Nothing?" *International Organization* 54:825–844.

Karol, David. 2007. "Does Constituency Size Affect Elected Officials' Trade Policy Preferences?" *Journal of Politics* 69:483–494.

Kawashima, Takeyoshi. 1967. *Nihonjin no hou ishiki* (Japanese Legal Consciousness). Tokyo: Iwanami Shoten.

Keck, Margaret and Kathryn Sikkink. 1998. *Activists Beyond Borders*. Ithaca, NY: Cornell University Press.

Keefer, Philip and David Stasavage. 2003. "The Limits of Delegation: Veto Players, Central Bank Independence, and the Credibility of Monetary Policy." *American Political Science Review* 97:407–423.

Kelemen, Daniel and Eric Sibbitt. 2002. "The Americanization of Japanese Law." *University of Pennsylvania Journal of International Economic Law* 23:269–323.

Keohane, Robert. 1984. *After Hegemony: Cooperation and Discord in the World Political Economy*. Princeton, NJ: Princeton University Press.

Keohane, Robert, Andrew Moravcsik, and Stephen Macedo. 2009. "Democracy-Enhancing Multilateralism." *International Organization* 63:1–31.

Keohane, Robert, Andrew Moravcsik, and Anne-Marie Slaughter. 2000. "Legalized Dispute Resolution: Interstate and Transnational." *International Organization* 54:457–488.

Kim, Moonhawk. 2008. "Costly Procedures: Divergent Effects of Legalization in the GATT/WTO Dispute Settlement Process." *International Studies Quarterly* 52:657–686.

Kindleberger, Charles P. 1986. *The World in Depression*. Berkeley: University of California Press.

King, Gary. 1989. "Event Count Models for International Relations: Generalizations and Applications." *International Studies Quarterly* 33:123–147.

King, Gary and Langche Zeng. 2001. "Logistic Regression in Rare Events Data." *Political Analysis* 9:137–163.

Kono, Daniel. 2006. "Optimal Obfuscation: Democracy and Trade Policy Transparency." *American Political Science Review* 100:369–384.

Kono, Daniel. 2007. "Making Anarchy Work: International Legal Institutions and Trade Cooperation." *Journal of Politics* 69:746–759.

Koremenos, Barbara, Charles Lipson, and Duncan Snidal. 2001. "The Rational Design of International Institutions." *International Organization* 55:761–799.

Kovenock, Dan and Marie Thursby. 1992. "GATT, Dispute Settlement and Cooperation." *Economics and Politics* 4:151–170.

Krauss, Ellis. 2004. "The U.S. and Japan in APEC's EVSL Negotiations: Regional Multilateralism and Trade." In *Beyond Bilateralism: The U.S.-Japan Relationship in the New Asia Pacific*, ed. Ellis Krauss and T. J. Pempel. Stanford, CA: Stanford University Press, pp. 272–295.

Krueger, Anne O., ed. 1998. *The WTO as an International Organization*. Chicago: University of Chicago Press.

Krugman, Paul, ed. 1986. *Strategic Trade Policy and the New International Economics*. Cambridge, MA: MIT Press.

Kucik, Jeffrey and Eric Reinhardt. 2008. "Does Flexibility Promote Cooperation? An Application to the Global Trade Regime." *International Organization* 62:477–505.

La Porta, Rafael, Florencio Lopez-de Silanes, Cristian Pop-Eleches, and Andrei Shleifer. 2004. "Judicial Checks and Balances." *Journal of Political Economy* 112:445–470.

Laird, Sam and Alexander Yeats. 1990. *Quantitative Methods for Trade-Barrier Analysis*. London: Macmillan.

Lake, David. 1988. *Power, Protection, and Free Trade: International Sources of U.S. Commercial Strategy, 1887–1939*. Ithaca, NY: Cornell University Press.

Larkins, Christopher M. 1996. "Judicial Independence and Democratization: A Theoretical and Conceptual Analysis." *American Journal of Comparative Law* 44:605–626.

Laver, Michael and Ken Shepsle. 1991. "Divided Government: America Is Not Exceptional." *Governance* 4:250–269.

Lawrence, Robert. 2003. *Crimes and Punishments? Retaliation under the WTO*. Washington, DC: Institute for International Economics.

Lee, Jong-Wha and Phillip Swagel. 1997. "Trade Barriers and Trade Flows across Countries and Industries." *Review of Economics and Statistics* 79:372–382.

Leipziger, Danny, ed. 1997. *Lessons from East Asia*. Ann Arbor: University of Michigan Press.

Lemos, Leany. 2010. "Brazilian Congress and Foreign Affairs: Abdication or Delegation?" Technical Report No. 58, Oxford University Global Economic Governance Program.

Leventoglu, Bahar and Ahmer Tarar. 2005. "Prenegotiation Public Commitment in Domestic and International Bargaining." *American Political Science Review* 99:419–433.

Liang, Wei. 2007. *China's Foreign Trade Policy*. New York: Routledge.

Lincoln, Edward. 1999. *Troubled Times: U.S.-Japan Trade Relations in the 1990s*. Washington, DC: Brookings Institute.

Lipson, Charles. 1991. "Why Are Some International Agreements Informal?" *International Organization* 45:495–538.

Lohmann, Susanne and Sharyn O'Halloran. 1994. "Divided Government and U.S. Trade Policy: Theory and Evidence." *International Organization* 48:595–632.

Low, Patrick. 1993. *Trading Free: The GATT and U.S. Trade Policy*. New York: Twentieth Century Fund Press.

Magee, Stephen, William Brock, and Leslie Young. 1989. *Black Hole Tariffs and Endogenous Policy Theory*. Cambridge, UK: Cambridge University Press.

Maggi, Giovanni. 1999. "The Role of Multilateral Institutions in International Trade Cooperation." *American Economic Review* 89:190–214.

Maggi, Giovanni and Andres Rodriquez-Clare. 1998. "The Value of Trade Agreements in the Presence of Political Pressures." *Journal of Political Economy* 106:574–601.

Maggi, Giovanni and Andres Rodriquez-Clare. 2007. "A Political-Economy Theory of Trade Agreements." *American Economic Review* 97:1374–1406.

Maggi, Giovanni and Robert Staiger. 2008. "On the Role and Design of Dispute Settlement Procedures in International Trade Agreements." Working Paper No. 14067, National Bureau of Economic Research.

Mansfield, Edward and Marc Busch. 1995. "The Political Economy of Nontariff Barriers: A Cross-National Analysis." *International Organization* 49:723–749.

Mansfield, Edward and Rachel Bronson. 1997. "Alliances, Preferential Trading Arrangements, and International Trade." *American Political Science Review* 91:94–107.

Mansfield, Edward, Helen Milner, and Jon Pevehouse. 2007. "Vetoing Cooperation: The Impact of Veto Players on Preferential Trading Arrangements." *British Journal of Political Science* 37:403–432.

Mansfield, Edward, Helen Milner, and Jon Pevehouse. 2008. "Democracy, Veto Players and the Depth of Regional Integration." *World Economy* 31:67–96.

Mansfield, Edward, Helen V. Milner, and Peter Rosendorff. 2000. "Free to Trade: Democracies, Autocracies, and International Trade." *American Political Science Review* 94:305–321.

Mansfield, Edward, Helen Milner, and Peter Rosendorff. 2002. "Why Democracies Cooperate More: Electoral Control and International Trade Agreements." *International Organization* 56:477–513.

Mansfield, Edward and Jon Pevehouse. 2006. "Democratization and International Organizations." *International Organization* 60:137–167.

Mansfield, Edward and Eric Reinhardt. 2003. "Multilateral Determinants of Regionalism: The Effects of GATT/WTO on the Formation of Preferential Trading Arrangements." *International Organization* 57:829–862.

Mansfield, Edward and Eric Reinhardt. 2008. "International Institutions and the Volatility of International Trade." *International Organization* 62:621–652.

Maoz, Zeev and Bruce Russett. 1993. "Normative and Structural Causes of Democratic Peace, 1946–1986." *American Political Science Review* 87:624–638.

Martin, Lisa. 1992a. *Coercive Cooperation: Explaining Multilateral Economic Sanctions*. Princeton, NJ: Princeton University Press.

Martin, Lisa. 1992b. "Interests, Power, Multilateralism." *International Organization* 46:765–792.

Martin, Lisa. 2000. *Democratic Commitments: Legislatures and International Cooperation*. Princeton, NJ: Princeton University Press.

Matsumoto, Ken. 2009. *The Future of the Multilateral Trading System: East Asian Perspectives*. London: Cameron May.

Mavroidis, Petros. 2000. "Remedies in the WTO Legal System: Between a Rock and a Hard Place." *European Journal of International Law* 11:763–813.

Mayer, Wolfgang. 1981. "Theoretical Considerations on Negotiated Tariff Adjustments." *Oxford Economic Papers* 33:135–153.

McCubbins, Mathew, Roger Noll, and Barry Weingast. 1987. "Administrative Procedures as Instruments of Political Control." *Journal of Law, Economics, and Organization* 3:243–277.

McCubbins, Mathew and Thomas Schwartz. 1984. "Congressional Oversight Overlooked: Police Patrols versus Fire Alarms." *American Journal of Political Science* 28:165–179.

McGillivray, Fiona. 2004. *Privileging Industry: The Comparative Politics of Trade and Industrial Policy*. Princeton, NJ: Princeton University Press.

McGuire, Steven. 1997. *Airbus Industries: Conflict and Cooperation in US-EC Trade Relations*. New York: Palgrave.

McNamara, Dennis. 2010. "IPR, Innovation and Asian Regional Integration— Japan's Challenge in China." Paper presented at the International Studies Association Annual Meeting, New Orleans.

Mearsheimer, John. 1994–95. "The False Promise of International Institutions." *International Security* 19:5–49.

Mertha, Andrew. 2007. *China's Foreign Trade Policy*. New York: Routledge.

Meunier, Sophie. 2005. *Trading Voices: The European Union in International Commercial Negotiations*. Princeton, NJ: Princeton University Press.

Milgrom, Paul R., Douglass C. North, and Barry R. Weingast. 1990. "The Role of Institutions in the Revival of Trade: The Law Merchant, Private Judges, and the Champagne Fairs." *Economics and Politics* 2:1–23.

Milner, Helen. 1988. "Trading Places: Industries for Free Trade." *World Politics* 40:350–376.

Milner, Helen. 1997. *Interests, Institutions, and Information: Domestic Politics and International Relations*. Princeton, NJ: Princeton University Press.

Milner, Helen and Benjamin Judkins. 2004. "Partisanship, Trade Policy, and Globalization: Is There a Left-Right Divide on Trade Policy?" *International Studies Quarterly* 48:95–119.

Milner, Helen and Keiko Kubota. 2005. "Why the Move to Free Trade? Democracy and Trade Policy in the Developing Countries." *International Organization* 59:107–143.

Milner, Helen and Bumba Mukherjee. 2009. "Democratization and Economic Globalization." *Annual Review of Political Science* 12:163–181.

Milner, Helen and Peter Rosendorff. 1996. "Trade Negotiations, Information and Domestic Politics." *Economics and Politics* 8:145–189.

Milner, Helen and Peter Rosendorff. 1997. "Democratic Politics and International Trade Negotiations: Elections and Divided Government as Constraints on Trade Liberalization." *Journal of Conflict Resolution* 41:117–146.

Milner, Helen and David Yoffie. 1989. "Between Free Trade and Protectionism: Strategic Trade Policy and a Theory of Corporate Trade Demands." *International Organization* 43:239–272.

Mitra, Devashish. 1999. "Endogenous Lobby Formation and Endogenous Protection: A Long-Run Model of Trade Policy Determination." *American Economic Review* 89:1116–1134.

Moe, Terry. 1990. "Political Institutions: The Neglected Side of the Story." *Journal of Law, Economics, and Organization* 6:213–253.

Moravcsik, Andrew. 1989. "Disciplining Trade Finance: The OECD Export Credit Arrangement." *International Organization* 43:173–205.

Moravcsik, Andrew. 2000. "The Origins of Human Rights Regimes: Democratic Delegation in Postwar Europe." *International Organization* 54:217–252.

Morrison, Wayne and Marc Labonte. 2009. "China's Currency: A Summary of the Economic Issues." Technical report, Congressional Research Service.

Morrow, James. 1989. "Capabilities, Uncertainty, and Resolve: A Limited Information Model of Crisis Bargaining." *American Journal of Political Science* 33:941–972.

Morrow, James. 1994. "The Forms of International Cooperation." *International Organization* 48:387–423.

Mulgan, Aurelia George. 2005. "Japan's Interventionist State: Bringing Agriculture Back In." *Japanese Journal of Political Science* 6:29–61.

Murphy, Sean. 2009. *The Sword and the Scales: The United States and International Courts and Tribunals*. Cambridge, UK: Cambridge University Press.

Naoi, Megumi. 2009. "Shopping for Protection: The Politics of Choosing Trade Instruments in a Partially-Legalized World." *International Studies Quarterly* 53:421–444.

Naoi, Megumi and Ellis Krauss. 2009. "Who Lobbies Whom? Electoral Systems and Organized Interests Choice of Bureaucrats vs. Politicians in Japan." *American Journal of Political Science* 53:874–892.

Nelson, Douglas. 1989. "Domestic Political Preconditions of US Trade Policy: Liberal Structure and Protectionist Dynamics." *Journal of Public Policy* 9:83–108.

Nielson, Daniel. 2003. "Supplying Trade Reform: Political Institutions and Liberalization in Middle-Income Presidential Democracies." *American Journal of Political Science* 47:470–491.

Noland, Marcus. 1997. "Chasing Phantoms: The Political Economy of USTR." *International Organization* 51:365–387.

Odell, John. 1993. "International Threats and Internal Politics: Brazil, the European Community, and the United States, 1985–1987." In *Double-Edged Diplomacy: International Bargaining and Domestic Politics*, ed. Peter Evans, Harold Jacobson, and Robert Putnam. Berkeley: University of California Press, pp. 233–264.

Odell, John. 2000. *Negotiating the World Economy*. Ithaca, NY: Cornell University Press.

Odell, John and Barry Eichengreen. 1998. "The ITO and the WTO: Exit Options, Agent Slack, and Presidential Leadership." In *The WTO as an International Organization*, ed. Anne O. Krueger. Chicago: University of Chicago Press, pp. 181–209.

O'Halloran, Sharyn. 1994. *Politics, Process, and American Trade Policy*. Ann Arbor: University of Michigan Press.

Okimoto, Daniel. 1989. *Between MITI and the Market: Japanese Industrial Policy for High Technology*. Palo Alto, CA: Stanford University Press.

Oye, Kenneth. 1985. "Explaining Cooperation under Anarchy: Hypotheses and Strategies." *World Politics* 38:1–24.

Pahre, Robert. 2008. *Politics and Trade Cooperation in the Nineteenth Century*. Cambridge, UK: Cambridge University Press.

Palmeter, N. David. 1996. *Anti-Dumping under the WTO: A Comprehensive Review*. London: Kluwer.

Panitchpakdi, Supachai and Mark Clifford. 2002. *China and the WTO*. Singapore: John Wiley.

Pastor, Robert. 1980. *Congress and the Politics of U.S. Foreign Economic Policy*. Berkeley: University of California Press.

Patel, Mayur. 2008. "Building Coalitions and Consensus in the WTO." Paper presented at the meeting of the International Studies Association, San Francisco.

Pekkanen, Saadia. 2001. "International Law, the WTO, and the Japanese State: Assessment and Implications of the New Legalized Trade Politics." *Journal of Japanese Studies* 27:41–79.

Pekkanen, Saadia. 2008. *Japan's Aggressive Legalism: Law and Foreign Trade Politics beyond the WTO*. Palo Alto, CA: Stanford University Press.

Pekkanen, Saadia, Mireya Solis, and Saori Katada. 2007. "Trading Gains for Control: International Trade Forums and Japanese Economic Diplomacy." *International Studies Quarterly* 51:945–970.

Pelc, Krzysztof. 2010. "Constraining Coercion? Legitimacy and Its Role in U.S. Trade Policy, 1975–2000." *International Organization* 64:65–96.

Persson, Torsten, Gerard Roland, and Guido Tabellini. 1997. "Separation of Powers and Political Accountability." *Quarterly Journal of Economics* 112:1163–1203.

Piper, W. Stephen. 1980. "Unique Sectoral Agreement Establishes Free Trade Framework." *Law and Policy in International Business* 12:221–242.

Posner, Richard. 1972. "The Behavior of Administrative Agencies." *Journal of Legal Studies* 1:305–347.

Priest, George. 1985. "Reexamining the Selection Hypothesis: Learning from Wittman's Mistakes." *Journal of Legal Studies* 14:215–243.

Priest, George and Benjamin Klein. 1984. "The Selection of Disputes for Litigation." *Journal of Legal Studies* 13:1–55.

Putnam, Robert. 1988. "Diplomacy and Domestic Politics: The Logic of Two-level Games." *International Organization* 42:427–460.

Ramseyer, Mark. 1985. "The Costs of the Consensual Myth: Antitrust Enforcement and Institutional Barriers to Litigation in Japan." *Yale Law Journal* 94:604–645.

Ramseyer, Mark and Minoru Nakazato. 1989. "The Rational Litigant: Settlement Amounts and Verdict Rates in Japan." *Journal of Legal Studies* 18:263–290.

Ramseyer, Mark and Frances Rosenbluth. 1993. *Japan's Political Marketplace*. Cambridge, MA: Harvard University Press.

Raustiala, Kal and Anne-Marie Slaughter. 2002. *The Handbook of International Relations*. Thousand Oaks, CA: Sage.

Ray, Edward. 1981. "Tariff and Nontariff Barriers to Trade in the United States and Abroad." *Review of Economics and Statistics* 63:161–168.

Reinhardt, Eric. 2000. "Aggressive Multilateralism: The Determinants of GATT/WTO Dispute Initiation, 1948–1998." Manuscript, Emory University.

Reinhardt, Eric. 2001. "Adjudication without Enforcement in GATT Disputes." *Journal of Conflict Resolution* 45:174–195.

Reinhardt, Eric. 2003. "Tying Hands without a Rope: Rational Domestic Response to International Institutional Constraint." In *Locating the Proper Authorities: The Interaction of Domestic and International Institutions*, ed. Daniel Drezner. Ann Arbor: University of Michigan Press, pp. 77–104.

Richardson, Bradley M. 1997. *Japanese Democracy: Power, Coordination, and Performance*. New Haven, CT: Yale University Press.

Rickard, Stephanie. 2010. "Democratic Differences: Electoral Institutions and Compliance with GATT/WTO Agreements." *European Journal of International Relations* 16:711–729.

Rodrik, Dani. 1989. "Promises, Promises: Credible Policy Reform via Signaling." *Economic Journal* 99:756–772.

Rodrik, Dani. 1995. "Political Economy of Trade Policy." In *Handbook of International Economics*, vol. 3, ed. Gene Grossman and Kenneth Rogoff. Amsterdam: North-Holland, pp. 1457–1494.

Rogowski, Ronald. 1987. "Trade and the Variety of Democratic Institutions." *International Organization* 41:203–223.

Rogowski, Ronald. 1989. *Commerce and Coalitions: How Trade Affects Domestic Political Alignments*. Princeton, NJ: Princeton University Press.

Rose, Andrew. 2004. "Do We Really Know That the WTO Increases Trade?" *American Economic Review* 94:98–114.

Rosendorff, Peter. 2005. "Stability and Rigidity: Politics and Design of the WTO's Dispute Settlement Procedure." *American Political Science Review* 99:389–400.

Rosendorff, Peter and Helen Milner. 2001. "The Optimal Design of International Trade Institutions: Uncertainty and Escape." *International Organization* 55:829–857.

Rubin, Donald. 1973. "The Use of Matched Sampling and Regression Adjustment to Remove Bias in Observational Studies." *Biometrics* 29:185–203.

Rubin, Donald. 1979. "Using Multivariate Matched Sampling and Regression Adjustment to Control Bias in Observational Studies." *Journal of the American Statistical Association* 74:318–328.

Sakakibara, Eisuke. 1991. *Parallel Politics: Economic Policymaking in the United States and Japan*. Washington, DC: Brookings Institution.

Sarat, Austin and Joel B. Grossman. 1975. "Courts and Conflict Resolution: Problems in the Mobilization of Adjudication." *American Political Science Review* 69:1200–1217.

Sartori, Anne. 2002. "The Might of the Pen: A Reputational Theory of Communication in International Disputes." *International Organization* 56:121–149.

Sattler, Thomas and Thomas Bernauer. 2011. "Gravitation or Discrimination? Determinants of Litigation in the World Trade Organization." *European Journal of Political Research* 50:143–167.

Schattschneider, E. E. 1935. *Politics, Pressures, and the Tariff*. New York: Prentice Hall.

Schelling, Thomas. 1980. *The Strategy of Conflict*. 2nd ed. Cambridge, MA: Harvard University Press.

Scheve, Kenneth and Matthew Slaughter. 2001. "What Determines Individual Trade-Policy Preferences?" *Journal of International Economics* 54:267–292.

Schoppa, Leonard. 1997. *Bargaining with Japan: What American Pressure Can and Cannot Do*. New York: Columbia University Press.

Schwab, Susan. 1994. *Trade-Offs: Negotiating the Omnibus Trade and Competitiveness Act*. Boston: Harvard Business School Press.

Schwartz, Warren F. and Alan O. Sykes. 2002. "The Economic Structure of Renegotiation and Dispute Resolution in the World Trade Organization." *Journal of Legal Studies* 31:179–204.

Shaffer, Gregory. 2003. *Defending Interests: Public-Private Partnerships in WTO Litigation*. Washington, DC: Brookings Institution.

Shaffer, Gregory and Victor Mosoti. 2002. "EC Sardines: A New Model for Collaboration in Dispute Settlement?" *Bridges* 6:15–22.

Shaffer, Gregory, Michelle Ratton Sanchez, and Barbara Rosenberg. 2008. "The Trials of Winning at the WTO: What Lies behind Brazil's Success." *Cornell International Law Journal* 41:384–501.

Sherman, Richard. 2002. "Delegation, Ratification, and U.S. Trade Policy: Why Divided Government Causes Lower Tariffs." *Comparative Political Studies* 35:1171–1197.

Shirk, Susan. 1994. *How China Opened Its Door*. Washington, DC: Brookings Institution.

Shugart, Matthew and Stephan Haggard. 2001. "Institutions and Public Policy in Presidential Systems." In *Presidents, Parliaments, and Policy*, ed. Stephan Haggard and Mathew McCubbins. Cambridge, UK: Cambridge University Press, pp. 64–102.

Simmons, Beth. 2000. "International Law and State Behavior: Commitment and Compliance in International Monetary Affairs." *American Political Science Review* 94:819–835.

Simmons, Beth. 2002. "Capacity, Commitment, and Compliance: International Institutions and Territorial Disputes." *Journal of Conflict Resolution* 46:829–856.

Simmons, Beth. 2009. *Mobilizing for Human Rights: International Law in Domestic Politics*. Cambridge, UK: Cambridge University Press.

Simmons, Beth. 2010. "Treaty Compliance and Violation." *Annual Review of Political Science* 13:273–296.

Snyder, Glenn. 1984. "The Security Dilemma in Alliance Politics." *World Politics* 36:461–495.

Spence, A. Michael. 1973. "Job Market Signaling." *Quarterly Journal of Economics* 87:355–374.

Srinivasan, T. N. and Philip Levy. 1996. "Regionalism and the (Dis)advantage of Dispute-Settlement Access." *American Economic Review* 86:93–98.

Staiger, Robert and Guido Tabellini. 1999. "Do GATT Rules Help Governments Make Domestic Commitments?" *Economics and Politics* 2:109–144.

Staiger, Robert 1995. "International Rules and Institutions for Trade Policy." In *Handbook of International Economics*, vol. 3, ed. Gene Grossman and Kenneth Rogoff. Amsterdam: North Holland, pp. 1497–1551.

Stephenson, Matthew. 2003. "'When the Devil Turns...': The Political Foundations of Independent Judicial Review." *Journal of Legal Studies* 32: 59–89.

Taniguchi, Masaki. 2000. "Defuenshibu na teiso: Nichibei fuirumu massatsu no seijigaku" (Defensive Complaints: The Politics of the Japan-U.S. Film Dispute). *Bōeki to kanzei* 4:110–121.

Tarar, Ahmer. 2001. "International Bargaining with Two-Sided Domestic Constraints." *Journal of Conflict Resolution* 45:320–340.

Tarullo, Daniel. 2004. "Paved with Good Intentions: The Dynamic Effects of WTO Review of Anti-Dumping Action." *World Trade Review* 2:373–393.

Thompson, Alexander. 2007. "The Power of Legalization: Explaining U.S. Support of WTO Dispute Settlement." Paper presented to the ISA Annual Convention, Chicago.

Tomz, Mike. 2008. "Reputation and the Effect of International Law on Preferences and Beliefs." Working paper, Stanford University.

Trachtman, Joel. 1999. "The Domain of WTO Dispute Resolution." *Harvard International Law Journal* 40:333–378.

Trefler, Daniel. 1993. "Trade Liberalization and the Theory of Endogenous Protection: An Econometric Study of U.S. Import Policy." *Journal of Political Economy* 101:138–160.

Tsebelis, George. 2002. *Veto Players: How Political Institutions Work*. Princeton, NJ: Princeton University Press.

Tyson, Laura D'Andrea. 1992. *Who's Bashing Whom? Trade Conflict in High-Technology Industries*. Washington, DC: Institute for International Economics.

Upham, Frank. 1976. "Litigation and Moral Consciousness in Japan: An Interpretive Analysis of Four Japanese Pollution Suits." *Law and Society Review* 10:579–619.

Upham, Frank. 1987. *Law and Social Change in Postwar Japan*. Cambridge, MA: Harvard University Press.

Upham, Frank. 1996. "Privatized Regulation: Japanese Regulatory Style in Comparative and International Perspective." *Fordham International Law Journal* 20:397–511.

Urata, Shujiro, ed. 2002. *Nihon no FTA senryaku* (Japan's FTA Strategy). Tokyo: Nihon Keizai Shimbunshya.

Verdier, Daniel. 1994. *Democracy and International Trade: Britain, France, and the United States, 1860–1990*. Princeton, NJ: Princeton University Press.

Vogel, Ezra. 1979. *Japan as Number One*. Cambridge, MA: Harvard University Press.

Vogel, Steven. 2006. *Japan Remodeled: How Government and Industry Are Reforming Japanese Capitalism*. Ithaca, NY: Cornell University Press.

Von Stein, Jana. 2005. "Do Treaties Constrain or Screen? Selection Bias and Treaty Compliance." *American Political Science Review* 99:611–631.

Waldfogel, Joel. 1998. "Reconciling Asymmetric Information and Divergent Expectations Theories of Litigation." *Journal of Law and Economics* 41: 451–476.

Waldmann, Raymond and Jay Culbert. 1998. "U.S. Trade Policy vis-à-vis the Aircraft Industry." In *Constituent Interests and U.S. Trade Policies*, ed. Alan Deardorff and Robert Stern. Ann Arbor: University of Michigan Press, pp. 173–181.

Wauters, Jasper and Hylke Vandenbussche. 2010. "China-Measures Affecting Imports of Automobile Parts." *World Trade Review* 9:201–238.

Weathers, Charles. 1997. "Japan's Fading Labor Movement." Working Paper, Japan Policy Research Institute.

West, Mark. 2001. "Why Shareholders Sue: The Evidence from Japan." *Journal of Legal Studies* 30:351–382.

Widner, Jennifer. 2001. "Courts and Democracy in Postconflict Transitions: A Social Scientist's Perspective on the African Case." *American Journal of International Law* 95:64–75.

Wilson, Bruce. 2007. "Compliance by WTO Members with Adverse WTO Dispute Settlement Rulings: The Record to Date." *Journal of International Economic Law* 10:397–403.

Wood, Dan and Richard Waterman. 1991. "The Dynamics of Political Control of the Bureaucracy." *American Political Science Review* 85:801–828.

World Bank 1993. *The East Asian Miracle*. Washington, DC: World Bank.

Yoshimatsu, Hidetaka. 2003. *Japan and East Asia in Transition: Trade Policy, Crisis and Evolution, and Regionalism*. New York: Palgrave.

Yue, Chengyan, John Beghin, and Helen Jensen. 2005. "Tariff Equivalent of Technical Barriers to Trade with Imperfect Substitution and Transport Costs." Technical Report No. 383, Center for Agricultural and Rural Development, Iowa State University.

Index